Architecture Laid Bare!

In Shades of Green

Robert
Brown
Butler

ISBN-13: 9781466345935
ISBN-10:1466345934

This book's text is set in BuBabel, BuHB, Bu2H, and other typefaces created by Robert Brown Butler. For more on these superior faces visit bufontforge .com. This book was printed and bound by Create-Space, Inc. of Charleston, South Carolina.

The logo signifies that this book's text, photos, drawings, cover art, typefaces, and page designs were all prepared by Robert Brown Butler.

The mission of the architect —of architecture—
is to help people understand how to make life
more beautiful, the world a better one for living
in, and to give reason, rhyme, and meaning to life.

Frank Lloyd Wright

I am here writing no more than the too specific
outline of a practical ideal perceiving Change as
already upon us.

Frank Lloyd Wright

Contents

Contents

Architecture Shapes Your Life

This book shows how you can lead a better life with better architecture. This undertaking is no mild matter, because architecture affects your every motion and mood more than food, drink, sex, and clothes combined. It is the great shaper of your activities, the ruling soother of your psyche, the essential provider that houses all your other provisions —and the better your architecture is, the better you will be.

You would think that crowds of inhabitants everywhere would have a fanatical urge to know all about this subject that is so central to our lives, the way people flock to rock concerts and athletic contests by the tens of thousands. Why don't they?

Based on my more than fifty years' experience in the "space trade": The nature of the rooms we inhabit generally seems so obvious that we give them little thought, or any problems that do arise seem too ponderous to overcome, or any discerning of their solemn amenities is obscured by one's more clamorous concerns for food, drink, sex, and clothes.

In fact, it takes a leap of abstraction to perceive how the relation between a stove and a counter can improve the food you eat. Or how water gushing from a pipe can be made safe to drink. Or how the acoustic construction around your bed can make your lovemaking more serene. Or how the size of a closet can improve your appearance at a business meeting miles away. But such abstractions can lead you to a wealth of dividends —and the lack of them can lead you to a poverty of grief. As a sample, do you ever feel like your life isn't going quite the way you would like? Or do you at times feel a little at odds with your loved ones or business colleagues when you don't think you should? If so, you may be suffering from crimes that are not yours —committed by unqualified professionals, phony promoters, and profiteering purveyors

Introduction

who prey on the patrons they so avidly claim to serve.

Here are a few more architectural crimes you may suffer from that aren't your fault. Today's homes often cost thirty percent more than they should. Most homes and workplaces today could be just as comfortable while being thirty percent smaller. Many of these habitations should cost a third as much to keep warm in winter and cool in summer. Due to poor construction many of our buildings are rotting around us as we speak. And many are so destitute of aesthetics that even a pickle jar designed by Heinz and Company is grander by comparison.

These are the curses this book must cope with. The crimes it must uncommit, for your benefit.

To begin with, bad architecture is like a cancer. As the insidious affliction takes root, you have no idea anything is wrong. As the degeneration spreads, you may have a strange apprehension that something is not quite right. When the dreadful rot is finally discovered, it may require extensive surgery to remove —or be too late.

So while we are in the foyer of this subject, what can we do to alleviate these incipient pains that can ravage your life if allowed to go unchecked? These easings will come not by delving into matters pertaining to history or culture, nor by dallying with transient styles or trendy motifs —they will come by burrowing to the very marrow of what architecture is about: those unchanging anatomical elements that make a building *function;* that make its structure stand up, its water run hot and cold, its electricity flow, and its interiors comfortable every hour of the year no matter how the weather rages outdoors. To this end, this 458-page text companied by 240 visually rich drawings combs through every essential material and construction that appears or is about to appear in today's buildings; and amid a mosaic of economic cues it acquaints you with what each element is, when to use it, and what its installation and use entails. By so doing this book lays bare the nature of this science of shelter, this Mother of the Arts, in a way that will lead you —by leaps of abstraction as well as revelations of truth— to the comfort, beauty, and economy you so richly deserve. With this approach you may even become like the ancient Chinese sage who set off on a journey today, and arrived yesterday.

Architecture Laid Bare!

When it comes to putting its knowledge to use, this book gives you another advantage: it employs the "hands-off" approach. This involves describing each part of a building's design and construction for those who haven't the time, knowledge, or experience to do the work themselves yet need to be sure the professionals who do this labor will do it right. Hence when this reference describes how to design or construct part of a building, it often ends by saying something like, "If you don't care to do this work yourself, hand these pages to a professional and he or she will know what to do." Then when it comes to dealing with the Caesars of architectural creation you will find yourself replacing the subservient "What should I do?" with the assertive "This is what I want." Aside from the authority you will gain, this will save you much expense and vexation by enabling you to articulate your architectural aspirations more clearly, reduce your hours of paid consultation, ensure that everyone's labor is a faithful transcript of your desires, and foster greater understanding between everyone on your design or construction team —so you will be *master* of your architectural fate, not its slave.

Due to this book's construction it is not meant to be read from cover to cover like a novel, but is meant to be referred to here and there like an encyclopedia; for every part is written independently of every other part. Hence you may find it easier to find the facts you seek by entering through the book's back door —its detailed index— than by opening its cover. However you use this $25 volume, it may save you many thousands of dollars during a long life in your library. Even if you never use it to design or build anything, it may provide you with many hours of delightful reading about an everyday subject. The knowledge you gain may also lead you to be the center of conversation at cocktail parties and other social gatherings.

The scope of this reference goes far beyond a layman's spatial concerns. It also hopes to lead architects, contractors, and merchants of building materials away from the confusion that confounds so much architectural thinking today. It also aims to

Introduction

influence manufacturers of building materials to make them sounder and safer, and it makes an appeal for more accessible and updateable information about building standards and environmental risks regarding architectural materials and methods of construction. And it hopes to influence senators and legislators to write logical and lucid laws for governing the use of products and practices in the building industry.

Though this book is about all kinds of buildings —commercial, recreational, and industrial as well as residential— most of its examples are residential because (1) people tend to be more familiar with their homes than commercial buildings; (2) homes are usually smaller and simpler than commercial buildings and the elements common to all are more easily elucidated; and (3) occupants of homes are often more able to implement any required or desired changes.

This volume has a final focus. Even under the most optimal circumstances, there is *no* way every citizen in this wide nation can take all the ideas in these pages and vacate all the millions of old bad buildings they inhabit and replace them with millions of new good buildings. Hence this book often emphasizes how to transform your *existing* confines from miserable to magnificent in ways that are more comfortable and durable at less expense. For this is the only goal that has a chance of working for the majority of citizens that comprise We the People of the United States.

Robert Brown Butler
robert3butler@gmail.com
blog ... architecturelaidbare.com

Notes

Acknowledgements

The author takes extreme pleasure in acknowledging those who helped him prepare this volume:

Emily Butler-Sessa, Jon Sessa, Harry Wirtz, Jim Phillips, Bert Brosmith, John Milnes Baker, Vic Daquino, Dana Chipkin, Rick Bondi, and Pat Byron; and especially David Bady, Stephen Jacoby, and the author's wife Janis Y. Butler.

About the Author

After graduating from the Cornell School of Architecture in 1964, the author returned to his native Atlanta, Georgia, to work for several prominent architects during the next two years. In 1966–7 he spent a year traveling through western North America visiting more than a hundred Frank Lloyd Wright buildings and other notable architecture, and settled in Big Sur, California. Between 1967 and 1973 he worked as a carpenter there and in Aspen, Colorado. In 1973 he moved to Mahopac, New York, where since he has worked somewhat chronologically as a carpenter, building contractor, and registered architect.

Down through the years Mr. Butler has received a variety of honors for his creative work. Since the early 1960s his paintings, sculptures, and other artwork have appeared in numerous public exhibitions. In the late 1970s he received two federal grants for his innovative environmental architectural designs. From 1978 to 1980 he taught architectural drafting and environmental design at B.O.C.E.S., a college in Westchester County. In 1986 and 1989 he received two U.S. Patents for architectural inventions.

In 1981 Mr. Butler published his first book, *The Ecological House*, which introduced many ideas that are further refined in this volume. In 1984 he authored the *Architectural and Engineering Calculations Manual*, published by McGraw-Hill, which was the first book of its kind whose algebraic formulas were formatted for easy use by computers. In 1998, after ten years of labor,

About the Author

he authored McGraw-Hill's *Standard Handbook of Architectural Engineering*, a massive 1070-page volume for the general architect that includes an interactive disk of the book's 1,000 equations which allows each to be solved quickly and error-free by computer; again the first book of its kind. In 2001 he published two books for professional engineers, totaling 1,540 pages, titled *Architectural Engineering Design: Structural Systems* and *Architectural Engineering Design: Mechanical Systems*, that also include computerized disks of the book's equations. In 2002 Mr. Butler authored the *Architectural Formulas Pocket Reference*, a scaled version of his two professional engineering books that includes "the formulas and nothing but the formulas" plus introductory text. The above six books, in addition to this one, may be viewed at Amazon.com ➡ books ➡ robert brown butler.

In preparing the last four volumes cited above, Mr. Butler designed a few simple computer typefaces which contained all the mathematical symbols that appeared in his books (a sampling is ℙ ₿ ¢ ☞ ◄ — ⚷ ► ⊕ ⊖ ➡ ⬅ ❸ ∠ 🖳). The present book freely uses these symbols, especially in its drawings. These typefaces' lowercase letters are also larger and more uniform than in standard faces (note the same point-size letters in this face's Sue Sugarman and Sue Sugarman from a standard face) which makes these typefaces more legible and comfortable to read than standard faces. This typography is fully described in this author's website, bufontforge.com.

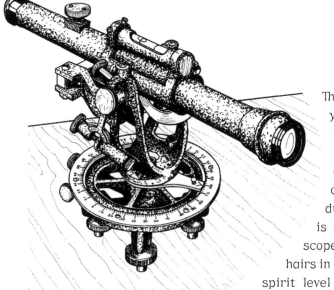

The instrument you see here is a *transit*, also known as a surveyor's level or dumpy level. It is a little telescope with crosshairs in its lens and a spirit level on top that rotates on a calibrated compass base mounted on a sturdy tripod. This instrument is indispensable for ensuring that every part of a building's foundation is level. Most models look more modern than this one, which was given to me by the previous owner of the property on which I built my house in 1973. It may have been old then, but it still works like new today. Being the first serious instrument one uses when constructing a building, it is appropriate to acquaint you with it at the outset of this reading —every part of which is "on the level".

Happy surveying!

Architecture Laid Bare!

In Shades of Green

Shades of Green

A building is a document. A written record, prepared by designers, carpenters, and other artisans in which the materials of its construction, the refinement of its lines, even the manner in which its utilitarian hulk is adorned, are all a grammar and syntax in which can be read an owners' propensities and felicities.

But often in these edifices is written a story of waste: resources depleted, environments degraded, landfills created, and attendant miseries and misdeeds — a fable of *"fin de siecle"* habitations whose seeming beauty is often the phosphorescence of decay, whose alleged grandeur is often the result of a comprehensive misapplication. Today we are receiving the invoices of these damages in the form of escalating energy costs, increased pollution, and other environmental debits which must be paid, either by us or our descendents. Not only is such construction unsustainable for more than the near future, it is slowly turning most interiors that today seem so invitingly and enduringly comfortable into traps —cages whose escalating energy and maintenance costs will someday by exhausting your funds to maintain them evict you from them. Then you may find that having this book may not be a luxury so much as a necessity; and, by conjecture accompliced with foresight, some of its directives may be worth incorporating into your own habitations, starting tomorrow.

Regarding the above-mentioned environmental debits, to many the chief concern is conserving energy. But if this is so, we must consider *all* the energies consumed in making and maintaining a building. This includes all the energies consumed in procuring, processing, and piecing together a product's constituent parts; all the energies consumed in packaging and transporting the product to the premises of its incorporation; all the energies consumed in operating and servicing the product during its use-

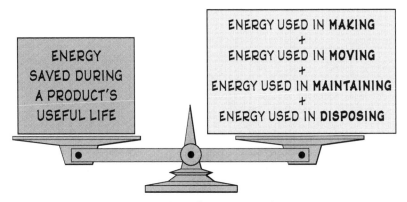

1-1. The scale of embodied energy

ful life; even all the energies consumed in disposing the product at the end of its life —altogether what is known as a product's *embodied energy*. If the sum of all these energies is *more* than the energy the product will save during its lifespan, using the product will only *worsen* our energy crisis instead of lessen it. Lamentably, such energy debits are the case for a number of presently promoted green products, materials, and constructions. For this reason, every building product should have its balance sheet of proven energy debits and potential energy savings assayed on the scales of embodied energy —and any article that tilts this balance adversely should be stamped REJECT.

Further, as the makers of building products extract raw materials from the earth, process them into finished products, and package and transport them to building sites, they often damage that larger foundation of architecture known as the environment beyond its ability to restore itself. Therefore we must use green building products not only in ways that preserve energy but preserve *every* environmental resource. Otherwise we are like someone sitting on an iceberg who, when s/he becomes thirsty, breaks off another chunk of ice to quench one's thirst. These days these dynamics are especially relevant for that subsector of the animal kingdom known as America.

Architecture Laid Bare!

Some solutions to these dilemmas have already been formulated. Their foundation has already been laid, no more able to be displaced than the architectural stylobates and spires of yore, and their enduring blueprints are being drawn as we speak. Indeed, today we are on the verge of an Environmental Renaissance, as culturally encompassing as the one that shook Europe several centuries ago, though the antiquity to be revived this time around may be more aboriginal in nature.

Presently the standard-bearer of this new architectural order is a loosely knit entity with a tightly knit code known as LEED (for Leadership in Energy and Environmental Design): an aptly eye-catching acronym if ever there was one. Since 1998, this agency has encouraged the creation of environmentally sustainable architecture by using a detailed checklist to count the number of environmentally desirable materials, products, and methods of construction used in a newly constructed or largely renovated residential or commercial building, then awarding the examined structure a silver, gold, or platinum certificate based on the number of points it has earned. Since this program's initiation it not only has made the public more aware of the ethical and practical benefits of sustainable architecture, it has stimulated environmental competition among designers and builders, promoted conservational construction practices which the manufacturer of no single building product could ever have done alone, recognized environmental leadership in the building industry, and transformed the building market from a complacent energy waster into a conscientious energy conserver. For those of you who may not want to sit still for a sermon on the fate of the earth, at least hear this: A "green" building that earns a high score on LEED's checklist is likely to be more comfortable, healthier to live in, less expensive to maintain, more durable, and have a significantly higher resale value. Here are a few environmentally benign building products and construction practices for which LEED awards points in new and remodeled buildings: [1]

Shades of Green

☞ Conserving natural areas and restoring damaged areas to provide habitats and promote biodiversity, and avoiding building on farmlands or wetlands.

☞ Using environmental resources more efficiently than they are used in conventional buildings.

☞ Using less energy and creating less waste during a building's construction and use.

☞ Installing permeable pavings that let rainfall seep into the soil instead of wash into storm drains and sewers.

☞ Installing high-R-value windows that reduce energy losses through the building envelope.

☞ Implementing automated controls for HVAC (heating, ventilating, and cooling) systems.

☞ Installing occupancy sensors to control lighting, ventilation, air conditioning and heating in intermittently occupied interiors.

☞ Installing efficient electric motors with variable-speed drives (these allow a motor to rotate slower, thus saving energy, when the required power is less than maximum).

☞ Using cisterns to collect rainwater for mechanical systems and irrigation.

☞ Using pendant instead of recessed light fixtures (pendant fixtures lose less heat through their mounts and are usually located nearer the tasks they illuminate where they use less wattage to maintain the same lighting).

☞ Using appliances and office equipment that carry the Energy Star Label.

☞ Installing composting toilets.

☞ Recycling graywater onsite.

No question about it: all these directives are laudable. However, even a perfect score on LEED's checklist will not lead our nation to a sustainable architecture because a number of this agency's directives are littered with flaws. Some are underinclusive, some fail to consider all the facts, and some are wrought with commercial bias; and there are a number of directives LEED should include but doesn't. Moreover, some "green" products LEED promotes are overly expensive in ways that seriously depreciate their cost-benefit ratios (the ratio of a product's initial cost versus its projected savings during its life of use) which for many consumers is the primary criteria for buying any so-called energy-efficient product. LEED certification also increases building costs: it typically adds 7 to 8 percent to a building's mechanical, plumbing, and electrical costs; and it generally adds 2 to 4 percent for each level of silver, gold, and platinum status a building may attain.[2] LEED's grading system is also inflexible and overly complicated, it involves excessive paperwork, and obtaining LEED certification is itself expensive: this "nonprofit" organization charges up to three thousand dollars just to evaluate a simple house ($600 for registration alone), it charges $200 for a reference guide that is thinner than this book plus $350 for its CD, and its annual membership dues (dues?) range from $300 to $5,000.

But the litany of liabilities that befall LEED's labors do not end here; for rumors persist that its ranks are being infiltrated by some of the same old hoggish profiteers who got us into this environmental mess in the first place: corporate entities who have adopted the rhetoric of green rather than its reality, who woo us with freshly minted environmental imagery while engaging in the same old resource-greedy paths of environmental destruction in hopes that they will be in the forefront of selling the next architectural generation of profit-making products.

Hence, to make it perfectly clear what LEED's shortcomings are —to leave no rationale for any dissenter to question, to quash what any incompetent may falsely claim, to refute what any misinformed person may spuriously assert, and in other ways to erase all possible doubt of what this book proclaims— every time these pages criticize one of LEED's directives, it makes every effort to articulate *how* the directive is underinclusive, *how* it fails to consider all the factors, and *how* it is wrought with commercial bias.

Shades of Green

These efforts begin by encapsulating LEED's most serious short-comings below, so no question may remain regarding their further articulation throughout this lengthy text:

☞ LEED awards zero points for efficient indoor spaces —or, as I have called this basic energy conserver since publishing in 1981 my first of six previous books on architecture: *Creating maximum comfort in minimum volume.* It makes little sense to stuff lots of insulation into a building's shell if its interiors are filled with useless corners, unused crannies, long gunbarrel hallways, seas of circulation around islands of furniture, and other conglomerations of excess cubage that consume energy to build and consume more energy to keep comfortable. A corollary to this is using efficiently designed furniture —what this text calls *furnitecture*— to make a smaller space more comfortable.

☞ LEED awards points for building on brownfield development sites; or, as it says in its reference guide: "building on sites that have been damaged by environmental contamination as a way of preserving undeveloped land." A more candid way of describing this point-getter is to say LEED encourages building on "Love Canal" sites in order to preserve natural habitats. What twisted logic is this? To whatever extent natural habitats may be lost by building on them, this simply cannot compare with building on land that could impair the health of those living on or near it or could lead to toxic wastes draining to neighboring acres. Even the slightest inclination in this direction is to encourage tomorrow's appalling environmental disasters. Here the rule should be if a site is "damaged by environmental contamination", DON'T BUILD ON IT —period! Far more feasible is Frank Lloyd Wright's directive: "Pick a site no one wants." [3] He meant to select land with steep terrain, big boulders, and other terrestrial challenges that would offer an architect a heightened opportunity to impart character to a building. Here we need think no further than how Wright built a certain house on a steep boulder-strewn hillside by a remote creek in southwest Pennsylvania to know how eloquent his directive is compared to this ill-fated creed of LEED!

☞ LEED awards points for a number of materials and methods that are simply good construction practice. Two such point-grabbers: a spray-on flexible waterproofing on foundation walls, and a woven plastic "shingle breather" that creates a quarter-inch airspace between cedar shingles and the underlying sheathing. When nearly forty years ago I built the house I live in today, I waterproofed its foundation not with a liquid applied with a sprayer but a gooey tar applied with a trowel, and I put a *three*-quarter inch airspace between the house's exterior siding and the underlying sheathing —and I didn't do these things for environmental reasons. Hear what one of America's most esteemed building scientists, Joseph Lstiburek, Ph.D, said of LEED's checklist containing a number of these bogus point-grabbers:

> Aren't these code requirements? Shouldn't these be "the standard of care"? Have we architects and engineers sunk so low that we now get points if we meet basic building requirements that all buildings should meet to be called buildings? ... Green programs waste a lot of time and money on stuff that is obvious and more time and money on stuff that is irrelevant or unimportant. [4]

☞ LEED also awards points for waterless urinals, which almost always waste more energy than they save.

☞ It awards points for using leather instead of vinyl as an interior finish, claiming that vinyl emits VOCs (volatile organic compounds, that nose-wrinkling plasticky smell which many finishes and furnishings emit when new) while asserting that leather is environmentally healthier apparently because it is a more "natural" material. But tanning leather uses chemicals that poison the environment; and procuring, piecing together, packaging, and transporting leather products harm the environment in other ways. Surely more environmentally benign finishes are available than either of these choices.

☞ LEED fails to award points for siting a building to utilize such proven natural energy conservers as desirable weather patterns, foliage, and topography.

☞ LEED awards points for irrigation when it shouldn't. Building irrigation systems typically destroys native environments, making these systems' materials destroys environments elsewhere, and the water they consume often depletes local water tables. Here LEED should *subtract* points for irrigations that nourish lawns and other alien vegetation, and add points only for acres that cultivate native flora sprinklered by the clouds.

☞ LEED says nothing about the huge amounts of energy our nation's businesses waste in lighting unoccupied buildings at night. It doesn't do any environmental good to install an occupancy sensor in a room if its lights are programmed to remain on all night when no one is there.

☞ LEED awards points for prefabricated homes, claiming they are less wastefully constructed than stick-built houses. Apparently none of LEED's acolytes ever visited the dumpsters of factories that make prefabs; they only noted the debris on construction sites. In a factory-built house I once remodeled, a header over a closet door was not a code-mandated double 2 × 4 but a scrap of 2 × 6 a factory worker had split lengthwise with a hatchet and nailed the split ends together. You'd be surprised at the number of modular units whose framing is inadequately fabricated and whose wiring and plumbing is similarly installed —all concealed behind finishes before leaving the factory so

Architecture Laid Bare!

local building inspectors cannot detect them. Moreover, these dwellings are often fabricated where hurricanes, tornados, and earthquakes are less severe and local codes are correspondingly more lenient than where the units are later sited —a big reason why modular homes are often so devastated by natural disasters. LEED could help here by awarding points to modular units that are fabricated without interior finishes. Then local inspectors can ensure that a prefab's structural and mechanical systems are legally adequate; and, as a bonus, installers or owners can apply interior finishes to their tastes.

☞ LEED awards points for clustering homes in ways that encourage walking, biking, and public transit, thereby minimizing dependence on automobiles and their adverse environmental impact. At first this may seem laudable because walking, biking, and busing to nearby schools, markets, and other community resources would use less energy. But a deception lurks here. This "habituated boxing of dreary human cages," [5] as Frank Lloyd Wright called such herding, invariably creates more noise, more dirty air, more crowds, more bumper-to-bumper traffic every morning and evening, and more parking lots between buildings that are never enough —all at a time when citizens today can do much of their schooling, buying, banking, and similar activities on the internet. Such crowding only feeds the affliction that freighted it. A more inspiring point-earner on any environmental checklist would be to encourage people to dwell where congestion and noise are minimal, where trucks can deliver purchased items to suburban and rural residences at less unit cost of fuel consumed than cars driven by individuals, where dwellings are surrounded by lots of air-freshening foliage that can bring the wonders of nature to one's windows, where you won't hear your neighbors through your walls, where you can grow a garden that won't be shaded by a neighboring rooftop or tramped on by strangers, where you can compost without the neighbors complaining, where hawks soar above the treetops, where you can hear the owls at night, where you can let the dog outdoors without a pooper-scooper in one hand and a leash in the other. Of such amenities Frank Lloyd Wright said: "You would enjoy all that you used to enjoy when you were ten to a block, and think of the immense advantages for your children and for yourself: freedom to *use* the ground, relationship with all kinds of living growth."[6] In fact, the more one lives in natural settings, the more one will likely embrace environmental precepts. A peerless measure here is a concept that appears in every ecology textbook, the *power density (PD) ratio*: the amount of biomass (foliage, natural materials, energies, etc.) an acre of land produces compared to how much it consumes. Clustered residences have high negative *PD* ratios because each acre consumes far more natural materials and energy than it produces; while wildernesses have positive *PD* ratios because each acre produces far more natural materials and energy than it consumes. This is a primary determinant of a property's environmental viability, one which clustered developments fail miserably. Moreover, every square mile of clustered development requires about 30 square miles of wilderness to purify its air, recycle its water, absorb its wastes, modify its climate, and provide a substantial portion of its occupants' food and fiber needs without economic cost or human management. This is the *wilderness ratio*. Urban square miles require about 50 square miles to do the same, and suburban square miles require about 17 square miles. This is why we need to preserve as much wilderness as possible; not so we'll have more spotted owls and snail darters someday, but so our grandchildren will be able to *breathe*.

One way LEED could minimize citizens' dependence on automobiles would be to award points for sidewalks in residential neighborhoods. Then people could more easily ride bicycles with baskets and saddlebags, pull wagons loaded with merchandise, and push their own shopping carts —all powered by foot force not fossil fuel.

☞ LEED recommends a number of "green" products that may contain toxins. We know that LEED-encouraged compact fluorescent lamps contain toxic mercury, and urethane in insulations can cause cancer. But how toxic are the newly developed low-VOC paints promoted by LEED? Or the recently developed spray-in foam insulations promoted by LEED? Or the phenol formaldehyde-based glues in OSB panels promoted by LEED? In 1982 —now a generation ago— urea formaldehyde foam insulation (known as UFFI) was banned by the U.S. Consumer Product Safety Commission due to "unreasonable risks to consumers from the irritation, sensitization, and possible carcinogenic effects of formaldehyde emitted by UFFI." Formaldehyde may be a fine preservative for undertakers, but not for occupants of buildings. Hear what the Environmental Protection Agency (EPA) has said more recently about the presence of this toxin in today's residences:

> In homes, the most significant sources of formaldehyde are likely to be pressed wood products made using adhesives that contain urea-formaldehyde (UF) resins. Pressed wood products made for indoor use include particleboard (used as sub-flooring and shelving and in cabinetry and furniture), hardwood plywood paneling (used for decorative wall covers and used in cabinets and furniture), and medium-density fiberboard (used for drawer fronts, cabinets, and furniture tops). Other pressed wood products, such as softwood plywood and flake or oriented strand board [the earlier-mentioned LEED-promoted OSB], contain red/black-colored phenol-formaldehyde resin. ... Formaldehyde, a colorless, pungent-smelling gas, can cause watery eyes, burning

sensations in the eyes and throat, nausea, and difficulty in breathing in some humans exposed at elevated levels above 0.1 ppm. ... Average concentrations in older homes without UFFI are generally well below 0.1 ppm. In new homes with significant amounts of new pressed wood products, levels can be greater than 0.3 ppm. ... Health effects also include fatigue; skin rash; severe allergic reactions. May cause cancer.

And all this is due to only one toxin in today's buildings! How many other poisons produced by man's own hand may be lurking in the sub-floors, shelves, cabinets, furniture, decorative wall covers, drawer fronts, furniture tops, softwood plywoods, OSB panels, and other materials that enclose occupants in newly constructed buildings? Are we to innocently lie prey to the kind of toxic disaster that struck possibly 50,000 homes in the South a few years ago that were built of Chinese sheetrock? This toxic product made these homes smell like rotten eggs on humid days; it dissolved copper in wires, pipes, appliances and electronic equipment; it caused occupants to have headaches, nosebleeds, and other illnesses; it lowered property values; and it forced home interiors to be gutted while owners had to continue paying mortgages while renting offsite housing. To pile insult on injury, many afflicted residents endured four economically and emotionally devastating years before their complaints reached the public ear. How many other citizens today await similar disasters before some appalling lottery selects them as the next big loser? And to what extent are the factory and construction workers who handle these products incurring health hazards? Certainly we should try to preserve the environment by the way we erect our buildings —but not at the expense of materially shortening our lives!

☞ A LEED-accredited building is evaluated just after construction, when this should be done after the building has been occupied for a while, say, six months; because a significant percentage of LEED-accredited buildings have proven to be energy-*deficient* after being occupied. Of this deceit Joseph Lstiburek, Ph.d., has stated, "You can get a LEED rating and not save any energy compared to traditional buildings." And the *New York Times* has said, "LEED standards sometimes reward large wasteful houses simply for using green technologies." [7] For a specific example of which there are many, a prominent engineer has said: "I have been asked to accept as green a $3,000 stainless steel outdoor griddle that uses less propane than a conventional grill." [8] All too easily LEED's directives are manipulated by profiteering businesses colluding with wealthy building owners to earn a credential that is fallacious on its face. If LEED evaluates a building before its performance is confirmed, its award plaque should come with removable screws. [9]

So this is the creed on LEED. This agency has done a lot of environmental good, but it still has a long way to go before it can claim to practice what its acronym preaches. Indeed, if you truly seek the essence of this agency's directives, you will presently achieve your objectives more quickly and inexpensively by using the unbiased reference you now have in your hands. Its directives won't cost you a few thousand dollars per building to implement, and they are untainted with commercial bias.

Another thing is sure: the solution we desperately need will not be laid at our doorstep by such Pollyanna measures as "a diverse array of technological innovations", "local and national policies aimed at reforming the energy systems around us",[10] and other excessively optimistic notions proposed by many authorities today.

So, bolstered by these disclosures, this book offers the following prescription for laying the foundation of a truly sustainable architecture:

Shades of Green

☞ **Find more environmentally sustainable ways to manu-
facture and assemble building materials.** This involves
consuming minimum energies and ravaging minimum environments in procuring and piecing together a product's
materials, packaging and transporting them to building
properties, and assembling them simply and durably.

☞ **Develop building envelopes that are thermally strong,
simple, economical, and durable.** Almost everywhere a
building's outer walls and roofs should contain not six
inches but at least *12* inches of insulation, this thermal
armor should be simple and economical to construct, and
it should last for decades.

☞ **Minimize wasted volumes in enclosed spaces.** It makes
little sense to fill a building with lo-flo showerheads, efficient light bulbs, and the like if its spaces contain room-
fuls of excess cubage that waste considerably more energy to construct and keep comfortable.

☞ **Develop and maintain up-to-date registers of toxic
substances in construction materials.** As past disasters have proven, a vigilant method of monitoring new
building products for possible toxins is urgently necessary. This includes short- and long-term risks of any sub-
stance that could be harmful to occupants in or around a
building or pose any dangers to adjacent properties; and
any material or product that fails this test should have a
skull and crossbones printed on it.

An even simpler prescription, especially for small buildings,
is to begin with efficient furniture (pages 95 ff), then create efficient indoor spaces (pages 87 ff), then you will have room inside
your exterior walls to add an extra foot of insulation (pages 357
ff), *ad posterus.* This work can be performed with present technology, requires no government policy reforms, can occur in
existing buildings, and be done one room at a time.

No matter how our environmental dilemma is dealt with, we

will never develop a sustainable architecture with minuscule efforts. In fact, if every American immediately began using *no* light bulbs and bathing in creeks and lakes, we *still* wouldn't solve our energy crisis because our buildings simply are hemorrhaging energy in too many ways. Even worse, if incorporating such minor economies into our buildings lull us into believing we need do nothing more, they will become more the problem than the solution. As Martin Luther King not long ago said of another movement in the making: "A beginning sincerely made is one thing, but a token beginning that is an end to itself is quite another." [11]

At the other extreme, if every suburban and urban dweller suddenly "sees the light" and flees their homes to live in straw-bale houses powered with solar panels on rural acres, how will these many millions even find the land they seek? There won't be near enough to go around. Neither will there be near enough excavators and carpenters and sheetrockers to build their abodes. And who would move into the vacated abodes? They would rot to ruin. The vacating residents would also give up their jobs, the businesses that depend on their patronage would fail, corporations would founder, the stock market would plunge to a thousand. This is why improving existing buildings one room at a time —which will allow inhabitants to avoid renting other places to live while possibly paying existing mortgages, will put local laborers back to work, and will enable local businesses to remain afloat— is eminently the best approach. And the best way to begin this work is to acquaint our citizenry with the buildings they presently live and work in and how they can most easily improve them, which is this book's chief objective.

Surely many limitations will loom in our efforts. But as Frank Lloyd Wright once said, "Limitations seem always to have been the best friends of architecture." [12] A corollary of this is: "Dig your well before you get thirsty" —meaning if you act early, you will likely end up with more comfort at less expense than will those who procrastinate until energy prices have risen five-fold before they decide the time has come to shift into action.

Shades of Green

Luckily, a few past examples exist here and there in this wide nation to remind us how at any time We the People can create a more sustainable architecture:

The Palace of the Governors in Santa Fe, New Mexico, a magnificent 250-foot-long commercial building whose walls are constructed of native adobe earth, whose impressive entrance facade is a colonnaded portico with fifteen thick wood posts capped with carved corbels, whose tall windows and transomed entrance doors are made of native woods, whose interiors are graced with floors of natural wood and ceilings of split boards set on log beams; built between 1610 and 1612.

The Henry Whitfield House in Guilford, Connecticut, whose facades and three forty-foot-tall chimneys are built of local fieldstone mortared with cement made of local clay and ground oyster shells, whose elegant staircase and clever second-story corner windows and tall third-story dormers projecting from a steep gable roof are constructed of locally obtained lumber; cornerstone laid in 1639.

The Hall of the Cloisters at Euphrata, Pennsylvania, a six-story residential building for a monastic community, whose mortised post-and-beam structure is built of local timber, whose clapboard siding is made of local wood, whose huge gable roof adorned with two dozen dormers is all made of local lumber; construction circa 1732.

Each of these buildings consumed virtually no fossil fuel in its making, and each —its anchoring base, welcoming entry, shape-giving corners, and sheltering roof— lyrically harmonizes its use of native materials with its stated purpose. These enduring examples show that if the day comes when we *really* have our backs to the wall, we needn't despair; because the answers we seek exist almost everywhere that developers haven't with their heavy machinery torn them down and the materials we'll need will forever be around our shoulders and under our feet.

Surely these fields of opportunity are green for the sickle.

Tools

This chapter describes the essential implements of architectural communication: the *Architectural Program*, *Architectural Plans*, *Specifications*, and the *Contract Bid*. These are used to articulate an owner's architectural desires whether the project is small as a bathroom vanity or large as a corporate skyscraper. In every case the client, we'll say it is You, is the axle that the wheel of architecture revolves around. It is essential to mention this, because so often in architecture all the words and numbers and pictures in a designed building's documents end up serving each other more than the occupants for whom they are intended.

So, let's say you have a spatial idea you want to bring to shape. What should you do first?

First, write down everything you can think of about the idea you hopefully, amorously, desperately would like to have. Probe your psyche. Get everything you can think of out in the open. Prod your thoughts with favored pictures from books and magazines. Collect them. Make a folder of them. Add to them every iota of interest you can think of. Below is a sketchy list:

☞ Do you have a property in mind? Or do you presently have no idea where the project will be built? If you have a site, what are its features (rocks, streams, foliage, etc.) and drawbacks? What trees and other foliage should be saved (list their heights, trunks and crown diameters)? Any views to be preserved? Any obscured views that could be opened? Et cetera.

☞ How many occupants will the building serve? Family? Employees? Customers? Guests? What are the known and anticipated numbers, as well as future prospects?

☞ What furnishings should each space have? This includes

any movable furniture as large as a chair, any built-ins such as cabinets and shelves, and any mechanical equipment like heaters, coolers, motors, even light bulbs (you'll learn later that the bulbs themselves aren't so important as the constructions around them).

☞ What about storage needs? Required and desired workspaces? Spaces for pets? Space for support staff (nannies, caregivers, custodians)?

☞ What kind of mechanical or computer equipment is required or desired? What amounts of heating, cooling, and ventilating will be needed to make the building comfortable? What is each interior area's lighting requirements? What heavy machinery should the building have? Any special drainage or ventilation requirements for spillages, fumes, dust, etc.? May any occupants have allergies or heightened sensitivity to conditions indoors?

☞ What should each entrance require due to local climate conditions (warm, cold, snowy, rainy, etc.)?

☞ What are the project's vehicular requirements? Cars? Trucks? Bicycles? Sidewalks for pedestrians? Desired parking for residents, guests, employees, customers? Full-day versus transient parking? Et cetera.

☞ How should the building relate to the surrounding neighborhood (an important consideration with many commercial buildings)?

☞ How will you finance all of this? Available funds, budget, bank, bonds, borrowing, etc.

☞ How involved will you be in the building's design and construction?

Next, you will try to find the proper professional(s) to bring your spatial idea to shape. If you plan to build a house, select an architect and/or contractor who specializes in residential construction; and if you want a solar house, don't select an architect who designs antebellum homes. When you have a list of candidates, (1) look at some of their work, (2) if possible talk to some of their previous clients, and (3) interview the candidates in their offices where you can look around for clues that indicate how they do business. Make a copy of the information you have assembled for each candidate. During this possibly lengthy conference you should ask:

☞ What are the candidate's fees and expenses?

☞ If you hire an architect, what will be his/her role in finding the contractor and other construction personnel?

☞ How long will the project take to design and/or build? What are the consequences if someone you hire takes too long or quits in the middle of the job?

☞ What kind of design and construction disputes are likely to arise, and how will they be resolved?

☞ What local laws and zoning ordinances will govern the project's design and construction?

With all the above, no one book could cover every nuance that could come into play here, especially when your own personality may influence the result as much as anything else. All this book can do is orient you in the right direction, and open your range of vision so the sweep of your comprehension aligns with the breadth of your desires, so your every concern can proceed unencumberingly in a logical chain of inquiry toward the finest solution you can expect that your budget will allow.

If a candidate with whom you confer is a contractor or carpenter or other tradesperson, s/he will likely look at your assembled information, make a few suggestions for improvements here and there, expound on his extensive knowledge of building materials and the latest construction tools, and say he will need a few days to prepare an estimate of how much the project will cost. He may show you a few standard plans that are suggestive of your expressed desires, and say he can revise part of any plan to satisfy your more specific needs. In essence his or her approach will likely be, "Okay, this is the way (i.e. your way) we'll do it."

Tools

However, if the candidate is an architect, s/he will likely take an entirely different approach. S/he will examine every item of information you have, and think not so much what it is like as your reason for liking it, and may suggest whole new ways to implement the essence of what you truly desire, and envision any potential conflicts that may occur. S/he will also know how to work with professional engineers to abstract your needs into optimally sized climate control and plumbing systems, desirable lighting levels, and other mechanical requirements. S/he may even sketch a few vertical sections to show how a certain space would look as you stand or walk around in it (something a contractor would rarely do); because an architect is more likely to see a group of related spaces not as a jigsaw puzzle but as a Rubik's Cube. An architect also has a document titled "Standard Form of Agreement between Owner and Architect" (known as A.I.A. Document B141), which details every aspect of an architect's business relation with a client. Usually the smaller the project, the more you might be inclined to hire a contractor; and the larger the project, the more you had better retain the services of an architect. Whatever you decide, don't think so much of saving money as getting maximum value for money spent; for a dime of design is often worth a dollar of construction.

An architect will also assemble all your information into a definitive *Architectural Program* which s/he will use to design the building. This document will describe the building's required spaces, how they relate to each other, and how you would like them to be furnished. While preparing this document the architect may interview a number of the building's other prospective occupants to determine what they also believe its spaces should have, and s/he may confer with the manufacturers of certain materials, products, or machinery that may be installed. The Architectural Program also deals with several other vital concerns of each essential space and the building as a whole, as follows:

☞ How big should each space be: its floor area, optimal

Architecture Laid Bare!

shape, and ceiling height. Architects have books, tables, and rules of thumb for determining the size of almost every indoor area (e.g. a queen-size bed for two is 60 × 78 inches, etc.); then s/he adds whatever adjacent space is needed for someone to use each area (e.g. a queen-size bed should have at least 17 inches of space on each side and at least 27 inches along its end, etc.). A more complex example: the access aisle on each side of a car in a garage should be at least 38 inches to allow a passenger to open a car door to get out then close the door and walk past it while carrying a bag of groceries. Sizing commercial spaces can run the gamut from simple to difficult. Dimensioning a basketball court is easy: one looks it up in *Architectural Graphic Standards*. But what about a museum exhibit area for a full-size dinosaur? I once had to dimension a space like this for a wildlife art museum I designed in 1983. I researched the length and width of a dinosaur, then added a 12-foot-wide viewing aisle around it: wide enough for two strolling people talking to each other as they pass two people strolling toward them plus a ring of people pausing to look at the exhibit.

☞ What storage does each space require? How much of the area should be adjacent to the space and how much can be located remotely? Required storage often adds 5 to 20 percent more area to each space.

☞ What kind of sidewalks, lobbies, halls, steps, ramps, elevators, escalators, and other circulation area is needed for occupants to move from outside the building to each essential area indoors? These spaces typically add 15 to 25 percent to the building's essential area.

☞ How much added floor area is required for a building's mechanical equipment? This may be as little as 10 percent in small buildings to more than 30 percent in large.

☞ What driveways and/or service roads does the building require from the nearest public street(s)? This includes

C. HONORS ROOM

CONCEPTUAL. If there is a "special place" deep within the Jonas Wildlife Center, this is it. This space will be used for entertaining guest speakers and visiting dignitaries, a reading room for visitors examining museum documents, and a conference room for administration meetings. This room should have access to the auditorium, office and lobby areas; and it should contain a large conference table with seats for 16, decorative foliage, perhaps a few small exhibits that require minimum security surveillance, and a large wall area for mounting plaques, awards, and life membership rosters. Nearby should be a kitchenette, and ample storage area.

VOLUME. Floor area of honors room + kitchenette + storage ≈ 450 sf + 50 sf + 50 sf ≈ 550 sf. Height of honors room = 12–13 feet. Height of minor spaces = 9 ft.

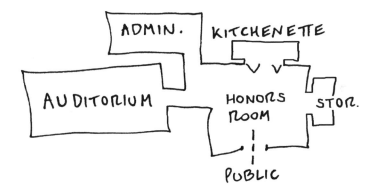

2-1. Page from an architectural program

This is a description of one room in an Architectural Program I wrote for a museum of wildlife art I designed in 1983. This document was a *preliminary* program, written primarily to attract funds to construct the project. If this had been the final program, prepared after acquiring the funds and before initiating the building's formal design, this space's requirements would have been more elaborately detailed.

Architecture Laid Bare!

lanes, curves, turnarounds, parking areas, and a host of related areas. A residential driveway may be no more than a strip of asphalt from the street to the garage, while the service area for a large factory would require far more.

☞ How should the building be protected from fire? This includes fires erupting inside the building as well as wildfires approaching from outside.

☞ How should the building accommodate the handicapped?

☞ What opportunities exist for using recycled materials in the building? Today this has become an increasingly relevant and opportunistic issue.

Even if you hire a handyman to install a towel rack in a bathroom, the two of you should write a little Program, even if only half a page long, that describes the work to be performed and the fees to be paid. You can also use this memorandum as court evidence if the builder doesn't satisfactorily perform the work required. However long an *Architectural Program* is (for a custom residence it may be fifty pages and for a large commercial building it may be several hundred) the owner should read it thoroughly. If you want the framed portrait of your great-grandfather in his Civil War uniform to appear above your grandmother's antique bowfront sideboard in the front hall, this is the time to make sure this desire is spelled out in the Program. Otherwise the architect can legally charge you extra to later redesign the space to include these furnishings. The same applies if you want a four-bedroom house, then later realize you have the funds to build only three. This document is vitally important, as evidenced by what Eugène Viollet-le-Duc, the famed French architectural theorist of the mid-19th Century, said:

> To every architect worthy of the name, a programme that is well drawn up and clear, and which is not liable to any false interpretation, is half the battle. ... To be true in respect of the programme is to fulfill exactly, scrupulously, the conditions imposed by the requirements of the case. [1]

Tools

Poorly written *Architectural Programs* are the root cause of many design and construction disputes. A subtle example of this occurred in the first architect's office I worked in, in 1960. The architect had designed a fine residence for a husband and wife during which the wife said she wanted the living room to be "about 15 by 20 feet". The architect duly included this data in the building's program and designed the space with these dimensions. But when the wife first stepped into the framed construction she looked around and said, "This room is too small!" She didn't have an accurate spatial idea of the dimensions she desired, and the architect hadn't been aware of this possibility. While this mistake wasn't the architect's fault, when a client makes such a suggestion, the architect should try to understand precisely what the client is thinking.

Once every detail of the Program is agreed on by all parties involved, the architect designs the building. This is typically an "educated trial-and-error process" in which the architect tries arranging the building's spaces in every way possible to find which is most functional, comfortable, beautiful, and affordable. On large buildings this may take the architect and a large staff months to complete.

When the architect is done, s/he presents the design of the building and its environs as a solution to the client in the form of a set of drawings known as the *Architectural Plans*, sometimes called the *Drawings*, or simply the *Plans*. This is a sheaf of large pages, bound along the left, which when opened may occupy most of a conference table. Each page, looking broad as a linen tablecloth, is covered with sketchy but photorealistic drawings accompanied by notes and symbols. Each page has a title box, typically in the lower right corner, that lists the building's address, addresses of the architect and owner, the page's title, and the date it was finished. Almost every drawing also has a scale which indicates its relative size, and every site plan and floor plan has a north arrow which orients it to the compass and each other. The aim of these drawings, as Frank Lloyd Wright once said, is "to render the composition in outline and form and suggest the sentiment

2-2. The planned building

of the environment."[2] When you examine this document you are looking at a copy: a *blueprint* (this word derives from the pre-World War II method of reproducing architectural drawings as white lines on dark blue pages). The original drawings are kept in a vault in the architect's office. The architect makes however many copies the owner, contractor, estimators, suppliers, financiers, and any business associates may require. The Plans include:

PERSPECTIVE ... A picture of the building and its environs, usually as viewed from the air (known as a bird's eye view) or
  from the ground before the main entrance. This is commonly the Plan's title page. Perspectives for large public
  buildings may be in color, and they often show people and
  vehicles as they would normally appear about the building. Figure 2-2 is a perspective of my house I designed in
  1974 as seen from the driveway below, and figure 2-3 is a
  photo of the finished house. If you look closely at each,
  you can see a few small differences between the planned
  building and the final result. This usually happens,

2-3. The final result

because when a design is being built, a more practical solution for a certain part may present itself that was difficult to visualize during the more conceptual, remote, and miniaturized design stage.

SITE PLAN ... This is a map of the property on which the building is located. It shows the property's boundaries and siting of the building plus its driveways, turnarounds, parking areas, any related construction, landmarks, landscaping, bodies of water, topography, nearest public road(s), and the like. If the terrain surrounding a planned building will be extensively revised, the drawings may have two site plans of the same scale: existing and revised. Figure 2-4 is part of the site plan for the house that appears in figures 2-2 and 2-3. This drawing also shows existing trees and rocks near the house that should not be removed, the building's foundation, the outline (in dotted lines) of the roof, and the locations of the drilled well slightly above the house and the septic tank below.

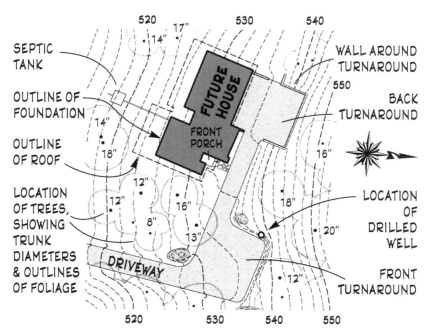

HEAVY DOTTED LINES ARE 10 FOOT CONTOUR INTERVALS (FEET ABOVE SEA LEVEL); LIGHT DOTTED LINES ARE 2 FOOT INTERVALS

2-4. Part of a site plan

ELEVATIONS ... These are pictures of the building that show how it will look from the outside. Each picture is of one facade, and it shows in addition to the building's shape its doors, windows, vents, and exterior finishes. Outlines of the floors, walls, and ceilings just inside the facades usually appear in dotted lines. Figure 2-5 shows part of the east elevation of the house appearing in figure 2-3. Next to each foundation and floor level in figure 2-5 is the symbol ⊕ with a number beside it, as in —⊕524.17. These are *elevation markers*. The lowest one says this level, the underside of the foundation, is 524.17 feet, or 524 feet 2 inches, above sea level. Above this marker is a second that says —⊕526.67. This is the level of the lowest floor, which, if you do the math, is 4 feet 6 inches above the underside of the foundation. Well above the second marker is a third, — ❸ 536.17, which says the second floor is 9 feet 6 inches above the first. The contractor uses these horizontal references to determine the height of the building. In lieu of using actual above-sea-level dimensions the archi-

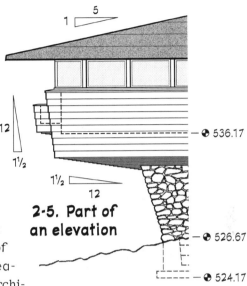

2-5. Part of an elevation

may use a common datum such as —❸ 100.00 for the lowest part of the construction. All elevation contours appearing on the site plan should relate to this vertical reference on all other drawings.

An elevation should show exactly how the designed building will look, in character as well as detail. I remember a four-story office building designed years ago in a nearby city whose drawings showed its long front facade as a curtain wall with rows of gracefully thin mullions between large areas of glass. But when constructed, the mullions were thick and made the building look like it was wrapped in bicycle tape: not the attractive article the owner thought he was paying for. This likely happened because the architect, after drawing the mullions to look attractive on paper, didn't try hard enough to find a mullion from manufacturers' catalogs that matched what was drawn. The owner put up a fuss which a local newspaper reported in an article about the size of a postage stamp. The best way to avoid this problem is for the architect to

43

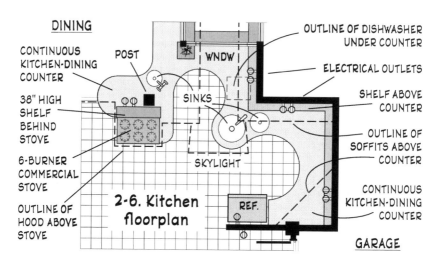

DINING

CONTINUOUS KITCHEN-DINING COUNTER

POST

WNDW

OUTLINE OF DISHWASHER UNDER COUNTER

ELECTRICAL OUTLETS

38" HIGH SHELF BEHIND STOVE

SINKS

SHELF ABOVE COUNTER

OUTLINE OF SOFFITS ABOVE COUNTER

6-BURNER COMMERCIAL STOVE

SKYLIGHT

OUTLINE OF HOOD ABOVE STOVE

2-6. Kitchen floorplan

REF.

CONTINUOUS KITCHEN-DINING COUNTER

GARAGE

show the client actual samples, obtained from the manufacturer, of what s/he plans to install in the building. This
is important not only for construction details in commercial exteriors, but for all kinds of details inside and outside any building. Models, mockups, and product samples
are often helpful here, though often expensive.

FLOOR PLANS or PLANS ... Each of these drawings, the most
familiar to most people, is a large picture taken at eye
level that looks straight down on a floor that shows the
size and shape of each space and how they relate to each
other, plus the location of walls, any built-in cabinetry,
immovable appliances or machinery, and the structure
that supports the construction above. Figure 2-6 is a
floorplan of the kitchen in the house that appears in figure 2-3. Since this is a geometrically complex space, figure 2-7 is a photo of the kitchen in figure 2-6 that helps
you visualize what appears in the plan. An architect can
draw a perspective of a space that is as realistic as a
photo *before* the space is built. Still, complex spaces usu-

2-7. Photo of kitchen whose plan appears in 2-6

ally require a number of auxiliary drawings and a few architect's visits to the site to make sure the contractor and all his or her subs (members of a specific building trade, such as a plumber or electrician, also known as subcontractors) builds them correctly. A plan's open areas typically appear in white and solid areas appear as solid colors or dark patterns representing different construction materials, somewhat as follows:

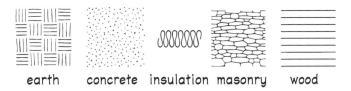

earth   concrete insulation masonry wood

Large buildings may also have ELECTRICAL, PLUMBING, and HVAC (heating, ventilation, and cooling) floorplans that detail these mechanical installations on each floor. Buildings with complicated ceilings may also have ceiling plans that show their construction.

SECTIONS ... These views are taken by slicing vertically through the building, conceptually removing one side, and looking into the other side to show what the interiors look like, what their vertical dimensions are, how the stacked spaces relate to each other, and how occupants relate to windows, doors, counters, cabinets, and stairs. Large buildings may have several sections cut from different directions. Figure 2-8 shows a section through the staircase of the house in figure 2-2.

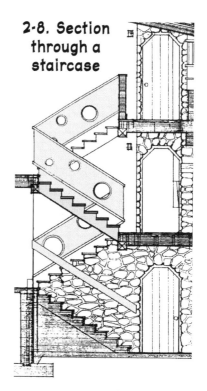

2-8. Section through a staircase

INTERIOR ELEVATIONS ... These are detailed sections of interior spaces that show locations of cabinets, counters, shelves, appliances, mechanical equipment, plumbing fixtures, electrical outlets and switches, tiled areas in bathrooms, towel racks, finishes, etc. These drawings are often meticulously detailed.

CONSTRUCTION DETAILS ... These are usually small drawings, often numbering in the hundreds for large buildings, that show how every part is constructed. Figure 2-9 shows the construction below the kitchen sink appearing in the plan in figure 2-6 and the photo in figure 2-7. These are also meticulously detailed. The title of each includes the number on its page and the page number, as in ⓑ-14, which is the "B" or likely second drawing on page 14. These notations in addition to appearing beside each detail also appear somewhere on a larger plan or section that shows where the detail is located in the building.

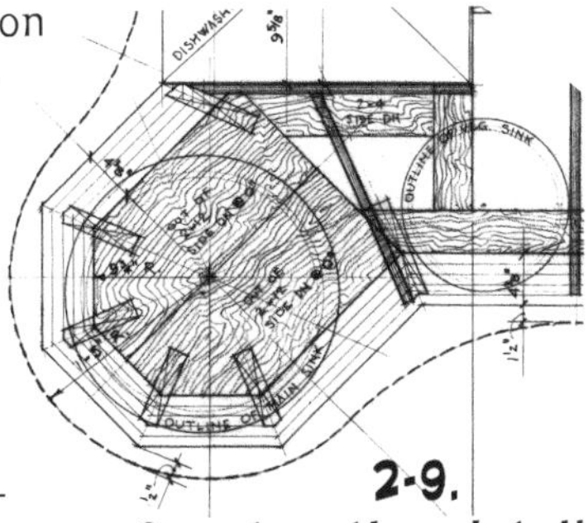

2-9.
Construction detail
of kitchen sink

To help you read a set of architectural plans, figure 2-10 shows a few symbols you'll find on them. These may vary depending on the architect's style of drawing.

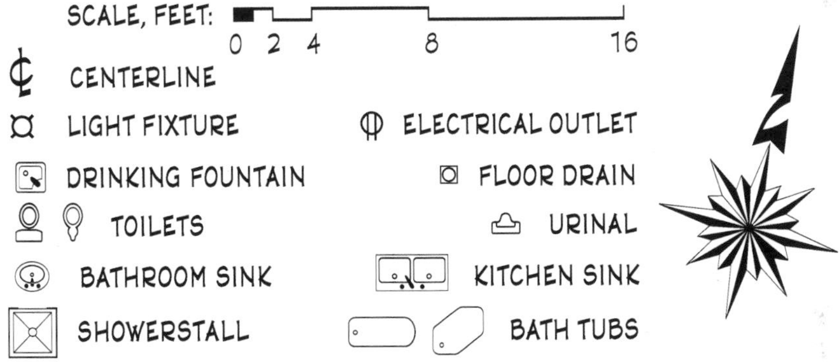

SCALE, FEET: 0 2 4 8 16

₵ CENTERLINE

☒ LIGHT FIXTURE   ⏀ ELECTRICAL OUTLET

DRINKING FOUNTAIN   ▣ FLOOR DRAIN

TOILETS   URINAL

BATHROOM SINK   KITCHEN SINK

SHOWERSTALL   BATH TUBS

2-10. A few architectural plan symbols

In these days of modern computer technology, an architect may sit you in front of a large computer screen and "walk" you through a 3-D replica of the proposed design, in which you step through spaces looking nearly as real as if you were in the finished building. These programs may allow you or others to:

☞ Zoom in or out of any view so you can look closely at details or gain a larger picture of the area.

☞ Operate the lighting, and see how the sun traveling across the sky brightens interiors during the day.

☞ Change wall colors, floor finishes, and decors so you can

47

see which combinations you like the most.

☞ Perform cost and performance analyses of heating and cooling systems.

☞ Route ducting, piping, and other mechanical networks through the building so contractors will be able to install them more economically.

Be warned that these attractive graphics can be seductive. They can hide imperfections, and they can make a space look larger or smaller than it really is.

When an architect designs a building, his or her labor may not always be exactly what you desire. If the designer veers from the material requirements of the program, or tries to allure you with embellishments that subtract from your pocketbook more than they add to your welfare, it may be time for you to assertively "put the engine back on the track". Hopefully all you have learned here so far will enable you to do this confidently and well. Certainly you may not know the nuances a professional acquires from having performing this labor for years. But if you have a firm conceptual grasp of what you want, and don't let yourself be sidetracked into situations that may seem alien to your desires, you will more often be master of your architectural fate, not its slave. At the outset it may take you two or three conferences, even a retainer, to learn how truly capable a candidate may be in your behalf, before you finally feel comfortable about steaming straight ahead or possibly cutting your losses before further damage may be done. On the other hand, when the architect's labor is a faithful transcript of your desires, and is the expression of an inventive intellect and refined artistry, you may be overcome with exhilaration as an amorphous concept suddenly comes to life and you suddenly imagine yourself inhabiting the building. There is so much about this relation that is subjective: at its best it really is a dance of harmonious personalities, of which this nor any other volume can predict any outcome whatsoever.

A more pragmatic matter is that a building's design and construction is rarely the result of vision, desire, talent, and perseverance as much as it is an accommodation to the forces of supply and demand, cash flow, and code compliance.

After the Architectural Program and the Plans come two more documents: The *Specifications*, which may be the size of a telephone book if the building is large, and the *Contractor's Bid*, which is usually thin enough to fit into a business envelope.

The *Specifications* describes the materials, equipment, appliances, and finishes plus the quality of every part of the work that is required to build the architecture. This document, written in construction language, is essentially a communication between the architect and contractor; but the owner should be somewhat familiar with it and may enjoy reading it. Most of a specification's language is industrial boilerplate, though some passages may be precisely tailored for the building it serves and include colors of materials, dimensions of installed appliances, model numbers of mechanical equipment, and the like. This document commonly has the following sections:

1. GENERAL REQUIREMENTS
2. SITE CONSTRUCTION
3. CONCRETE
4. MASONRY
5. METALS
6. WOOD & PLASTICS
7. THERMAL & MOISTURE PROTECTION
8. DOORS, WINDOWS, & SKYLIGHTS
9. FINISHES (paints, trims, adhesives, floors, walls, ceilings, etc.; both indoors and outdoors)
10. EQUIPMENT (items like laundry facilities, parking gates, patient care systems, scoreboards, etc.)
11. SPECIALTIES (items like shower curtains, fireplace inserts, signage, closet hardware, etc.)
12. FURNISHINGS (items like bookcases, cabinets, window shades, stadium seating, office furniture, etc.)

13. SPECIAL CONSTRUCTION (generators, saunas, security devices, blast-resistant protection, swimming pool covers, intrusion detection, computer control centers, etc.)
14. CONVEYING SYSTEMS (elevators, escalators, dumbwaiters, chutes, hoists, cranes, etc.)
15. MECHANICAL (plumbing, heating, cooling, ventilation, snowmelting, hangers, supports, etc.)
16. ELECTRICAL (electrical, lighting, phone, telecom systems)

To give you an idea of how meticulous the *Specifications* are, in a commonly used standard Specification one boilerplate section of item 9 above, FINISHES, is 46 pages long, one section of which is *Gypsum Work*, which is 15 pages long, a small part of which reads,

Part III of *V, Execution*:
Section 3.3 of 9, Applying Interior Gypsum Board:
Subsection 2 of 6, Single-Layer Application:

1. On ceilings, partitions, and walls, apply gypsum panels at right angles to framing, unless otherwise noted or required by fire-resistance-rated assembly.
   a. Stagger abutting end joints not less than one framing member in alternate courses of panels, and minimize all end joints.
2. Fastening Methods: Apply all gypsum panels to supports with drilled steel screws.
3. Cover all seams, joints, and screwheads with coats of joint compound according to standard practice.

The purpose of this detailed language is to make absolutely clear what the contractor is required to do to construct the building to the owner's satisfaction. It is the FINE PRINT of the contract between the Owner and Builder, as enforced by the Architect. Normally this document is a notably boring tract lined with the dullest prose and suffering from a paucity of pictures. But consider this. The book presently in your hands is a glorified manual of specifications, more than four hundred pages long, which, if you like, you could take to a professional and say, "I would like you to design and construct every functional part of the building the way these pages say."

That's the written guarantee the "specs" are meant to make.

Finally comes the fourth document, the culmination of often months of labor and the entree to constructing the building: the *Contractor's Bid.* [3] This is the price the builder has placed on his or her envisioned labor. This offer is written on letterhead stationery, slipped into a business envelope, and opened before all interested parties in a legal proceeding known as the Bid Opening Ceremony. Some bidders, instead of stating a specific price for the work to be performed, may state that s/he will perform the work for "time and materials": the cost of one's labor plus that of one's crew and subcontractors, plus the cost of materials, plus an honest profit added thereto.

Whatever amount a contractor's bid may be, the owner should never consider it to be the only funds that will be needed to erect the building. The owner will require added funds for all kinds of landscaping around the building, all kinds of furnishing inside, unforeseen add-ons, cost overruns and possible mistakes, unexpected economic occurrences, and a host of other contingencies. For a normally upscale residence, an owner would be wise to allot only about 70 percent of available funds to erect the building and reserve the rest for all other considerations. For larger projects this reserve may generally be less, and for smaller projects it may be more.

A crucial act on the part of an architect or owner is selecting the best contractor to construct the design. If you entertain several candidates, (1) see that each is provided with exactly the same information, including a complete set of Plans and Specifications; (2) at the end of the day drive by a project each contractor is building and note how clean and tidy the site is (a professional outward appearance often indicates how "professional" hidden aspects of the work may be); (3) try to find if each bidder pays his laborers good wages and benefits (contractors tend to exercise the same integrity toward their clients as they do toward their crews); (4) during any telephone calls you may have with a bidder to clarify any details, try to note the caller's knowledge, grasp of the situation, and depth of inquiries; and (5) do the usual inquiring about each contractor's skills and ethics. Here are a few things to avoid. (1) Refrain from sharing insights you have gained from discussing the project with one bidder with another, so that all bidders will remain on an equal footing (sharing such information may also conceal the second bidder's ineptness). (2) Don't select more than four bidders: good contractors spend a lot of time preparing an estimate, and with each effort they have a right to believe they have a reasonable chance of winning the work. (3) After the bids are in, never use a lower bid to renegotiate a lower price from a higher bid.

The object of all the above is not to select the lowest bidder, but the lowest *responsible* bidder. Exactly what is this? This is best answered with a few examples. Say the lowest bidder has an office-in-home, has been working for a year, and employs inexperienced labors who receive no wage benefits; while a slightly higher bidder has a large office in a commercial building, has been in business for twenty years, has several supervisors who direct a number of ongoing projects, and employs experienced laborers who receive wage benefits? It is easy to say all candidates should be similar in size, scope, background, and experience; but in sparsely populated areas during times of prosperity when all local contractors may be fully employed, this often is not an option. Here are a few other examples that will give your powers of judgment plenty of exercise when trying to select the most responsible contractor for a given project:

☞ A higher bidder may possess the kind of integrity and knowledge that would be critical in constructing difficult parts of the building.

☞ During an initial interview an honest experienced contractor may give you an accurate appraisal of how expensive a project will be, and when a later contractor says s/he can do the work for less as an enticement to win the work, his labor eventually costs more than the first contractor had quoted.

☞ A youthful "inexperienced" contractor who has a real talent and passion for the work may go to almost any extreme to do it well in hopes of gaining a reputation for oneself.

☞ An accomplished "best of bread" gentleman who has been working for decades may be highly skilled at making favorable impressions during initial conferences —but once s/he wins the work, s/he may be more skilled at being evasive, oppressive, argumentative, and inclined to take sudden vacations when s/he doesn't get his way. It is easy to say: obtain references. But ...

☞ An incompetent contractor who does twenty jobs may do eighteen badly and get excellent references from the other two (who may be relatives or receivers of favors) and thus render a false impression of his competence.

☞ Don't over-estimate experience. The best contractor I ever worked for, Reeford Shea, for several years around 1970, once said, "It takes only five or six years to be a good carpenter, and I've seen people who've done it for thirty years who still don't know what they are doing."

In each case, if you can, seek a contractor's references and interview *them*. Ferret out those who, out of a sense of timidity or loyalty, may have said good things about a bad character; or who out of pique or embarrassment may have criticized a conscientious candidate who said what an owner needed to know but didn't want to hear. Another clue: Ask how the candidate will keep a record of the Work. Contractors who take daily stock of their affairs, who keep regular accounts of their work, whose books are up-to-date, whose credit is firmly established at local lumber companies and other outlets, who seek advantageous bargains for materials, who buy the best materials, who buy largely on favorable terms, who always know where they stand with their suppliers, whose dealings are bona fide, who carry no debts, and who always seem to be well-informed about the latest events and trends deserve higher commendations and compensation than those don't do these things. Still another clue: Try to find out what they like to do in their spare time, and what hobbies they might have enjoyed when they were young. I often think that one of my finest "qualifications" as an architect is not my ivy-league architectural education or my decades of experience in both design and construction, but that when I was a kid I loved to make model airplanes (not ones of molded pieces of plastic but of carved and sanded pieces of balsa) and displayed dozens of them from my bedroom ceiling in various attack positions. Try to learn things like this about each candidate if you can.

On the good side, almost anywhere you can find one or more experienced contractors who really know what they are doing and who down through the years have assembled a competent team of contractors and subs. Though they may be more expensive, they will more likely give maximum value for money spent. However, it often seems there aren't enough of the good ones to go around; because they tend to get snapped up by the wealthiest clients on the choicest projects; and well they deserve this accommodation. But sometimes this can leave slim pickings for the majority of owners who have small projects with modest budgets.

Another tip for owners about to embark on any construction project, large or small, is to keep a *Book of Entries*. This is a record of every material delivered and every hour of work performed, as suggested in figure 2-11. If you can't obtain the listed information from the contractor, insist, if you can, that s/he keep a similar record for the project, and insist, if you can, to be allowed to examine it when you want. Better yet, you keep such a record and have the contractor keep one, and compare them occasionally, perhaps during weekly conferences. This is one of the most thorough ways an owner can show an interest, keep

Tools

2-11. Book of Entries

INVOICE	DATE	QUANTITIES	COSTS	RECEIVER	WAGES	REMARKS
NAME OF	MONTH,	LENGTHS,	UNIT	CONTRACTOR	HOURLY	
SUPPLIER,	DAY, YR,	WEIGHTS,	PRICES,	OR REP WHO	WAGE,	
HANDLER	TIME OF	NUMBERS,	AMOUNTS,	ACCEPTED	HOURS,	
OF ORDER	DAY	ETC.	SUMS	GOODS	WITHHLD'G	

informed, be involved, and have the confidence to assert oneself when necessary. Also if any construction or legal dispute arises, you will likely have a needed record of all that transpired.

Once construction begins, the contractor or a foreman should be on the jobsite at all times, while the architect and owner periodically visit the site, perhaps once a week and more often at critical stages of construction. Examples of the latter are before concrete will be poured (so you can see that everything is located where it should be before it is concealed by the concrete), after the building is framed (the first time you can see the interiors full-size before the framing and structure are concealed with finishes), and after any kitchen appliances and plumbing fixtures have arrived (so you can make sure they are what you want before they are installed).

At any time during construction, if the architect or owner believes part of a building "isn't being constructed correctly as described in the Plans," the contractor has the right to say, "Show me where the Plans describe how the part should be constructed correctly." If the architect can do this, the contractor typically corrects the construction at his expense. If the architect cannot do this, the contractor typically corrects the construction at the architect's or owner's expense. Another difficulty arises if the owner visits the construction and, on seeing the polydimensional reality in full size, may realize there are things s/he wants that s/he had been unable to express or visualize earlier when the project was in miniature, on paper, and remote from the site. Then the architect, owner, and contractor must confer. Ideally the contractor informs the owner how much the revised construction will cost, the owner decides if s/he wants to pay for it, and if so the architect draws the revised construction as an addenda to the Plans. There are two legal methods of resolving the above disputes: *Change Orders* and *Field Orders*:

Change Order ... a written order issued by the architect to the contractor authorizing a change in the work, an adjustment in the contract sum, or extension of the contract time as originally defined by the contract documents that **is not** the fault of the contractor; wherein the contractor is paid for the extra work required.

Field Order ... a written order issued by the architect to the contractor authorizing a change in the work, an adjustment in the contract sum, or extension of the contract time as originally defined by the contract documents that **is** the fault of the contractor; wherein the contractor pays for the extra work required.

On the whole, there are many competent contractors and subcontractors (these specialize in part of the construction such as plumbing or electrical work) who do their best to give their clients their money's worth, who do not cultivate adversarial relations with them, and who try to see that the job gets done the way the owner wants. But there is a tendency for a small but significant few to be *incompetent* (their initial claims overestimate their abilities), *manipulative* (they take advantage of your inferior knowledge of the situation), *exploitative* (they overcharge for their work), or *dishonest* (they lie about what they will do and you won't discover it until they are long gone). If an owner hasn't a professional knowledge of the work to be performed, or is unable to spend every waking hour watching the work, or cannot afford a trusted overseer, s/he is prey to these rogueries in the form of excessive billing and deficient work. A few examples appear below, in hopes that they will improve your ability to deal with the same if ever the need arises.

Regarding being incompetent ... in 1974 I hired a mason to

build three innovative fireplaces I had designed for my house (they are detailed in a later chapter). He was a burly callous-handed man with decades of experience: all favorable signs of the competence I sought. The morning he was to begin building the first fireplace, we met by the hearth and discussed in thorough detail my meticulously drawn plans. I then left to supervise other parts of the job and about eleven o'clock returned to see how he was doing.

I was mortified to see him building a conventional fireplace! "Hey," I yelled, "you're building it wrong."

He looked up at me wide-eyed and replied: "I've been building fireplaces for 21 years, you think I don't know what I'm doing?"

After overcoming my apoplexy, I pulled myself together and told him to tear it down and start over. Thereafter I constantly had to keep an eye on him to make sure he followed the plans. But what does an owner do who *hasn't* years of construction experience, and *can't* spend every hour of the week watchdogging the work? If you live in an area where skilled artisans are scarce and you don't want to wait a few years to get the job done right, you may simply have to go with the "best" available. Or else, shore up your patience and wait. You may even find it more soothing to your psyche and more economical to your pocketbook to take a leave of absence from your job, buy a few good books on construction, and perform or oversee the work yourself.

Regarding being manipulative ... a few all-too-common ploys are that once construction begins, on bid jobs a contractor may cut corners when s/he thinks he can get away with it, and on time-and-material jobs they may "stretch things out" so they work more hours and make more money than they should. As for cost-plus jobs, they may tell you how something should be done that is faulty if they believe you are ignorant of the situation, then later when the fault is discovered they'll likely get to do it again. Hear what one construction engineer, a top forensic authority in his field for decades, has said of this willfully negligible practice:

Architecture Laid Bare!

> A few contractors construct work in a manner that they know to be in violation of the engineer's [or owner's] intent and even against a normal interpretation of contract drawings, as long as they have some argument to justify doing so. They believe they will get paid three times —twice to install and once to remove the faulty work— and they often do. Specialty subcontractors in particular generally know their area of the specifications exceptionally well and that these types of errors always seem to generate extras for them. ... This is not the business model of best-of-bread contractors, but it also is not so rare that it doesn't deserve mention. [4]

In such cases you really have to know what the builders are doing, and know when an effort to paint their side of the fence white is black as hell, and find the time to observe them; or you must hire an overseer who is highly competent and who you can trust.

Regarding being exploitative ... in 1979 when I was building a large addition for a woman's residence that included installing thirty kitchen cabinets as storage units throughout the house, the client and I visited a local lumber company that carried a line of fine cabinets. While we discussed the project with the manager at his desk, he quoted the price of the cabinets displayed in the showroom in the next room as $162 each. When the client stepped into the showroom to look at the cabinets, the manager leaned way over his desk and whispered to me ... "93 to you."

He didn't know the client's and my career paths were headed toward matrimony. Needless to say, she got her cabinets for 93 dollars each. The difference in profit between the two prices was more than two thousand dollars for thirty cabinets. In 1979! That's a lot of payola for delivering a pickup truckload of case-work. Such huge markups on building products by suppliers to contractors "happen all the time" in these venues. Perhaps the best antidote for owners who don't plan to marry their contractors is to make an educated guess of what a markup may be (here you might guide your thoughts with the "93/162" rule), then bargain the contractor down as best as you can. Another useful yardstick is the "10-18-28" rule: these numbers I obtained from a lumber company manager in 1975 who confided that the lumber he then sold for 28 cents a board-foot he bought from a wholesaler for 18 cents a board-foot and directly from the mill for 10 cents a board-foot. Down through the decades, these price ratios appear to have remained fairly constant.

Even more exploitative is the price pyramid that underlies many of today's construction projects, especially residences. A successful residential contractor recently confided to me that he typically (1) includes a wage for his time spent on the jobsite which may be from 30 to 50 dollars an hour; (2) he adds 15 percent to all wages (including withholding, insurance, etc.) that he pays himself, his crew and his subs; (3) he adds 15 percent to the price of all the materials he orders; (4) he adds 15 percent to #2 and #3 above as a "job" profit; (5) he adds another 15 percent to #4 above as a "contractor's" profit; then (6) he tries to sell the completed construction for as much as a realtor can get —which may be another 20 percent! The contractor makes even more if s/he purchased the raw land and developed it. Of course when it comes to such faithless manipulations, the realtors all have their feet on the accelerator and not the brake. The biggest jump in these profits came in the early 1990s when Congress passed laws allowing banks to lend more money to homeowners —whereupon contractors, being no fools, simply raised the price of their labor to the limits of what buyers could borrow. So the homeowner's mortgage crisis is not a "debt" crisis so much as it is the result of a widespread oligopoly conducted by contractors working in collusion with realtors. For example, in 1975 around here, you could buy a raised ranch on an acre of land for $50,000. Today the price for the same construction around here is more like $450,000 — and inflation has *not* increased nine times since 1975. In 1975, lumber used to sell (as mentioned above) for about 28 cents a board foot, and today it usually sells for 60 to 65 cents a board foot. Using 62 cents as an average, according to this index a raised ranch on an acre of land today should sell for around $111,000. Certainly land values have risen out of proportion to this ratio during the last forty years, but by far the biggest reason for the difference between this price and $450,000 is the huge increase in contractors' profits. As an ethical comparison, back around 1970 the contractor I worked for, Reeford Shea, a moral man, charged 25 dollars an hour for his work plus 10 percent of all material and other labor costs. If today's prices are about 3 times what they were in 1970, a contractor's hourly wage today would be about 75 dollars an hour, plus material and labor commissions. If s/he worked 40 hours a week, this wage alone would be 3,000 dollars a week. In my book, that's good pay.

If you ever wonder why a three-bedroom house these days costs three or four hundred thousand dollars —*after* the mortgage crisis has significantly lowered their pricetags— now you know. Still, these prices should drop another one-third *or more* if a contractor's profits are to become anywhere like what the rest of us hard workers earn. If these prices should ever lower to equitable levels, I lament the losses that millions of homeowners would incur who in past years had to buy houses when their prices were inflated.

Regarding being dishonest ... in 1981 my gravel driveway needed grading, which it does every few years. When a dump truck with a big JESUS SAVES sign mounted over the cab delivered gravel to a neighbor across the street, I assumed the driver was an honest man, walked over and introduced myself, and asked if he could deliver 20 yards of gravel to my driveway. He quoted a reasonable price, and we set a delivery date two days hence.

The morning of the delivery, a different truck arrived with a different driver, who turned out to be the first driver's brother. During the usual introductory civilities, I slipped a tape measure from my belt and stepped over to the truck and measured the dump body's length, height, and width, then did some quick math in my head. I said to the driver, "This truck holds only 16 yards when I ordered 20." He nodded a quick Yessir and proceeded to satisfactorily grade my driveway. No problem there. But when he handed me the invoice it listed 20 yards of gravel delivered. I said, "You delivered only 16 yards. What are you billing me 20 for?"

"That's what my brother said. Are you going to pay me?"

"I'm not going to pay you for 20 yards when you delivered only 16, but I'll write you a check for 16."

He huffily refused my equitable offer and drove off with the parting words, "You'll hear from my brother tonight."

That night I heard from the brother. When I explained that I refused to pay for 20 yards of gravel because only 16 was delivered, the brother, amid a few deific referrals to the big sign on his truck, replied, "Oh, we agreed that I would deliver you 20 *tons* of gravel, not 20 *yards*." Now I had known for years that a cubic yard of gravel weighs about 2,800 pounds, which means (if you do the math) that 16 yards of gravel weighs about 22 tons —which would suggest this fellow had delivered more than what we had agreed. But I angrily replied that I had been in this business twenty years and I —— well knew the difference between a yard and a ton of gravel and he was knowingly trying to *cheat* me —and I later mailed him a check for sixteen yards of gravel, minus a ten percent "lie factor."

You can do this too. If you do the following:

Whenever a truck delivers a load of gravel, dirt, asphalt, or any other such material to a project you own or manage, (1) know the terminology, which may involve doing a little research in advance; (2) don't be fooled by pious references to religions, experience, degrees, pedigrees, and other exhibits of alleged integrity; (3) clip a 20-foot tape measure on your belt, and when the truck arrives step over and measure the dump body's length, width, and height; (4) write the numbers down (a good pencil and pad here is a ballpoint pen and the palm of your hand) and compute the yardage *in situ*. With the facts firmly in hand and your knowledge firmly in mind, you will stand a fighting chance of seeing that justice is done. I know it may be hard for some of you to summon the gumption to measure such a truck when it arrives.

Architecture Laid Bare!

But if you feel the *slightest* timidity in such situations, consider this to be the *first* sign that you must *immediately* pull yourself together and *force* yourself to do what you know you should do, and worry about any stammering and embarrassment later. As further testimony of what such assertion can lead you to, witness this:

Five years ago I contracted to have part of my driveway paved. When the contractor arrived with a truckload of asphalt, I, with tape measure in hand, stepped over and asked, "Mind if I measure the dump body of your truck?"

"Measure it, touch it, feel it all you want," he scorned. His truck turned out to be the size he said it was and he proceeded to pave my driveway in a way that was honest and competent in every way. Then a year ago he and another man drove up to my house unannounced. On my front porch the contractor explained that his friend had a clever architectural idea he wanted to patent. Owning a few patents myself, I invited them in and spent an hour giving the man some excellent advice. During our conversation I mentioned to the contractor, "Remember when I measured your truck?"

"Yeah," he laughed, "I remember that." The point here is he remembered it well enough that when a friend of his needed some important advice he came to me first. *That's* the kind of respect that facing up to contractors will gain you.

In summary, when dealing with any of the above rogueries, you need three weapons: *knowledge*, *facts*, and *boldness*. Usually the amounts of the first two will exponentially increase your amount of the third.

However, there is a final roguery, sporadically exhibited by contractors and their construction kin, that defies categorization, which is dishonored here with the following accounting ...

Back in the old days, when my backbone wasn't as strong and my tongue wasn't as sharp as it is now, my chimney had a large TV antenna mounted on it which needed a lightning rod from the flue down the side of the house to the ground. I researched the required installation, consulted the yellow pages, and discussed the matter with an installer who knowledgeably answered every question I asked. When he arrived at my house, we discussed the work in detail, and he replied with the kind of quiet confidence that struck me as admirable in the building trades. So I gave him the go-ahead and stepped back to watch the show.

I was surprised to see him run a solid (not stranded) copper wire, one thin as coathanger wire (not a half inch in diameter), down the side of the house to a pencil-thick (not a half-inch thick) copper rod, which he hammered a foot (not several feet) into the ground.

I complained.

He brusquely inquired what did *I* know of these things.

I cited my sources.

He scoffed and exclaimed that he had been installing these systems for twenty years and had never had a complaint; that his installation was recommended by Underwriter's Laboratories, had been tested by ASTM, and underwent twelve years of onsite testing by the National Fire Protection Association which has been testing such equipment on every structure from horse barns to missile silos since 1908; that his installation complied with ANSI safety standards for lightning protection as well as NFPA 780, UL 96, and UL 96A; and that his method of installation was the first choice of every building inspector in the county, each of which would gladly vouch for his integrity —all from memory in a voice so overbearing I couldn't get in a word edgewise. When he finally paused for breath I asked if he had "anything in writing?"

He replied, "Of course I do, but it's all in the other truck which is in the garage today. Besides, you don't need anything in writing for this, it's all so obvious; just look at it."

What do you do with such slithery trickery?

First, have your knowledge, facts, and boldness on the tip of your tongue. "Knowledge" and "facts" here include written copies with pictures of what is to be installed, which is fairly easy these days if your computer has access to the internet and a printer.

Architecture Laid Bare!

Then show the worker your specs and ask, "Is this the way you will do the work?" If he says yes, fine, then sit back and enjoy the view. If he says No, or beats around the bush, or at any time while he is working you begin to feel uneasy at what you see, *force* yourself to say the simple word, "Stop," and voice your concerns. If he is evasive or otherwise fails to allay your concerns, be insistent, and try your best to be firm. If at any time you start to feel flustered, or tongue-tied, or like you're the dumbest person in the world, consider this to be the *first* sign that the fault is *anything* but yours and say, "Sir, there is something about this that worries me, and I must ask you to stop right now until I can get my thoughts together about what is going on here." If he refuses to leave, tell him he is trespassing on your property and order him off the premises immediately or you will call the police. This is one power every owner in one's castle has.

Certainly it is hard to muster the courage to turn a skilled artisan away just when s/he is about to do the work you desperately need. But consider this. If you order the person away before he starts or soon thereafter, you may look for someone twice and pay only once. But if you don't order him away, you may look for someone twice and pay three times (as earlier described): once to do the work, once to remove the mistake, and once to do it right.

As an addenda to these deficiencies, a more benign yet more commonplace dilemma, not only with contractors but subcontractors, handymen, even architects, and indeed many people in any line of work, is the *form-factor syndrome*. I first learned of this debility when I tried to find a manufacturer for a "pocket-size computer with a full-size keyboard" I patented a few years ago. On visiting the corporate headquarters of one of the largest computer companies in the world in Silicon Valley, California, a corporate officer there told me they weren't interested in my invention because it didn't "fit their form factors": meaning they had already sunk a few million dollars into plastic-injection-molding the housings, building the computer motherboards, et cetera, for the products they had; and if my invention couldn't use their already-made parts —their form factors— they weren't going to retool their assembly lines to make a new kind of product no matter how good it was.

And how true it is in the construction trades that a perfectly capable contractor, honest and reliable in every respect, simply can't perceive a new way of doing things because it doesn't "fit his form factor": his "tried-and-true" method of putting bread on his table possibly dating back several decades to his early adulthood when he "tooled" his "mental assembly lines" to fit what seemed at the time the most logical and sensible way to get the job done.

Unfortunately, one of the biggest hurdles to overcome with many of the ideas in this book, especially the more revelational ones, is getting contractors, subcontractors, and even many architects to "retool" their "mental assembly lines" to fit the new "form factors" that will be required to truly solve the momentous architectural problems our society faces today.

There is one more deceit, one more lie, that you might have to deal with on a construction site: a contractor who says, "Yeah, I've heard of that guy, and he doesn't know what he's talking about."

Then you'll *really* be glad you have this book in your hands.

Notes

Design

Last night my wife and I were washing the dishes after dinner when a paring knife with a round handle rolled off the counter by the sink and fell on the floor. My wife shook her head and said, "Never make knives with round handles."

"Bad design," I cried, uttering that mantra which marks all things imperfect in architecture that every second-year apprentice knows.

How many times have you used a furnishing that was clumsy, been in a room that was uncomfortable, or walked too far from one space to another because you were forced to use a "knife with a round handle" —part of a building whose designer didn't put enough thought into making it function properly?

This lengthy chapter is simply a number of analogues, some large, some small, that describe how to "design knives with handles that won't roll off a counter" in ways that satisfy that elementary directive spoken by Vitruvius in ancient Rome: *commodity, firmness*, and *delight*. The intent of this text isn't to train you to be the next Frank Lloyd Wright, only to enable you to see that those professionals you entrust to do this work will do it right.

Driveways

A driveway is a building's tether to the outer world. Each typically connects to the building at a public entrance and a private or service entrance, it may be decorative in ways that public roads are not, and it includes driving lanes, parking areas, service entrances —every surface a tire will tread on. You can't enjoy using a building unless it has a driveway, nor can you enjoy using any furnishings, groceries, or office supplies in the building either.

Design

A driveway should be straight and flat as possible. Where topography, trees, and other disruptions make them curve or go up or down, the lane should nestle into the terrain and gently skirt obstacles. Straight lanes should be 11 feet wide and curved ones 13 feet, and both should be 2 feet wider if curbed. If narrower they will be more difficult to drive on; if wider they will encourage motorists to drive too fast. On long driveways every 100 feet should have space for oncoming cars to pull over, and along both sides should extend a four-foot aisle to allow walkers, bikers, and playing children to move aside when a car passes. In cold climates these aisles are also needed for depositing plowed snow. Ideally no branches should extend over the driving surface, especially on inclines, because falling leaves can make the surface slippery. A driveway should slope no more than 6 or 8 per cent where it may be icy in winter, and no more than 12 percent anywhere. Alleys between buildings should be at least 16 feet wide. [1]

Where a driveway meets the street beyond the property, the angle between the intersecting roads should be at least 60 degrees, the corner radii should be at least 20 feet (30 is better), and the area at least 30 feet back from the curb should be clear of foliage, solid fences, and other visual obstructions.

A driveway can have four kinds of curves:

Flat curve: a horizontal curve where the driveway turns right or left. Minimum radius is about 60 feet. Any less, and a motorist may need to decelerate quickly to keep from being pulled off the road by centrifugal force.

Crown curve: a vertical curve where a road rises over the crest of a hill. Each should be gentle enough so a motorist won't experience a queasy airborne feeling or sudden reduction in visibility as s/he mounts the crest.

Sag curve: a vertical curve where a road descends into a dip or depression. Each should be gentle enough so a motorist won't experience a whiplash sensation or believe the road ahead is farther away than it really is as s/he

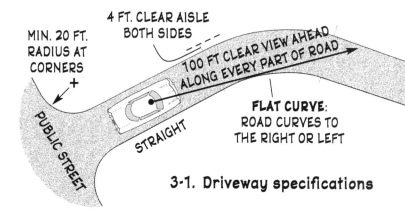

3-1. Driveway specifications

enters the dip. When possible, crests should be lowered and dips filled to create nearly planar driving surfaces.

Cross-slope: a side-to-side crown in a road. Its chief purpose is to drain rainwater to the road's sides. Optimal slopes are $\frac{3}{16}$ to $\frac{1}{4}$ inch per linear foot down from the crown. If less, vehicles tend to hydroplane during heavy rain; if more, vehicles tend to skid during icy or snowy weather.

A driveway should have shoulders along its sides and sideslopes beyond its shoulders. Shoulders should descend at about a 1:12 pitch sideways from the road and be 8 to 12 feet wide so vehicles can pull over in emergencies. A firm and attractive shoulder construction is turf grass planted in 4 inch topsoil spread on 4 inch crushed rock. Utility networks such as lightpost wiring and sprinkler piping should be at least six feet outside the road so they can be serviced without tearing up the road and obstructing traffic. Utility networks should also sleeve through thick-walled conduits that picks and shovels can't damage and vehicles cannot crush, and each should be laid in a bed of gravel and buried at least 15 inches below grade. Where a shoulder slopes steeply downhill, it should have reflector markers or guardrails located three to four feet from the road. Where a shoulder must slope uphill, a drainage ditch must extend between the edge of the road and the base of the rising terrain. If you leave out the ditch you

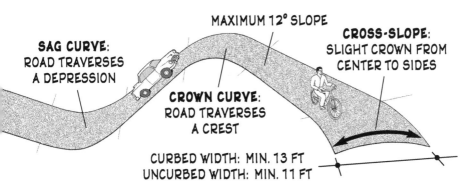

MAXIMUM 12° SLOPE

SAG CURVE: ROAD TRAVERSES A DEPRESSION

CROWN CURVE: ROAD TRAVERSES A CREST

CROSS-SLOPE: SLIGHT CROWN FROM CENTER TO SIDES

CURBED WIDTH: MIN. 13 FT
UNCURBED WIDTH: MIN. 11 FT

might as well leave out the road, or a tributary of Noah's flood may someday remove it for you. As for sideslopes, each should be 15 feet wide to provide space for errant vehicles, be clear of foliage and other objects that could obstruct driver visibility (especially along the inside of curves), be covered with plants to deter erosion, and slope about 1:6 pitch to drains and depressions.

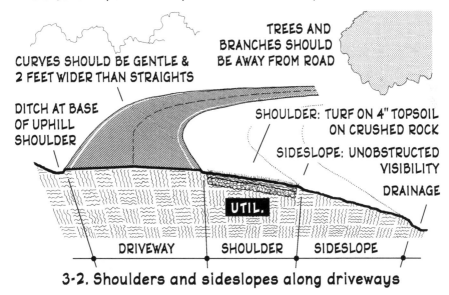

TREES AND BRANCHES SHOULD BE AWAY FROM ROAD

CURVES SHOULD BE GENTLE & 2 FEET WIDER THAN STRAIGHTS

DITCH AT BASE OF UPHILL SHOULDER

SHOULDER: TURF ON 4" TOPSOIL ON CRUSHED ROCK

SIDESLOPE: UNOBSTRUCTED VISIBILITY

DRAINAGE

UTIL.

DRIVEWAY   SHOULDER   SIDESLOPE

3-2. Shoulders and sideslopes along driveways

If a driveway crosses a stream, it should do so at nearly right angles, where the streambed is stable and straight, and where the opposing banks are strong. If the stream is small, it may flow through a culvert whose diameter is professionally sized to receive maximum floodwaters from the stream's watershed. A culvert should *always* have a flared end fitting on *both* ends, as sketched below; then erosion won't occur at the upstream end by the inflow washing under the culvert nor at the downstream end by the outflow eddying under it. If the stream is large, it may be bridged by a small trestle whose ends rest on foundation walls built into each bank, every part of which should be sized by a professional engineer.

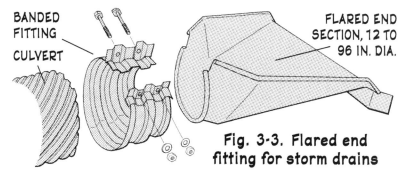

BANDED FITTING

CULVERT

FLARED END SECTION, 12 TO 96 IN. DIA.

Fig. 3-3. Flared end fitting for storm drains

If a driveway requires roadsigns, they should be the same as on public roads. Centerlines, crosswalks, direction arrows, and the like are usually applied to paved surfaces with stencils and spraypaint. These can also be made with a big roll of adhesive tape known as *thermoplastic pavement marking tape*. This sticky-backed material is thick, up to twelve inches wide, easily applied, cut with scissors, economical, durable, made in three colors (white for crosswalks, yellow for cautionary markings, blue for handicap designations), and your county highway department usually carries it. It can also be used to tape a basketball key-hole on your turnaround, replicate a business logo on your entrance drive, even locate information on a vertical facade or roadsign. I did this once when I needed a deer crossing sign by my driveway. I went to the local highway department, bought a 12-inch strip of this tape, drew a six-point buck on it, cut it out, peeled off the backing, and taped my trophy on a traffic sign the department also sold. It's looking at you in figure 3-4.

Design

3-4. Custom roadsign

A driveway may be illuminated at night with *lamp posts*, *bollards* (waist-high posts with lights on them that also serve as vehicle barriers), footlights (low lights mounted along the road), and *landscape lighting*. All lights, fixtures, foundations, and wiring should be designed by architects or professional engineers, who usually have plenty of manufacturers' catalogs to help you select almost any fixture you may desire.

Every driveway needs adjacent places to park. Each may be perpendicular, angled between 45 and 60 degrees, or parallel to the lane; and each should generally be about 9 feet wide and 20 feet long. Regarding commercial parking dimensions, *Architectural Graphic Standards*, an encyclopedic volume used by architects (your local library probably has one) lists parking dimensions for all kinds of vehicles plus bicycles, motorcycles, motor homes, delivery trucks, busses, even golf carts and baby carriages.

Many driveways also have turnarounds so drivers won't need to back into the street when pulling out of a garage. A turnaround should be dimensioned as sketched in figure 3-5 on the next page. The area outside the garage door should be paved and descend $\frac{1}{2}$ inch per foot at least four feet beyond the door, and the soil beneath this heavily traveled area should be compacted to minimize settling, cracking, freezing, and heaving.

Even more meticulous is the design of a commercial service entrance. This is a world of loading docks, security entrances, approach aprons, truckable sills, and trailer turning radii, every detail of which must be professionally sized. Here thousands of dollars can be lost at the stroke of a drafting stylus if any part is

71

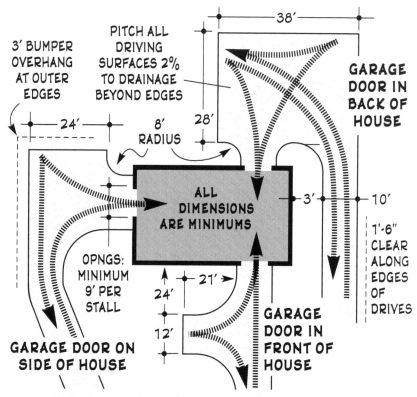

3-5. Dimensions for residential turnarounds

too large, or thousands can be lost at the bump of a truck if any part is too small. If you are ever responsible for are otherwise involved in the design of a commercial service entrance, be as familiar with its operation as you can, and learn as much as you can about daily and seasonal weather patterns, lighting requirements, and security concerns.

An important consideration in designing turnarounds and parking areas is drainage, whether rain, snowmelt, hosewater, or even chemicals emptying from nearby industrial or agricultural operations. Every drop should descend gently toward a depression, which may be small as a bathtub or large as a hundred-foot-wide waterway weaving between two subdivisions. Conservationists have dignified the latter mires by giving them an ecological-ly impressive name —*bioretention areas or bioswales*— and preparing environmental specifications for their construction.

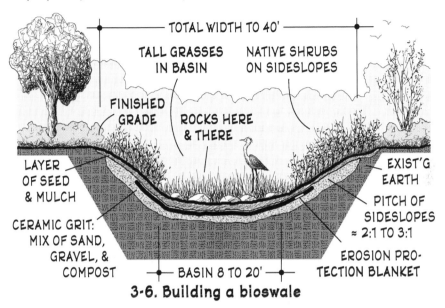

TOTAL WIDTH TO 40'

TALL GRASSES IN BASIN   NATIVE SHRUBS ON SIDESLOPES

FINISHED GRADE   ROCKS HERE & THERE

LAYER OF SEED & MULCH

CERAMIC GRIT: MIX OF SAND, GRAVEL, & COMPOST

BASIN 8 TO 20'

EXIST'G EARTH

PITCH OF SIDESLOPES ≈ 2:1 TO 3:1

EROSION PRO-TECTION BLANKET

3-6. Building a bioswale

A bioswale is a scientifically designed and carefully con-structed water retention area that collects runoff from nearby turnarounds, parking lots, public roads, even large flat roofs. It is usually long and narrow, has gently sloping sides planted with low-maintenance and deep-rooted wetland vegetation and native shrubs, and has a central depression filled with riprap or other rocks. These basins slope very gently in one direction (usually about 0.1 percent) which allows silt, automotive greases, chemi-cals, pathogens, and other pollutants in the water to settle with-out stirring up already-settled matter. Bioswales retain pollu-tants, minimize erosion, and clarify the residing water, which nourishes plants, recharges local water tables, and supplies nat-ural watercourses downstream with slow purified seeps instead of turbulent polluted surges. In addition to being ecologically desirable, bioswales save money by eliminating paving, curbs, gutters, pipes, and stormwater collection systems —plus they look pretty, especially when herons stalk through the sedges and turtles bask on the rocks. In public settings they are often bordered by walkways, bike trails, trees, and other natural amenities. LEED even awards points for constructing them (if they include educational signage, which should *not* be required). Some large bioswales even have underground vaults that trap bottles, cans, and trash for later removal as well as *oil absorbent booms, big* sausage-like devices several feet long and several inches thick that soak up oils, solvents, paints, and the like, then are periodically replaced. To learn more about these products, visit www.sbprojectcleanwater.org/improvements.html, or google each product to find companies that sell it.

Two accessories for upscale driveways are *de-icers* and *security notifiers*. De-icers are usually electric heating wires located under concrete surfaces in front of building entrances and in flat pedestrian areas where puddles of water could freeze in winter. Security notifiers are alerting devices installed along a driveway. One may be embedded in the pavement and its wiring extended inside the building, or the device may be a battery-powered or remote-controlled motion detector mounted by the driveway. Two other security devices for those who can afford them are gates that open and close by intercoms or approaching/departing drivers, and gatehouses containing security guards.

Since a driveway supports a lot of weight and is exposed to a variety of weather extremes, it must be carefully designed and built. Each has a *bed* (its subconstruction) and a *topping* (its surface). A driveway's bed is built as described below. If you don't have the knowledge or equipment to do this work yourself, give these directions to a professional and s/he will know what to do.

1. Remove the topsoil from the road and shoulder areas and set it aside to cover exposed terrain after construction.
2. Remove all stumps and roots down to four feet below finished grade.

Design

3. If part of the bed is soft or unstable, dump a few truck-loads of fist-size rocks (known around here as *crusher run*) whose sharp edges knit together to form a nearly solid surface that won't be dislodged by spinning tires. In 1974 when I built the driveway to my house, part of the lane passed over a marshy area 150 feet long. I unloaded fifteen truckloads of crusher run up to 18 inches deep before the soil stabilized. To this day this vehicular foundation is nearly as solid as concrete.

4. If the area contains wet soil that is constantly recharged with groundwater, it may require a network of profession-ally designed perforated drains that empties into nearby depressions or groundwater recharge basins.

5. If the road is packed dirt or gravel that will be paved, it may need a base of only 2 inches of added gravel.

As for a driveway's topping, the simplest are unpaved earth and gravel. While these are inexpensive, earth tends to form ruts due to erosion and tiretread wear and they are muddy dur-ing and after rain, and gravel tends to form washboard-like sur-faces on inclines that can damage vehicles unless they drive really slow. The best toppings are concrete and asphalt. These are smooth and durable, and after snowfalls you can plow them without tearing them up. Concrete makes the strongest and longest-lasting road; but it requires formwork, control joints, and reinforcement; it is difficult to pour on inclines; and it takes a week to cure. Asphalt, also known as *blacktop*, requires no formwork or control joints or reinforcement, is easily laid on inclines, takes only 2 or 3 days to cure, and melts ice and snow quicker in winter. But asphalt is not as durable as concrete, it is softer in hot weather, and petroleum products (like the ones that leak from under your car) will dissolve it. The last reason is why gas stations have concrete aprons around the pumps and con-crete floors in the service bays.

Since a reinforced concrete driveway should be at least five

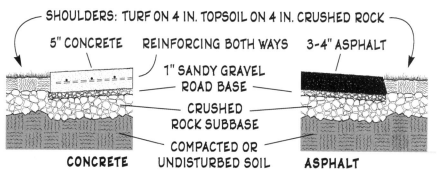

SHOULDERS: TURF ON 4 IN. TOPSOIL ON 4 IN. CRUSHED ROCK

5" CONCRETE   REINFORCING BOTH WAYS   3-4" ASPHALT

1" SANDY GRAVEL
ROAD BASE

CRUSHED
ROCK SUBBASE

COMPACTED OR
UNDISTURBED SOIL

CONCRETE   ASPHALT

3-7. Durable concrete and asphalt driveways

inches thick, which is overkill for a residential or small commercial driveway, these lanes are usually paved with asphalt. A common notion is that an asphalt drive can be as little as two inches thick, which obviously costs less than three or four. However, while a two-inch asphalt drive may cost eighty percent as much as three inches and sixty percent as much as four inches, two inches will be only about *30 percent* as strong as three inches and *12 percent* as strong as four. This is because the microstresses occurring within the asphalt's small tar-soaked stones will more easily tear them apart when the layer is thin, as appears below.

WHEN TIRE BRAKES,
ASPHALT PULLS APART ON UPHILL SIDE
AND PUSHES TOGETHER ON DOWNHILL SIDE.
WHEN TIRE ACCELERATES, THE REVERSE OCCURS.

RESULT:
CONSTANT
PUSH-PULL MAKES
THE TAR-SOAKED
STONES CRUMBLE

THIN ASPHALT

ASPHALT
PULLS APART

ASPHALT
PUSHES TOGETHER

3-8.
Why thin asphalt wears out much faster

Design

A driveway may also be paved with cobblestones, bricks, and Belgian block. These materials look elegant, discourage speeding, and make braking easier when the surface is icy; but they are expensive and tend to loosen in prolonged subfreezing weather.

If you plan to asphalt a driveway, here's a trio of tips:

1. On graph paper, measure the area you want to pave.

2. Knowing the topping's thickness, compute the volume of blacktop required. Example: if the driveway is 150 feet long, averages 12 feet wide, and the topping will be 4 inches deep, a little algebra says you'll need about 22 cubic yards. If you do this, you can tell the contractor how much you want and not the other way around.

3. When the truck(s) arrive, as mentioned earlier, measure the dump body to make sure the yards you need are the yards you get. If you want four inches, a dishonest contractor can compact it with a steamroller until its edges are four inches thick while its center (whose thickness you can't see) may be one inch thick; and when you learn about this a year or two later the contractor will have retired to Florida. An honest paver can't make every square foot equally thick; but if you know the yardage you need and ask to see the paver's batch plant receipts before writing your check, you'll know that what you bought is in there somewhere, and you'll stand a fine chance of your driveway lasting not years but decades.

Regarding vehicles that use driveways, LEED awards points for providing "preferred parking and alternative refueling stations for fuel-efficient vehicles." Since this directive is used to add credence to green buildings, it is pertinent to examine it here, as detailed below.

Many "fuel-efficient vehicles" are anything but when you consider that elemental yardstick of environmental efficiency: embodied energy. For example, the electricity used to run gas/electric hybrids is an average *36 percent* of utility-generated electricity (the rest is lost in transmission from power plant to plug) and the engine is nowhere near 100 percent efficient.[2] Hydrogen fuel is even worse. It delivers only about *27 percent* of the embodied energy it typically takes to make it. Every hydrogen-fueled vehicle success story seems to come from Iceland, where the huge amount of energy required to split water molecules into hydrogen atoms is geothermal energy —free energy gushing from the ground.[3] As one authority says about this fuel: "Our energy problems certainly will not be solved by *wasting* energy." Also, hydrogen fuel is stored in tanks at a pressure of 3,500 psi! Think of what will happen if one of these vehicles has a serious accident. It will be like a bomb exploding in an Iraqi marketplace. Another reason why electric and hydrogen vehicles are often more "economical" is that electricity and hydrogen are taxed less than gasoline. Ethanol is another counterfeit. *National Geographic* says, "Producing ethanol from corn consumes about as much fossil fuel as ethanol itself replaces, growing the corn requires nitrogen fertilizer made with natural gas and uses farm machinery, and the process gives off large amounts of carbon dioxide." [4] Why not use cellulose wastes: weeds, crop residues, logging and paper wastes, textile remnants, sawgrass, kudzu and other nuisance plants? *Scientific American* says we have enough of these kinds of recoverable cellulose to make enough "grassoline" to replace half the oil we use! Then we can have our corn and eat it too. Another possibility is algae. This fast-growing pond scum can be harvested daily, can produce 15 times more per acre than corn, and absorbs lots of CO_2 as it grows.[5] That should spark some interest in this subject.

What is so amazing about this is that we've had an energy-efficient replacement for gasoline and the infrastructure to dispense it for decades: natural gas. Back in 1969, the subcontractor who installed the natural gas system for a house in California I helped build ran his truck on propane. The gas line entered a special carburetor —all it took, he said. The fuel burned so clean that he hadn't tuned his engine in 30,000 miles. 1969, you remember, was the year we put a man on the moon.

Certainly we should road-test emerging biofuel technologies because many improvements down the road one or more may become the energy answer we are looking for. Meanwhile, let's not pretend these efforts are the answer when they are only *an experiment*.

Circulation

In many a building, up to thirty percent of its floorspace is devoted to lobbies, foyers, halls, stairs, elevators, and other passageways occupants traverse from outdoors on their way to essential interior spaces. Architects know how to minimize these areas and make them do double-duty by lining them with closets, shelves, and cabinets that are out of the way yet easy to reach. The most common such spaces are described below.

Sidewalks. A sidewalk is an outdoor hallway typically made of concrete, asphalt, brick, or pavers. A nice walk has broad curves lined with foliage, benches, kiosks and wide entrance aprons to buildings. Each should slope no more than one foot in ten, and should drain at least $1/8$ inch per foot sideways to nearby depressions to prevent puddling in rain and icing in snow. One's width should appear as in figure 3-9. Add $1^1/_2$ feet for a viewing corridor where the walk passes storewindows or points of interest; 2 feet for poles, hydrants, trash bins, and

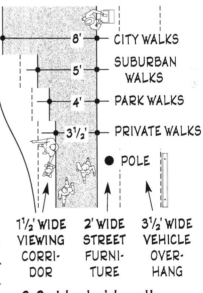

3-9. Ideal sidewalk dimensions

other street furniture along a street; and $3\frac{1}{2}$ feet where parked vehicles overhang curbs. Curbs should be 6 to 8 inches high.

Steps. Steps may be single, as in curbs, or in groups, as in stairs. In a stair each step has a horizontal tread and a vertical riser, and the stair's incline is the ratio of each riser's height versus each tread's width; or, as the noted art theorist Rudolf Arnheim put it, "the ratio of victorious advancing versus laborious lifting."[6] The more victorious the advancing the longer should be the treads; the more laborious the lifting the lower should be the risers. In floor-to-floor stairs avoid straight-flight steps — too dangerous. Instead turn the second half around so the last step aligns vertically and laterally with the first. This creates shorter falling distances for stumblers and allows quicker access to the rooms above and below. This may put a wasteful landing halfway up the stairs, but this area can be divided into four big pie-shaped steps which shortens the stairs' length: a construction known as the *horseshoe staircase*, as sketched in figure 3-10.

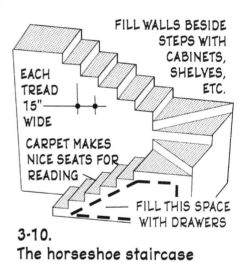

3-10.
The horseshoe staircase

A staircase can be made safer by increasing its rectangular treads from the usual 10 or 11 inches to 16 or 17 inches. A fine model for this is the grand staircase in front of the National Gallery of Art in Washington, D.C. Its steps have 17 inch treads and $6\frac{1}{2}$ inch risers, which allows a descender to enjoy the views and the Mall in front of this majestic building without nervously looking at one's feet. Frank Lloyd Wright was another advocate of wide-tread steps. A number of his residences have several

Design

entrance steps whose treads are 16 or 17 inches and risers are only 4 inches. Such inclines look generous to the eye while being gentle to the foot. Indoor stairs can be made more useful by lining the side walls with bookcases, framed photos and other mementos —all easily reached from the floors above and below. How's that for victorious advancing?

The normally useless cranny under a stair's lowest steps can also be fitted with the kind of sliding drawers installed in pickup truck beds. These units can convert a space buried three feet in a wall into one that's as easy to use as an opened drawer. Here are some companies that make this movable storage:

www.roll-a-bed.com ... makes a sliding truck bed that can fit
    into the end of a half-staircase.
www.cargobed.com ... makes sliding truckbed extenders from 19
    to 34 inches wide and 30 to 90 inches long.
www.slim-track.com ... makes drawer slides up to 20 feet long.
www.tuffyproducts.com ... makes drawers that are 10 and 16
    inches high, 24 inches wide, and 4, 6, or 8 feet long.

Ramps. Where steps obstruct wheelchaired pedestrians, they may be replaced with ramps. Each should slope no steeper than one foot in ten, be broken every thirty horizontal feet by a 5 × 5 foot landing, and have a railing on at least one side. The design of ramps in and around buildings is described in the *ADA Guidelines*, accessed by googling ADA Accessibility Guidelines. Indoor ramps are a superb means of moving many people up or down, a spectacular example being the quarter-mile long helix in the Guggenheim Museum in New York City.

Escalators. An escalator is a giant revolving chain, with each three-foot-wide step a link, that is fitted into an inclined truss that bridges two floors. Each tread rests on rollers attached to the gliding chain, and on each side runs a flexible rubber handrail that wraps around a large half-round newel projecting from each end. Every part of this machinery is meticulously designed to thwart any accident that human carelessness could devise. This is the most efficient vertical circulation for heavy pedestrian traffic in buildings with six floors or less. Compared to elevators they cost less, require one-third the floorspace to deliver the same passenger loads, can deliver many riders quickly, need no space-gobbling pits or penthouses, and don't have complex controls; but they are expensive and heavy. An escalator should be located in a direct line of traffic (though many retailers like walkarounds at landings since they force customers to step past merchandise), and passengers should be able to look around and see where they are going while moving up or down.

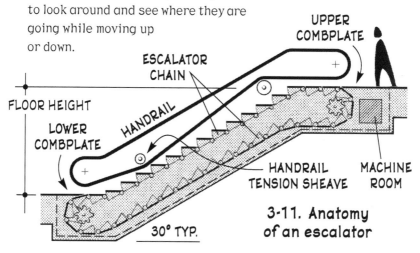

3-11. Anatomy of an escalator

Related to escalators are *moving walks*. Here the steps are replaced by long skidproof belts that may slope up to 11 degrees. They can carry large numbers of pedestrians over long distances in airports, sports arenas, and shopping malls. Moving belts also convey baggage in airports, ore in mining operations, and products assembled in industrial facilities.

Elevators. These moving rooms carry people and objects up and down in multistory buildings. They can be as simple and plain as a showerstall-size cab in a two-story house, or as complex as the vertically-to-horizontally moving cabs in Eero Saarinen's Gateway

Design

Arch in St. Louis or as showy as the glass-caged pods in one of John Portman's hotels that allow passengers to gaze at a huge central atrium as they woosh through the height of the hotel.

An elevator usually carries *passengers* or *freight*. A passenger elevator typically has an attractive interior backed with acoustic insulation that keeps its loud motors, vibrating ropes, and squeaking brakes from annoying riders in the cab and occupants around the shaft. A freight or service elevator is a utilitarian construction with sturdy rails, thick wood floors, caged ceiling lights, and a strong frame that can carry heavy loads (big ones can lift a loaded trailer truck or a railway freight car). Every elevator has electronic activators that reopen closing doors if a late arriver touches the jamb, safety contacts that keep doors from opening unless the cab is level with the landing, and automatic levelers that keep a cab's floor aligned with a landing as the cab's load varies when passengers enter and leave. An elevator may be *hydraulic* or *traction*, as detailed below:

Hydraulic Elevators. Here the cab is hydraulically raised and lowered by a telescoping plunger mounted beneath the cab or along a side. They are quieter and less costly than traction elevators and have smaller shafts, no penthouses, fewer controls, and lighter structural supports. But their height is limited to about 60 feet, they cost more to operate, and are slower. They are best suited for low-rise offices and hotels, buildings that accommodate occupants with disabilities, and industrial facilities

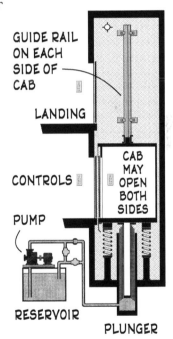

GUIDE RAIL ON EACH SIDE OF CAB

LANDING

CONTROLS

PUMP

RESERVOIR

CAB MAY OPEN BOTH SIDES

PLUNGER

3-12. Section thro' hydraulic elevator

83

where maintenance personnel often carry tools and equipment.

Traction Elevators. Here the cab hangs from steel ropes that pass over a traction sheave driven by a geared motor, then the ropes descend to a counterweight on the sheave's other side. When the cab goes up, the counterweight goes down. This vertical circulation costs less to operate in buildings more than 60 feet tall and is durable; but it costs more, is heavy, and the shafts and penthouses take up much space and are major building expenses.

A miniature version of a traction elevator is the *drum elevator*. Here a small cab hangs from a cable that passes over a pulley at the top of the shaft then descends to an electric motor-driven drum mounted on a heavy bedplate that acts as a counterweight. You may have seen one of these rise out of a city sidewalk in front of a storefront. They are also used as home elevators and dumbwaiters where lifts do not exceed about 50 feet.

In a *home elevator*, the cab may be small as a showerstall or big enough to hold a wheelchaired passenger and an attendant: typically about 25 square feet. Each requires a mechanical equipment area usually located next to the shaft above or below. The cab may rise through an open area such as a stairwell, or the top landing may be a floor door that opens upward as the cab rises through the floor; then the cab door remains locked until its

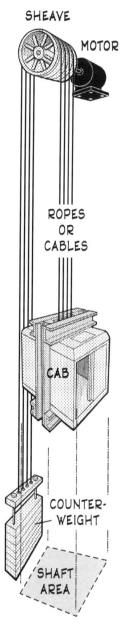

3-13. Traction elevator

threshold is level with the floor outside. Lifting capacities are 500 to 1000 pounds. They can have corner seats, illuminated operating buttons, on/off interior lighting, windowed doors, even intercoms that play music.

Home elevators are becoming more popular as our nation's population ages, but installing one in an existing residence can be a trial. First you must find a good place to put it. This necessitates a vertical shaft of about 4 × 6 feet from the lowest floor to the highest ceiling of the floors to be served, plus an area on each floor to serve as a vestibule on the door side of the cab. If an open well exists by a staircase whose landings can double as elevator vestibules, you may be in luck. The shaft could also be located outside the building, but this often looks ugly and usually requires converting upperstory rooms into vestibules. Solving this polydimensional puzzle usually requires an architect. The architect designs the spaces and specifies the elevator, a carpenter frames the shaft, a sheetrocker finishes the shaft with fire-code drywall, and the elevator's manufacturer installs it.[7]

If installing a home elevator would be too expensive, a more economical possibility is a *stair chair*. Also known as a *stairlift*, this is a chair mounted on an inclined track

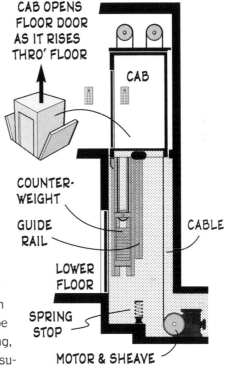

3-14. Home elevator

Architecture Laid Bare!

installed along one side of a staircase on the treads or against the wall. When the seat is not used it folds against the wall to allow normal use of the stairs. In addition to operating on straight one-story stairs, a stairlift can wrap around a volute at the foot of the stairs, ascend curved staircases, or rise through two or three stories. Some even have facing chairs for two riders. Travel is activated by button switches on an armrest or small push-button panels at each landing. One company, Jameson Medical, Inc., has a fine website (www.jamesonmedical.com/stair_lifts) that includes 12 helpful hints for the consumer.

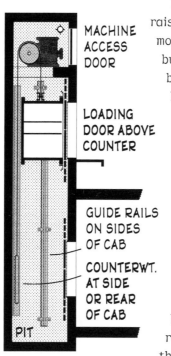

MACHINE ACCESS DOOR

LOADING DOOR ABOVE COUNTER

GUIDE RAILS ON SIDES OF CAB

COUNTERWT. AT SIDE OR REAR OF CAB

PIT

3-15. Dumbwaiter

In a *dumbwaiter*, the cab is raised and lowered by an electric motor. One's controls may be push-button, call-and-send intercom between floors, or phones at each landing. The cab's floor may be 2 to 3 feet square, its height may be $2^{1}/_{2}$ to 4 feet, it often has shelves and lights inside, and its doors may be hinged on one side or vertical biparting (half goes up, half goes down). Landings are often at counter height, the cab cannot move while any door is open, and a door cannot open unless the cab's floor is aligned with its landing. They are used in stores, resorts, luxury residences, and the like, and can move loads up to 500 pounds.

To learn more about the above products, google *elevators*, *home elevators*, *dumbwaiters*, or *stair chairs* on the internet.

Occupancies

Every indoor space has an optimal floor area based on its number of occupants and what they do. Examples are two people sleeping in a bedroom, and twelve people sitting around a table in a conference room. Each such space should provide *maximum comfort in minimum volume.* This involves removing any useless corners, unused crannies, excess doorways, gunbarrel hallways, seas of circulation around islands of furniture, and other chubby cubic footage from a floorspace. This strategy is central to all that is Green in architecture, because efficient spaces consume less energy and material to build, and they consume less energy to keep comfortable.

A fine way to create maximum comfort in minimum volume is to *make wasted corners useful.* Consider figure 3-16. In a suburban kitchen I installed a tall revolving cabinet between the refrigerator on one side and a wall oven on the other. This rotating cylinder has five 34-inch-diameter shelves enclosed by a tall sheet of formica that keeps items from sliding off the shelves when they revolve. It has 30 cubic feet of storage where before existed only 6.

In this residence I employed a second space-saving trick: a corner kitchen cabinet whose door opens into the dining room outside. As you can see in figure 3-17 on the next page, this makes every part of the corner under the kitchen counter more accessible. To see more ideas like these, take a peek at crosscreek.kraftmaid.com/storage ➡ Harmony Storage Solutions. Other habitations apt

3-16. A tall revolving cabinet

to have clever space-savers are mobile homes, recreational vehicles, and celebrity busses.

3-17. A clever corner cabinet

In many interiors, doors are blank on both sides. For a shrewder use of these swingers take a gander at figure 3-18. This 2×3 foot pantry has four little doors with sixty big shelves inside. Door hinges loaded as heavily as these must be carefully designed: the hinge screws must be long enough to penetrate the stud framing behind the shimmed doorframe, and the wood in both door and frame must be thick and solid. Never screw hinge screws into the

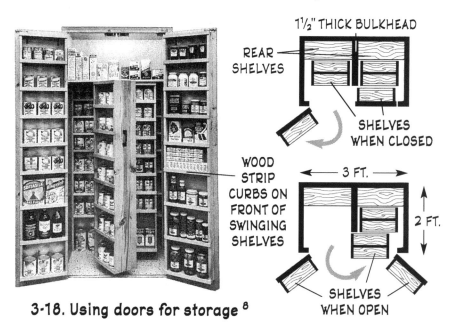

1½" THICK BULKHEAD

REAR SHELVES

SHELVES WHEN CLOSED

WOOD STRIP CURBS ON FRONT OF SWINGING SHELVES

← 3 FT. →

↕ 2 FT.

SHELVES WHEN OPEN

3-18. Using doors for storage [8]

edge of plywood, because the wedgelike screws will split the plies apart. Doors are also great for mounting clothes hooks, bulletin boards, mirrors and the like. If you don't want to use a door as storage, think of doing the opposite: cut a big hole in it and fill the opening with translucent glass. Then the light on one side will brighten the other, privacy is preserved on both sides, and the brighter spaces will look larger.

3-19. Making spaces look bigger than they really are

This last idea works well on walls. By making a large opening in a wall between two rooms, the space on each side may seemingly double its size, which can give you four rooms for the price of one hole. Two examples of this spatial legerdemain appear in figure 3-19. The deletion on the left opened a wall between a dreary hallway and a dark stair, which made each space look larger and allowed one descending the stairs to see the hall around the corner and vice versa. In the wall on the right I removed every other stud, doubled the remaining studs, and mounted cantilevering shelves on them. In addition to the openings making the spaces look larger, air and light pass from one space to the other.

A space-doubling cousin of big wall openings is *large mirrors*. These work best when the glass is large, when it is located so you don't readily see yourself in it, where two walls of glass meet at a corner, and when a roughly textured object is placed close to the glass in the corner. A good example of all this is a planter shaped like a quarter-circle (you could get a potter to make this for you) with a tall leafy plant in it. The reflection of the plant in the quarter-circular pot on each side will look like a bushy plant mounted in the middle of a large room. This could make a small household hallway look like a spacious hotel lobby.

Another visual trick is to mount a large pictureframe over an opening in a wall between an entrance hall and a living room. The apparent picture in the frame will, on closer inspection, be a view of the room beyond.

Another illusory enlarger is *wallpaper murals*. A full-wall photo of a tropical seashore or a mountain lake can make a small indoor room look like the great outdoors. Wallpaper murals are typically made in panels that together measure 8 feet 4 inches high by 12 feet wide. Two of many companies that sell them are wallpaperstore.com and creativewallcovering.com. If you're into trompe l'oeils, paint a ceiling sky blue and add a few clouds and perhaps a wavy chevron of geese flying south. Then the roomtop may look eight thousand feet high instead of eight.

A clever way to make a room look larger and be more useful at the same time is to *build long shelves around the top of its walls*. In almost every room a band of bare wall wraps around the walls between the tops of the doors and windows and the underside of the ceiling. In an average bedroom this space could hold fifty linear feet of boxes and books! This construction is performed with the hidden bracket trick, kin to the magician's floating lady trick. If you would like to see this sleight-of-hand performed by a local magician, hand the directions on the next two pages to a carpenter. This trick can be used to install shelves on any wood stud wall.

Design

1. Where the shelves will be installed around the room, $^3/_4$ inch above the level of the molding over the room's doors and windows locate the studs behind the walls by gently hammering a 16 penny finish nail into the sheetrock or other wall finish until you find both sides of each stud. Locate each edge within a tolerance of $\pm$ $^1/_{16}$ inch.

2. Center a vertical line on each stud, and through this line draw a horizontal line along the center of the shelf that will rest against the wall to create a cross (**+**) at the intersection of the two lines. The shelf should be at least 1 actual (not nominal) inch thick. 5/4 white pine works well here.

3. Drill a $^1/_4$ inch hole 3

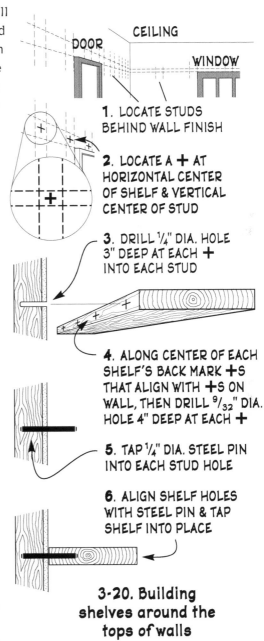

CEILING

DOOR

WINDOW

1. LOCATE STUDS BEHIND WALL FINISH

2. LOCATE A **+** AT HORIZONTAL CENTER OF SHELF & VERTICAL CENTER OF STUD

3. DRILL $^1/_4$" DIA. HOLE 3" DEEP AT EACH **+** INTO EACH STUD

4. ALONG CENTER OF EACH SHELF'S BACK MARK **+**S THAT ALIGN WITH **+**S ON WALL, THEN DRILL $^9/_{32}$" DIA. HOLE 4" DEEP AT EACH **+**

5. TAP $^1/_4$" DIA. STEEL PIN INTO EACH STUD HOLE

6. ALIGN SHELF HOLES WITH STEEL PIN & TAP SHELF INTO PLACE

3-20. Building shelves around the tops of walls

inches deep into each **+** on each stud.

4. Align each shelf against the wall where it will be installed. Where the studs' **+**s occur along the back of the shelf, mark a matching row of **+**s along the center of the shelf's back edge, then drill a $^9/_{32}$ inch diameter hole 4 inches deep into each **+** along the shelf.

5. Tap a $^1/_4$ inch diameter 7-inch-long steel pin (the hidden bracket) into each stud hole until $3^1/_2$ inches of each pin protrudes from the wall. Each pin diameter should be exactly $^1/_4$ inch.

6. Align the shelf holes with the pins and with a rubber hammer tap the shelf into place.

7. Fit pieces of cornice molding beneath the shelves on the wall between the doors and windows. These aren't necessary, but they add an elegant touch.

In addition to creating lots of storage these ledges will make the room look larger; because by locating the usual 8-foot high cornice molding beneath the shelves a little less than 7 feet high all around, the 7 foot height will look more like 8 feet. This illusion will also make *you* feel taller.

3-21. Ceiling shelves

A spacesaving cousin of above-the-door shelves is across-the-ceiling shelves, as in figure 3-21. These work best in small semiprivate rooms where the shelves can be located just above head height. In a private study a library of books could be mounted within arm's reach, close to your eyes so you can read the

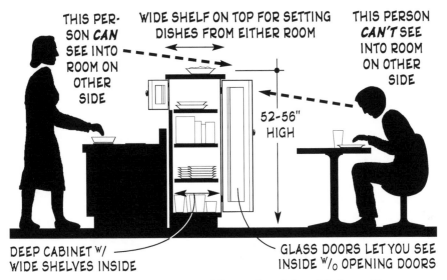

THIS PER-
SON *CAN*
SEE INTO
ROOM ON
OTHER
SIDE

WIDE SHELF ON TOP FOR SETTING
DISHES FROM EITHER ROOM

THIS PERSON
CAN'T SEE
INTO ROOM
ON OTHER
SIDE

52-56"
HIGH

DEEP CABINET ʷ/
WIDE SHELVES INSIDE

GLASS DOORS LET YOU SEE
INSIDE ʷ/ₒ OPENING DOORS

3-22. Saving space with a shoulder-high wall

spines, and out of the way of everything below. In the 6½ by 7 foot pantry of my house I built three shelves like this. Their undersides are an inch above my cowlicks, their length between the shelves is 41 inches, and they hold light bulky objects like paper towels, toilet paper, and boxes of cereal. The shelves' ends rest on the wall shelves on each side.

A clever way to make two rooms more useful at the same time is the *shoulder-high wall*. As you can see in figure 3-22, when this visual barrier rises between a dining room and a kitchen, it can keep seated eaters from seeing into a messy kitchen while allowing a standing cook to see the eaters: a welcome scenario for cooking mothers who need to keep an eye on the kids at the table. If the intervening wall is a deep cabinet with a wide flat top and doors on both sides, you can set prepared dishes from the kitchen and dirty dishes from the dining room on the wide top and store the dinnerware below where it can be reached from both sides. If the doors are glass, you can see inside when they're closed. Now you might need only one dining area instead of two:

another way to "double" a room's function. This idea works because when you enter a room you are standing and usually orienting yourself outward as you walk, then when seated your eyes are about 18 inches lower and you usually orient yourself inward toward the task before you; so a shoulder-high wall makes a space look larger when you stand and feel cozier when you sit. Since this cabinetry is essentially new, if you want one you won't find it at your local furniture outlet. But you can take these pages to a cabinetmaker and say, "This is what I'd like," and s/he will know what to do. A common use of shoulder-high walls in commercial buildings appears between office cubicles in corporate work areas, where they allow two people to converse on each side while standing and work in private when sitting.

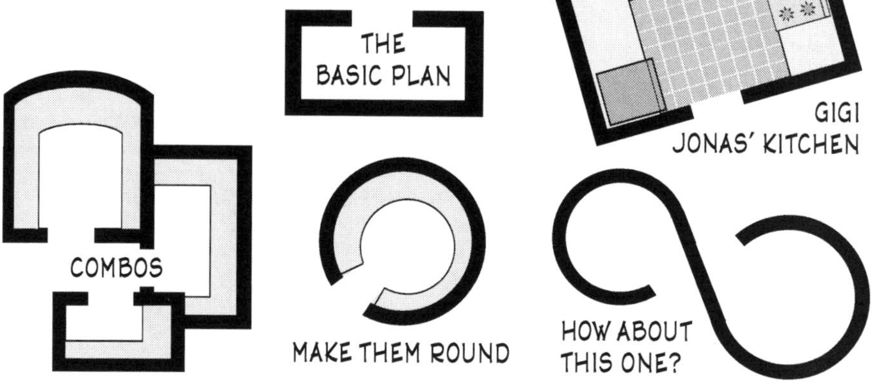

THE BASIC PLAN

GIGI
JONAS' KITCHEN

COMBOS

MAKE THEM ROUND

HOW ABOUT THIS ONE?

3-23. Clever uses of cul-de-sacs

Another efficient indoor space is the cul-de-sac. This is a U-shaped wall with only one door that allows minimum circulation to reach maximum storage. Examples are walk-in closets in homes and walk-in freezers in restaurants. One of the most efficient kitchens I ever saw was a cul-de-sac with wraparound cabinets and counters that an artist designed for herself. It appears in figure 3-23. A cul-de-sac can also be round or oval with a door in one side: shapes easily built with bricks on masonry floors.

In many a bedroom lies another few dozen cubic feet of wasted space. Think of that monstrous boxspring under that mammoth mattress. If you raise a bed's sleeping surface until it is level with the base of your buttocks as you stand, you can more easily lie down on your bed and get up. This is why the berths of kings and hospital patients are about thirty inches high. If you replace the mattress and boxspring (which often are 20 inches high) with four inches of foam plus a memory foam topper (a 2-inch mat that soothingly enmolds your reclining torso) and add a 3-inch toe-space at the bottom, you would have 20 inches of emptiness between the top of your toes and the bottom of the foam. That's enough room to fit two rows of long deep drawers on the bed's side from head to foot. You want a double bed? Place two units side-by-side with the drawers facing out on both sides, as sketched below. If you add a cedar-lined trunk at the foot of the bed (so folded sheets and blankets can rest inside and pulled-back ones can rest on top instead of falling on the floor) and add a headboard with a few long shelves above the pillows, you could almost move

TWO SINGLE UNITS SIDE-BY-SIDE MAKE A DOUBLE BED

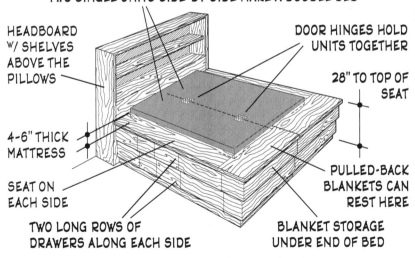

HEADBOARD W/ SHELVES ABOVE THE PILLOWS

DOOR HINGES HOLD UNITS TOGETHER

28" TO TOP OF SEAT

4-6" THICK MATTRESS

SEAT ON EACH SIDE

PULLED-BACK BLANKETS CAN REST HERE

TWO LONG ROWS OF DRAWERS ALONG EACH SIDE

BLANKET STORAGE UNDER END OF BED

3-24. The noble bureaubed

your attic under your mattress. Here's a bed fit for a king *and* a queen! Now those bureaus across the room can be replaced by a long desk with shelves above and cabinets below: a quiet place for a hobby or small office. Then in two steps you could rest while you read, or take a nap when your deskwork grows weary. Then you could use this room during the other two-thirds of the day when it is normally vacant. For double beds this furniture should be built in two halves or you'll never get it through the bedroom door. The two halves are held together by a pair of door hinges mounted on top; one leaf of each hinge is mounted on one bed, the other leaf is mounted on the other bed, and the pin is inserted through the leaf knuckles to hold the beds together.

Replacing the above bureau with a long desk utilizes one of the biggest space-savers in any building: the counter. A bed is a counter you sleep on. A table is a counter you eat or work on. A desk is a counter you work or play on. Most counters are not their ideal length. Take desks. Most are a puny three or four feet long. But imagine having a lengthy desktop like the one in figure 3-25. This is a long plywood counter with a row of cabinets and plenty of legroom located below, with more cabinets and shelves mounted above. This would transform the room! Here the long plywood counter simply lays on the cabinets which don't need to be fastened together —so all these pieces can be rearranged like Lego bricks as the need arises. How nice for growing children whose interests change, for grownups who change jobs or hobbies, and for families or businesses when they move. Here's a few more facts about this versatile furnishing:

☞ The long countertops are built of one or more pieces of $3/4$-inch thick plywood, and underneath their front and back edges are fastened 1 × 1 inch angles that support the plywood and align it on the cabinet units below.

☞ The cabinet units can be ordered from lumber company catalogs. Anyone can buy them. If you do, remember the earlier-mentioned "93/162" contractor's discount.

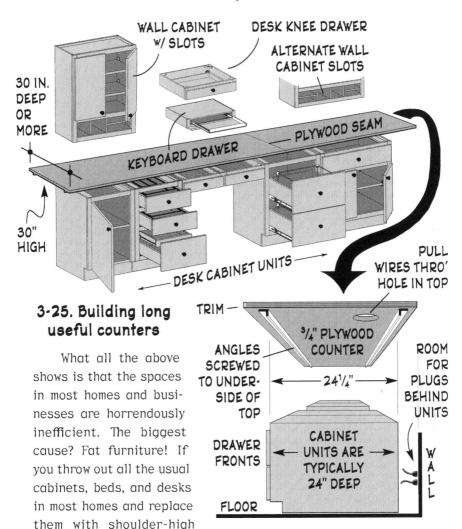

WALL CABINET w/ SLOTS

DESK KNEE DRAWER

ALTERNATE WALL CABINET SLOTS

30 IN. DEEP OR MORE

KEYBOARD DRAWER

PLYWOOD SEAM

30" HIGH

DESK CABINET UNITS

PULL WIRES THRO' HOLE IN TOP

TRIM

ANGLES SCREWED TO UNDER-SIDE OF TOP

¾" PLYWOOD COUNTER

24¼"

ROOM FOR PLUGS BEHIND UNITS

DRAWER FRONTS

CABINET UNITS ARE TYPICALLY 24" DEEP

WALL

FLOOR

3-25. Building long useful counters

What all the above shows is that the spaces in most homes and businesses are horrendously inefficient. The biggest cause? Fat furniture! If you throw out all the usual cabinets, beds, and desks in most homes and replace them with shoulder-high walls, bureaubeds, and long counters, this *furnitecture* could make 2,000 square feet of floorspace feel as roomy as 3,000 normal square feet. Think of all the money and energy you'd save if you could be just as comfortable in two-thirds the space? What's a few *CFL*s and lo-flo showerheads compared to this!

Furnitecture is more than a clever way to make spaces more useful. It is *the* elemental method of creating a truly sustainable architecture. It is the primary green energy domino that pushes over all the others —because it leads to smaller rooms, which leads to having enough room around the insides of exterior walls to add a foot of extra insulation around an *existing* building, which leads to smaller heating and cooling bills every minute you are in it. Furnitecture is also less expensive than many furnishings that hold half as much, it won't force you to live elsewhere while it is being built, and you can do a little at a time.

Another big way to create maximum comfort in minimum volume is to *double a room's function*, as in the earlier "library staircase". A few other candidates for assigning double duty are:

☞ *Garages*. If one adds a corridor around a parked car and lines the outer edges with shelves, cabinets, and a long workbench, this area can become a busy workshop for a family of do-it-yourselfers. I did this in my garage, as you can see below.

**3-26.
A de"light"ful
garage workbench**

In front of the bumpers is a long workbench with an electrical plug strip on the wall above, above this is a long ribbon window that lets in plenty of light with a wide overhang that obstructs the sun, and above the windows is a long shelf installed with the hidden bracket trick described a few pages ago.

☞ *Hallways*. If a typical gunbarrel hallway is widened a foot

Design

or so and kitchen cupboard cabinets are stacked three units high along the walls on one side, this usually thrift-less slit of space can hold a basement of belongings. This idea works well against any blank wall —in houses, offices, classrooms, factories, and studios. The cabinets should have adjustable shelves and glass doors so you can see what's inside without opening them.

☞ *Dining rooms.* In many homes this space with a big table in the middle and a long buffet on one side and lots of walls all around is often used only once a day. Think of how useful this space would be if the walls were lined with cabinets, shelves, a sewing machine, even the washer and dryer with that big folding table close by.

An outstanding example of doubling, even tripling and quad-rupling, a room's function exists in a tiny apartment in Hong Kong. There Gary Chang has installed in his 344 square-foot loft rolling walls up to 2 feet thick, 12 feet long, and 10 feet high that can be moved to create 24 different spaces. Instead of his going from one room to another, the rooms come to him. Sitting in the kitchen, he touches a button ... quicker than he can walk down a hall he's in his bedroom. If he wants a large living room, the shelves roll to the sides. If he wants a bookshelf within arm's reach, it's there with another tap of a button. Too close? A finger-tap inches the shelf back. This is not so much maximum comfort in minimum volume as spatial prestidigitation. [9]

If you incorporated all these space-savers into half your house you might find the other half empty. Then you could:

☞ Build in one room a small gymnasium, with a treadmill or exercycle on one side, a few dumbbells on the other, and a wide floormat in the center —and damn the driving and dues-paying to a health club miles away.

☞ Store lots of furniture and other belongings in another room —and damn more driving and monthly payments to a public storage unit miles away.

Architecture Laid Bare!

☞ Install a work center. In this era of office-in-homes this could become the busiest place in the house. This space would include a long table for packaging, a photocopier for copying invoices and receipts, space for several sizes of boxes and perhaps a bulk bag of styrofoam peanuts, and, if necessary, space for storing inventory.

☞ Create a recycling center. Here we're not talking about a row of garbage cans in the garage; we're talking about a bedroom-size space with a long sorting counter with a deep janitor's sink on one wall, a concrete floor thick enough to absorb manual compaction with a screened drain in the center, a 6-inch integral curb around the floor, a wall-mounted hose bibb with a hose rack alongside for washing the counter and floor, cabinets and shelves all around, two openable windows for cross-ventilation, an exhaust fan, eight bins for recycling

Newspapers	Cardboard	Other papers	Metals
Glass	Plastics	Compost	Other outgoing,

and a wide entrance door with a strongbox lock to discourage theft.

In almost every area in a home or place of business, a few rules of thumb known to architects can lead to efficient and comfortable design. Some appear below.

Entries, also *foyers* and *front halls* ... Here an occupant transforms from an "outdoor" to an "indoor" person and back again. Hence this space is best designed as an "airlock entry" with two doors: one leading outdoors, one leading in, with the floor between at least six-by-six feet in size to allow a person to maneuver into or out of an overcoat. If the person is wearing a hat and galoshes while carrying two bags of groceries, this chamber should have a large waist-high shelf for divesting burdens, a head-high shelf for setting the hat, a shoulder-high row of hooks for

100

hanging the coat (hooks are better than a closet when the garment is wet and they take up less space), a small seat for removing the galoshes (the space below should be open for storing the footwear), and a hard, durable, easy-to-clean floor. Along one side should be a wide closet for storing year-round outdoor wear, and nearby should be a powder room. This compartment's two opposing doors can be opened one at a time which will keep heat from flowing through when the weather is hot or cold outside.

Kitchens ... an efficiently arranged kitchen sink, stove, and fridge should form a triangle whose perimeter is no more than 22 feet. On each side of each vertex should be at least two feet of counterspace, and ideally much more. A clever arrangement is the kitchen with large circular counters between the stove and sink and fridge that appears on page 45. This design minimizes the triangle's perimeter while maximizing the areas beside each vertex. If the kitchen has a dishwasher it should be close to the sink, and dish and silver storage should be close to both. A kitchen should also be near a garage so one can quickly carry groceries from car to counter.

Living areas ... in residences, instead of fitting together a boxy living room, dining room, and den in the old Victorian way, think of the activities occurring in these spaces. Then you may prefer a FORMAL area for pleasant conversation (this needs several upholstered seats, each near a low table); a PASSIVE area for reading books, listening to TV and music and the like (these need lots of shelves and counters in front of a few seats and sofas); and a PLAY area for light physical activity (this suggests exercise equipment, musical instruments, and the like). Each area should have plenty of storage close by.

Laundry areas ... instead of cramming a clothes washer and dryer into a corner of a clammy basement infested with spiders and mildew, locate the machines in an area as nice as the living room. This should have a large sink, contain plenty of counters for folding clothes, and be close to where clothes and linens are donned and shed.

When all the spatial ideas described above are organized into a coherent plan, they will likely expose a marketing ploy that has snared many a homeowner the past few decades: When you want a nice house, you don't spend days analyzing every activity that may occur within; no, you're more likely to spend the same number of days driving around the countryside looking for the "best" already-made home, one that typically offers you thirty percent less useful space and costs thirty percent more than it should . Realtors and developers have trained you to do this. It's taken them a few billion dollars of marketing to pull it off —but look around you: have they succeeded? Hopefully the last fifteen pages will give you a script that will help you dodge this ploy, and lead you and your loved ones and business colleagues to the kind of comfort you truly deserve and can better afford.

Fire Safety

Seventy-five percent of all fire deaths in buildings are caused by smoke and gas inhalation. Pushed outward by the expanding heat of flames, these toxins spread to areas well beyond their source, often faster than a person moving at a brisk walk. Consider the Happy Land nightclub fire near New York City in 1990 in which 87 people breathed their last. During a conversation I once had with the insurance claims adjustor for this fire, he said some people who died on the lower floor at the bar were found slumped in their seats with cigarets and drinks in their hands [10] —because they had inhaled an invisible gas with no odor and one lungful was all it took.

As a fire produces smoke and toxic gases, it also depletes the oxygen supply. Though oxygen comprises about 21 percent of air, reducing this to 10 percent leads to faulty judgment and rapid fatigue, and reducing it to 6 percent results in collapse. It is of little solace to any victim that oxygen levels lower than 7 percent usually do not support combustion.

Considering that many buildings today are essentially stacks of firewood and plastic, it may surprise you that designing them not to burn is *not* the first rule of fire safety design. Fire safety rule number one is *Design the building so occupants can escape in case of fire.* Here the architect asks: Will the building be residential or commercial? Will it be tall with a small base? Or low with a large base? Will it have a few large spaces? Or many small ones? Any atriums inside? Balconies outside? Any open escalators or stairwells? Are the windows large, small, sealed, openable? Each such scenario has code mandates for making it safe to escape from in case of fire. Since fires often quickly disable electrical circuitry and ventilation systems, alarm systems and emergency exit lighting should be battery-operated, and fire-control ventilation should be activated by two emergency generators located well apart from each other.

Fire safety rule number two is *Design the building to quickly detect a fire.* When a fire erupts indoors, a hot region exists at the flames —the *fire zone*— and adjacent areas fill with toxic gasses —the *smoke zone.* Many commercial buildings today have computerized sensors installed throughout that (1) detect fires and smokes the moment the first fume curls into the air, (2) activate fire suppression systems that smother the fire, (3) close supply air ducts in the fire zone so fresh air won't flow to the fire, (3) open exhaust air ducts in nearby smoke zones so smokes and gases can escape outdoors, and (4) activate alarms that alert occupants and notify the fire department. Even in residences, smoke detectors are often required.

Fire safety rule number three is *Design the building so a fire can be quickly put out.* In commercial buildings this is done by locating fire sprinklers, firehose racks, and fire extinguishers throughout the building. Two other fire extinguishers in any building are toilets and faucets with hose connections on them,

Architecture Laid Bare!

as pictured in figure 7–4 on page 280.

Fire safety rule number four is —finally— *Design the building so it won't burn.* Since steel and concrete rapidly lose strength when they heat up, in steel and concrete structures every beam and column is clad with fireproofing. Where small commercial interiors are framed with metal studs and joists, the framing is covered with firecode-rated drywall. As for finishes and furnishings, if you are the owner or a manager that is involved in the design or construction of a building or part thereof, take a thumbnail-size chunk of each planned interior finish (including furniture fabrics and insulation) outside, put a match to it, and take a whiff of the fumes. You may think twice about installing some of these materials in areas where you, your loved ones, or business colleagues may live and work.

In suburban and rural areas, fires may spread from one building to the next due to *wildfires.* Each may be a *surface fire* (the flames spread along the ground), or a *crown fire* (the flames race through the treetops). Advancing flames can also kill a house by *firebrands* or *flamefronts.* Firebrands are burning debris lofted into the sky by strong convection currents that can carry these sparky items far ahead of the advancing flames. In intense wildfires these embers can fill the sky and ignite any woody object they fall on. Flamefronts are walls of fire that usually pass a given area in 1 to 5 minutes. Since it normally takes 2 to 3 minutes of flame exposure to ignite most wood exteriors, a passing flame front may leave one house undamaged while the house next door burns to the ground. Even noncombustible materials are no guarantee of protection. Exposed plastics such as vinyl gutters and vinyl siding quickly melt; and though metal roofing or siding won't burn, during an intense fire these thin sheets conduct heat so well that wood sheathing beneath them can ignite. Though masonry facades and clay tile roofs won't burn either, a spark or ember can enter an attic vent, plastic plumbing vent, or broken window in these surfaces and ignite curtains and drapes and gut the construction from the inside.

Design

A wildfire's temperature can also be so hot that a building spontaneously combusts before any flames reach it. Witness the Oakland, California, fire in 1991 that literally vaporized 3,000 homes in a 1,500 acre suburban area and killed 24 people. I once stood a quarter mile away from a forest fire whose flame front was a half mile wide and must have been sixty feet high. I was sweating like a leaky sieve. Imagine being fifty feet from those flames. You would fry to a crisp in a minute. And sometimes the sky can become so foggy with smoke, even miles from the blaze, that you find it hard to breathe. In fact, large fires can suck all the oxygen out of the air for hundreds of feet around; so even if you find a damp or cool place to hide you could suffocate. Another myth is that a good-sized creek running nearby would be an excellent source of water in case of fire; but a forest fire upstream can suck the creek dry. Also any stream less than 30 feet wide is usually a poor fire barrier because foliage usually grows high along streams which allows advancing flames to leap across them. Finally, if the wind is briskly blowing, a wildfire can race across the ground faster than a horse can gallop.

So wildfire safety rule number one is if a fire approaches a building you are in, *get away fast and far*. Before you flee, close the garage door and all doors and windows and turn off any fuel lines. If you have a chainsaw, brush saw, or axe, bring them along; then if you come to a burning tree fallen across the road you might be able to remove it. Also, on hillside fires, heated rocks can burst and roll downhill where they can start new fires below and collect on roads where they can keep occupants from evacuating and firefighters from reaching the fire. To give you an idea what can happen here, three days after I witnessed the wall of flames mentioned above (this was a huge fire that eventually burned 63,000 acres), I was shoveling from a local highway rocks and boulders that had rolled from a steep hill covered with fire alongside when a golfball-size rock sailed off the hill and struck me in the forehead. The next thing I knew my eyes were filled with blood and I couldn't see what I was doing. Fortunately the cut was small and I had a towel in the car and several people were nearby. If the rock was large and I was alone, you might be reading my obituary. So a few more items to throw into your car before fleeing a fire are a shovel, hardhat, towels, first-aid kit, and a couple friends. Some of these ideas may seem arcane, but on rare occasions they may help you live to tell the tale.

In areas threatened by wildfires, consider building or improving houses and small commercial buildings as described below.[11] Due to a building's other design directives it may be understandably impossible to implement all these suggestions.

☞ Locate the building on level land at least fifty feet from the bases and crests of hills.

☞ Remove branches extending above driveways and roads. If they catch fire they could fall and block the road. Also remove branches extending over any buildings.

☞ Have at least 40 feet of space between trees within 100 feet of the building, and remove all branches within 12 feet of the ground (this greatly reduces the chance of a surface fire becoming a crown fire).

☞ Create a fifty-foot-wide fire-free zone between buildings and surrounding vegetation with driveways, turnarounds, terraces, swimming pools, low stone walls, and the like. The lower and lesser the foliage, the better. Avoid shrubs and meadows close to the building. A mowed lawn slows advancing flames better than flowerbeds and ground covers, especially during prolonged dry weather.

☞ Mount spigots with hose racks on two opposite facades. In the above-mentioned wildfire, I used a hose to save a house by starting a backfire on the house's lawn and controlling the fire's spread completely around the house with the hose until the whole lawn was charred; then I went into the kitchen, got an icepick, stabbed dozens of holes along the hose, climbed a ladder onto the roof and looped the hose back and forth along its peak, then turned the hose on before leaving the premises. The wild-fire swept through the area and burned to the ground every house within half a mile except this one.

☞ In areas prone to grassfires (where a person can more safely remain at home to protect it) a good firefighting tool is a swimming pool and a gasoline-powered pump. Do not rely on electrical tools, because power lines far from where you are can be severed by a fire.

☞ Build facades and roofs of fireproof materials: facades of stucco, brick, and stone; roofs of metal, slate, clay tile, and concrete shingles. Eave overhangs should be minimal and their vents located close to the outer edge.

☞ Where large windows are on the side of a house that faces prevailing winds, fit their outer faces with noncom-bustible shutters that are easy to reach, are easy to latch and unlatch, and cover the frames. This is a good idea for all windows. The most fire-resistant glazing is low-e glass, followed by tempered glass, laminated glass, double panes, and single panes. The more fire-resistant the glazing, the less likely it will break when exposed to intense heat and allow flames to enter inside.

☞ Fit all exterior vents with $1/4$-inch metal mesh screens to keep flying embers from entering indoors. This includes plumbing vents. Fit chimneys with $1/2$-inch mesh screens. This meshing will also keep rodents and other unwelcome critters from moving indoors.

☞ During dry seasons, keep gutters clean of leaf litter. One of the quickest ways a wildfire can kill a house is by ignit-ing dry pine needles in a gutter. Metal gutters are better than vinyl ones. Better yet is no gutters at all.

☞ Fit all barbecue and incinerator flue tops with $1/2$ inch mesh spark arrestors.

☞ Clear away all flammable debris around the house, under the house, and inside the house (especially in the attic).

Accessibility

Commercial buildings today must be designed to accommodate the handicapped. But they should be the same for such encumbered occupants as small children, pregnant women pushing strollers, and retirees carrying groceries. Hence accessibility is not design for the "Disabled" so much as for the "Encumbered", which can be almost anyone anytime. One of the finest ADA-compliant buildings, though not promoted as such, is New York's Guggenheim Museum. Of this seven-story helix Frank Lloyd Wright said: "It would be easy to go up in the elevator in a wheelchair and come down again without undesired interruption." [12] Here is eloquent proof that a building needn't look like a physical therapy ward to accommodate the disabled. The same is true for Wright's gorgeous sink faucets that appear on page 279.

Designing buildings for the disabled is described in the *ADA Guidelines*, which may be accessed by googling ADA Accessibility Guidelines. Here is a sampling of these directives:

Wheelchair dimensions. Minimum clear opening width for wheelchairs is 32 inches. A circular or T plan area (see figure 3-28) that allows wheelchairs to turn around should exist in each residential kitchen, in one toilet stall per public restroom, in front of one closet in each lodging and institutional bedroom, and along every 50 linear feet of hallway. Each water fountain and vanity should have a 32-inch wide knee-space under it. By the way, a baby stroller is a type of wheelchair, one that requires a second person to push it.

It is wise to design any building, public or private, according to ADA guidelines. Here are two excellent design rules for encumbered occupants: (1) select doorknobs and faucet handles that can be operated with a closed fist (i.e. levers, not knobs); and (2) locate bathtub handlebars, soap dishes, mirrors, faucets, paper towel dispensers, and other wall-mounted items so occupants can reach them while seated.

Design

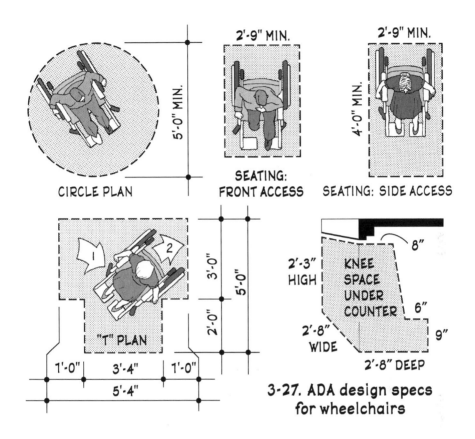

2'-9" MIN.

2'-9" MIN.

5'-0" MIN.

4'-0" MIN.

CIRCLE PLAN

SEATING:
FRONT ACCESS

SEATING: SIDE ACCESS

"T" PLAN

3'-0"
5'-0"
2'-0"

1'-0" | 3'-4" | 1'-0"

5'-4"

2'-3"
HIGH

KNEE
SPACE
UNDER
COUNTER

8"

6"

2'-8"
WIDE

9"

2'-8" DEEP

3-27. ADA design specs
for wheelchairs

The Genesis of Ornament

Ornament has little to do with a building's function. Surely ornament can make an ordinary space look more attractive; but when it is stuck on a building like post-it notes reminding you of how nice it would be to live in early Greece or Rome, it has nothing to do with the building itself and is an inglorious masquerade that only blots whatever beauty the building may truly have. Such frilly appliqués also cost money in ways that only make things worse, and they unnecessarily use materials that degrade the environment in their making, packaging, and transporting to the site —so ornament is anything *but* green architecture.

109

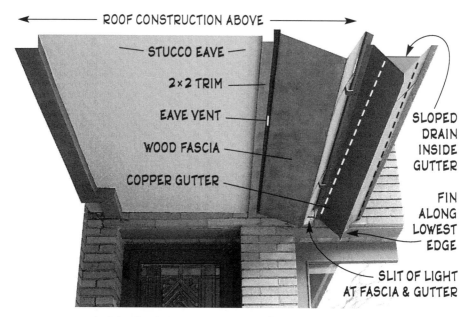

← ——— ROOF CONSTRUCTION ABOVE ——— →

— STUCCO EAVE —

2 × 2 TRIM ———

EAVE VENT ———

WOOD FASCIA ——

COPPER GUTTER ——

SLOPED
DRAIN
INSIDE
GUTTER

FIN
ALONG
LOWEST
EDGE

— SLIT OF LIGHT
AT FASCIA & GUTTER

3-28. Evolving ornament from function

If ornament must exist on or in a building, it should be spare, and it should evolve from a functional aspect of the building's construction. One architect was exemplary in doing this: Frank Lloyd Wright. When he ornamented a building, he wouldn't borrow from the almsbasket of ancient and outmoded styles; he would typically evolve the motif from a functional part of the building. Let's see how he did this.

Figure 3-28 shows the roof above the entry of the George Barton residence in Buffalo, New York, which Wright designed in 1904. The roof shelters the porch in front of the door from Buffalo's considerable annual rain and snow, and it has three functional requirements. (1) The roof needs an eave vent which, combined with the vent at the roof's peak, removes moisture from the roof. (2) The roof's eave requires a gutter with a downward pitch to carry the collected rainwater away. (3) The gutter needs a downspout at its lowest part to carry the rainwater to the ground.

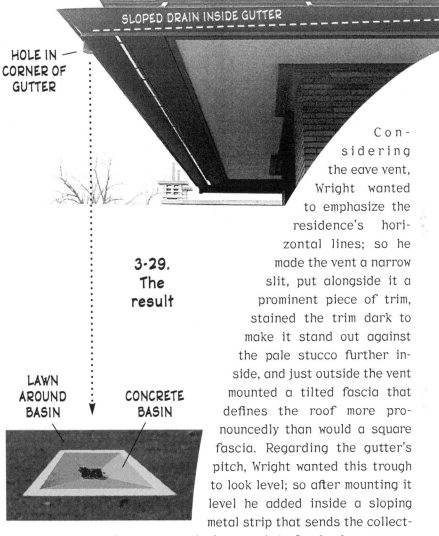

SLOPED DRAIN INSIDE GUTTER

HOLE IN CORNER OF GUTTER

**3-29.
The
result**

LAWN AROUND BASIN

CONCRETE BASIN

Considering the eave vent, Wright wanted to emphasize the residence's horizontal lines; so he made the vent a narrow slit, put alongside it a prominent piece of trim, stained the trim dark to make it stand out against the pale stucco further inside, and just outside the vent mounted a tilted fascia that defines the roof more pronouncedly than would a square fascia. Regarding the gutter's pitch, Wright wanted this trough to look level; so after mounting it level he added inside a sloping metal strip that sends the collected water to a downspout at the lower end. As for the downspout, a vertical pipe would disrupt the horizontal look Wright desired — so he omitted it, and put a hole in the gutter's lower end and located a concrete basin in the lawn fourteen feet below.

Wright ornamented this architecture in other functional ways. He gave the gutter a V section and added a fin along its low-

111

est edge to make it stronger, both of which further accent its horizontality. And instead of fastening the gutter against the fascia he located it two inches away —to create a poetic slit of light that makes the gutter look like it is reaching out to the sky to gather the rain. Also in figure 3-29, note that the projections and indents of the gutter, fascia, and eave vent together look like the molding of a large horizontal pictureframe that extends under the roof around the house, and the wide strip of stucco acts as a manilla matting between the frame and the facades. Of this construction Wright said: "The underside of the roof projections was flat and light in color to create a glow of reflected light that made upper rooms not dark, but delightful." [13] Again, the building's decor stemmed from functional directives.

The bricks beneath the porch roof in figure 3-28 gave Wright another chance to enhance this architecture's horizontal lines. Here he didn't use standard bricks but longer and thinner Roman bricks, then he made the vertical mortar joints narrow and flush with the bricks' surfaces and the horizontal joints wide and deep to give the masonry a horizontal look, as appears in figure 3-30.

In this and many other ways, Wright evolved a building's ornament from some aspect of its function —what he called his "æsthetic fodder" [14]— the way a flower blossoms from a bud. Early in his career he stated that "Form follows function". But decades later he revised this directive by declaring that "Form and function should be one, joined in a spiritual union, as efflorescence is to a tree." [15] This was at the core of his philosophy of organic architecture, and it is Green Architecture at its best. Wright knew the loveliest architectural ornament is not produced in a factory so much as it evolves on the site, amid all the other beauties Nature provides. Regarding more excessive decor, Wright scorned it as "Aesthetics dyspeptic from incontinent indulgence in 'Frenchite' pastry." [16] His genius often appeared in his writing as well as his architecture. So if you are looking for a simple way to lessen our nation's energy crisis, then campaign against money-draining, energy-wasting, ocularly aching appliqué —

especially when there is a better way of doing the same, one that carries an elegant pedigree.

Wright occasionally designed ornament for its own sake in some of his buildings. But the way he did this usually aligned with his philosophy of organic architecture in a manner that is also worth noting. When he designed such ornament, he would evolve it from a local plant, or as Viollet-le-Duc once said,

STANDARD BRICK

— NORMAL VERTICAL & HORIZONTAL JOINTS

ROMAN BRICK

VERTICAL JOINTS ARE NARROW & FLUSH; HORIZONTAL JOINTS ARE WIDE & DEEP

3-30. How Wright emphasized horizontal lines with bricks

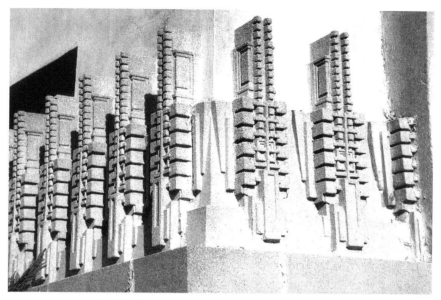

3-31. Botany as a basis for ornament

"Seek the flora of the fields." A superb example is the stylized hol-lyhocks in the frieze around the living room and second floor of the Barnsdall Residence he designed in Los Angeles, California. The hollyhock is not a local plant (it is a native of China) but it was the owner's favorite, of which Wright said: "A bit sentimental, Miss Barnsdall had prenamed the house for the Hollyhock she loved for many reasons, all of them good ones, and called upon me to ren-der her favorite flower as a feature of Architecture how I might."[17] The result appears in figure 3-31. This is one feature of Wright's architecture that other designers could emulate anywhere.

Sadly today, architectural æsthetics have veered far from these functional directives. Many highly publicized buildings today are littered with garishly excessive ornament that not only looks ugly and out of place but has inflicted serious damage to the environment. Take Frank Gehry's titanium freeforms, one of which appears in figure 3-32. The front of this building, a center for the performing arts at Bard College ninety miles north of New

3-32. Where's the beef?
View of a Gehry "freeform" from where you park

York City, has a huge titanium roof, 60 feet wide and equally as high, that from a distance looks like a few pieces of tinfoil were swept up in a swirling dust devil and deposited on the roof. This weird shape tilts so precariously over the entrance that it looks like a stiff breeze would topple it to the ground. What if a foot of snow falls on this slick surface as it does every year or so? It would avalanche to a pile in front of the doors —and woe to anyone who may be standing there. Such gilded rags are an immense expense that has no rationale, a monstrous example of frilly appliqué. Shakespeare described such ugliness as a "Harlot's cheek, beautied with plast'ring art." [18] Here Gehry's art is nothing but a harlot's cheek. I would gladly call it Gehry garbage, but elsewhere in these pages I have put garbage on a pedestal.

This building has other architectural debits. The above portal isn't even the building's main entrance; this is around the side of the building next to a parking lot where playgoers park during performances and employees park during work. This is the view that appears in figure 3-32. High above the right of this facade appears the edge of the titanium freeform that looks so oppressively prominent from in front. Where do you think this facade's main entrance is? The big dark rectangle near the ground in the middle of the building? Guess again. It's the two little double doors at ground level off to the right. This deception violates three more axioms of well-designed architecture: (1) a building's openings should have a human scale (the faux entrance makes the facade look much smaller than it actually is); (2) every part of a building should look like what you think it is; and (3) every part should be where you expect it. In these respects good architecture "reads" as clearly as a dictionary definition —and this building does anything but. Also, one can photograph a building from an angle that makes it look beautiful when from a slightly different angle it looks ugly. Regarding this, the most publicized photo of this building is the front of the titanium freeform; but from where most people enter the building it looks like a huddle of ugly boxes. How different this is from Frank Lloyd Wright's architecture, which usually looks beautiful from *every* angle: right, left, near, far, inside and out. The snapshot in figure 3-33 also says little about parts of the building's interior being clumsy to use, that mining the huge quantity of titanium cladding was extraordinarily destructive to the environment, and that the freeforms out front led this building to cost far more than it should have. Viollet-le-Duc described such debits as well as anyone when he said:

> Whom are we trying to please in thus expending immense sums in reproducing forms of which no rational explanation can be given? [19]

Clearly computers have opened new horizons for architectural expression —but because you *can* do something doesn't mean you should. Indeed, Le Corbusier's chapel at Ronchamp, Saarinen's TWA Terminal, and Wright's Guggenheim Museum —all designed before 1960— were as curvy as Gehry's computer-aided designs and they didn't need computers.

Design

The Grandeur of Garbage

For every thousand square feet of floor area built in America today, a few acres of land somewhere in the world have usually been destroyed. At the same time, for every thousand square feet of floor area built in America today, a truckload or two of trash is usually hauled to a landfill. All this waste coming and going doesn't stabilize that larger foundation under a building known as the environment. LEED has done well to address this problem. It awards points for such green construction practices as "maximize the use of building products that include recycled materials" ... "minimize construction waste" ... "divert waste materials from landfills and incinerators to recycling centers" ... and "use salvaged, refurbished, or reused materials". Indeed, if anything could be called the soul of sustainable architecture, it is rescuing and reusing old materials in new construction. After all, it is not the mighty dinosaur or mastodon that has survived through the ages, but the scavenging buzzard and shark.

An elemental way to think of recycling is to look at the property you live on. The landscape you see outside contains a certain cubic yardage of material. The building you are in also contains a certain cubic yardage of material. Both those yardages are more alike than you think; after all, one did come from the other. Extend this idea to the materials a few miles away at your local landfill, and possibly a few places in between and beyond, and you get a glimmer of the opportunities that await someone who considers using natural or old materials in new construction.

A fine way to map these logistics is to think of the most beautiful marbles or hardwoods you've seen in an expensive residence or corporate office. Those materials came from someone's backyard that was a lot like yours, and their essence is no different than the essence of any material found anywhere. The challenge is not reclaiming materials to work with —that is easy— but finding ways to bring out each material's essence so it displays the same kind of beauty you see in the finest marbles and hardwoods.

Architecture Laid Bare!

For example, it takes little more than money to bring out the beauty of a finely grained hardwood in a building; but it takes a refined insight to bring out the beauty in an old board found in someone's back yard, and people know and love this quality when they see it. Furthermore, if you reuse an old board in a building, that's recycling; and that achievement is noble enough; but if you clean that board in a way that makes its weathered grains gleam so lustrously that someone says, "You can't buy wood like that in a lumberyard"—then you have tapped into a more kingly essence. Done like this, recycled building materials won't look like reshuffled trash; they will exhibit the kind of class and erudition one associates with elegant lifestyles and sophisticated people. It almost seems incidental that such efforts can help keep a few corners of our world Green, and could save you some of that green you put in your pocket. And we all admire beautiful work made with things someone obtained for free.

Let's elucidate this idea with an example. Figure 3-33 shows a corner of one small room in my house that I built in 1974, the master bath. The fieldstone wall rising above two sides of the sunken tub was constructed of rocks I collected from a two hundred year-old stone wall on my property. When building these walls, all I did was preserve the material's essence —its strength and rugged character— from where the rocks once sat in the woods to where they now sit around this room. I also used this natural material collected on my property to build the exterior wall around the first floor, eighty linear feet of walls completely indoors, and the chimney mass with three fireplaces that rises through the heart of the house.

Another example of bringing out a discarded item's essence is the round pieces of glass you see mounted in the fieldstone wall above the tub. These tiny windows are empty liquor bottles. The essence of this material is that light passes through the glass but you can't see clearly through it, which allows a bather to see what she is doing while preserving her privacy. After collecting a couple dozen bottles from the dumpsters of several local bars

3-33. The grandeur of garbage

one Sunday morning, I arranged the bottles in matching pairs, removed their tops with a bottle cutter bought from the Whole Earth Catalog, mated the matching tops, duct-taped the tops of each pair together to make a cylinder about three inches thick and ten inches long, and mounted these cylinders of thermopane here and there in the stone walls as the mason built them.

I employed a simpler tactic with the hexagonal slate shingles on the wall to the right of the tub. The essence of these thin slabs of stone is that they shed water. After finding them in a back yard

119

ten miles away (the owner was glad for the Hamilton I laid in his hand and having a cleaner backyard), I nailed them on the wall around the tub much the way one nails shingles on a roof.

One material I had to pay for and do a lot of work to exploit its essence is the sunken tub's bluestone floor and side walls. On visiting a local masonry supply yard (not to buy rocks, to be sure) I spied two huge slabs of bluestone, 36 × 48 inches in size and 3 inches thick, marked 70 percent off because they had a coppery blush on their bluish surfaces that someone thought was unsightly. The better the fool. Also considered unsightly were the long cracks along the slabs' edges which indicated the slabs were delaminating. After bringing them home, I carefully tapped a row of oak wedges into the delaminating edges and split each three-inch slab into three one-inch slabs. I didn't break a piece. After mounting a diamond-tip masonry blade in my circular saw, I cut and assembled the six slabs into a sunken tub that's 48 inches wide by 74 inches long which is big enough for a family to bathe a dog in if it wanted. In fact, here is where we wash our dog and it is the perfect place to do so. I cut the tub's side pieces at slight angles so they incline 10 degrees outward toward the top, and I clad the concrete pedestal under the barn beam post with three narrow slabs of bluestone whose edges I mitered at a 45 degree angle so the pieces fit together as neatly as the corners of a pictureframe. The masonry blade I used can be bought in almost any hardware store, it fits into any electric handsaw, and using it requires no more skill than it takes to cut plywood. The blade does cut through masonry much slower than through plywood and it raises a cloud of dust behind the saw; so if you do this work, make sure you are outdoors and facing the wind. That's all an amateur needs to know to do professional work with this material. In fact, every part of this bathroom's construction was routine carpentry and masonry performed with common hand tools, much of it done by the one who is typing this text.

One of the biggest troves of recyclable treasures I found for my house regards the little steel railing on the near side of the

Design

tub. This railing's pieces came from a factory that had gone out of business. After driving my Chevy Blazer inside, I folded down the back seats, picked pieces of scrap off the floor, and loaded them in. When the metal was only three inches deep I noticed my tires were half flat from the accumulating weight! I stopped loading and slowly drove home. I drove back for one more load. I could have had a half dozen if I wanted. Onsite, after trying my hand at welding and blacksmithing (two skills I had no previous experience in), from the metal I collected I not only built this railing around the bathtub, I constructed a 32-foot-long railing for my house's three-story staircase, a 37-foot long drainage grate in front of the garage, a 13-foot-long drainage grate at the top of the driveway outside, a 31-foot-long tool hanger in the garage, and many smaller items throughout the house. That's a lot of architecture for 80 miles of gasoline, wouldn't you say?

Another recycling adventure that ended in this bathroom concerns the thick wood post above the mitered bluestone pedestal and the weathered boards on the front of the vanity and around the mirror. These came from a 250-year-old barn seventy miles away. I reused one of the barn's handhewn beams for this post, and I reused many more of the barn's beams and posts as exposed structure throughout the house. As for the vanity fronts and the mirror's frame, I made these out of the barn's siding —which I also fashioned into cabinets, shelves, and base molding throughout the house in every room. I even reshaped some of the old barn door hinges into toilet paper holders, as appear in figure 3-34. Since the siding was very dirty, I brought out its essence by (1) lightly wire-

3-34. Toilet paper holder

brushing each piece on all four sides in the direction of the grain (where the grain was swirly I matched the swirls with my brush-strokes), (2) tapping the piece vertically on a concrete block a few times to knock out the dirt, (3) hosing the piece down (it was amazing how dirty the water was that flowed out of each board), and (4) sun-drying each board for two days. This is a simple, superb method of turning the oldest filthiest board you ever saw into an attractive finish you will never have to paint.

In the old barn I dismantled for this house, I also cut the barn's long slim rafters into mullions and placed them 4'-0" apart in six ribbon windows, one of which is 161 feet long, that wrap around the house. Figure 3-26 on page 98 shows what these ribbon windows look like from the inside.

Another wonderful recycling experience I had with this house concerned a small mill only three-tenths of a mile away where a man made oak stakes and wedges for local contractors and the public utility. (We used to send new laborers out to "Fred's steaks and wedges" to buy lunch their first day on the job). Behind Fred's mill was a pile of oak lumber cutoffs, some of them fourteen feet long. After relieving Fred of these scraps I ran them through my tablesaw and created lengths of $1/8 \times 1^1/_4$ inch oak trim that became 170 linear feet of edging around a dozen built-in countertops throughout the house. For years afterward I hauled away Fred's lumber scraps and cut them into oak firewood to warm my house. Fred and I got along real well together.

When it comes to recycling, two personality traits are important that require no innate skills, though they do tend to be more eloquently expressed if constantly exercised. These are *reputation* and *obsession*. Reputation involves having a congenial demeanor and letting your friends and their friends know you are looking for trash to build a house with. Reputation is what led a friend of a friend of mine to tell me about the slate shingles in someone's back yard ten miles away, a friend of a friend who led me to the steel scraps on the floor of the company going out of business, and a friend of a friend who told me about the big barn

Design

70 miles away that I used to build my house. Obsession is acting with heightened inspiration when spying a potentially useful item. Many times while driving somewhere I have seen a nice-looking rock along the road and stopped to pick it up. These rocks now appear in 370 linear feet of walls averaging three feet high that I built around two turnarounds, two patios, and a beautiful three-terraced garden next to the house. Once while driving along a country road I saw a small half-collapsed barn clad in weathered siding. Instantly I envisioned converting the old siding into new trim in my house. The farmer who owned the barn was pleasantly surprised when I offered him forty dollars to remove it "before somebody got hurt there." Obsession is also what led me to gather the rocks on my property, the liquor bottles in the dumpsters behind the local bars, and Fred's oak lumber cutoffs.

Obsession can find other avenues of expression. As a sample, in figure 3-33 see the shower curtain hanging by the left of the bathtub? For years after constructing this tub in 1974 I couldn't find a shower curtain that was long enough and whose top would slide smoothly around the tub. Then in 1986 while working on a remodeling job, I was cutting some molding on my table saw when a piece got hung up in the blade and —*wham*— the next thing I knew I was staring at a red hole an inch long and half as wide on the underside of my forearm. Tablesaw kickback! I knew I'd bought a few sutures at the local ER; so after finishing up work (yes, I wrapped a cravat around my arm and worked another four hours until I was done), I drove to the hospital where a nurse led me to an examination room with a bed in the center and curtains all around and told me to lie on the bed and wait for the doctor. While I rested on my back staring at the ceiling, my eyes wandered over to the surrounding curtains ... up to the little chain connectors at the curtains' tops ... around the metal track the connectors were mounted in. Suddenly I cried, "There's my shower curtains!" When the doctor stepped in, he found me standing on a chair looking up at the curtains' ceiling connectors. My first words to him had nothing to do with my injury but were, "Where's the custodian?" After the doc sewed up the cut in my forearm with seven sutures he phoned the custodian, who came up and gave me the address of the company that supplied the curtains; and the rest of the story you know.

The above experiences reveal another recycling truth. Although a building's construction is described in a set of plans before ground is broken, many recycled materials may not be found until after construction has begun, which can lead to plan changes during construction. Hence recycling often requires flexibility by the architect, contractor, and owner.

Now some recycled materials may cost nearly as much as analogously new materials purchased retail. For example, regarding the old barn I used in my house, I paid a carpenter who lived near the barn to dismantle it, a crew of four men to help me load the barn beams and siding onto my excavator's backhoe trailer, the excavator to haul these materials 70 miles back to my house, and a couple laborers to clean the beams and siding onsite; and all these outlays together came near to what I would have paid for similar-size beams and boards at a commercial lumberyard. But here's another truth about recycling: the checks I wrote for this lumber went not to merchants and managers in other parts of the country, even the world, but to local people. Indeed, the money spent in procuring, packaging, transporting, and preparing such materials is a local "stimulus package" of which any American president would be proud.

The recycled lumber, reused rocks, retrieved liquor bottles, recovered shingles, and reclaimed steel in my house have another quality that is missing in new construction materials: the older they get the better they look. Admittedly a lot of imagination was required to create this architecture —but the more of this resource you consume, the more that remains!

In the above residence, LEED's recycling directives were taken to a higher level of fulfillment and refinement than what would have earned a top score on any environmental checklist. Indeed, this dwelling not only *is* environmental, it *looks* environ-

Design

mental: it plays the part, it practices what it preaches, inside and out. From the living room, the barn-rafter mullions between the long ribbon windows wrapping around three sides of this space look like the trunks of the trees outside, the weathered wood trim around the windows looks like the trees' branches, and the rocks in the chimney mass behind look like the rocks on the ground outside —all of which make you feel like you're outdoors when you're in. As if untrammeled Nature flows in through one side of the house and out the other. As if the wind has blown through the place for a century. A few weeks ago an outdoorsman who makes his living conducting ecotours around the world visited my house. While standing in the front hall he said the place *smells* like the outdoors. Buildings like this need no scorecard to judge them by —a penned effort to render their values as exemplary— and they can be built by any amateur with common hand tools.

When I was in architecture school, my history professor showed color slides of Simon Rodia's monumental Watts Towers, two of them nearly a hundred feet tall, built by one man in Los Angeles; and he showed slides of Antoni Gaudí's gorgeous serpentine benches rimming the large public terrace of the Park Güell in Barcelona, Spain. These architectural wonders were built of trash —shattered china, defective tiles, collected seashells, broken bottles— yet they are studied in the halls of academia as examples of the finest architecture in the world. Look on these mighty works at wiki.watts_towers and wiki.park_guell. You'll be delighted at what you see.

Notes

Structure

Structure is what holds a building up. It is a building's most important system —because if it fails, all else fails.

A building's structure is essentially a lattice wherein each piece collects the weight of everything resting on it plus its own weight, then delivers its total weight to the members it rests on, down through the height of a building from the peak of its roof to the underside of its foundation. Each member in this skeleton must be carefully sized to support the maximum load it could conceivably carry: if too small, the member will fail under maximum stress; if too large, material and money will be wasted.

Foundations

A building's structure doesn't begin in the sky but in the ground. This is because a building's lowest construction bears the heaviest loads and needs the strongest support. This occurs where the flat underside of a building's footing rests on an equal area of earth immediately below. A footing should be wider than the construction just above to give it a pedestal to rest on, and footings are made of concrete because this material is strong as rock and won't rot or rust.

The soil beneath a building is rarely uniform. Each cubic foot may contain different earths, rocks, silt fissures, lava brecciations, and ancient shorelines that have evolved during the past billion or so years. Hence *every* linear foot of footing under *every* building —even one-story cottages on hard level soil— should contain at least two lengths of half-inch-diameter steel reinforcement known as *rebar*. The cost of this life insurance policy is pennies compared to what its omission could cost later.

A common dirt dilemma exists where soil freezes in winter.

Structure

Then the soil's volume increases by 9 percent and exerts a pressure of 150,000 pounds per square inch in every direction — that's three times stronger than tensile steel. Hence building codes mandate that the bottom of a building's footing should lie below the ground's deepest frost penetration in winter. However, Frank Lloyd Wright said a building doesn't need a deep foundation, only a trench a foot deep and two feet wide whose bottom drains to lower elevations; then you fill the trench with a foot of gravel and build on this.[1] I would chance this on *very* well-drained soil.

Another dirt dilemma exists where strong soil lies over weaker soil. A footing bearing on the stronger soil can punch a hole through it and settle into the softer soil below. This is what caused the Tower of Pisa to lean. After it started to tilt, a strata of soft clay was discovered ten meters below the hard soil under the sinking side of the building. If this tower were built today, test borings would be made around the planned foundation to learn what lurks deep below. Then the tower would be built elsewhere, or long thick poles known as *piles* would be sunk deep into the ground until their bases rested on firmer soil, in this case a stratum of granite beneath the soft clay.

4-1.
What caused the Tower of Pisa to lean

10 METERS

SANDY SOIL

SOFT WET CLAY

GRANITE

Another aqueous disaster awaits buildings rising on hills of clay. If the clay slopes more than about 27 degrees and becomes saturated with water, it can cleave from the underlying soil and become an avalanche of mud, and any houses rising on the soil get an expensive ride downhill. Californians know about this.

Soil also flows with water, settles with gravity, is moved by ice, and even drifts with the continents. Indeed, we sailors live on an ocean of earth. This figure is apt, because in most places the earth a few feet below its surface is saturated with moisture. The liquid's highest level is the local *water table*, above which the soil is dry. During dry spells this level falls and during wet spells it rises. If it rises higher than a basement floor and no drainage exists around its perimeter, the basement can become a wading pool. In such conditions, empty in-ground swimming pools have been known to pop out of the soil.

Another dirt disaster awaits when a building's foundation is dug deeply too close to an existing building. Witness what happened to a narrow thirteen-story apartment in Shanghai in 2009 after an underground parking garage was excavated along one side. The removed earth was piled on the apartment's other side, heavy rain created uneven soil pressures beneath the building's sides, its pilings snapped —and the building toppled like a felled tree. [2]

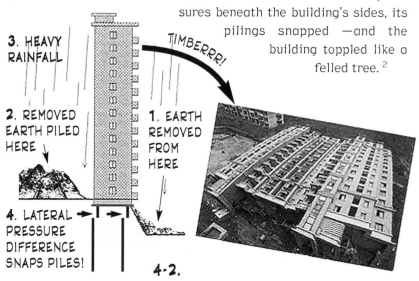

3. HEAVY RAINFALL

TIMBERRR!

2. REMOVED EARTH PILED HERE

1. EARTH REMOVED FROM HERE

4. LATERAL PRESSURE DIFFERENCE SNAPS PILES!

4-2.

How uneven soil pressures can collapse a building

Here's a few thumbnail notes on how certain features on or above the ground can tell you what lies below:

Rock outcrops. Bedrock may lie just below. Bad for excavating foundations, good for supporting buildings.

Foliage. Some species (willow, skunk cabbage) indicate moist

soil and poor places to build. Sparse foliage in a verdant
area suggests solid ground.

Gentle slope. Easy sitework, good drainage.

Steep slopes. Costly excavating, erosion and sliding soils.

Level terrain. Easy sitework, poor drainage.

Convex and concave terrain. Sloping terrain typically undu-
lates laterally in a series of shallow ridges (convex terrain) and depressions (concave terrain). Since rain
drains from ridges into depressions, convex terrain is
usually a firm dry strong place to build and concave terrain is usually a soft wet weak place to build, as below.

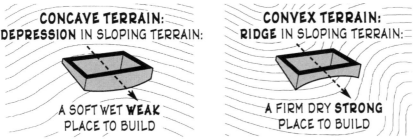

CONCAVE TERRAIN:
DEPRESSION IN SLOPING TERRAIN:
A SOFT WET **WEAK**
PLACE TO BUILD

CONVEX TERRAIN:
RIDGE IN SLOPING TERRAIN:
A FIRM DRY **STRONG**
PLACE TO BUILD

4-3. Convex terrain and concave terrain

However, even if you're only going to dig a post hole you need
more information about subsoils than this. With small buildings
such data is normally obtained as follows:

1. The contractor locates the building's foundation on the
   site according to the Plans.
2. The excavator digs the foundation's footings.
3. The contractor and excavator examine the exposed earth.
   The owner might want to attend this party too. If any
   ledges, boulders (common), centuries-old treestumps
   (very common), springs (fairly common), or buried debris
   (rare) occur, onsite adjustments are made. Ledges may
   require dynamiting or redesigning the foundation. Small
   boulders are removed, and large ones with wide bases
   that lie below frost level are left undisturbed. Springs

require draining, either by digging a trench to lower levels or pumping out the rising water.

For larger buildings, deep holes may be bored in the area of the foundation and long thin cylinders of soil are removed and analyzed by an engineer. If these *soil test borings* indicate that the soil beneath the planned building isn't strong enough to support it, long column-like *piles* may be sunk deep into the earth

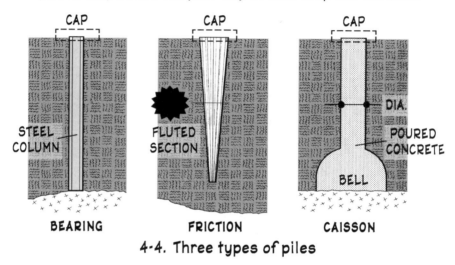

4-4. Three types of piles

below. There are three kinds: *bearing piles*, *friction piles*, and *caissons*. A bearing pile is a thick steel column driven into the ground like a huge nail until its bottom rests on firmer soil below. A friction pile is a tapered steel column with fluted sides which gains its strength by the friction developing between its deepening shaft and the enveloping soil. A caisson is a big hole drilled with a huge augur whose base is excavated to create a bell-like cavity, then the void is filled with concrete. After all piles are in place, a concrete cap is built on each cluster to create adequate bearing for the building above.

A bad place to build is a site contaminated with toxic chemicals. Strangely, LEED awards points for building on sites like this, what they call *brownfield development* sites, i.e. "Sites that have been damaged by environmental contamination as a way of preserving undeveloped land." Who would want to live on land like this? A better approach is Frank Lloyd Wright's earlier-mentioned "sites that no one else wants": land with challenging features that could *enhance* the character of a building there. A variation to Wright's approach is an *infill site*: a lot that normally can't be built on. Example: In 1978 when I was field engineer for a 160-house development in New York, one lot sloped so steeply from the street that a driveway couldn't legally be laid to the building site thirty feet below. So the developer (1) built a poured concrete basement wall on the legal building site, (2) dumped truckloads of excess earth excavated from other homesites in the development around and inside the basement wall until the ground was level on top, (3) built a second basement wall on the first, (4) dumped more earth from other homesites until the ground was again level on top, (5) built a *third* basement wall on the second —and *that's* where he constructed the house. LEED, take heed.

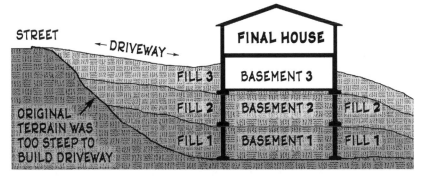

4-5. A cleverly developed infill site

A building's foundation should be constructed as follows:

1. Cover the outside with thick gooey tar applied with a trowel —not "liquid asphalt" applied with a brush or spray.
2. Install a large pipe with penny-size holes along it (known as *perforated drain tile*) alongside the footing to collect water accumulating around the foundation.

131

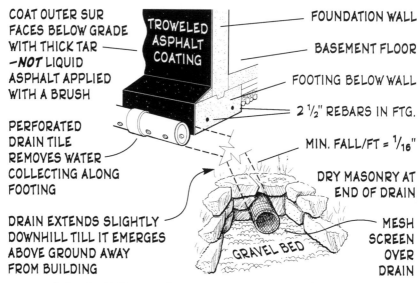

COAT OUTER SUR
FACES BELOW GRADE
WITH THICK TAR
—*NOT* LIQUID
ASPHALT APPLIED
WITH A BRUSH

TROWELED
ASPHALT
COATING

FOUNDATION WALL

BASEMENT FLOOR

FOOTING BELOW WALL

$2\frac{1}{2}$" REBARS IN FTG.

PERFORATED
DRAIN TILE
REMOVES WATER
COLLECTING ALONG
FOOTING

MIN. FALL/FT = $\frac{1}{16}$"

DRY MASONRY AT
END OF DRAIN

DRAIN EXTENDS SLIGHTLY
DOWNHILL TILL IT EMERGES
ABOVE GROUND AWAY
FROM BUILDING

GRAVEL BED

MESH
SCREEN
OVER
DRAIN

4-6. Building a foundation that won't leak

3. Backfill the excavation around the foundation with ¾ inch gravel up to within six inches of finished grade.
4. Lay rosin paper (a water-resistant reddish-brown paper that will keep silt from filling the spaces between the gravel) on the gravel three feet from the foundation.
5. Spread 6 inches of topsoil on the rosin paper. The owner should examine the outside of a foundation just before it is backfilled —and bring a camera.

Structural Members

A structural member may be a *beam, column, brace, connection*, or combination thereof, as detailed below.

Beams. These are usually horizontal members that collect weights resting on them, then they carry these loads plus their own weight down to their supports. Beams are usually the principal load gatherers in a building. They include

Structure

Girders ... large beams that support a row of smaller beams.

Cantilevers ... beams extending beyond their supports at one or both ends.

Arches ... curved beams.

Rafters ... beams that support roofs.

Joists ... beams that support floors.

Lintels ... heavy beams over fireplaces.

Headers ... short beams over windows and doors.

Stairs ... inclined beams with steps on top.

Trusses ... networks of triangularly arranged struts. These include *peaked trusses* (low triangular shapes), b*oxed trusses* (low rectangular shapes), and *longspan steel joists* (long low trusses of small steel shapes). Trusses can span long distances and pipes, wires, and ducts can be installed through their open webs.[3]

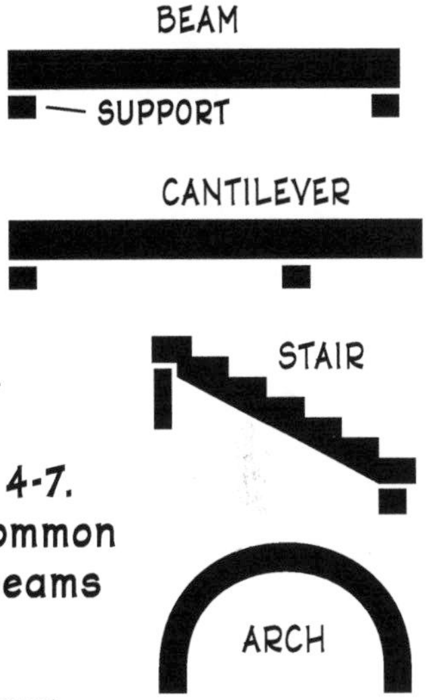

BEAM

SUPPORT

CANTILEVER

STAIR

**4-7.
Common
beams**

ARCH

STRUT

CHORDS

PEAKED WOOD TRUSS

BOXED WOOD TRUSS

LONGSPAN STEEL JOIST

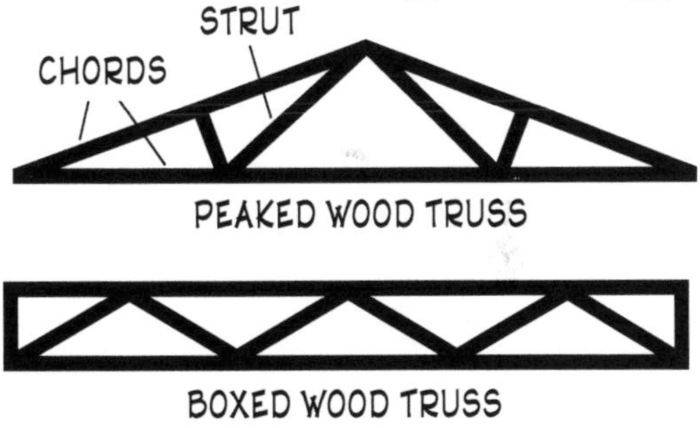

Although peaked wood trusses as shown above are mostly used to construct boxy buildings, their geometry can be exploited in far more imaginative ways. An amazing example was created by Frank Lloyd Wright in 1948, a time when this structure had hardly been developed, in the Unitarian Meeting House in Madison, Wisconsin. The structure above the nave is a series of light wood trusses whose construction is illustrated below and whose exterior appears in figure 4-9.[4] The reason why many of Wright's buildings look so exciting is that (1) he was an astonishing structural genius, and (2) after creating an ingenious structure, he *conceals* it. He's like a magician who pulls a rabbit out of a hat and doesn't

1. Begin with a gable roof truss outline:
2. Make the truss's top chords assymetrical:
3. Mirror the first truss with another alongside:
4. Raise the trusses' inner corners until the long top chords are flat and aligned and the short side chords form mansard-like sides:
5. Make a second pair of trusses with the top chords short and side chords long and parallel to the first trusses' chords:
6. Locate the two low trusses over the nave's back and the two tall trusses over the pulpit, then arrange between them seven more pair of trusses so the flat top chords progressively shorten and the sloping side chords similarly lengthen to form a soaring roof over the nave.

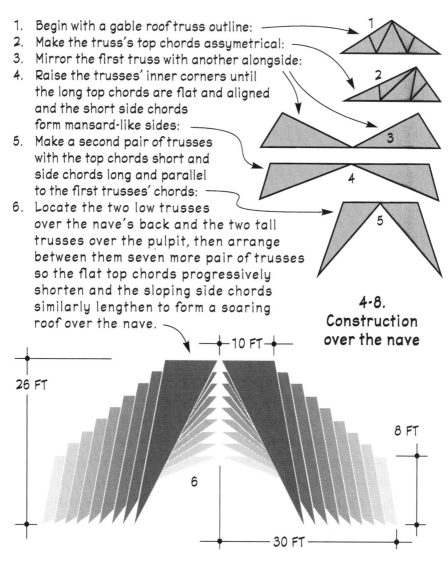

**4-8.
Construction
over the nave**

10 FT

26 FT

8 FT

6

30 FT

tell the audience how he performs his tricks. In the Unitarian Meeting House he clad the trusses' undersides in plaster and their tops with copper roofing until nary a clue remains of the bones within. He performed such structural legerdemain in hundreds of buildings during his long career.

VIEW OF ROOF OVER THE NAVE

THE ROOF FROM THE FRONT

4-9. The Unitarian Meeting House from the outside

Have you ever wondered why architects today don't copy Wright's work? They can't! He was so profoundly ingenious that hardly anyone since can fathom his brilliant designs, let alone duplicate them in their own projects. As Wright himself said, his architecture "can never become a formula for the tyro." [5] How different he was from another great architect of his time, Mies van der Rohe. Mies's 1927 Barcelona Pavilion and early European residences were also profoundly innovative, but his iconic use of steel and glass could be easily copied by others; so much so, that most of today's urban skylines were forged on a Miesian anvil. Eero Saarinen described this well when he said: "The followers of Mies codified his style into a very simple vocabulary of architecture which was to have universal application." [6]

Before we leave Wright's Unitarian Meeting House, we should acknowledge the contribution of Frank Tetzlaff, the carpenter foreman who fabricated the trusses. This reveals another outstanding trait of Wright: his ability to find talented artisans and bring out the best in them. How lucky we are to have had him —to dote on his works, to enjoy continuing revelations of his genius, so we can better understand the monuments of innovation he made and the obstacles he overcame in making them.

Columns. These are usually vertical supports that collect the weight of the beams and the loads resting on them, then they carry these loads plus their own weight down through the height of the building into the ground. Columns essentially hold the building up. Each can also be expressive of its function, as the Greeks eloquently demonstrated twenty-five centuries ago when they built the Caryatids, the draped females who hold up the roof of the Erechtheum at the Acropolis in Athens. These ladies show that columns can serve two architectural purposes: act as structural support, and be a mannikin for ornament. A column also doesn't have to be vertical. Consider the inclined pillars at Eero Saarinen's Dulles Airport in Washington, D.C. and the angled struts between the bubbles in the Watercube in China. Columns include

4-10

Structure

Posts ... freestanding columns with usually rectangular cross-sections.

Pilasters ... columns that protrude partly from the wall to which they are attached.

Walls ... columns that are very thin in one direction and very long in the other. They can be straight or curved.

Stud walls ... several rectangular wood posts held together by a sheet of plywood, itself a very long thin column, which together support much more weight than the studs could carry alone.

Footings ... columns whose heights are very short compared to their lateral dimensions.

Piers ... small footings that are usually square or nearly so. A large thick pier is often stepped so its center can be thick without wasting a lot of concrete.

Piles ... deep below-grade columnar supports for large buildings.

Steeples ... tapered columns that support nothing on top.

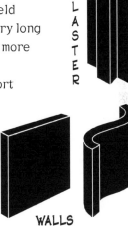

WALLS

The most common columnar construction listed above is the wall. One has two functions: structure, and an enclosure of spaces. However, some walls support no structure above (these are *nonloadbearing walls*), while others do support structure above (these are *loadbearing walls*). In renovation work you would want to know which is which before removing one, or you might get a few tons of rubble down your neck. One way to tell the difference is to look at the structure above. If you can't see this because of the ceiling finish, remove part of the finish until

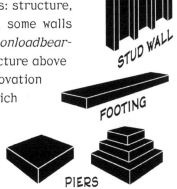

STUD WALL

FOOTING

PIERS

4-11. Common columns

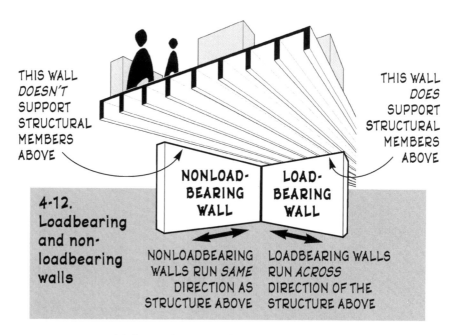

THIS WALL
DOESN'T
SUPPORT
STRUCTURAL
MEMBERS
ABOVE

THIS WALL
DOES
SUPPORT
STRUCTURAL
MEMBERS
ABOVE

NONLOAD-
BEARING
WALL

LOAD-
BEARING
WALL

**4-12.
Loadbearing
and non-
loadbearing
walls**

NONLOADBEARING
WALLS RUN *SAME*
DIRECTION AS
STRUCTURE ABOVE

LOADBEARING WALLS
RUN *ACROSS*
DIRECTION OF THE
STRUCTURE ABOVE

you can see which way the rows of beams, joists, or rafters extend above. Or look at the building's plans. If you have trouble with this, call in a contractor or architect. Also helpful may be figure 4-12. A loadbearing wall is part of a building's structure and cannot be moved without first firmly bracing the structure above.

Braces. We all know what a house of cards is: a little building with lots of floors and walls but no bracing to keep them from falling down. If you so much as breathe on such a structure it will collapse. This is why wind is Public Enemy Number One to many buildings. Since these Aeolian forces can blow from any direction, every beam and column in a building must be laterally braced in every direction —north, east, south, west— to withstand strong winds. We're not talking about breezes here —but tornadoes and hurricanes. Another lateral force is just as lethal: earthquakes. They move a building back and forth from its bottom while winds do the same from the top. To give you an idea of what these forces can do, here is how one of them tears buildings apart.

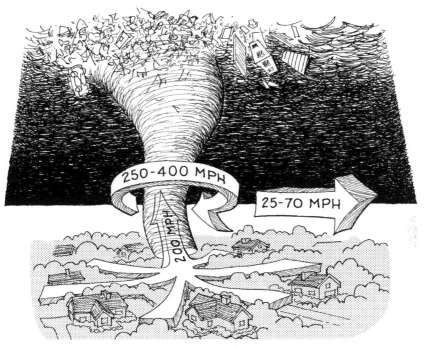

4-13. Tornado forces

A tornado is a writhing serpentine funnel that usually travels east to northeast at speeds of 25 to 70 miles an hour and often takes an erratic skipping path, its tapered end hopping randomly over one area then descending furiously on another. The funnel's walls of water droplets mixed with dust and debris whirling counterclockwise at speeds up to 400 miles an hour can scour building exteriors of finishes and send them flying through the air. The funnel's whirling walls also create a vacuum inside which draws the surrounding ground air rapidly toward the funnel's mouth, often at 200 miles an hour —then the vortex sucks up everything it passes over like a huge vacuum cleaner, sending clouds of fragments spouting into the sky, leaving behind floors and furnishings exposed to barrages of high-velocity debris and heavy rain. In flat open country the funnel can be seen from afar, but in wooded areas the deadly cone may be upon its victims before they have a chance to seek shelter, the only warning being a dark sky and a characteristic roar that makes you wonder, what is a freight train doing around here?

It takes some mighty clever braces to withstand these terrific forces. Here's a rundown of the best structural engineers have yet devised.

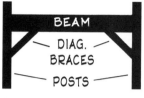

DIAGONAL BRACING

Diagonal bracing ... this is a diagonal strut located near the corner of a beam and a post that makes the corner rigid; they are usually installed as inplane pairs at each end of a beam. You've probably seen these braces in old barns. These diagonal supports keep networks of beams and columns from swaying and toppling.

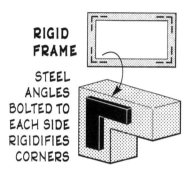

RIGID FRAME

STEEL ANGLES BOLTED TO EACH SIDE RIGIDIFIES CORNERS

Rigid frame ... this is strengthening the corners of a wall framed by beams at the ceiling and floor and columns at the ends. An example is a pair of steel angles bolted to each side of a timber post-and-beam connection.

VERTICAL: BRICK FILL IN CONCRETE FRAME

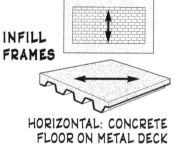

INFILL FRAMES

Infill frame ... this involves filling an area of wall or floor with a solid material that keeps the area rigid. An example of a vertical infill frame is a brick wall

HORIZONTAL: CONCRETE FLOOR ON METAL DECK

THIN-WALLED CORES

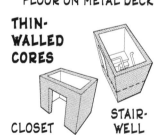

CLOSET   STAIR-WELL

4-14. Common braces

between a floor and a ceiling beam and two columns on each side; here the masonry keeps the frame from leaning right or left. An example of a horizontal infill frame is a concrete floor poured onto sheets of formed metal known as *metal decking* or *composite decking*; this bracing is unsurpassed for resisting racking stresses that occur in high-rise buildings. You've probably walked on this bracing whenever you've been in a tall building (it's usually covered with carpet).

Thin-walled core ... this is a small room whose walls have strong corners-in-common that essentially create a fat hollow column that can hold up twenty or thirty tons of architecture. Common thin-walled cores are closets, bathrooms, stairwells, and elevator shafts. They are relatively safe shelters during hurricanes and tornados.

A final structural load to consider here is rain or snow remaining on a flat roof. Ponder what can happen here. An inch of rain weighs more than five pounds per square foot of area. On a large flat roof this can be a lot of weight that depresses the roof's central area, which can cause more rain to collect, which depresses the area even more, ad infinitum —until tons of collected water collapse the roof. Ponding is especially dangerous in regions that receive lots of snow in winter, because if the temperature of the room under the roof is above freezing (usually the case), the lowest snow will melt to water that no one can see and after a few snowstorms the roof may collapse —usually on a sunny day when this is the last thing one would expect. Hence all flat roofs should slope at least $3/8$ inch per linear foot ($1/2$ inch is safer), which is done by tilting the roof toward one edge or crowning the roof at its center or between any interior drains. Some authorities may say a $1/4$ inch pitch is enough; but there are too many construction weirdities (from settling foundations to warped rafters) that can make a $1/4$ inch pitch become flat enough to puddle water, and the safer incline is as easy to build.

In snow country, steep roofs can create other problems. If an area of thick snow starts to slide — again usually initiated by the lowest layer melting— it can shear whole chimneys and dormers from the roof, then beyond the eave the avalanching snow can flatten a deck or a truck. To prevent these calamities:

1. Locate chimneys at or near roof peaks.
2. Fasten dormers to the roof framing below with plenty of Strong-Ties.
3. Locate decks and balconies below gables, not eaves, unless the roof extends over them.

Connections. These are the ligaments that hold together the bones. They include nails, screws, bolts, welds —anything that holds one structural member to another. Without these fasteners a house would look like a pile of lumber. A versatile connector is the sheetrock screw. They won't pop out of the sheetrock a few decades later, and they have spawned the use of stamped metal fasteners in wood framing. These bent pieces of zinc-coated

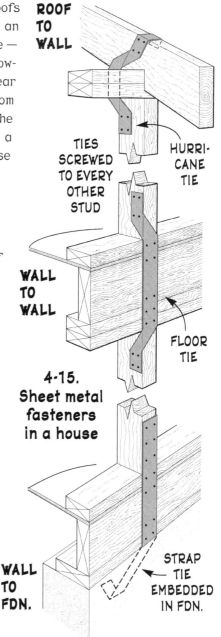

ROOF TO WALL

TIES SCREWED TO EVERY OTHER STUD

HURRI-CANE TIE

WALL TO WALL

FLOOR TIE

4-15. Sheet metal fasteners in a house

WALL TO FDN.

STRAP TIE EMBEDDED IN FDN.

sheet steel dotted with holes are made in dozens of different shapes, and with stout screws and the guns that drive them they are about as easy to install as poking holes in a potato before microwaving it. They can fasten roofs to walls, walls to floors, and floors to foundations in every way imaginable. Figure 4-15 shows a few. A tornado would come in second place in a wrestling match with this construction. These little prizes are familiarly known as Simpson Strong-Ties, after the company that makes more than anyone else. They'll make a house three times stronger for a few hundred dollars. That's the wisest storm damage insurance a homeowner can buy. If you would like an interesting book to read, one you can get for free, go to your local lumber company and ask for a Simpson Strong-Tie catalog. It is "fastenating" reading.

Structural Materials

Each material used as structure in a building has a certain innate strength. Exceed this, and the material will fail and whatever rests on it will fall. Each material also has a personality which if you offend you may also regret. Common structural materials used today are wood, steel, concrete, masonry, and fabrics. Their various strengths and personalities are detailed below.

Wood. From cradle to coffin, we are embraced by wood. Its fibers are hard and tough yet warm to the touch, and they are emblematic of all that is natural in the world. Wood forms through its length irregular striations known as *grains* and through its width concentric *growth rings* of alternating hardness and softness. Each species has a distinct pattern of grains and rings which have slightly different strengths. Wood is stronger along the grain than across, so it typically acts as structure in a direction parallel to its grain. Though wood burns, its surface initially forms a char that temporarily protects the deeper fibers from further damage. Hence heavy timbers are usually safer during the first hour of a fire than steel or concrete,

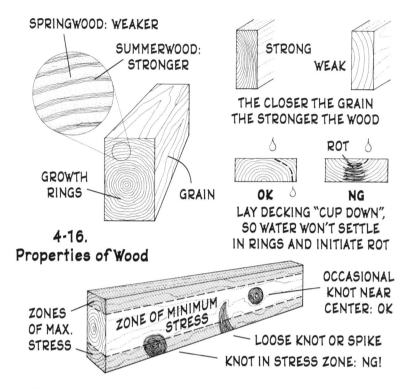

SPRINGWOOD: WEAKER

SUMMERWOOD: STRONGER

STRONG

WEAK

THE CLOSER THE GRAIN
THE STRONGER THE WOOD

GROWTH RINGS

GRAIN

ROT

OK

NG

LAY DECKING "CUP DOWN",
SO WATER WON'T SETTLE
IN RINGS AND INITIATE ROT

**4-16.
Properties of Wood**

ZONES OF MAX. STRESS

ZONE OF MINIMUM STRESS

OCCASIONAL KNOT NEAR CENTER: OK

LOOSE KNOT OR SPIKE KNOT IN STRESS ZONE: NG!

which lose their strength quickly as their temperature rises.

Another characteristic of wood is that it contains water. When a tree is felled its fibers are saturated with moisture, which after the wood is sawn into lumber much of the moisture exits through the wood's surfaces at a rate of about 1 inch of depth per year: a process known as *curing*. Hence a 2 × 4 will take about a year to cure and a 6 × 6 timber will take about three years. But even after wood has cured, its fibers still absorb moisture and swell when the surrounding air is humid and shrink when the air is dry. This is why your front door may stick in its frame on a hot humid summer day and leak air around its edges on a cold winter night. Moisture in wood creates another problem. Its presence is like the Colonel's eleven secret herbs and spices to hungry termites, carpenter ants, molds, mildew, and a host of other bugs and fungi that love the nourishment of lignin. Imagine eating the dirt from a hole you dig. That's what a termite does. I suppose we would do the same if our homes were made of chocolate cake. When you finally discover any of the above destructive agents in your home or place of work, it may be too late to do anything but replace their repast.

If wood is to endure as structure, any moisture it may contain should be allowed to escape as follows:

☞ Locate all wood framing at least 18 inches above ground, especially over crawl spaces in humid climates. This makes it hard for termites and other pests to reach the wood. Every crawl space should have an entrance door (this needn't be much bigger than the rabbit hole in *Alice in Wonderland*), so someone can crawl around inside and look for telltale signs of wood-eating pests.

☞ Locate screened vents on each side of crawl spaces, attics, and any other areas enclosed by wood construction, so air can flow through the space and carry away any accumulating moisture.

☞ Do not install wood siding directly against plywood sheathing but on 1 × 2 inch furring strips; then air can circulate behind the siding, which minimizes its discoloring, curling, nail-popping, and rotting later on.

Here is a final directive that ought to be written into every building code: Wherever surfaces of wood, metal, or masonry contact each other, *insert a layer of 90-pound roofing felt —**not** tarpaper— between the two materials.* This is because wood, metal, and masonry absorb moisture in different ways; and moisture collecting on the surface of one can enter the other and degrade it. One exception is copper flashing in masonry chimneys, as here the adjacent materials are aqueously compatible. Anywhere else, and this thick rough asphaltic barrier will halt transfer of moisture through the surface-in-common. Tarpaper is too thin and smooth, and plastic sheet is worse than nothing, because its slick surface collects moisture then cracks which opens the door to the very damage it intends to prevent. Here is what can happen when the above directive is disobeyed. Once when I visited a beautiful small stone church in western North Carolina, the pastor on learning I was an architect asked if I would look at a problem in the belfry. After we stepped under the belfry, he pointed twenty feet overhead to the underside of the belfry's floor. It was supported by several timbers whose bare ends were embedded in the belfry's thick stone walls —and there they had rotted until the floor above was too weak to walk on. If the timbers' ends had been clad in 90-pound building felt before embedding them in the masonry, they would be strong today.

One questionable wood preservative is chemicals. Opinion on these products fumes with controversy, but here are the facts. Most chemical preservatives are poisonous. They poison the environment in their making, they poison the wood they impregnate, and they poison you when you touch them. A common preservative over the past few decades has been chromate copper arsenate. CCA-treated wood is used to build decks, playground equipment, and other outdoor construction that must stand up to warm humid weather. But CCA leaches arsenic over time. [7] Do you want your children playing on this? Apparently CCA will be phased out for residences by 2012, but that won't phase out the suffering by people in the past who have been exposed to this toxin. CCA's proposed replacements are an alphabet soup of products with names like ACQ-C, ACQ-D, CBA-A, CA-B, and SBX/DOT; of which one respected company has said: "Whether these new chemicals will turn out to be less dangerous in the long run is anyone's guess." If you want to learn all you never need to know about wood preservatives, visit www.strongtie.com/productuse/PTWoodFAQs.html.

Another chemical you don't want to put on wood is paint. This clogs the wood's pores, which keeps them from breathing and makes the fibers brittle, which shortens wood's life rather than lengthens it. Besides, why hide something beautiful and make it

146

look like plastic? And once you've applied the first coat you're shackled to a lifetime of maintenance. The finest color for wood is "lumber umber". Making paint also damages the environment, and some paints emit toxic gases after they are applied. If LEED was on the ball here, it would subtract points from buildings with painted wood. If you must coat wood to protect it, stain it. This brings out its grain while allowing its fibers to breathe. All this is particularly sad when four fine preservatives have been around for years and will be for a long time to come. They are:

1. *Optimal site conditions* ... dry or well-drained terrain exposed to prevailing breezes that can remove accumulating moisture. And don't think that using redwood for foundation plates will prevent rot or termites. I have personally seen termite infestation in redwood. It was due to suffocating assembly and saturated moisture.
2. *Superior materials* ... strong and decay-resistant woods. Where site conditions are poor, use masonry.
3. *Proper assemblies* ... simple constructions that allow each piece to breathe —and inserting 90-pound roofing felt between where wood touches metal or masonry.
4. *Attentive workmanship* ... doing more than saying "Uh-huh" to the above directives.

Whenever wood is used as structure, it is carefully selected according to *species* and *grade*. Species are classed as *softwoods* (coniferous trees like pine, fir, and redwood) and *hardwoods* (deciduous trees such as oak, hickory, and maple). Softwoods are usually lighter and softer and are more easily sawn, while hardwoods tend to be stronger and more durable. In this country, professional lumbermen examine every pallet of lumber that leaves a sawmill and give it a grade depending on the wood's number of knots, splits, warps, wanes, pitch streaks, and other structural defects or blemishes; then the grade is stamped on the lumber. Lumbermen can read these stamps the way an orchestra leader reads sheet music. Three lumber stamps appear in figure 4-17. Below are listed common grades of wood (some vary in different parts of the country):

4-17. Three lumber grading stamps

CLEAR ... has beautiful grains with not a knot in them. This wood is used for exposed floors and windowframes and is generally too valuable to use as structure.

SELECT STRUCTURAL ... has tight grains with at most a few small tight knots. This is premium structural wood.

STRUCTURAL ... defect-free lumber with a few blemishes.

DECK ... slightly blemished but structurally sound lumber commonly used for decking.

STUD ... small pieces with unsightly blemishes that still are structurally sound.

UTILITY ... typical of knotty studs these days. These are borderline structural. Stud grade 2 × 3s are acceptable in stud walls but utility grade 2 × 3s are not.

INDUSTRIAL ... laths and other woods usually dotted with defects.

ECONOMY ... hardly strong enough to build a crate with.

When an architect needs a certain strength of wood for a given structural situation, s/he selects a species that is strong enough, looks up its allowable stress in a table, notes its grade, and specifies it in the Plans.

Lumber is sold in *nominal* dimensions, which aren't the same as *actual* dimensions. Consider the 2 by 4 you buy at a lumberyard. Its actual size is not 2 by 4 inches but about $1^1/_2$ by $3^1/_2$ inches. The larger, nominal, dimension is the wood's original size

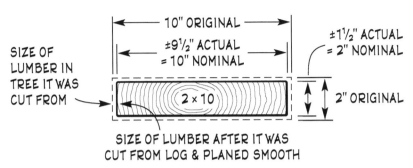

4-18. Nominal and actual dimensions

as scribed in the tree it was cut from while the smaller, actual, dimension is the wood's size minus the thickness of the saw blade that cut the piece from the tree and minus the depth of a planar blade that peeled the roughsawn surface from each side to make the wood smooth to the touch. One-inch-thick lumber loses only about a quarter inch of its thickness to the saw and plane, so a 1×4 is about $^3/_4 \times 3^1/_2$ inches. You would want to know these things before, say, laying an oak floor with 1×4s. Otherwise you might end up with ten percent of the floor still uncovered when you've used the lumber you ordered, and when you call to reorder more the company is out of stock.

Another common lumber measure is the board foot. This is a piece of wood 12 by 12 inches in area and one inch thick. Thus a 2×10 that is sixteen feet long contains (2 × 10 ÷ 12) × 16 = 26.7 board feet. If a pallet of 16-foot-long 2×10s is 6 pieces wide and 10 pieces high, your calculator will tell you the pallet contains 1,602 board feet of lumber. If a lumber company sells structural hem-fir 2×10s for 63 cents a board foot, your calculator will inform you that the pallet of this lumber will cost $1,009. Easy, eh? Might be easier doing this number-crunching than paying a contractor this price plus 15 percent wage withholding plus 15 percent job profit plus 15 percent contractor's profit plus another 20 percent retail markup. This might even make you think of building your own house someday.

Architecture Laid Bare!

A common structural wood is plywood. When sheets of this are fastened to a row of studs, the assembly may be up to 14 times stronger than the studs standing alone. However, since plywood is made from essentially defect-free logs that are becoming scarce these days, plywood is slowly being replaced by OSB. This "was-wood" is made by impregnating wood chips with a strong resinous glue and compressing the mash into plywood-like sheets. LEED even claims that OSB is environmentally "green" since the wood chips are a waste product.

But wait a minute. OSB glue contains toxic phenol formaldehyde. Although plywood contains this too, it has only a few paper-thin layers compared to the stew of phenol in OSB. OSB is also factory-sealed with waterproof paint, and when a sheet is cut the exposed edges allow moisture to enter, and if the edges aren't quickly resealed the invading moisture will reduce the material's strength. Hence OSB cannot be exposed to rain after it is framed and before it is enclosed —a tall order on building sites where it rains a lot. OSB also should remain dry after construction, which poses a problem if fire sprinklers may soon be required in new residences. Think how hard it would be to replace a few hundred square feet of drenched OSB subfloor under an activated fire sprinkler, and possibly a row of I-joists just below whose webs are also made of OSB. [8]

An attractive wood structure is *timber frame construction*. Also known as *post-and-beam*, it replicates the strength and craftsmanship of the old barns built of handhewn posts and beams a couple centuries ago. Characterized by exposed timbers and tall cathedral ceilings with long ridge beams at gable peaks and lots of diagonal braces to keep the timbers in place, this native-looking structure looks nice in rural homes, ski lodges, rustic dining halls, and other outdoorsy architecture. The posts (typical sizes are 8 × 8 and 10 × 10 inches) and beams (usually 4 × 8 to 6 × 12 inches) may have mortise-and-tenon joints secured with pegs or sawn ends held together with bolts and steel plates much as appears in figure 4-19. The timbers are usually pre-assembled

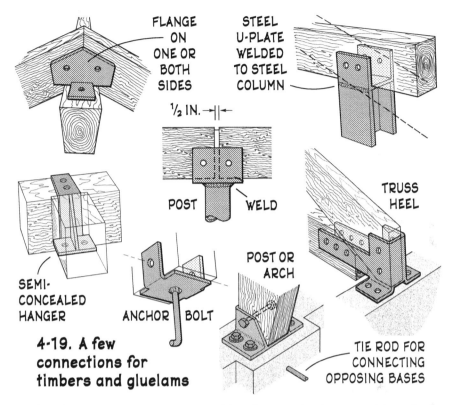

FLANGE ON ONE OR BOTH SIDES

STEEL U-PLATE WELDED TO STEEL COLUMN

½ IN.

POST   WELD

TRUSS HEEL

SEMI-CONCEALED HANGER

ANCHOR BOLT

POST OR ARCH

4-19. A few connections for timbers and gluelams

TIE ROD FOR CONNECTING OPPOSING BASES

in a factory to make sure everything fits snugly, then are shipped to the site and erected with a crane. Since this construction is usually exposed, ill-fitting joints and hammermarks on the timbers are very undesirable.

Another "timber" construction is *glulams*. These are glued and laminated (hence glulams) $^3/_4$ or $1^1/_2$ inch planks arranged end-to-end and layer-on-layer and occasionally side-to-side to form solid beams up to eight feet deep, a foot thick, and a hundred feet long. One's top if flat usually tapers slightly to one or both sides, and its underside may be *straight* (⬭), *pitched* (⬭), or *curved* (⬭). A flat underside typically has a slight camber to eliminate the illusion that the beam sags in the center. Glulams are usually straight, but they can be curved to form arches that are connected with hinged pins. Their connec-

151

tions tend to be thick plates held by big bolts, as sketched in figure 4-19. Glulams typically appear in churches, conference centers, and other upscale commercial buildings. This structure is designed as follows. The architect, knowing the load of each member, selects its profile and sizes it according to tables found in manufacturer's catalogs, then the contractor orders them from a fabricator who makes them and trucks them to the site.

A more prosaic wood structure is *poles*. Here telephone pole-size posts are mounted in the ground usually 12 to 20 feet apart and enclosed with facades and roofs. This is a rugged way to build barns and other boxy architecture up to 30 feet tall that has few columns inside, lightweight roofs, and no basements. Lately though, this structure's facades have been dandied up with fancy windows and frilly arcades and its roofs have been duded up with rows of dormers and multiple gables. No longer can sanctimonious zoning boards reject this architecture on the grounds that its rural pedigree could lower upscale property values.

But it must be said, a wood pole whose base is buried a few feet in bare ground is inferior construc-

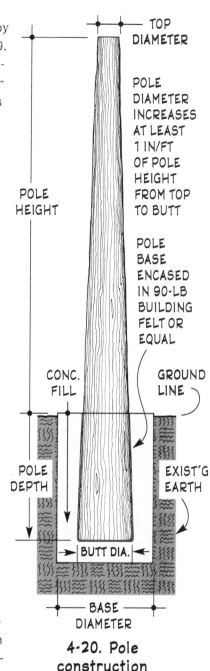

TOP DIAMETER

POLE DIAMETER INCREASES AT LEAST 1 IN/FT OF POLE HEIGHT FROM TOP TO BUTT

POLE HEIGHT

POLE BASE ENCASED IN 90-LB BUILDING FELT OR EQUAL

CONC. FILL

GROUND LINE

POLE DEPTH

EXIST'G EARTH

BUTT DIA.

BASE DIAMETER

4-20. Pole construction

tion. It may be okay for cattle but not for people. Better is to encase the pole's base in 90-pound roofing felt, mount it in a water-resistant cardboard tube known as *sonotube*, fill the void between pole and tube with concrete, peel the sonotube from the concrete after it has set, then backfill the void around the concrete with gravel, as in figure 4-20. This structure is more durable, ballasts the pole with a heavy anchor, and keeps it from working upward due to constantly flexing winds. Pole structures are best suited for elevated well-drained sites in dry cool regions, and least suited for depressed elevations in warm humid areas.

Steel. This material is strong and springy, its uniform molecularity makes every member virtually the same as every other, and when experiencing extreme stresses steel won't suddenly crack as will wood and concrete. But steel has an Achilles' heel: it greatly weakens when exposed to fire. At 1,500° Fahrenheit steel is soft as warm chocolate. In the steel column pictured on the right, fire heated the column until it could no longer support the several floors above, then it sunk a couple feet. Also, at –60° F steel tends to shatter like glass when struck with a hammer.

4-21. How fire can melt steel [9]

But the latest alloys have enabled steel to partly recover from this weakness. Still, structural steel is thermally mollycoddled by cladding it in materials that resist extreme heat and cold.

Structural steel is made in a variety of standard shapes, as appears in figure 4-22. Each shape is an end view, and each varies greatly in size. As a sample, a **W** shape can be 4 to 36 inches deep. If you see on an architectural plan a structural member with the note **W 10×45** beside it, this is a wide-flange shape that is 10 inches deep and weighs about 45 pounds per linear foot. This notation allows architects to use the members' weights in structural calculations and contractors to estimate how much a building's steel construction will cost. Anyone can buy these shapes. If you ever need a bar, rod, angle, or other piece of steel, say a channel that is 3 inches deep but you don't know its other dimensions or its weight, google SSS-steel.com to get a mill inventory of every structural steel shape known to man, then look in the yellow pages under *Steel Products* or *Metal Specialties* and call the number. You might say, "I need a steel channel three inches deep that's about 1½ inches wide whose web is an eighth of an inch thick. It weighs about 3.5 pounds per foot." The clerk on the phone will think you're a pro. He may even give you a contractor's discount.

Steel has a few structural cousins of lesser mettle, the chief being aluminum. This is lighter than steel and won't rust; but it is only about half as strong, it corrodes when it contacts concrete, and it tends to sag under prolonged stress.

Common steel structures appear below.

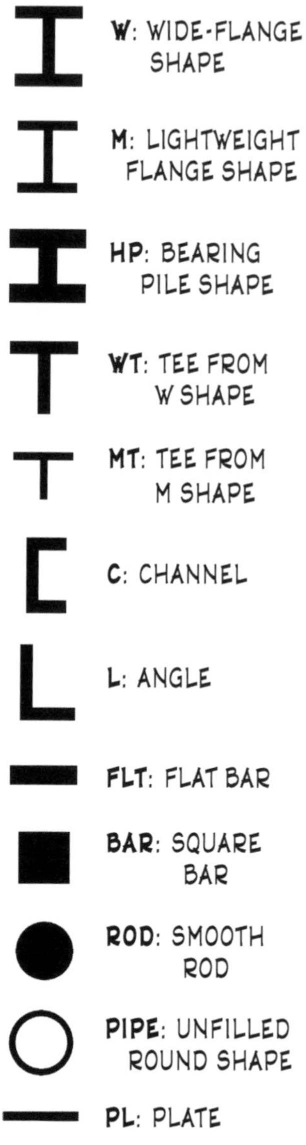

STRUCTURAL STEEL FRAMING. This is used in large buildings as beams and

W: WIDE-FLANGE SHAPE

M: LIGHTWEIGHT FLANGE SHAPE

HP: BEARING PILE SHAPE

WT: TEE FROM W SHAPE

MT: TEE FROM M SHAPE

C: CHANNEL

L: ANGLE

FLT: FLAT BAR

BAR: SQUARE BAR

ROD: SMOOTH ROD

PIPE: UNFILLED ROUND SHAPE

PL: PLATE

4-22. Standard structural steel shapes

154

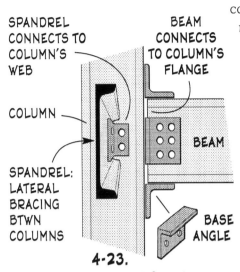

SPANDREL CONNECTS TO COLUMN'S WEB

COLUMN

SPANDREL: LATERAL BRACING BTWN COLUMNS

BEAM CONNECTS TO COLUMN'S FLANGE

BEAM

BASE ANGLE

4-23.
Structural steel framing

columns. A crane lifts each member toward its final rest, then as it hangs from a cable a few muscular iron-workers push it daintily into place and insert a bolt through predrilled holes to hold it while they assemble the rest of the connection. This structure looks most exciting just after erection, when its skeleton brandishes its bones against the sky before being clad in fire-proofing and finishes.

OPEN-WEB STEEL JOISTS. Also called *longspan steel joists*, these lightweight trusses are assemblies of usually horizontal top and bottom chords connected with diagonal struts, all made of small steel angles and rods. This structure is economical for light uniform loads on long spans, and ducts and pipes can pass through their voids. You've probably seen rows of these members in the ceiling of your local supermarket or health club. They can be up to 144 feet long and 72 inches deep. They require lots of lateral bracing to keep them from buckling.

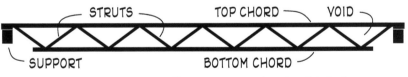

STRUTS   TOP CHORD   VOID

SUPPORT   BOTTOM CHORD

4-24. Anatomy of an open-web steel joist

SPACE FRAMES. This structure has an aerodynamic nature that captures the essence of the space age. Each is an assembly of struts and joints that extends in two directions to create

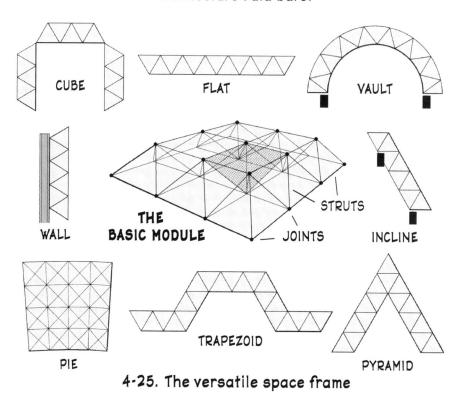

CUBE

FLAT

VAULT

WALL

THE
BASIC MODULE

STRUTS

JOINTS

INCLINE

PIE

TRAPEZOID

PYRAMID

4-25. The versatile space frame

loadgathering assembly that is very strong for its weight. It typically spans 30 to 120 feet, is available in many colors and finishes, requires no lateral bracing, and allows ducts and pipes to fit within the frame. Since they cannot support heavy concentrated loads they are usually built as unoccupied roofs; and since they experience large deflections they usually have no ceiling finishes on their undersides so they are usually open from below, which makes them unsuitable above dirty, dusty, or corrosive environments. Expansion joints also cannot exist within a space frame, so large frames have rollers under where they rest on supports. By varying a space frame's strut lengths and joint connections, walls, trapezoids, vaults, cubes, and domes can be made, culminating in the geodesic domes conceived in the fertile mind of Buckminster Fuller.

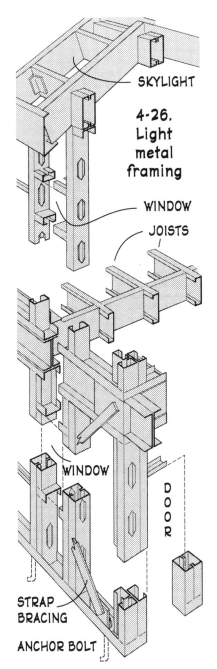

4-26. Light metal framing

SKYLIGHT

WINDOW

JOISTS

WINDOW

DOOR

STRAP BRACING

ANCHOR BOLT

LIGHT METAL FRAMING. In many commercial buildings wood framing is not allowed because it is considered a fire hazard. Enter light metal framing. Its studs, joists, and rafters have the same nominal dimensions as wood, but they are sheets of galvanized steel bent into hollow rectangular sections. These shapes are lighter and won't burn, wires and pipes can be fitted inside them, and termites can't eat them. Sheet metal shapes are also easier to make into very small assemblies because you can cut little pieces of metal with tinsnips and easily screw or tack-weld them together, while it is hard to nail together little chunks of wood without splitting them. However, a large picture or bookshelf can't be mounted on a wall of light metal studs without special connectors.

Concrete. This is a mixture of cement, water, and aggregate wherein the cement and water form a paste that coats each aggregate, then the coating around each particle sprouts microscopic needles that entwine with the needles from other directions (a process known as cur-

157

ing) to create an interlocking mass that is hard as rock. But the needles can be pulled apart comparatively easily, so concrete is about one-seventh as strong in tension as it is in compression. Where part of a concrete structure will be stretched, as along the underside of a beam, steel reinforcing (strong in tension) is placed to hold the concrete together.

The most important ingredient in concrete is the cement. The most common is *Portland ASTM Type I*, which reaches required strength in about 28 days. *ASTM Type III* costs more but cures faster, so it is used in cold weather or where forms must be removed quickly. *ASTM Type IV* produces less heat when it cures, and is used in warm regions and large masses of concrete.

CEMENT

WATER

SAND

GRAVEL

ROCKS

WIRE MESH

REBAR

4-27. Ingredients of concrete

As for the water mixed with the cement, if it's not clean enough to drink, it's not clean enough to make concrete. Increasing the water-to-cement ratio makes concrete thinner and flow more smoothly but reduces its strength, while decreasing this crucial ratio makes concrete thicker and harder to work but increases its strength.

As for aggregates, most are crushed rock, from sand to boulders. An aggregate must contain no silt or organic matter. Rough rocks are better than smooth, because they offer the enveloping cement a better grip which makes the concrete stronger. Aggregates typically comprise 60 to 80 percent of concrete's volume.

As for steel reinforcing, this is usually *wire mesh* (rectangular patterns of steel wire generally six inches apart) or *rebar* (steel rods covered with tiny lugs that interlock with the enveloping concrete). All reinforcing must be "clean enough to eat on", but a little rust is

158

desirable since it pits the metal's surface which makes it bond better with the concrete. Contractors often let rebars sit out in the rain a few weeks before installing them. Reinforcing must be placed at least $1^1/_2$ inches from any outer surface of the concrete or water may reach it and initiate corrosion.

All kinds of admixtures can be added to concrete to make it set faster, improve its workability in cold weather, increase its resistance to freezing, allow it to withstand higher temperatures, make it insulate better, increase its moisture resistance, make it lighter or stronger, change its color, make fresh concrete stick to old, even enable it to bend. And this just in from Beijing or there-abouts: adding sticky rice soup to concrete makes it stronger and more stable. The Chinese have been using this in pagodas, tombs, and city walls for 1,500 years. [10]

As important as concrete is the form it is poured in. A concrete form is a tank that holds a liquid —one that weighs about 150 pounds per cubic foot, which happens to be $2^1/_2$ times heavier than water. Imagine an aquarium that's eight feet tall, forty feet long, and eight inches thick: that's what the formwork for only one side of a residential basement is like. Since this container must be very strong and cannot leak, its sides (usually sheet metal or plywood) are thick and shored by rows of vertical posts, horizon-

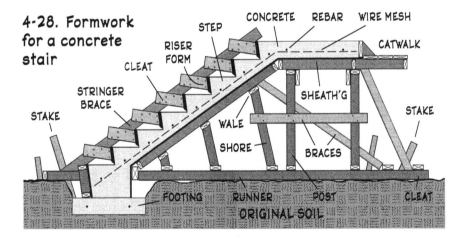

4-28. Formwork for a concrete stair

STEP CONCRETE REBAR WIRE MESH
RISER FORM CATWALK
CLEAT
STRINGER BRACE SHEATH'G
STAKE STAKE
WALE
SHORE BRACES
STAKE
FOOTING RUNNER POST CLEAT
ORIGINAL SOIL

tal walers, and diagonal braces. A form may even have catwalks along its top so workers can easily place rebars and pour concrete into them. The formwork for a concrete stair appears in figure 4-28. Unless you are a professional you wouldn't want to build this yourself. Since formwork essentially involves erecting a second structure to house the first, concrete construction is most feasible where a form is reused many times, as in hotels, warehouses, and parking garages with many small areas of the same size.

No debris should ever be tossed into a concrete form before it is filled with concrete. No wads of chewing gum, no cigaret butts —nothing. I remember one reinforced concrete building, a well-publicized museum designed by a famous architect, that developed serious corrosion problems several years after it was built. The cause? Beer cans thrown into the formwork by the laborers.

If you ever have to pour concrete, be prepared for weird things to happen. One anecdote will serve here. When I poured the floor slab of my house's garage and the turnaround outside, the transit mix truck was scheduled to arrive at 9 A.M., but the batch plant got its orders mixed and the truck didn't show up until 3:30 in the afternoon. We finished the pour about five, but the concrete still needed to cure 4 to 6 hours before its surface could be smoothed and if we waited till morning the surface would be too hard to work. So we all went home, had dinner, returned at nine, parked our cars and trucks with our headlights shining across the slab, and by eleven were done.

When concrete is stripped of its forms, the texture on the forms' inside appears on the concrete's outside. If the forms are knotty plywood, the concrete will look like a black-and-white photograph of knotty plywood. Le Corbusier, the great French architect of the mid-Twentieth century, used rough boards for his formwork which after they were removed made the concrete look rugged: a technique he called *béton brut* (brute concrete). Another architect who knew a thing or two about building forms to make concrete look interesting was Frank Lloyd Wright. An example appears in figure 4-29 (another appears in figure 3-31 on page

4-29. Wright's concrete columns at Florida Southern University [11]

114). The insides of the column forms were built to resemble alligator hide, an appropriate organic motif since the building is in southern Florida. In his architecture Wright used all kinds of natural elements —cactus, thistles, grapevines, ivy, mushrooms, butterflies, flowers— as inspirations for ornament in his buildings. His method went something like this: (1) What's a common animal or plant around here? (2) What pattern or imbrication is typical of this organism? (3) Use this pattern as a template for ornament. Now that you know the drill, you can do this too.

A simple form used for small buildings is *slip-forms*. These are plywood or aluminum sections often 8 feet tall and 1 or 2 feet wide whose vertical edges fit together and the connected pieces are braced along the outside. A slip-form subcontractor can carry all the pieces for one house on a medium-size truck.

While concrete can be shaped into exciting structure, it is a poor insulator. A new product that does something about this is *foxblocks*. The outer and inner walls of each block are made of rigid foam insulation about 2 inches thick, each weighs less than ten pounds, and is about 48 inches long. The blocks are dry-

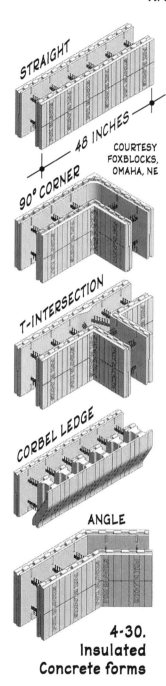

STRAIGHT

48 INCHES

90° CORNER

T-INTERSECTION

CORBEL LEDGE

ANGLE

**4-30.
Insulated
Concrete forms**

stacked up to four feet high and interlock like Lego bricks; then rebars, sleeves, anchor bolts, and other inserts are fitted into the voids which are filled with concrete. Five variations of these blocks appear in figure 4-30. After the concrete has cured, the blocks' rigid foam sides remain to receive the interior and exterior finishes. To build higher walls the above steps are repeated after the lower concrete has cured. These walls provide respectable insulation, are structurally and acoustically superior, are virtually impervious to penetration by air and water, and bugs can't eat them. However, on visiting a chat room about this product I found one owner to say, "The plumber, electrician, and drywaller all wanted more money because this is new." This is what we improvers are up against, folks. But another person said, "The learning curve is more common sense than education." For more information on this product see www.foxblocks.com, www.arxx.net, and www.amvicsystem.com.

This section on concrete structure would be remiss if it didn't mention *warped planes*. Also known as *shell structures* and *hypars*, these reinforced concrete shapes have large thin curved surfaces that are very strong for their weight. Their great strength and lightness is revealed by a simple experiment: hold a sheet of paper in front of you by one edge. Note how the far edge droops down. But if you crimp the

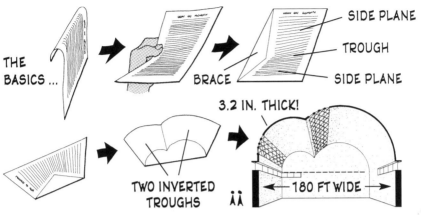

EDUARDO TORROJA'S JAI ALAI FRONTON, MADRID,SPAIN

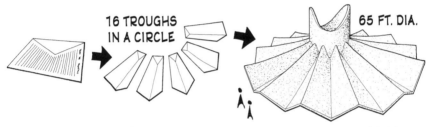

FELIX CANDELA'S UMBRELLA BAZAAR, CUERNAVACA,MEXICO

4-31. Masterly examples of warped plane bracing

edge you hold, the crimp's depth forms a low V-shaped cantilever that extends through the paper's length and holds the outer end up. These origami-like foldings have spawned some of the most exciting forms in architecture. Two masterly examples appear in figure 4-31. Warped planes can cover large areas because they are free to expand and contract during changing temperatures, but any openings in them must be minimal. The shells typically have opposing bases between which extend footings filled with tensile steel that keep the bases from spreading apart, and the bases and footings are usually buried so their bulky shapes won't sully the nature of the soaring forms above.

Reinforced concrete is also used to construct *earth build-*

ings. These shell-like shelters are buried in the ground, usually in sloping terrain so one facade is above grade so natural light can enter the cavern within. The roof should be nearly flat (a 3 to 5 percent pitch sheds water without promoting soil shifting), and the soil on top should be 12 to 18 inches deep (including a bed of 6 inch gravel between soil and roof) to allow the growth of thick ground covers that will absorb moisture and minimize erosion. This construction's advantages and drawbacks are:

➕ Low heating and cooling bills, no wind load problems.
➖ Much environmentally destructive excavation needed to create the look of undisturbed soil above. Massive structure required to support heavy roof loads whose weight can double when saturated with rain, to which must be added any snow loads in winter. Interiors fill with moisture and mildew. Trees can't grow on top. Few windows. Few views to enjoy.

Masonry. This is an interlocking assembly of rock-like units, natural or manmade, typically held together with mortar. This structure can be almost any shape, from the marble drums stacked in the columns of the Parthenon, to the interlacing ribs in the rose windows in the Cathedral of Chartres, to a garden wall in your back yard. A common masonry product today is the concrete block. When numbers of this precast concrete unit are mortared together into interlocking masses, to many this construction possesses all the beauty of a basement wall. But hear what Frank Lloyd Wright said of this homely material:

> We would take that despised outcast of the building industry —the concrete block— out from the gutter, find a hitherto unsuspected soul in it, and make it live as a thing of beauty —textured like the trees. [13]

Wright eloquently proved his point in the residence that appears in figure 4-32. This building shows his genius about as much as anything he designed. He also cast decorative blocks with pat-

4-32. A Wright house built of concrete blocks [12]

terned facings and assembled them into a number of "texture-block" houses and commercial buildings.

Masonry mortar joints may be *troweled* (excess mortar is sliced off with a trowel), *tooled* (a rounded steel tool is pressed into the joint), or *raked* (the outer mortar is removed to create an indented joint). Troweling and tooling make the masonry more resistant to weathering. Raking makes the units look sharper.

Masonry is strong in compression but weak in tension, and except for adobe blocks the mortar is weaker than the units. Hence masonry, to be stable, should be built with as much stone and as little mortar as possible: i.e. big rocks and thin seams. A number of other rules for building masonry that will live longer than your grandchildren are:

☞   Investigate subsoil conditions below any planned mason-ry construction, which is heavy, to avoid creating any "Pisa" structures someday.

☞   Don't build masonry when temperatures are likely to fall below freezing during the next two days, as the moisture still in the mortar may freeze and weaken it. If this is unavoidable, shroud the masonry with a tarp and place a heater underneath to keep the curing mortar warm.

☞   Make walls at least one-sixth as thick as their height.

☞   Avoid long straight walls, which can topple. Add corners, curves, piers, pilasters, and abutting walls to increase the construction's lateral stability.

☞   Don't place doors, windows, and other large openings near corners.

☞   Wet the rocks or blocks before mortaring in place, or they will absorb water from the mortar which saps its strength. For this reason good masons keep a bucket of water and a sponge near their work. The warmer the weather, the more important this is.

☞   Bury metal embedments deep in the masonry. If water reaches them, corrosion may weaken them and cause the enveloping mortar to spall. The best metal is stainless steel, followed by bronze, brass, copper, and galvanized metal. Use the same metal for all parts in one connection.

☞   The open cells in concrete blocks and some kinds of clay tile can be laid vertically or horizontally. If vertical, the masonry is nearly twice as strong; if horizontal, light and air can pass through the construction.

Another adaptable masonry product is chimney flue tile. A clever chimney cap can be made from a flue tile by removing a side with a masonry blade in an electric saw and mounting the cap on the chimney, as in figure 4-33. Chimney cleaners can remove these

4-33. Flue tile chimney cap

caps easily. If you're up to it, you can make your own masonry products. I did this in my house. Once twenty years ago while reading a Richard Scary story to my then-little daughter, I saw a chimney cap that looked like an owl —and I had to have one. After enrolling in a local pottery class I made what I wanted. It's looking at you in figure 4-34.

The most common masonry in many American residences is the fireplace. It should be near the center of the house, so it will radiate heat into interior spaces in every direction, and never in an exterior wall where some of the heat will radiate through its back directly outdoors. From the outside a centrally located chimney should look like a big nail that holds the house to the ground: a nice aesthetic touch.

4-34. Owl chimney cap

Actually, there's no sense having a fireplace if it isn't efficient. Yet even today, in a society known for its "Yankee ingenuity" that is enduring an energy crisis, most fireplaces are woefully inefficient. This was not so during colonial New England. Then a house usually had a high, wide, shallow hearth that threw much heat into the room it faced. Necessity was the mother of this invention, because in those days firewood was cut by hand and an efficient fireplace allowed a day's work to create a lot more heat. This hearth remained the domestic standard well into the

4-35. Yesterday's and tomorrow's fireplace today

Nineteenth Century, until the mining of coal and making of steel led to easier-to-make cast iron stoves and sheet metal chimneys. Then in Victorian days a nostalgic version of the colonial hearth evolved that was dreadfully inefficient, which of course became the American standard that endures to this day. But Frank Lloyd Wright saw through the glimmer of this woeful heat waster and vilified it as "a mantel that frames a few coals in a grate." [14]

When I designed the fireplaces in my house, I decided to emulate the efficient colonial models. The one facing the kitchen appears above. As the colonists often did, I hung a swinging crane on the left and built a dutch oven in the firebox wall on the right. This hearth has worked superbly well for more than thirty years. I even took a bath on this hearth during the historic snowstorm of October 29, 2011, which left us without power a few days. On the crane I hung a cast-iron kettle, filled it with water from the pond

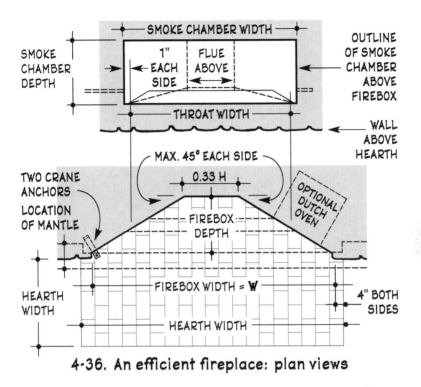

4-36. An efficient fireplace: plan views

below the house, built a fire under the kettle, and on the hearth set a sitz bath I have downstairs. When the water was hot I started at the top and worked my way down, then poured the dirty water residing in the sitz bath into the kitchen sink ten feet away.

So that others may enjoy this fireplace's beauty and utility, the following describes their construction, with drawings that any architect or contractor will understand.

1. In figures 4-37 and 4-38, select a height (dimension **H**) for the firebox opening. A good number for normal-size fireplaces is 48 inches. Locate the hearth at the same level as the floor in front, otherwise the air below will remain cold.

2. Make the firebox's width between 1.0 and 1.6 **H** (dimension **W** in figures 4-38 and 4-36). The firebox in figure 4-35 is 54 inches high and 78 inches wide.

169

3. Make the firebox's hearth depth, backwall width, and backwall height = $^1/_3$ H.

4. In the front view of figure 4-38, locate the throat (the narrow opening at the top of the firebox where smoke rises into the chimney) 12 inches above the top of the firebox opening. Next, in the side view of figure 4-37, align the $\dot{\mathbb{C}}$ (centerline) of the throat's depth directly above the $\dot{\mathbb{C}}$ of the firebox and make the throat's front-to-back dimension = $^1/_{12}$ H, then round this number to the next highest $^1/_2$ inch: likely 4 to 5 inches. Then extend the firebox's sides upward to locate the ends of the throat.

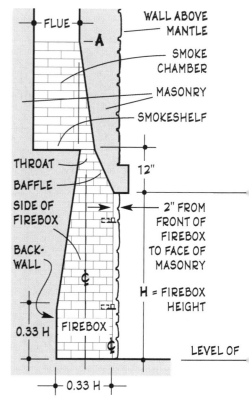

4-37. Section thro' hearth

5. In figure 4-37, locate the baffle above the firebox. This is the inclined face behind the mantle that extends up from the mantle's underside to the throat. The baffle's bottom edge is 2 inches in from the front of the firebox. The baffle should be coated with heatproof mortar or equal.

6. Knowing the length of the throat, find the length of the smokeshelf (the smoke chamber's floor) by adding 1 inch to each end of the throat, as in figures 4-38 and 4-36.

7. Size the flue. Its section should be square or slightly rectangular. If square, the length of each side may be found from $S^2 \geq 0.1\,A\,B$, where

Structure

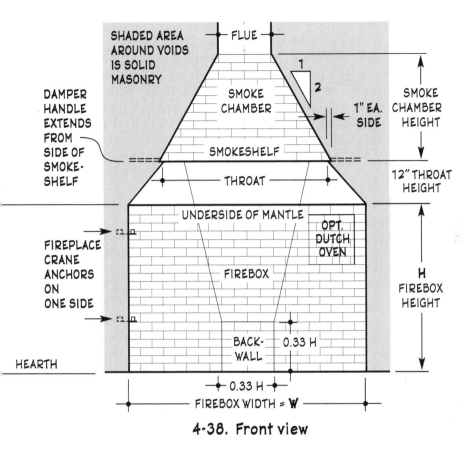

4-38. Front view

S = side of flue if square, in. (interior measure)

A = width of fireplace opening, in.

B = height of opening, in.

Example: if S = 15.2 in, select the next larger locally available size: likely 16 inches. If the flue is rectangular (i.e. 16 × 20 inches), locate the narrow side front-to-back.

8. Find the height of the smoke chamber; this is where the smoke collects above the firebox before rising up the chimney. Designing this space correctly is the secret to creating a good draft in the flue. Looking at the front of

171

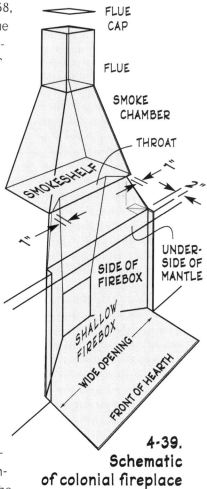

the smokeshelf in figure 4-38, align the center of the flue with the center of the fire-box, then from the bottom of the smokeshelf's sides extend two lines upward at a vertical pitch of 2:1 until the lines intersect the two lines located at the sides of the flue, then draw a horizontal line through the two intersections. The vertical distance between this line and the smoke-shelf is the smoke chamber's height.

9. In figure 4-37, locate the smoke chamber's top front edge. This is at the smoke chamber's height directly above the back of the throat, and is point **A** in the side view of figure 4-37, which also becomes the front of the flue above. Now, knowing the front-to-back dimension of the flue, locate the

4-39. Schematic of colonial fireplace

back of the smokeshelf by extending a vertical line down from the back of the flue.

10. Add the missing dimensions. Figure 4-39 shows a schematic of this fireplace, and figure 4-40 shows a few details that are difficult to portray in the plans. The above dimensions can be adjusted slightly (an inch or so either way) if the fireplace's design and construction must satisfy other criteria not mentioned here.

172

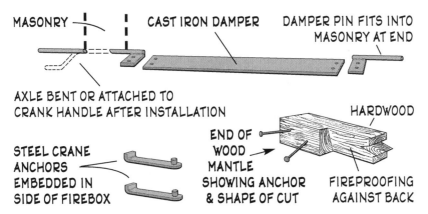

MASONRY --- CAST IRON DAMPER DAMPER PIN FITS INTO MASONRY AT END

AXLE BENT OR ATTACHED TO
CRANK HANDLE AFTER INSTALLATION

END OF WOOD
MANTLE

STEEL CRANE
ANCHORS
EMBEDDED IN
SIDE OF FIREBOX

SHOWING ANCHOR
& SHAPE OF CUT

HARDWOOD

FIREPROOFING
AGAINST BACK

4-40. Fireplace construction details

A tip from years of experience: in these shallow hearths use andirons that are short, no more than 12 inches front to back. They will hold the fire closer to the backwall and smoke will be less likely to curl into the room in front.

As marvelous as this hearth is, grander versions can be made. In the medieval castles of England, fireplace mantles were often six feet high, the firebox was wide enough to roast a hog on a spit, and on each side rose masonry inglenooks whose seats enabled a shivering nobleman to warm his body close to the flames, the stately but chilly hall at his back. If such a large hearth was built today, the base of its smokeshelf could be near the level of the second floor. If made of copper, this thin, light, heat-conducting truncated pyramid would absorb much heat rising to the chimney and deliver it to adjacent spaces indoors.

Recently the *New York Times* published an article about fireplaces[15] that sadly was an example of the misinformation that all too often appears in today's newspapers, magazines, and books. Hear what this article said, and what it *should* have said, to offer the knowledge the public urgently needs today ...

Near the beginning of the article it says: "For the last several years, TheDailyGreen.com, an online magazine, has advocated replacing all wood-burning fireplaces with electric ones." Does this supposed authority believe that generating electricity is efficient and doesn't cause pollution? An average 66 percent of the electricity that would run such a fireplace is *lost* in transmission between the power plant and plug, and the remaining energy produced at the plant causes pollution in its vicinity.

Two lines later this article quotes another supposed authority, a journalist who wrote an article on fireplaces who said: "There is no such thing as an environmentally responsible fire: Switching one type of wood for another is still use of a natural resource that otherwise could have been spared." Untrue! The truth here is that trees often die or are downed in storms, and where they cannot remain and naturally decompose it is environmentally *commendable* to use them as firewood, which also reduces consumption of fossil fuels. A good example of this happened last October on my own property when twelve inches of wet snow fell before the leaves had fallen and broke at least twenty large branches around my house and driveway. My wife and I spent fifty hours cutting the fallen branches into three cords of firewood and branchlets (these we hauled to remote areas of our property to serve as shelters for small animals). This was far more economical and ecological than letting the branches sit in my front yard till they rotted a dozen years from now or paying a landscapist a thousand dollars to haul them to a landfill.

Then, of all things, the author uses the above quote in her very next sentence as a basis for quoting a third "authority", a writer of articles on an environmental website who says: "Wood-burning fires are a direct pollutant to you, your family and your community." Here the botanical truth is that burning wood produces (1) smoke, which is mineral particles that mostly deposit on nearby foliage then are washed by subsequent rain into the soil below the foliage where the minerals nourish the plants; (2) steam, which when it rises above the chimney quickly cools to water; (3) carbon monoxide, which above the chimney quickly combines with oxygen to form carbon dioxide; and (4) carbon dioxide, which is absorbed by nearby plants via transpiration which is how plants breathe. This is the kind of information a competent and responsible journalist would have been quick to report.

Then the author in her next sentence says: "Organizations like the American Lung Association ... recommend that consumers avoid wood fires altogether," and she quotes this organization's chief medical officer as saying, "Wood smoke contains some of the same particulates as cigaret smoke ... as well as known carcinogens ... and has been linked to respiratory problems in young children." Instead of employing such scare tactics —itself unethical— to erroneously imply that every consumer who dares step near any wood fire risks suffering from cancer and respiratory problems, this article should have said that (1) inefficient wood fires should be replaced with efficient ones and describe how this can be done; (2) fireplaces should have shorter andirons that keep the fire closer to the back wall where smoke will be less likely to enter the room in front; and (3) people shouldn't sit within five feet of an open fire. This part of the article does say: "The association strongly advises people not to use the traditional fireplace." Now *this* gets to the point! But this should have been a central premise of the article from which evolved a plethora of supporting evidence and conclusions.

A few lines further down this article cites another "authority", one Karen Soucy, "an associate publisher at a nonprofit environmental magazine" by saying she "refuses to enter a home where wood has been burned, even infrequently." A line later we learn that Ms. Soucy's chief reason for doing this is because she suffers from asthma. This author should not have reprehensively used this one individual's illness as representative of all people everywhere to condemn all homes that burn wood.

Amid this article's atrocities it does have a few accuracies. Just below Ms. Soucy's commentary the article says: "For those who still want to build a fire, there are several ways to make it more environmentally friendly." Then the next 44 lines of her 215-line article (a little over 20 percent) mention several positive aspects of burning wood indoors. But then she negates all she just said by quoting a builder of wood fires as saying: "She feels too guilty about the damage it may do to the environment."

The article then spends eight commendable lines describing the importance of using seasoned firewood. But this passage ends by inaccurately stating that "wood should be stored for at least six months before being burned." Wood stored this long is only about one-third cured. I know an experienced woodsman who has been cutting, stacking, curing, and burning his own firewood for 37 years (need I mention his name) who knows the best time to cut and stack firewood is early spring before the foliage blooms, then the wood should be stored in a fairly dry place and burned the second and third winter afterward. Here a competent and responsible journalist would have ferreted out the facts.

The final thirteen lines of this article admirably cites a few efficiently woodburning achievements of an experienced environmentalist. But *again* the author negates her positive remarks by saying of the environmentalist: "Every time she builds a fire, it causes 'inner conflict. It's a guilty pleasure.'"

How can the population of a great metropolis, and the nation beyond, ever learn what it urgently needs to know about an environmental issue when it is exposed to such logical fallacies, harmful distortions, and outright lies as appeared in this one article in an important newspaper? Here the greatest blame is not to be heaped on the article's many stupid sources but on the one source who contorted incorrect data to support a wrongful conclusion instead of doing what a competent and responsible journalist would have done: objectively collect the pertinent facts, and let the conclusion speak for itself.

Earth. Earth is one building material the world will never run out of. Its viability increases with every decrease of other materials, and any post-construction waste can be recycled in a garden. In this country earth construction dates at least back to the Pueblos of the 1300s. It can be built anywhere there is dirt if you know the recipe, which is: Take 1 cup of dirt. Add 1 cup of water.

Structure

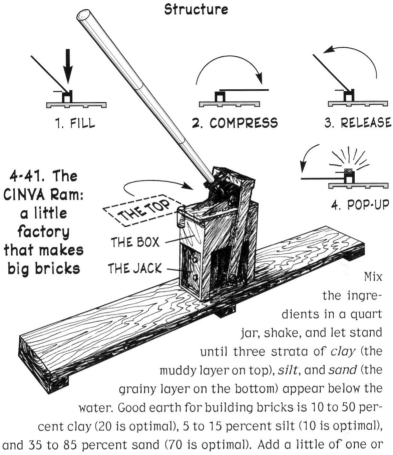

1. FILL

2. COMPRESS

3. RELEASE

4. POP-UP

4-41. The CINVA Ram: a little factory that makes big bricks

THE TOP

THE BOX

THE JACK

Mix the ingredients in a quart jar, shake, and let stand until three strata of *clay* (the muddy layer on top), *silt*, and *sand* (the grainy layer on the bottom) appear below the water. Good earth for building bricks is 10 to 50 percent clay (20 is optimal), 5 to 15 percent silt (10 is optimal), and 35 to 85 percent sand (70 is optimal). Add a little of one or the other until the ratios are right, then for every nine shovels of the mixed ingredients add one shovel of Portland cement. Finally add a little water and mix well, until a squeezed handful forms a slightly slippery ball that holds its shape and leaves little residue on your hand when you open it.

As for the forms that will make the bricks, they may be wall forms or checkerboard-like molds into which the mix is tamped; but the best is the CINVA RAM, an adobe brick-size metal box with a cover on top and a jack below that compresses the soil placed in the box. After filling the box with the prepared earth and covering it, by swinging a long handle from one side of the box over to the other you compress the earth into an adobe brick. A few molds can be fitted into the box to create bond beams, hollow-core blocks, tiles, tapered blocks for arches, and other shapes. After the bricks are formed, place them on a flat clean surface such as plywood (not bare earth) in a warm shaded area, cover them with used cement bags or sheets of polyethylene to protect them from rain and keep moisture from escaping too fast from the curing clay, and finely spray them with water three times a day for a week or ten days. After curing about three weeks, they may be assembled and mortared as bricks.

Adobe brick does have some drawbacks. It is very heavy while not being very strong, and it doesn't stand up well against lots of rain. These debits are reduced by erecting low buildings, having roofs that project sufficiently to keep wind-driven rain from dashing against the facades, and sealing outer surfaces.

Fabric structures. A fabric structure is typically a sail-like cloth held aloft by three or more cables tautly attached to masts or other firm structure so the fabric looks as if it is floating in the air. Such membranous construction can

☞ Be the ultimate suspended ceiling or curtain wall.

☞ Shade the sun and maintain privacy.

☞ Lower heating and cooling costs by reducing an interior's volume.

☞ Reflect sound when mounted above a stage and be quickly adjusted for different performances.

☞ Act as a movie screen, with the projector on one side and the viewers on the other.

☞ Create shade and let in light at the same time, a property exploited beautifully by Frank Lloyd Wright in his canvas drafting room roofs at Taliesin West.

☞ Be shaped into tubular ducts whose airflow passes through the fabric along its length.

Hear what one authority has said about this modern structure's marvelous possibilities:

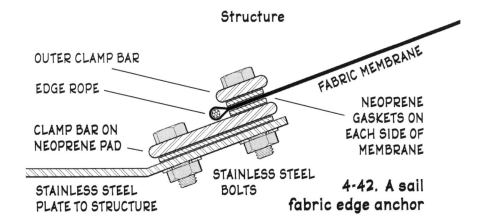

OUTER CLAMP BAR

EDGE ROPE

FABRIC MEMBRANE

NEOPRENE GASKETS ON EACH SIDE OF MEMBRANE

CLAMP BAR ON NEOPRENE PAD

STAINLESS STEEL PLATE TO STRUCTURE

STAINLESS STEEL BOLTS

4-42. A sail fabric edge anchor

Imagine a future in which surfaces manifest themselves as translucent, receptive membranes, shimmering with light and movement. Our everyday lives will be transformed by walls, ceilings and floors that respond to movement and changes in the weather. Building facades will come alive with floating, abstract forms and moving images capturing our attention and expanding our imaginations.

June Bisantz [16]

A fabric sail is typically made in rolls from 60 to 150 inches wide (wider shapes are made by hemming strips together with fishing line); and it is specified by its *tpi* (threads per inch each way), seam construction, weight of an added layer of waterproofing, and weight of a UV topcoat. A typical fabric specification is 120 inch 18/18 tpi cotton with lapped seams, 6.5 ounces per square yard (oz/yd^2) silicone waterproofing, and a 0.3 oz/yd^2 fluorex UV topcoat. Light fabrics weigh about 8 oz/yd^2, heavy ones about 30 oz/yd^2.

As important as the fabrics are the cables and anchors that hold them aloft. Each cable has two end fittings; one connects to the sail, the other to the anchor. The edge anchor appearing in figure 4-42 above connects to both the sail and the anchor and has no intervening cable. The cables are stranded corrosion-resistant flexible steel; and the bolts, clamps, and plates are usually hot-dipped galvanized steel plate or stainless steel.

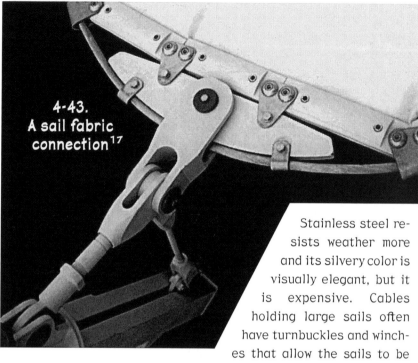

**4-43.
A sail fabric
connection**[17]

Stainless steel re-
sists weather more
and its silvery color is
visually elegant, but it
is expensive. Cables
holding large sails often
have turnbuckles and winch-
es that allow the sails to be
kept taut during changes of weather. These adjusters should be
located where they can be easily reached. All these parts are
designed by engineering specialists who know the hardware and
the microstresses that occur in every nut, bolt, plate, clamp, and
cable through which a fabric's forces blindly find their way from
the sky to the ground. Here is truly a case of a chain being only
as strong as its weakest link. The masts are often a prominent
sculptural element, or they are hidden so the fabric looks like it
is soaring in the air.

But fabric structures have flaws:

☞ Outdoor sails do not like snow. Drifts and deposits from
eaves and parapets above can turn them into rags.

☞ They don't like high winds. In windy areas use tough fabrics with strong connections and locate near the ground.

Structure

☞ An outdoor sail can drain lots of rainfall into a small area. Drainage patterns from sail fabrics should be mapped and ground surface runoffs channeled safely.

☞ Indoor sails must be fireproof. Also a good idea outdoors.

☞ Sails can obstruct the spray of fire sprinklers.

☞ They can ignite if located near lights. Place them away from heat-producing fixtures and devices.

4·44. A sail fabric anchor [18]

Fabric sails are designed as follows. The designer begins with an outline of the sail's shape, a summary of site conditions including wind and snow loads, and the fabric's specifications. S/he draws and specifies every connection in exact detail and requires that the contractor adhere precisely to every part of the design, because many fabric failures are caused by inexperienced contractors who select what they believe are "or equal" fittings or assemblies that are inadequate. Key design issues are size, shape, supports, cost, durability, and collaboration with all involved parties. Some things never change.

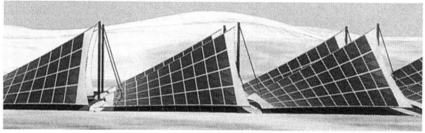

4-45. Solar sail hypars mounted in a desert [19]

Architectural fabrics can be other than cloth. Three are insect screen, hardware cloth, and cyclone fence. These flexible meshes are used as sunscreens, railing fillings, and porous walls that allow ventilation while maintaining privacy, and at night a light shining obliquely across a metal fabric can give it a luminescent glow. For more ideas on metal fabrics, stroll through the galleries at Cambridge Architectural (www.cambridgearchitectural.com) and MechoShade Systems (www.mechoshade.com). Two more fabric websites are www.tensinet.com and www.ifai.com. When considering a fabric design, always ask a supplier for a sample.

While many fabric structures are held aloft by cables, a second kind is held aloft by air pressure from below. You've probably seen such *bubble fabric structures* mounted over swimming pools and tennis courts. Each is a domed enclosure whose bottom edge is typically fastened to the top of a low foundation wall, then air is pumped into the bubble to hold it up. These structures can cover very large areas (a major league baseball stadium has one), and they have four general components:

1. The *envelope* (the domed fabric, usually rubberized canvas).
2. The *inflation system* (two or more motor-driven blower fans).
3. *Anchorages* (sealed perimeter top plates on a foundation).
4. *Access portals* (one or more sealed entrance doors where the occupants enter and leave the enclosure).

Bubble fabrics are usually designed by the companies who make them. After dimensioning the bubble, they size the inflation

Structure

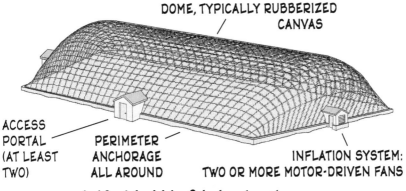

DOME, TYPICALLY RUBBERIZED CANVAS

ACCESS PORTAL (AT LEAST TWO)

PERIMETER ANCHORAGE ALL AROUND

INFLATION SYSTEM: TWO OR MORE MOTOR-DRIVEN FANS

4-46. A bubble fabric structure

system by (1) estimating the leakage at the bubble's fabric seams and its perimeter base, (2) determining the leakage of the access portals, (3) determining the system's operating pressure based on the bubble's design wind loads (usually 80 mph), and (4) sizing the blowers to produce the airflow required to maintain a slightly greater atmospheric pressure inside than outdoors. Each system must be fully automated, include reserve blower capacity, and have an emergency backup in case the primary power fails.

Notes

Electrical

This chapter describes the kinds of electrical systems you will find in today's buildings. But before we begin, I feel moved to tell you something that may shock you (no pun intended): The most economical, enjoyable, and environmentally desirable building I ever lived in, one I resided in for all the four seasons of a year — had no electricity.

Enjoyable? I wouldn't believe it myself, frankly, if I hadn't actually experienced it.

It began in 1969 when the contractor I worked for, Reeford Shea, started building a large house on a mountainside in one of the remotest areas of California's Big Sur, itself a remote area, near a narrow winding highway fifty-five miles from any urban area. The only practical way to build the house was for the crew to live on the site, so Reeford and I began by camping in a small clearing two hundred feet below the foundation. While Reeford

5-1. The visqueen house: living area, looking west

lived with his wife in a miner's tent by the campfire, I moved in under a nearby redwood sapling shaped like a big Christmas tree that was eighty feet tall. Around the base of its trunk I built the framing for a small house from scraps of lumber salvaged from the job and wrapped the framing in clear polyethylene (known locally as visqueen) vapor barrier. The east and west ends of the main room appear below. Mind you, *this dwelling was built from scrap*. The white porcelain sink you see in figure 5-1, I found lying beside some garbage cans at the end of a driveway (it had a large chip in one corner), and the stove you see to the right I bought for twenty dollars in a thrift shop. The propane that fueled the stove was supplied by a five-gallon "jug" I replenished about every three weeks from a large propane tank on the property. I even built two small bedrooms off the living area, one for me and a woman who moved in with me, the other for her two small children. In other words, not just one person, but a *family of four* lived here, willingly, gladly, even luxuriously considering the beauty of the environs and the comfort of the accommodations. In the stove Rosemary baked all kinds of bread; and many of our vegetables were miner's lettuce, nasturtium, and other natural foods the

5-2. The visqueen house: living area, looking east

children collected within a hundred feet of our door. For a refrigerator, we didn't have one because we didn't need one. For lighting at night, we used kerosene-run Aladdin lamps, which produce an adjustable and beautiful bright light, and each of us had a flashlight. All the other electrical contrivances that populate modern homes we had none of, because we found our natural trappings to be more interesting and just as easy to live with. For a toilet, the backhoe operator who cleared the site for the main house dug a pit for an outhouse just uphill of the campfire area behind a chest-high clump of shrubbery that offered privacy; then Reeford built over the pit a seat-high wood frame box about three feet square, mounted on the box a toilet seat, and constructed above the seat a little gable roof and covered it with a poncho, the assembly as a whole looking like a wishing well. A user of this toilet sat behind the shrubbery and enjoyed above its neck-high crown a million-dollar view of the Big Sur coast, of huge thirty-foot combers rolling in from China and smashing on the rocks into fifty-foot arcs of spray, the kind of view many slave for fifty weeks a year to enjoy as a vacation thrill for a few days.

Regarding economics, we paid no rent, no utility bills, and no real estate taxes. After I subtracted withholding and all living expenses from my salary of $5.50 an hour, I banked more than a hundred dollars a week. Never have I done that since. As for the rigors of commuting, I would wake up at quarter to eight, dress, take a large thick slice of Rosemary's bread covered with six patties of butter and drenched with honey, eat this breakfast "on the fly" while commuting a hundred steps to work, and arrive maybe thirty seconds before eight. At the end of work at four-thirty I would be home two minutes later. So I spent less than five minutes a day commuting to and from work. Altogether the experience was anything *but* destitute, anything *but* fraught with anxiety. It was lively, interesting, fun, and —probably its finest testimony— the kids loved it. When we pined for finer luxuries, we drove down the driveway from our house-under-the-boughs and picnicked a mile away at a small state park that offered a gorgeous sampling of the wild Big Sur coast.

Certainly this experience indicates that living without electricity isn't so traumatic as many may believe, and that one gains more than one gives up when inviting the environment into one's home. But its inclusion here is for two other reasons.

First, in this era when LEED has promoted the concept of a sustainable architecture which cannot possibly be achieved according to its own directives, in figures 5-1 and 5-2 you see a bona fide example of sustainable architecture. Architecture that consumed virtually no embodied energy in procuring its materials; architecture which actually *reduced* environmental waste in its making. When all the promoting and sugarcoating is stripped away, when it gets right down to what we really need to do to create a sustainable architecture in this nation, this is the kind of effort it will likely take. Sobering, isn't it?

Second, you can go to Al Gore's movie, and read his books, and come to the realization that, yes, all we hear about creating an environmentally sustainable economy is really important. But living happily for a year in the wilderness in a house built of scraps that has no electricity drives the lesson far deeper into one's soul, and pins the badge of experience on one's chest like no movie or lecture or course or passion ever could. It was through these experiences on these remote premises that I grew to know first-hand the nature of the forces that form our buildings' larger foundation; and it is these experiences, more than my ivy-league education and long career in architecture offices and on construction sites, that enables me to offer you the wisest counsel on environmental architecture. If any leading light or acolyte of LEED or any its fervent affiliates can claim an environmental experience equal to this, I will avidly seek his company and heartily shake his hand.

Now let's describe an "alternative" energy that can make buildings useful and comfortable, one that has been around for a brief century or so —and may still be so a few decades hence!

Architecture Laid Bare!

The Basics

The electricity generated by your local utility arrives at your house or place of work via a thick *primary cable,* or *primary*, that carries a certain voltage and amperage. Typical for homes these days is 240 volts at 200 amps. The cable's voltage multiplied by its amperage is its *capacity* (what is available if you need it), which is not its actual usage, which is seldom more than one-third its capacity. The primary arrives at the building's service entrance either high overhead or deep underground, but never on or near the ground because in wet weather its current could electrocute anyone who touches it. If the primary arrives overhead, it enters a *weatherhead*, a mast-like projection mounted at least sixteen feet above the ground against the side of the building from where the cable descends into the building. If the primary arrives underground, it enters the building below frost level through a thick conduit whose ends are sealed to keep out water and rodents. Typical overhead and underground service entrances appear in figure 5-3. Whether arriving from above or below, the primary runs through an *electric meter* just outside the building where the public utility periodically records the electricity used. In commercial buildings the meter may be mounted just inside a service entrance due to the possibility of vandalism.

After the meter the primary runs through a *service entrance* (a switch where the current for the whole building can be turned on or off) then the primary enters a *panel box* (also a *circuit box* or *breaker box*) which in small buildings is a wall-mounted metal box resembling a medicine cabinet. Inside this container the primary divides into a couple dozen or so conductors known as *circuits*, each of which runs first through a *circuit breaker* (a protective switch that automatically turns the current off if the circuit is suddenly overloaded or shorted), then each cable extends to part of the building where it supplies power to several electric outlets in the area. An example of one circuit, which electricians often call a "home run", appears in the lower right of figure 5-3. In

188

Electrical

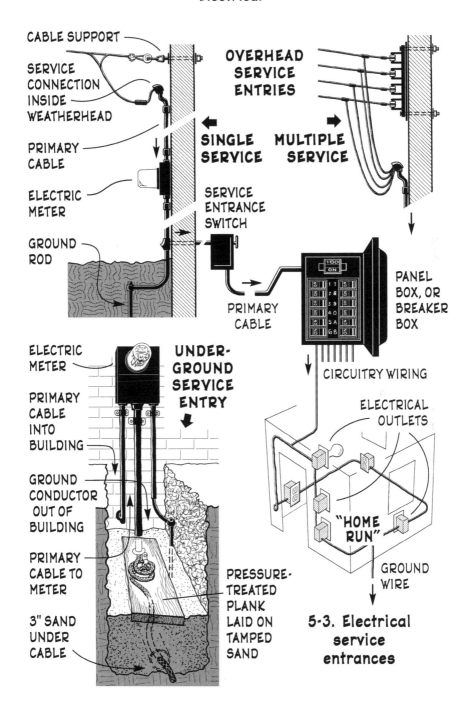

CABLE SUPPORT

SERVICE CONNECTION INSIDE WEATHERHEAD

PRIMARY CABLE

ELECTRIC METER

GROUND ROD

OVERHEAD SERVICE ENTRIES

← **SINGLE SERVICE**   **MULTIPLE SERVICE** →

SERVICE ENTRANCE SWITCH

PRIMARY CABLE

100 ON

PANEL BOX, OR BREAKER BOX

ELECTRIC METER

PRIMARY CABLE INTO BUILDING

GROUND CONDUCTOR OUT OF BUILDING

PRIMARY CABLE TO METER

3" SAND UNDER CABLE

UNDER-GROUND SERVICE ENTRY ↓

PRESSURE-TREATED PLANK LAID ON TAMPED SAND

CIRCUITRY WIRING

ELECTRICAL OUTLETS

"HOME RUN"

GROUND WIRE

5-3. Electrical service entrances

large commercial buildings the primary has a much higher capacity, then just before or after entering the building it passes through a transformer that steps down its power to a number of 240- and 120-volt conductors that extend to panel boxes throughout the building, then each panel box and its circuits look much like the one that appears in figure 5-3.

In each circuit, its voltage and amperage multiplied equals the electricity's power in watts (amps × volts = watts). If your toaster runs on 110 volts and 8 amps, its power is 880 watts. Since 1 kilowatt equals 1,000 watts, 880 watts can also be written as 0.88 kilowatts (kW or kVA). The most common electrical wiring is copper, followed by aluminum. Copper costs more, but it is 64 percent more conductive than aluminum; so a copper wire can be significantly thinner and carry the same current. But aluminum is 30 percent lighter, which makes it more desirable where weight is a factor. However, aluminum has a high rate of thermal expansion which can cause its connections to loosen over time, so it usually requires special connections.

A conductor (also known as a *cable*) contains at least three wires, each of which is either a solid strand or several hairlike strands that are more flexible and conduct electricity more efficiently. The three wires are clad in different colors of insulation: a black *positive* wire carries the current to the outlets, a white *negative* wire brings the current back, and a green *ground* wire collects any stray electrons that could damage the wiring or nearby construction. The three wires are then clad in a second larger insulation, of which there are three general kinds:

5-4. NM or Romex cable

NM (nonmetallic) cable: the wires are clad in a plastic jacket
   which is color-coded depending on the conductor's
   capacity. This is also known as *Romex cable* due to its
   1922 invention in Rome, New York, as an experimental

wire. The experiment was obviously a success because the company now sells 10 million pounds a month.

5-5. UF Cable

UF (underground feeder) cable: the wires are clad in a purple-gray jacket that can be installed underwater or underground. Two subtypes are *SE (service entrance)* cable and *USE (underground service entrance)* cable.

5-6. BX cable

BX cable: the wires are clad in a spiral metal jacket. This is used where the wiring could be damaged by physical force or fire, and is required in commercial buildings.

Two other conductors are *busbars* (copper or aluminum bars that carry large amounts of electricity in large buildings) and *flat conductor cables* (ribbonlike conductors that carry electricity under carpets to outlets located away from walls).

BUSBAR, WITH OUTLET TAP BOX

5-7. Two other conductors

FLAT CONDUCTOR CABLE

When a wire connects to a terminal, the electricity conducts only between the metals' mutual points of contact plus a microscopically small 'jump' area immediately around each contact. In a solid wire curled around a threaded screw (a common electrical connection), the area of contact is very small because the wire touches the screw threads in only a few places. The contact is almost as small between two solid wires twisted inside a wire nut. Better is two stranded wires twisted inside a wire nut. Better yet is a stranded copper wire bolted to a holed lug. Better still is a stranded or braided wire crimped to a sleeved lug. Even better is a soldered connection that fuses the conductors together. Best of all is an *exothermically welded connection* that fuses the wire to the terminal. This won't loosen or corrode, will resist repeated surge and fault currents, and will conduct high-voltage current safely between two different metals (as when a grounded conductor is bonded to a steel column).

Another excellent electrical conductor is the human body. Though your skin doesn't conduct electrons well unless wet, once it is penetrated it's all downhill, so to speak —because all the electrons want to do is find the quickest way to the ground. If this happens to be through your hand, arm, lungs, heart, and foot set on the ground, your hand and arm muscles may contract (then you can't let go), your respiratory muscles may become paralyzed (then you can't breathe), and your heart muscles may stop flexing (then you die). This is why every part of a building's electrical

SOLID WIRE CURLED
AROUND A SCREW:
THE WORST

SOLID WIRES
TWISTED IN WIRE NUT

STRANDED WIRES
TWISTED IN WIRE NUT

STRANDED WIRE
BOLTED TO HOLED LUG

STRANDED WIRE
CRIMPED TO SLEEVED LUG

SOLDERED CONNECTION

WELDED CONNECTION:
THE BEST

**5-8. Electrical
connections**

system is clad with insulation, often threaded through metal enclosures, and typically buried in walls and ceilings and floors, its closest emergence to the outer world being buried a half-inch deep in plug outlets —so no one can touch a bare wire.

Circuits

A building generally has five kinds of electrical circuits:

Convenience circuits. These include the familiar 110-volt outlets for operating small appliances and light fixtures.

Appliance circuits. These are outlets for electric ranges, clothes dryers, office photocopiers, theater projectors, and other large equipment. In apartments and homes at least two 20-amp appliance circuits are usually required in kitchens, pantries, dining rooms, and family areas. A gas stove typically requires a 120-volt outlet for clocks, lights, and minor appliances related to cooking. Behind every gas stove should be a 240-volt outlet in case a future tenant may prefer electric cooking.

Lighting Circuits. In commercial buildings with lights operated by wall switches or occupancy sensors, the lights require separate circuits. Wherever a light is operated by a wall switch, the usual lever is a *snap switch*. Other choices are a *press switch* (this has a rocker that is easier to operate), a *dimmer switch* (this has a slider that varies a light's intensity), or an *illuminated switch* (this contains a tiny light that turns on when the switch is off so it is visible in the dark). Wall switches should be mounted about four feet above the floor within two feet of the knob side of an entry door. When more than one door enters a room, two-, three-, and four-way switches may be mounted by each door so someone entering or leaving any door can turn the light on or off without walking back across the room. Where several wall switches are mounted together, consider labeling them and arranging them vertically so the outlet boxes will fit into the stud framing.

193

Architecture Laid Bare!

Motor circuits. In commercial and industrial buildings, large electric motors run elevators, pumps, and all kinds of other machinery. An electric motor can have 200 horsepower and weigh 2,200 pounds, and each has several critical dimensions as sketched in figure 5-9. The chief criteria for selecting an electric motor is the required wattage or horsepower and its speed in rpm. Many different kinds are available, a few being variable-speed motors for elevators and other machines with varying power requirements, motors for rapidly accelerating loads, explosion-proof motors where flammable vapors may be present, and chemical-service motors for corrosive environments. Electric motors have a number of accessories, a few being rodent screens, lint-proof covers, thermostats that cut power when the motor over-heats, weatherproofing for outdoor installations, fungus-proofing for tropical installations, and shaft modifications for industrial applications.

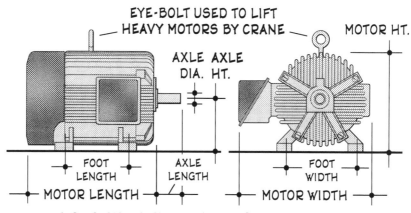

5-9. Critical dimensions of electric motors

A large electric motor should be surrounded by a service aisle, its cooling and ventilation loads must be known (this may require ducting and a nearby thermostat), its weight must be added to the structure it will rest on, and its mount may require a thick base that minimizes sound transmission to adjacent areas.

Electrical

Signal circuits. These are low-voltage circuits (12 volts is common) that operate phones, faxes, and the like. Decades ago a household's signal circuitry served only the doorbell and a phone. But nowadays this low-voltage wiring may include a variety of computerized sensors, operations, and controls. In a large commercial building, hundreds of signal circuits may govern the operation of light fixtures, thermostats, fire detectors, TV surveillance monitors, and other equipment located throughout the building, all collectively known as a *TBM* (total building management) *system*. These circuits can be programmed to streamline almost any business activity. Here's a sampling of what they can do:

☞ A hotel has an occupancy sensor in each room that notifies the front desk when the room is occupied, notifies security personnel if anyone but registered guests or the maid enters the room, activates thermostat setbacks when the room is vacant, and notifies fire controls if a fire erupts so firefighters need to search only occupied rooms.

☞ A home improvement center with 100 outlets throughout the United States has a central office with programmed controls that turn on each store's lights in stages beginning when its earliest employees arrive before the store opens, similarly stages them off after closing, downloads all sales data at the end of each day, and allows central management to try various energy-saving strategies for a any store.

Even owners of homes and small businesses today can have signal circuitry that automates appliances, climate control systems, indoor and outdoor lighting, security systems, surveillance videos, and vehicle detection and also have battery backup during blackouts and vacation controls from remote locations.

But all this e-wizardry has a dark side. When electricity runs through a conductor, it generates a magnetic field around it even if insulated; and if two conductors are laid close to each other, the field around each will induce a current in the other. These

fields cause little trouble if the currents are nearly the same —
but if one is significantly larger, say, when a 240-volt heavy
equipment wire lies next to a 12-volt signal wire, the larger current can so severely disrupt the smaller current that it can cause
computer databases to crash, electric motors to trip circuit
breakers, fax transmissions to fail, and phone calls to fill with
static. Sound familiar? This wayward wattage is known as *electromagnetic interference* (EMI) —and it can occur wherever big wires
bully little wires with reactive power. Even in a household living
room where a 110-volt wallbox is located next to a 12-volt signal
outlet, the magnetic field around the larger wire can disturb the
operation of an electronic device served by the smaller wire. In
fact, this is the way transformers work: two wires of significantly
different voltage are located close to each other with the sole
conductance between them occurring through their radiating
fields of electrons; hence when two wires of significantly different conductance are placed near each other, the stronger wire
will increase the voltage of the weaker one —and if that smaller
wire can't carry the load, something is going to "fry".

How can this molecular mayhem be minimized? Two ways. (1)
Locate conductors of different voltages and amperages 12 to 36
inches apart depending on the number of wires and the difference
in power. But this can take up a lot of space. A closer solution is
(2) install cables of different conductances in metal enclosures
that contain the EMI. Known as *wireways*, these long thin enclosures have openable tops or sides which enable easy lay-in or
removal of a conductor when necessary. In really large buildings,
dozens of wireways may be mounted along the walls and ceilings
of long hallway-like spaces known as *backbones* that are wide
enough to accommodate two service persons pushing a four-
wheeled cart loaded with tools and equipment. These spaces are
even air-conditioned the same as public hallways, because flowing
electrons produce heat and hotter wires create more EMI.
Wireways have a variety of aliases: trench ducts, wall ducts,
lay-in raceways, overhead raceways, cable trays, plugmolds, and

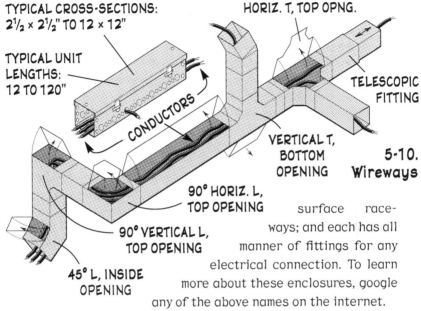

TYPICAL CROSS-SECTIONS:
$2\frac{1}{2} \times 2\frac{1}{2}$" TO 12 × 12"

TYPICAL UNIT
LENGTHS:
12 TO 120"

CONDUCTORS

HORIZ. T, TOP OPNG.

TELESCOPIC
FITTING

VERTICAL T,
BOTTOM
OPENING

90° HORIZ. L,
TOP OPENING

90° VERTICAL L,
TOP OPENING

45° L, INSIDE
OPENING

**5-10.
Wireways**

surface race-ways; and each has all manner of fittings for any electrical connection. To learn more about these enclosures, google any of the above names on the internet.

As further protection against EMI, many buildings today are equipped with refrigerator-sized power conditioners known as *switchgear*. In large buildings these units may number in the dozens and together look like the refrigerator sales section at Sears. These "amptraps" also contain batteries that maintain power during blackouts and recharge when the power returns. The solutions to these disturbances in large buildings offer clues for eliminating them in homes and small businesses, as follows:

☞ *Don't bury those wires!* Threading Romex cable through holes drilled in studs hidden behind interior finishes is fast becoming passé. Instead, locate conductors so they are accessible for servicing and upgrading, and install conductors of different power in separate enclosures.

☞ Make room for the enclosures. We're not talking about a few inches alongside a row of studs or rafters, but aisle-like areas big enough to accommodate a strolling worker carrying a tool box. This is easier than it sounds, because some enclosures (two being the above-mentioned plug-molds and surface raceways) are small and can be mounted above counters and wall baseboards where they can be easily reached for servicing As well as inserting plugs into outlets spaced along their lengths.

☞ Install near computers, photocopiers, lamp ballasts, and any device with a microchip in it a miniature switchgear known as a *UPS* (for uninterruptable power supply). These harmonic filters maintain smooth electron flow and many contain a backup battery. Most office supply stores sell UPSs for homes and small businesses.

Another way to minimize EMI in a room containing a lot of electronics is with an *EMI inhibitor*. An example is metal insect screen. Staple this to a room's studs, joists, and rafters before applying the finishes and you have a superb EMI inhibitor. Even if you slip a piece of metal insect screen between that 110-volt wallbox mounted next to the signal box in your living room, you will appreciably reduce the EMI occurring between them. Another EMI inhibitor is lead-lined drywall, the kind installed around X-ray areas in hospitals. A company named Less EMF Inc. sells such esoteric EMI inhibitors as Staticot™, VeilShield™, and Ex-Static™ Conductive Fabric. Most are metallic cloths that can be shaped into curtains and drapes. One of this company's customers fashions these fabrics into scarves which she wraps around her head to ward off EMI radiating from her cellphone. Could EMI-inhibiting bikinis be next? If you're in a vacation mood, visit this company's entertaining website at lessemf.com.

With the advent of computer electronics, those little ground wires that run from outlet to outlet in a room and gather stray electrons have become very important. In commercial buildings with lots of electronic equipment, these wires may be replaced by giant *signal reference grids* that connect every circuit and piece of equipment to sub-floor grids of copper straps or braided cables bonded to steel columns, ducts, piping, and other metal

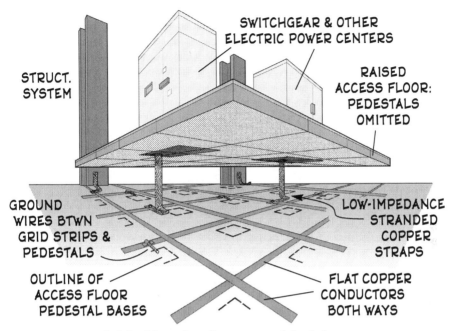

SWITCHGEAR & OTHER ELECTRIC POWER CENTERS

STRUCT. SYSTEM

RAISED ACCESS FLOOR: PEDESTALS OMITTED

GROUND WIRES BTWN GRID STRIPS & PEDESTALS

LOW-IMPEDANCE STRANDED COPPER STRAPS

OUTLINE OF ACCESS FLOOR PEDESTAL BASES

FLAT COPPER CONDUCTORS BOTH WAYS

5-11. Signal reference grid wiring

networks in the building. One such system appears above. These conductors carry the collected electrons back through the building's electrical service entrance where just outside the building the primary groundwire typically connects to a copper rod driven into the ground.

A ground rod is another part of this circuitry that has become significantly more important these days. The usual text says this long slender post should be hammered eight feet into the ground. But unless the soil is a squishy bog you won't drive a half-inch copper rod anywhere near this deep without bending it first. In homes most contractors make this terminal short —two feet, maybe— figuring this is good enough and knowing nobody is going to pull it up to see how long it is. Better is to drill a hole 8 feet deep with a 4 inch-diameter power auger, slip the rod into the hole, and fill the surrounding void with rock salt or copper sulfate —while the owner watches.

Architecture Laid Bare!

Also important is the ground around the ground rod. If this earth is excessively dry, hard, or otherwise unable to absorb the collected electrons, in worst-case scenarios the 4 inch-diameter hole mentioned above may need to be 12 inches, and you may need one of these holes every 20 feet around the building, and you may need to dig a trench between each hole, and you may need to fill all these cavities with rock salt, copper sulfate, or other electrolyte that ionizes the soil.

A more common problem you may encounter in building a home or business filled with the latest computer electronics is finding an electrician who is up-to-date on installing such equipment. As a sample, a computer-literate friend of mine who is a prominent sculptor with a large shop filled with tools including welding equipment and an overhead crane (meaning he is a proficient tool-user), recently built an addition to his house in which he wanted the latest computer technology. He did extensive research on the systems he desired so he could discuss the situation intelligently with the installers. Still, he had trouble getting his electrician to install such systems as ethernet cables and wide-band-width lines; and he later lamented to me that, "I had to push him ... If I wasn't home all day things wouldn't have been done right ... It's hard to track the right things down unless you know what you're looking for and how to find them." Sound familiar? If *he* had these troubles, how much harder would it be for someone who isn't computer-literate, isn't a proficient tool-user, hasn't done plenty of research, and can't stay home all day? Even the esoteric terminology needed to understand what is available and the people who install it can tax a lay-

PRIMARY
GROUND
WIRE FROM
BUILDING

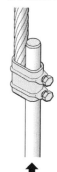

↑
½" DIA.
COPPER
ROD 6-10
FEET LONG
↓

**5-12.
Ground
rod and
clamp**

5-13. Lightning rod details

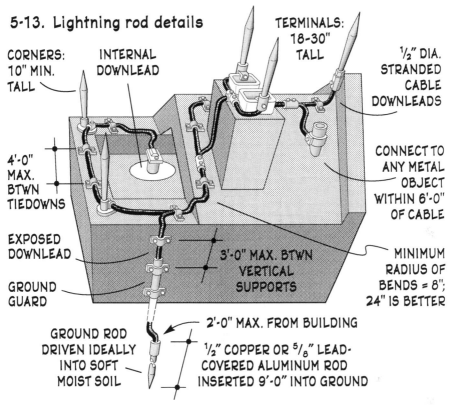

CORNERS: 10" MIN. TALL

INTERNAL DOWNLEAD

TERMINALS: 18-30" TALL

½" DIA. STRANDED CABLE DOWNLEADS

4'-0" MAX. BTWN TIEDOWNS

CONNECT TO ANY METAL OBJECT WITHIN 6'-0" OF CABLE

EXPOSED DOWNLEAD

3'-0" MAX. BTWN VERTICAL SUPPORTS

MINIMUM RADIUS OF BENDS = 8"; 24" IS BETTER

GROUND GUARD

2'-0" MAX. FROM BUILDING

GROUND ROD DRIVEN IDEALLY INTO SOFT MOIST SOIL

½" COPPER OR ⅝" LEAD-COVERED ALUMINUM ROD INSERTED 9'-0" INTO GROUND

man's intellect. One can find a modicum of solace at www.lan-shack.com/cat5-tutorial.aspx, which defines key electronic terms and lists a few electronic installation guidelines.

One final threat remains to electric wires and all the construction that surrounds them: stray electrons from the sky. A lightning bolt may carry six trillion volts and 20,000 amps and be thick as a quarter. They have been known to split trees, destroy submersible water pumps, shatter roof vents, fry power panels, explode fluorescent light ballasts, and wipe out thousands of dollars of computer equipment in a flash. The best we can do with these violent blasts of electricity is to make it easier, not harder, for them to blindly find their way into the ground. This is done by fitting a building with *lightning rods*, as appears in figure 5-13.

Architecture Laid Bare!

These are solid $\frac{1}{2}$ inch-diameter copper or aluminum terminals with pointed tips that are mounted on the building's peaks, ridges, chimneys, cornices, and other prominences. From the base of each terminal extends a $\frac{1}{2}$ inch stranded cable downward (never upward) that conjoin with other cables until two or more primaries descend down opposite sides of the building to ground rods driven at least 9 feet into the earth.

In large commercial buildings a few circuits must still conduct electricity if the utility power fails. These are known as *critical electric loads*; they include emergency and exit lights, one elevator, fire and security alarms, intercoms, hospital life-support systems, command centers, and orderly shutdown of all other systems. This electricity is supplied by onsite generators, or *gensets*. Each is an internal combustion engine that has an axle-in-common with a dynamo, both of which are mounted on a heavy sound-absorbing base near the building's electrical service entrance. Each unit is generally designed as follows:

☞ The radiator fan's intake air duct and the engine's exhaust pipe have short straight runs to the outdoors.

☞ The exhaust pipe has a muffler.

☞ The unit's base and all connecting pipes, ducts, wires, etc. are acoustically isolated from the rest of the building.

☞ An access aisle encircles the unit.

☞ The room the unit is in is spacious and well-illuminated.

☞ The room requires cooling to remove heat produced by the engine and keep the area at "room" temperature.

In office towers and similarly large buildings three gensets may be installed: two to satisfy momentary loads, and a standby unit in case one malfunctions or needs servicing. Some units operate during off-peak hours when electric utility rates are lower and the produced electricity is stored in batteries for use during peak hours. The engine's cylinders and exhaust pipe also offer opportunities for heat reclamation.

Residences and small commercial buildings may have smaller

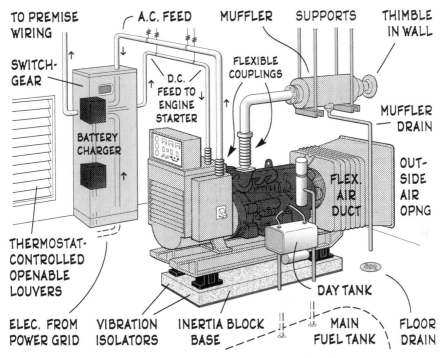

TO PREMISE WIRING

SWITCH-GEAR

BATTERY CHARGER

THERMOSTAT-CONTROLLED OPENABLE LOUVERS

A.C. FEED

D.C. FEED TO ENGINE STARTER

MUFFLER

FLEXIBLE COUPLINGS

SUPPORTS

THIMBLE IN WALL

MUFFLER DRAIN

FLEX. AIR DUCT

OUT-SIDE AIR OPNG

DAY TANK

ELEC. FROM POWER GRID

VIBRATION ISOLATORS

INERTIA BLOCK BASE

MAIN FUEL TANK

FLOOR DRAIN

5-14. Good onsite generator design

gasoline generators that satisfy the occupancy's critical electric loads when the utility power is out. Each is best located in a shed built against the outside of the building. Never put one of these units inside a utility area or near an exterior door, window, or vent. If the following anecdote won't scare you from doing this, nothing will. After a homeowner had "carefully" left his garage door open one night to ventilate a gasoline generator operating in the garage, while he was asleep a strong wind blowing through the garage door blew the kitchen-to-garage door wide open and the resulting draft carried the generator's monoxide exhaust indoors —and killed the owner in his bed.

When it comes to designing a building's electrical system, the owner and/or managers usually huddle with the architect and make a detailed list of all planned electrical use (including every

Architecture Laid Bare!

item's voltage and amperage) in and around the building. Often this list cannot be completed at this stage due to the nature of flexible-use tenancies and other unknown factors; but the more complete this accounting is at the outset, the less trouble everyone will have later on. Below is a conceptual checklist of a building's electrical outlets, which should be part of a planned building's Architectural Program:

☞ *Exterior*: garage door opener, entry lights, walkway, parking lights, landscape lighting, floodlights for outdoor activities, signage, ground fault interruption (GFI) outlets, time-controlled sprinklers.

☞ *Entry*: doorbells, addressor devices, occupancy sensors, security systems, video surveillance, time clocks, fire detection/alarms, emergency exit lights, elevators.

☞ *Lighting*: switches (1, 2, 3 way), fixtures, energy-saving lighting, programmed dimmers, occupancy sensors, timers, automatic switches, emergency lighting.

☞ *Communication*: closed-circuit TV, modems, voice/teledata networks, fiber optics, telephones, intercoms, etc.

☞ *Climate controls*: thermostats, humidistats, supply and exhaust ventilation, static air sensors, CO_2, VOC, and airborne particulate sensors.

☞ *Electrical/mechanical equipment*: service panel, heating and cooling, humidifiers, dehumidifiers, dampers, water heater, well pump, sump pump, fans, thermostat-controlled vents, onsite electrical generators.

☞ *Occupant-operated equipment*: computers, printers, disk drives, copiers, motors, industrial equipment, microcontrols for machine tools and industrial applications.

☞ *Baths*: fans, heat lamp, timer switch, Jacuzzi, exerciser.

☞ *Kitchen*: stove, hood fan, fridge, dishwasher, garbage disposal, microwave, special appliances, dumbwaiters.

☞ *Laundry*: washer, dryer, ironing.

☞ *Grounding devices/systems*: lightning, equipment.

204

Electrical

☞ *TBM systems*: tailor to specific needs.

☞ *Industrial occupancies*: thoroughly research all operations that use electricity, and list nameplate voltages and amperages of every piece of equipment.

☞ A 20 percent "future factor".

After the building is designed, the architect or an engineer organizes the electrical outlets into convenient circuits of required voltage and amperage, then sizes the conductors upstream from the outlets to the service entrance.

Renewable Energies

Generating electricity with coal, oil, and uranium not only depletes the world's energy reserves; it creates more than 60 percent of our nation's emissions of sulfur dioxide (the leading cause of acid rain), nearly 40 percent of our emissions of carbon dioxide (the leading greenhouse gas), and about a quarter of our emissions of nitric oxide (a key component of smog). On the other hand, generating electricity with sun, wind, and water saves energy and produces virtually no pollution. But manufacturing natural energy systems consumes energy and degrades the environment somewhere; so consideration of each should compare the embodied energy consumed in its making and installation with the nonrenewable energy it may preserve during its useful life.

These systems have a few other "drawbacks". They require a lot of time, considerable money, and usually a change in lifestyle by their users. These systems are not for everyone, mostly due to adverse site conditions; and the purpose here is not to woo you to their use but to wisen you to their nature, so you can be conversant with professionals and friends about what they are like.

Using natural energy in a building does not begin with harnessing the heat of the sun, the force of the wind, or the weight of falling water. It begins with constructing thickly insulated building envelopes, creating maximum comfort in minimum volume indoors, and installing energy-efficient appliances. Only after you have minimized the energy you will need are you ready to go to all the labor and expense of satisfying those needs with natural energy. Then you should:

1. Analyze the site's potential to harness natural energy. This begins —and often ends— by asking three questions:

    i. Does the site receive a fairly high percentage of sunshine year round, especially in winter?

    ii. Does wind blow strongly over the property?

    iii. Does a stream of water descend a significant vertical distance on the property?

2. If the answer to one or more of the above questions is yes, the site may have the potential to harness natural energy. Next, list the occupancy's *critical electric load*: the electrical uses that must be satisfied to make the occupancy habitable, such as running water, a few lights, and a refrigerator. If this load will include any appliances, use highly efficient ones.[1] If firewood is available, consider installing an efficient fireplace or a woodstove with a flat cooktop and an insulated flue.

3. Determine the natural energy's patterns of availability. On a site near Seattle the sun may shine an average 63 percent of the day in July but only 28 percent in January, when clouds and fog often obscure the sun when you need it most. And a creek in California may flow swiftly in March but be dry in September.

4. Will the system be *off-grid* or *on-grid*.[2] In off-grid systems the building doesn't have access to local electric power, then the system requires batteries to store its generated electricity for when more is needed than the system can supply. In on-grid systems the local utility provides electricity when more is needed than the system can supply, and when the system generates more than you need you

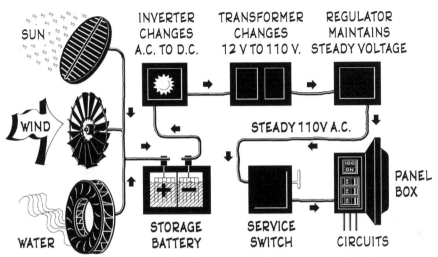

INVERTER CHANGES A.C. TO D.C.

TRANSFORMER CHANGES 12 V TO 110 V.

REGULATOR MAINTAINS STEADY VOLTAGE

SUN

WIND

STEADY 110V A.C.

WATER

STORAGE BATTERY

SERVICE SWITCH

CIRCUITS

PANEL BOX

5-15. Onsite generation of electricity

can sell the excess back to the utility. Some won't pay you nearly as much as you pay them while others will pay even more; so check. Batteries for off-grid systems typically add 20 to 40 percent to their cost and they require more maintenance; but off-grid properties often have notably lower land values which alone can make these systems economical. The most reliable system is on-grid with battery backup; but its dependability comes at a price.

5. Investigate incentive programs. Many governments and public utilities offer lower electric use rates, rebates, low-interest loans, cash subsidies, tax credits, property tax exemptions, permit fee reductions, and other incentives for natural energy systems that will serve residences and small businesses. These financial reductions can tip the scales of feasibility from negative to positive.

6. A presently little-considered aspect of producing electricity from natural energy is that each system supplies electricity for only one building or, as with the huge windmills built today, hundreds of buildings. There is virtually

Architecture Laid Bare!

nothing in between, while in many places a stream, hilltop, or large field could satisfy the energy demands of several neighboring houses. Then a system that would supply, say, six families might cost only three times more than a system for one.

Only now are you ready to analyze the site's potential to harness solar, wind, or water energy, as detailed below.

First, a word about "rules of thumb". Every system described below has a few general rules for economizing its installation and operation, which may be misleading. Example: "A wind prop should be at least 30 feet above any treetops or other landmarks within 500 feet of its tower." But when I can feel a stiff breeze while standing on the ground beside my house I begin to wonder if there's a better way to harness this energy. I also have seen plenty of pictures of windmills in Holland and on the Great Plains whose tops were hardly thirty feet above the ground and which had foliage and/or buildings nearby. To further support this claim, take a look at figure 5-16. This windmill was designed in Wisconsin in 1897 by a young architect who was singularly untrammeled by all the rules of thumb that have tied the minds of those who have designed and built wind towers from that day to this. Note this mill's shortness of height, the tree rising near its base, and the enclosed

5-16 [9]

208

Electrical

base that houses a staircase which in icy windy weather can be quickly and safely climbed by someone carrying a toolbox. This century-old solution shows that today's experts may have hardly scratched the surface when it comes to combining beauty and utility in their efforts to harvest natural energy.

Solar Power. The sun's rays can be utilized to generate electricity, make hot water, and heat indoor spaces. The efficacies of these methods are compared below:

☞ If the surface exposed to the sun is photovoltaic (PV) cells, about 100 square feet mounted perpendicular to the sun will produce 1 kilowatt-hour of electricity.

☞ If the surface is a solar water heating panel, about 22 square feet will produce the equivalent of 1 kilowatt-hour of electricity.

☞ If the surface is south-facing windows, about 16 square feet of glass will produce the equivalent of 1 kilowatt-hour of electricity.

Obviously, using the sun to generate electricity is much less efficient than using it to make hot water or heat indoor air. So an important design strategy is to use PV cells *only when you need electricity*. If you need hot water, obtain as much as you can from solar panels and the rest from other power sources. If you will warm indoor air, get as much as you can directly from the sun and the rest from other sources. Conversely, if a solar water heating system requires electricity to pump the water through the panels, consider installing a few PV cells to run the pump; and if south-facing glass requires a small motor to open and close insulated panels mounted behind the glass, think of installing enough PV cells to run the motors.

Using the sun to make hot water is described in chapter 7, using it to heat indoor spaces is in chapter 8, and using it to generate electricity is discussed below.

When electricity is generated by the sun, the elemental component is the PV cell. Each is typically a bluish-gray wafer of chemically treated silicone about 6 × 6 inches in size and less than a half inch thick. A few dozen are typically wired together to create a flat surface of almost any size and shape that is fronted with a tough transparent film that sheds moisture and minimizes impacts from above, backed by a structural substrate, and fitted with mounts. Some of these sandwich constructions are translucent, which allows some sunlight to pass through them; they have been mounted over porches where the cells collect added energy from sunlight reflected from the floor below. A catalogue of 28 companies that make PV panels appears in the Dec/Jan 2009 issue of *Home Power* magazine, and the Dec/Jan 2011 issue has an article titled "PV Purchasing, Top 10 Considerations." PV cells are also assembled as asphalt-like shingles and narrow rolls that fit between the fins of standard-seam metal roofs. A detailed article on shingle PV arrays appears in *Home Power* magazine, Apr/May 2009.[3] Every part of these systems should be accessible for servicing and possible repair or replacement; because if a wire between two PV modules breaks or disconnects, a whole row or panel of cells could become inoperative and you wouldn't want to tear up part of your roof to find the disconnect.

Although PV arrays convert around 12 to 15 percent of incident sunrays into electricity, their actual output is often nearly halved because (1) a panel's power is typically tested at 77° F but the sun typically heats it to 115° which reduces its efficiency 15 percent or so; (2) when rain doesn't fall for long periods the panel surfaces tend to collect dust which further reduces their output (try to mount them where they can be hosed); (3) their peak power typically decreases 20 percent during their 30-year life; and (4) stationary panels collect only about 70 percent of the sun's daily incident energy. These deficiencies can make the difference between a planned system eventually being cost-effective or a waste of money. Another factor that often has a decided effect on a system's feasibility is if one of the occupants is a savvy tool user.

Electrical

Here are a few design tips for the solarly advantaged: [4]

☞ Try to orient stationary panels within 15 degrees east or west of due south. Regarding the panels' vertical angle, or tilt, for maximum annual production the optimal tilt is the site's latitude plus 5 degrees, and for maximum winter production (when lights and appliances are used more) the optimal tilt is the latitude plus 20 degrees. Since varying the tilt angle 5 degrees up or down reduces the collected energy by less than 5 percent, it usually costs less to mount the panels flat on a roof of less-than-optimal pitch than have them protrude above the roof where a stiff wind could send them into a neighbor's yard.

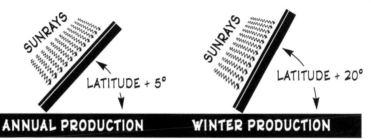

ANNUAL PRODUCTION   WINTER PRODUCTION

5-17. Optimal panel tilts for PV arrays

Regarding lateral orientation, if the panels face 30 degrees east or west of due south they will still collect 87 percent of what they will collect if they face due south; so a few degrees off from due south makes little difference.

☞ Consider sun-tracking panels. These have movable mounts with photoelectric eyes that keep the panels facing the sun as it moves across the sky. Though these systems cost more, due to the added energy they collect the extra initial cost is often returned in a few years.

☞ Consider mounting the panels on or near the ground. [5] They will be easier to install and less apt to be damaged by wind, servicing is easier and safer, and dust and snow collecting on the glass can be easily removed. A clever

Architecture Laid Bare!

way to remove any accumulated snow is to mount the panels so the snow's weight makes the panels tilt vertically and the snow slides off. Where a lot of snow falls in winter, ground-mounted panels can collect 30 percent more solar energy reflecting off the snow in front of them. However, ground-mounted panels are more likely to be obstructed from the sun by nearby trees and buildings. One fellow in Idaho solved this by mounting his PV array on a 60 foot pole. No word on how he serviced them. [6]

☞ Consider mounting the panels as awnings above south windows. If the facade above is smooth and lightly colored it will reflect considerable radiance onto the panels below when the sun is high, plus the panels will shade the windows. This works well in buildings with ribbon windows that have several feet of facade above. [7]

Wind Power. [8] There are many ways a gust of wind can make a light bulb glow. In 1980 an issue of *Wind Power Digest* described nearly fifty different wind generators that were available in that year alone. Little wonder, since the tank that holds this fuel is as big as the sky. But scooping these vagabonding electrons out of the azure is not for the faint of heart. First you need a tower with a heavy generator on top. Then someone needs to climb the tower once a month to maintain it. Third, wind towers attract lightning. Fourth, Murphy's Law states that these machines fail only during storms when the tower's ladder rungs are coated with ice and the nearest technician is on vacation. Fifth, a wind prop is at most only 59 percent efficient, because when wind strikes the blades at least 41 percent of the energy is deflected outward while the other 59 percent pushes the blades around. But low engine efficiencies never stopped Henry Ford. His secret (and yours) is knowing the facts in advance and exploiting the benefits of each. On the plus side, wind power increases according to the cube of the wind speed; so a 15 mph windspeed is not 50 percent more powerful than 10 mph but $(15/10)^3$ or 338 percent more powerful.

212

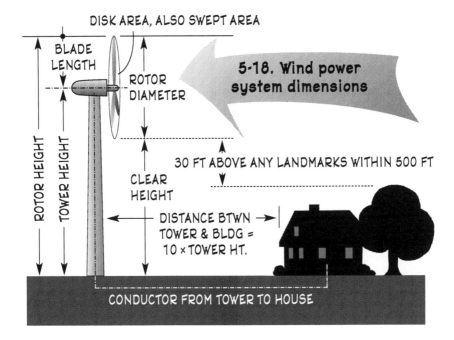

DISK AREA, ALSO SWEPT AREA

BLADE LENGTH

ROTOR DIAMETER

5-18. Wind power system dimensions

ROTOR HEIGHT

TOWER HEIGHT

CLEAR HEIGHT

30 FT ABOVE ANY LANDMARKS WITHIN 500 FT

DISTANCE BTWN TOWER & BLDG = 10 × TOWER HT.

CONDUCTOR FROM TOWER TO HOUSE

This is why wind prop feasibility increases rapidly above about 11 mph and decreases rapidly below this. The minimum average wind-speed for feasible generation is usually 8 to 10 mph, and 15 to 25 mph is optimal. Optimal terrain is a large flat open area with few or no obstructions such as trees and buildings. High-resolution wind maps, similar to topographic maps, that list typical wind-speeds for certain areas of the country are available that may help you quickly decide whether wind generation would be a boom or bust on your property. Take a look at www.windpowering ameri-ca.gov/wind_maps.asp#us.

A wind generator's blades typically have a feathering mech-anism that reduces their angles so in high winds they won't spin too fast and fly apart. The blades of small systems may be up to 12 feet long, while the blades of large utility-built turbines may be 90 feet long and can electrify 200 homes. *Headwind* models have the props mounted in front of the motor, while *tailwind* models have the props located behind. Headwind models require a large tail vane to keep the blades facing the wind, but they are more efficient. The tower cannot be mounted on a building because the prop's vibrations can damage the building and its rotation interferes with TV reception. Every tower must also be designed or approved by a licensed engineer, and each requires an access road to its base. Notwithstanding Frank Lloyd Wright's enchanting Romeo and Juliet windmill that appears on page 208, there are three general kinds of wind towers today: [10]

Tilt-up tower ... this is raised and lowered by a truck-mounted winch that allows the machinery on top to be serviced without anyone climbing the tower. It is usually cable-guyed in four directions and requires a clearing in one direction for raising and lowering. The winch truck's monthly visit may be a significant maintenance cost.

Guyed lattice tower ... this is a single truss-like structure similar to a radio broadcast tower that is held upright by cables extending in three radial directions to a distance of about 60 percent of the tower's height. These are the lightest and least expensive towers, but the guy wires require a lot of area.

Free-standing tower ... this is typically a pole or spire that requires no guy wires. Each is anchored by a large concrete foundation. These require only a small area around the tower's base and they are sturdy, but they are usually more expensive than the other two.

Whatever tower a system has, consider mounting on it every 50 feet upward anemometers that track wind speeds, directions, and gust peaks.

Before a wind power system is installed, its design is submitted to the building department and the local utility. The utility will require you to (1) submit an *interconnection contract* before you connect to the local grid (this is mostly a legal formality but it includes the specifications of your system for their records); (2) install an *external disconnect switch* on the line

5-19.

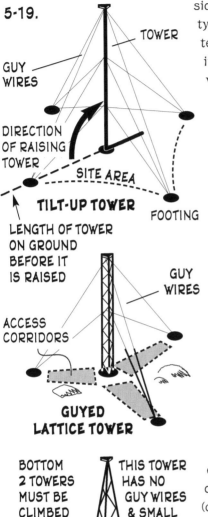

TOWER

GUY WIRES

DIRECTION OF RAISING TOWER

SITE AREA

TILT-UP TOWER

FOOTING

LENGTH OF TOWER ON GROUND BEFORE IT IS RAISED

GUY WIRES

ACCESS CORRIDORS

GUYED LATTICE TOWER

BOTTOM 2 TOWERS MUST BE CLIMBED MONTHLY

THIS TOWER HAS NO GUY WIRES & SMALL SITE

CONCRETE BASE

FREESTANDING TOWER

side of your electric meter so utility personnel can turn off your system when they work on power lines in your neighborhood; and (3) provide a certificate of insurance.

When it comes to living on wind power, you might not want to go as far as Maurice Seddon of Datchet, England, but it's worth noting. In cold weather he keeps warm in a jump suit sewn with thin wires, like those in an electric blanket, whose 12-volt current comes from a wind tower in his garden. When it gets really cold, he also wears gloves and shoe insoles that are similarly wired. When he wishes to move from one room to another, he unplugs his conductor-clad snuggly from one electrical outlet and replugs it into another. He says his method of keeping him warm indoors uses 1/13th the energy normally needed to heat his house. He also designs a line of heated apparel (chiefly long johns, gloves, and insoles) for motorcyclists that are powered by the cycle's alternator, and he has equipped his own motorcycle with an alternator-operated electric oven which he uses to cook stews when he is on the road.[11] That's moving in the right direction!

215

Architecture Laid Bare!

Water Power.[12] Generating electricity with water involves damming a stream to create a reservoir whose surface is well above the water at the dam's base, then a pipe called a *penstock* carries the impounded water from the top of the dam's upstream side to the bottom of its downstream side where the pressurized water turns the blades of a turbine connected to a generator that creates the electricity. These are known as *microhydro systems*, and one's key dimension is the vertical distance, or *head*, between the top and bottom of the penstock. These systems are most feasible in hilly country with mild wet climates, and least so in flat dry country with long cold winters. One's chief components are:

Water source. The larger and steeper the streamflow, the more power it will generate. The water's pattern of flow is also important. A stream that flows plentifully in winter may be dry during droughts or when summer foliage along its banks sucks up the flowing water. Conversely, a severe storm can turn a lazy brook into a torrent filled with boulders and uprooted trees that can destroy the dam. Hence where the stream enters the reservoir above the dam, try to position a few big boulders that will obstruct large floating or rolling objects while letting normal waterflow pass between them. It is crucial to know the stream's waterflow, which can be found as follows. (1) Where the stream flows smooth and straight for ten feet, throw a piece of bark on the water and time how many seconds it takes the bark to flow ten feet; (2) estimate the stream's cross-sectional area in square feet (sf); (3) multiply the velocity times the sectional area to obtain the stream's waterflow in cubic feet per second (cfs), cubic feet per minute (cfm), or gallons per minute (gpm). If possible do this several times a year, to become familiar with the stream's variable waterflow.

Reservoir. This is the water retained behind the dam. If possible it should be long and narrow in the direction of the

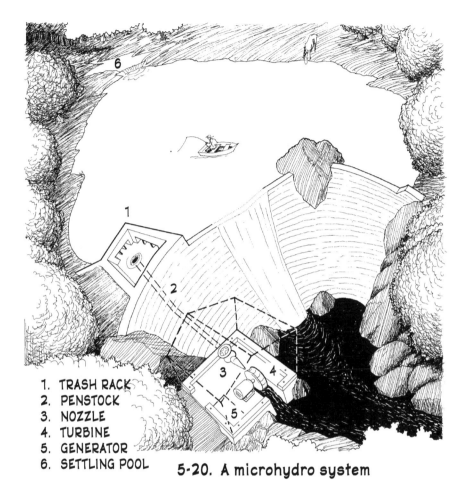

1. TRASH RACK
2. PENSTOCK
3. NOZZLE
4. TURBINE
5. GENERATOR
6. SETTLING POOL

5-20. A microhydro system

stream; then during storms any silt entering the reservoir will have more time to settle before reaching the penstock. For the same reason a small settling pool accessible by a backhoe should be located above where the stream enters the reservoir, then every decade or so this basin can be dredged of sediment. Before damming the reservoir, locate its shoreline with a surveyor's transit and remove all foliage from inside. In addition to powering the turbine, the reservoir can supply water to the occupancy served and be used for swimming, boating, fishing, fire protection, irrigation, and watering livestock.

Dam. This barrier creates the vertical distance, or head, between the penstock's intake and the turbine. The dam should be as narrow (reduces construction costs) and as high (increases power) as possible. The best site is where a steeply descending stream flows between steep terrain on both sides. The dam should be considerably thicker at its base than its crest, it should be slightly concave facing downstream, its ends should meet the banks on each side at an elevation above the stream's highest flood stage level, part of the crest should have a spillway that conveys floodwater safely over the dam, and enough normal streamflow should bypass the penstock to maintain a habitat for existing stream life. The dam must be designed by a licensed engineer. If the stream is small and steep, another way to create a tall head for generating electricity is simply to locate the penstock's upper end well upstream, pile some rocks in the water to divert part of its flow into the penstock, and screen its inlet with $1/_4$-inch galvanized wire mesh or equal. Such a small system may be constantly damaged by storms, but would be easily repaired.

Penstock. This is an inclined pipe, typically 2 to 6 inches in diameter, that runs from the top of the reservoir to the base of the dam. To keep objects from entering the pipe and lodging in the nozzle or damaging the turbine, the inlet must be screened and around it should be built an immovable *trash rack* that can easily be cleaned and repaired. Where the stream and dam are small, another type of inlet is a *Coanda-effect shear screen*, a sloped stainless steel mesh with narrow slots that allow much of the water to pass through the slots while any debris larger than 1 millimeter washes over them (see www.hydro-screen.com). The penstock should have a handwheel valve

218

just after the inlet so the water can be turned off and one's hands won't be sucked into the inlet when cleaning it of debris.

In cold regions this pipe must be buried below frost level (unless you want to insulate and heat it). Although flowing water generally won't freeze, if part of the system malfunctions during subfreezing weather and the water must be turned off to repair it, the penstock could crack. This pipe is usually copper if laid above grade and heavy plastic if buried, because steel can rust (unless expensive stainless steel), copper can degrade when buried, and plastic will be chewed on by wild animals from rats to bears. But burying the pipe can be difficult, because steep terrain (desirable) is usually rocky (undesirable). The pipe should be straight as possible, because at bends the flowing water's momentum can tear the pipe apart; then an engineer-designed thrust block must be constructed against the bend in alignment with the pipe above. If any part of the penstock flows uphill, each sag requires a cleanout valve to remove trapped sediment and each peak needs a air-release valve to remove entrained air bubbles.

Nozzle. This is a tapered spout located at the base of the penstock where it jets water onto the blades of the turbine. Each system should have two or three nozzles of different orifice diameters; then when the streamflow is high a larger nozzle can fully utilize its power, and when the flow is low a smaller nozzle won't let the penstock become partly empty which would reduce its power. Mounted on the penstock just before the nozzle should be a water pressure gauge, a hose bibb to allow cleaning of the area, and a valve so the water can be turned off when the system needs servicing.

Turbine. This is a wheel with spooned blades mounted around it. One appears in figure 5-21 on the next page. When the nozzle shoots water against the blades it rotates the wheel and a generator connected to the wheel's axle. YouTube shows several of these whirlers in action. Their blades turn so fast they are a blur. The water's velocity will wear holes in most blades in about a year, so you should have an extra set of blades on hand and they should be easy to replace. The nozzle, turbine, and generator should be sheltered from the weather. After the power water strikes the blades, the tailwater should fall quickly from the blades and flow freely downstream.

5-21. Penstock and turbine assembly

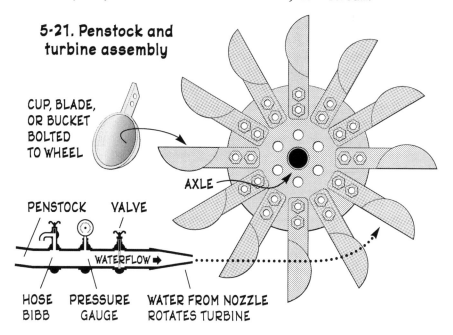

CUP, BLADE, OR BUCKET BOLTED TO WHEEL

AXLE

PENSTOCK   VALVE

WATERFLOW ➡

HOSE   PRESSURE   WATER FROM NOZZLE
BIBB   GAUGE   ROTATES TURBINE

Wiring. This conducts the generated electricity to the occupancy. The shorter the wiring, the lower its cost and the less line loss it will incur. The wiring may require an inverter, transformer, regulator, and other power conditioners. This componentry is well-known to professionals in the business.

Electrical

Batteries.[13] Often a natural energy system's production will vary so greatly between extremes of resource availability that a bank of batteries may be necessary to collect the electrons when the system produces a surplus and dispense them when the system has a deficit. Today's battery technology is dependable and widely available. As a sample, near my home is a supermarket-size building filled with hundreds of suitcase-size storage batteries which the local phone company uses to keep telephones operating if the utility power fails. I inspected this building in 1978. They are all over America today. But batteries have a few minuses. They are expensive, dangerous, messy, and heavy. They also need constant attention, have a limited life, and require precise design to work well; because a little inefficiency goes a long way backward with batteries. Three general kinds are available today:

Flooded lead-acid deep cycle. Low initial cost, short life.
Sealed maintenance-free lead-acid. Not as messy, need less
    maintenance, but expensive.
Nickel-cadmium. High performance, long life, high cost.

The best batteries for natural energy systems are deep-charge batteries. In them a large percentage of the electrolyte can be depleted before they have to be recharged. Car batteries are a poor choice because they take only a shallow charge (all they do is spend a few seconds starting the engine then the rest of the time the engine's alternator recharges the battery while the engine runs). If a system with these batteries experiences several days of cloudy weather you'll likely end up with a row of dead batteries. Also avoid sealed batteries. Though they require virtually no maintenance, won't leak, and won't build up corrosion on the terminals, they cost a lot, take only shallow charges, and are easily damaged by overcharging.[14] A better choice than either of the above are golf-cart batteries. These typically take a deep charge, can take a lot of abuse including chronic undercharging, and usually last 4 to 5 years. One also weighs only about 60 pounds, which is light enough to carry down a flight of stairs to a battery box in a basement. An even more cost-effective model may be L-16 batteries. These commercial storage cells take deep-cycle charges, cost relatively little, and typically last 5 to 8 years, all of which makes them useful for small to medium-sized systems; but each weighs 120 pounds. They were originally designed for floor-scrubbers in supermarkets where they ran for hours each night and were recharged from the utility power grid the next day. Even more economical in the long run are industrial batteries used in fork lifts. They are expensive and weigh as much as 300 pounds, but typically last 15 to 20 years. A few companies that make batteries for natural energy systems are:

Fullriver Battery (www.fullriverdcbattery.com)
MK Battery (www.mkbattery.com)
Sun Xtender (www.sunxtender.com)
Surrette Solar Batteries (www.surrette.com)
Trojan Battery Company (www.trojanbattery.com)
U.S. Battery (www.usbattery.com)

An important part of a battery-backed system is the number of batteries it should have. The chief criteria for determining this is the occupancy's daily *critical electric load* and its *days of autonomy*. The latter is the number of days the occupancy might be without power, which with off-grid systems would depend on the patterns of availability of natural energy, and with on-grid systems would be the number of days the occupancy might be without electricity when the utility power fails. A system's critical electric load multiplied by its days of autonomy equals its *supply load*, which then is matched by the batteries' *storage load*, which indicates the number of batteries the system should have. For example, if an occupancy's critical electric load is 60 amps at 110 volts, which equals 6,600 watts, and the days of autonomy is 3, the supply load is 6,600 × 3 = 19,800 watts. If you plan to use 12-volt batteries with a capacity of 85 amp-hours (a common size); then, since 12 volts times 85 amps equals 1,020 watts, you would need 19,800 ÷ 1,020 = 19.4 ➡ 20 batteries. Easy, eh? A few other criteria for numbering a system's batteries are best dealt with by a professional engineer, as follows:

☞ The deeper the discharges between a battery's charges, the fewer cycles the battery will endure before it dies, then the more batteries you will need to maintain adequate electron flow.

☞ A battery's discharge rate is influenced by the surrounding temperature. A battery stored at 32° F will last only 70 percent as long as a battery stored at 78°. If located where it will be cold in winter, they are best placed in an insulated enclosure that contains a thermostat and a small heater, which requires more energy, which requires more batteries. And since batteries give off hydrogen which is flammable and lighter than air, the enclosure must be sealed and its top slope to a peak that vents to the outdoors —all of which require expert design.[15]

☞ A bank of batteries requires a regulator (usually a DC-to-AC inverter) to maintain even electron flow, and possibly an automatic watering system to maintain the electrolyte. These also slightly reduce the system's overall efficiency and require expert design.

☞ The smaller and more numerous the batteries, the lighter each will be. But the more batteries a system has, the more likely it may experience *electrical dyssmmetry*: unequal electron flow between two or more parallel conductors. When this happens, a defective cell or corroded terminal can cause a whole row of batteries to receive less charge; and since replacing one defective battery only aggravates any inequalities, usually the whole row of batteries needs replacing. Solving this "equation" is another detail that requires an expert.

All the above microeconomics show how important it is to know a natural energy system's hidden drawbacks as well as its promoted advantages before you plunge any time and money into them. The stakes are bigger than you may think. When someone tries to "go solar" and finds it doesn't pay, they spread the word that these systems don't work. This is what happened to the Solar Energy Movement of the late 1970s. The centerpiece of that technology was arrays of flat plate collectors mounted on house roofs from where the sun's collected energy was piped or ducted into basement rock storage units from where the heat was ducted into interior spaces. When word got out that these expensive systems were so inefficient that they rarely recouped their initial costs, the Solar Energy Movement died on the vine. If Green Architecture isn't to experience a similarly short-lived popularity due to revelations of adverse economics, its advantages and debits must be portrayed accurately from the start.

The best way to learn if a system will pay for itself in the long run is to determine its *cost-benefit ratio*, then compare this with other economic opportunities. For example, if you spend $20,000 for a system that will save you $600 a year, you will save 600/20,000 = 3 percent of your initial investment per year. No deception there. But what if you invest the same $20,000 in interest-bearing stocks and bonds that yield an annual dividend of $4\frac{1}{2}$ percent? You would save $900 every year with probably less trouble. Of course the only surefire tool for making such adept comparisons is a crystal ball. Still, whether you can predict the future or not, only if a renewable energy system's annual savings compared to its original cost will "beat" the going interest rate will it be worth investing in over the long haul. And there are other "variable interest rates" at work here: our governments' varying interests in conserving energy, which can lead congresses and legislatures to offer rebates and tax credits during one administration, and revoke them during another.

Regarding the above honest disclosures of generating electricity with natural energy, each of these systems' number of debits may give you a gloomy picture of their feasibility. But an inequity lurks here. Consider coal. Mining this fossil fuel also has a number of debits: a long and sordid history of ruining workers'

Electrical

lives, crippling communities, creating mountains of waste, poisoning rivers and streams, and devastating landscapes while at the same time coal companies habitually enjoy favorable legislation, receive tax subsidies, and are granted government giveaways while they consistently ignore regulatory guidelines. If all these debits were added to these companies' balance sheets so their bottom line truly reflected what it takes to procure, process, package, and transport every lump of coal in one form or another from deep in the earth to your doorstep, our nation's citizens would form lines longer than the gas lines of the 1970s to grab every natural energy plum while supplies were available. It would be a feeding frenzy!

How will these inequities end? Will the public continue to be tempted by artificially low prices that do not fully reveal the environmental cost of an energy until a few more Montcoal mine disasters have occurred, until a few dozen more Deepwater Horizon wells have exploded, until a few hundred more Love Canals have poisoned our lives —until the businesses to blame are finally forced to make honest accountings of their labors that the public can base rational decisions on?

The answer tells how difficult our dilemma really is.

Notes

Lighting

Unless you live in a mausoleum, architecture is merely light reflecting off surfaces. No light, no architecture!

Inside a building this space-shaper may arrive from several sources. The sun. The sky. Light bulbs. Combinations of these. As a sample, if you step through a doorway in a museum toward a sculpture illuminated by two lights mounted in the ceiling, the sculpture may be further brightened by light entering a window, light arriving through the door you entered, and light from these sources reflecting off all the enclosing surfaces of the space the sculpture is in. But lighting is subtler than this. Hear what one of the twentieth century's leading authorities on illumination, Louis Erhardt, said of what else transpires here:

> Lighting does more than illuminate "to make visible." It sets the appropriate adaptation, adds to clarity or creates illusion, and leads the eye and the mind to the scene's salient features in an orderly, composed fashion. The purpose of lighting is to achieve the desired atmosphere and inspire a response, mental or emotional, in keeping with the space and the activity.[1]

If doing all of this only was as easy as screwing a bulb into a socket! But it isn't. To begin with, the light you see by should arrive plentifully but not harshly. The arriving photons should arrive from directions that won't create annoying shadows, and they should reveal colors accurately (you'd be surprised that some lights make blue look like turquoise and red look like lavender). Every light bulb should also be energy-efficient, it must be located where it won't ignite any materials nearby, and since bulbs burn out each should be easy to replace. A light bulb also dims as it ages, it collects dust, its voltage may vary, and it even

Lighting

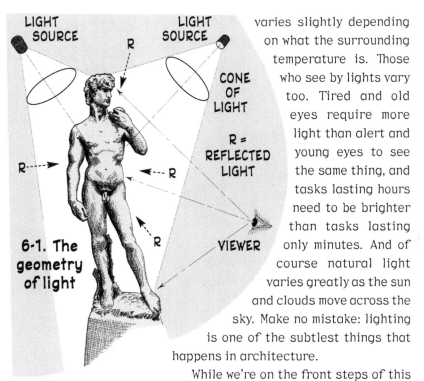

6-1. The geometry of light

varies slightly depending on what the surrounding temperature is. Those who see by lights vary too. Tired and old eyes require more light than alert and young eyes to see the same thing, and tasks lasting hours need to be brighter than tasks lasting only minutes. And of course natural light varies greatly as the sun and clouds move across the sky. Make no mistake: lighting is one of the subtlest things that happens in architecture.

While we're on the front steps of this subject, we should define five general kinds of lighting:

Task ... This is the light that shines directly on something you are doing. This illumination brightens desks, counters, workbenches, a book you are reading, and the like.

Accent ... This light reveals a featured detail, such as a painting on a museum wall or an ornamental tree in your yard.

Ambient ... This is general illumination that fills every part of an area between its task and accent lighting; it is also called *fill light*. It makes every part of a space at least slightly visible, it softens shadows, and generally adds a warm feeling to what you see.

Decorative ... This is lighting that adds an attractive element to normal lighting. Examples are chandeliers, Tiffany lampshades, and neon lights.

Glare ... this is too much light. It can range from a bright
sheen on a page you are reading to a streetlight outside
that shines through a window to annoy someone inside.

Daylighting

Daylight is the king of light fixtures, certainly the largest,
one whose lordly rays and princely reflections arrive from that
one big bulb that shines so beneficently from afar. Daylight is the
primary prism to which artificial light is added, not the other way
around. It may enter windows, skylights, clerestories, French
doors, and the like in a building's shell. Each such source could
be called a nuclear-powered dimmer-operated daylight fixture
with a recessed mount and a transparent facing.

Daylighting varies in the four directions of the compass.
South light is brightest, because that's where the sun is most of
the day. North light is soft and shadowless: it is ideal for illuminating deskwork and similar activities. East light in the morning
and west light in the afternoon are low bright lights that can
shine directly into your eyes. They can be blocked with foliage
located outside east and west windows and/or drapes mounted
inside. Architects know other ways to coax light indoors when you
want and cloak it when you don't, as you shall see.

Wherever any kind of light comes from, the amount that
strikes what you are looking at is measured in *footcandles*. One
footcandle is the amount of light given off by a candle flame when
it is a foot from your eyes. Desirable lighting levels for a number
of visual tasks appear in figure 6-2.

The primary lens for creating daylighting in today's buildings is glass. Whether window or skylight, transparent or translucent, small or large, in outer surfaces or inner ones like interior
French doors, this skin-like material allows the day's brightness
to enter every nook and cranny of the space further within. But
daylighters lately have a new lens to work with: a $1/10$ inch thick
translucent membrane known as EFTE that also is flexible, elastic,

Lighting

OUTDOORS

Direct sunlight 10,000

Clear sky overhead 8,800

Medium overcast sky 2,000

Clear north light 1,200

Clear sky at dawn or dusk ... 40

Smoggy sky ... 70-85% of above

INDOORS

Surgical operating room   2,000

Color matching, TV studio 300

Fine machine work 200

Tailoring, proofreading 150

Private office 100

Classroom, office, museum
   exhibit, applying makeup ... 75

Reading a novel, computer
   work, conference room 50

Public elevator, bedroom 30

Freight elevator, pantry,
   toilet area 20

Assembly, hallway, lobby,
   hotel room, stairway 15

Service entrance, intimate
   dining, showering 10

Garage, stockroom, linen
   closet 7.5

Emergency exit 5

Basement 3

Candle flame 1 foot away 1

Theater seating 0.5

Full moon, clear cold night .. 0.2

6-2. Desirable lighting levels, footcandles

UVA-resistant, durable, lightweight, and environmentally benign. You may have no idea what this is until you are cued that it covered the facades and roof of the Watercube, the facility that hosted the aquatic events in the 2010 Olympic Games in Beijing, China. 7.7 acres of this translucent material covers the building's roof and from the air it looks like patterns of soap bubbles in a bubble bath, an apt metaphor for this aquatic facility, and it allows soft natural light to brighten nearly 17 acres of floorspace below. Although EFTE has been around since 1982 and has often been used in Europe for atriums, exhibition halls, gas station roofs, and the like, its appearance in the Watercube has added this material to the palettes of architects around the world, and brought its wondrous light-emitting properties to your doorstep.[2]

Some of the finest examples of daylighting in the last century were created by Frank Lloyd Wright and Le Corbusier, as you can see in

229

Architecture Laid Bare!

figure 6-3. In the skylights of Wright's Johnson Wax Building and above the entrance of a house he designed in Illinois, he used daylight in ingenious ways. As for Le Corbusier, look at the shape of a window he designed at the top of a staircase of a monastery in France; and the south facade of his Chapel at Ronchamp in France is one of the finest window compositions ever. As Corbu said: "Recognize then the primordial importance of the location of windows: here the decisive architectural impressions are born." Nearly as important as light is its complement, shadow. Of these Wright said: "Shadows have been the brushwork of the architect when he modeled his architectural forms."[3]

Two rules we can learn from these geniuses is give windows unusual shapes and don't be afraid to put them in unusual places. Another rule is that the higher a window, the more light it throws deeply into the room. I followed all

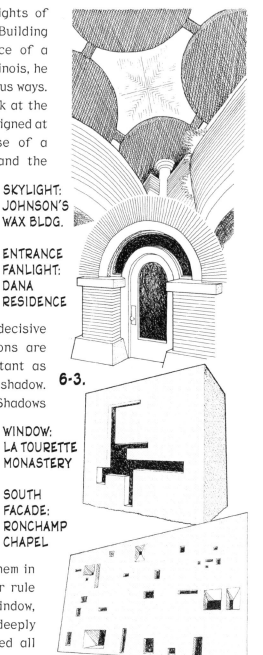

SKYLIGHT:
JOHNSON'S
WAX BLDG.

ENTRANCE
FANLIGHT:
DANA
RESIDENCE

6-3.

WINDOW:
LA TOURETTE
MONASTERY

SOUTH
FACADE:
RONCHAMP
CHAPEL

FIXED PANE ⟶|⟵ OPENABLE PANE

6-4. Maximum light and minimum heat loss

these directives in my house I built in 1974 with several windows like the one you see above. This opening is wide at the top and narrow at the base so it throws more light more deeply into the room while less heat flows through the smaller area of glass, and the narrow low sill allows children and the family dog to look outside. This window was made of plexiglass twenty feet from where it was installed by a local carpenter (need I mention his name) who used an electric saw mounted with a plastic-cutting blade bought at the hardware store. If you would like to do this, you'll need a car, a driver's license, and about ten dollars. Or you can show these pages to a carpenter who likes to do interesting work. Also note that this window has no bulky expensive frame: a useless contrivance, promoted by sellers more than users. A frame usually does nothing for the wall nor the window. By omitting the frame, I kept some money in my pocket and created a more intimate relation between indoors and out. Any carpenter can make windows like this, as follows:

1. Nail pieces of $3/4 \times 2$ inch (actual, not nominal) wood against the stud framing around the inside of where the plexiglass will go.

2. Cut the plexiglass $1/4$ inch smaller than the opening all around.

3. Nail 1-inch (actual) exterior trim around the outside of the pane.

4. Install gypsum (or other) interior finish around the inside of the wall to the pane.

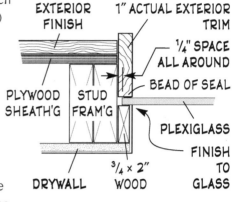

EXTERIOR FINISH
1" ACTUAL EXTERIOR TRIM
$1/4$" SPACE ALL AROUND
BEAD OF SEAL
PLYWOOD SHEATH'G
STUD FRAM'G
PLEXIGLASS
FINISH TO GLASS
$3/4 \times 2$" WOOD
DRYWALL

6-5. Framing elegant windows on the cheap

&

6-6. Making part of the above window openable (below)

Part of the window in figure 6-4 is openable, as appears in figure 6-6. The high-silled rectangular pane on the right in figure 6-4 is $1/2$-inch plexiglass, which is thick enough to insert screws into its edge. So I installed a piano hinge along the pane's top, added a sash lock and eye catch at the bottom, and hung a screen door latch on a chain from the ceiling inside. To open the

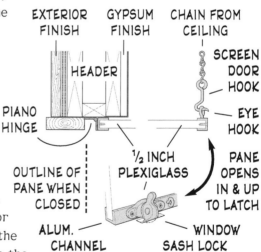

EXTERIOR FINISH
GYPSUM FINISH
CHAIN FROM CEILING
HEADER
SCREEN DOOR HOOK
PIANO HINGE
EYE HOOK
OUTLINE OF PANE WHEN CLOSED
$1/2$ INCH PLEXIGLASS
PANE OPENS IN & UP TO LATCH
ALUM. CHANNEL
WINDOW SASH LOCK

Lighting

window I undo the sash lock, lift the pane in and up, and fit the hook hanging from the ceiling into the eye at the base of the pane. This assembly appears in figure 6-6. Plexiglass won't condense on the inside during cold weather the way vitreous glass does. But don't use plexiglass for skylights, because its rate of thermal expansion will cause the pane to leak around its edges.

The long ribbon windows in my house are also simply framed, as figure 6-7 shows. This barebones construction allows a 161-foot ribbon of glass to wrap around three sides of the house and makes you feel like you're in the woods outside when you're indoors. Figure 3-26 on page 98 shows what part of this window looks like from inside. Ribbon windows enable daylight to enter more evenly and deeply into the rooms behind.

6-7. Framing ribbon windows

Another place to mount windows is in interior walls. Then the light on each side enters the other side in both rooms to give you four times the light for the price of one hole. This would work well above interior doors by replacing the wall over the header with a glassy transom. And while you're at it, replace the solid door below with a fancy French door with a translucent pane. A few other methods of letting light through walls are glass blocks, translucent glass showerstalls, liquor bottle windows (like the ones on page 119: I also mounted few of these near the tops of the interior masonry walls in my house), interior stud walls filled with batt insulation with the foil face removed (a small amount of light will pass through this) and sheathed with translucent plexiglass on both sides, and even light-emitting concrete (take a peek at www.litracon).

Two more ways to coax daylight deeply into buildings are the *sawtooth roof* and the *light well*, as sketched in figure 6-8. These

233

SAWTOOTH ROOF

LIGHT WELLS

6-8 work well where temperatures are equable year-round as in Hawaii and on the California coast. But in hot or cold regions a lot of heat will flow through these openings; then it would make more sense to replace each large area of glass and the construction around it with a simple roof containing thick insulation and a light fixture just inside. The energy to light the bulb would be less than what would otherwise escape through the glass.

Another de"light"ful daylight deliverer is the Sunpipe®, a domed tube with mirrorlike walls that can send light as deeply as three floors below.[4] Each unit is installed much like a stovepipe, diameters are 10 to 21 inches, and 45 degree elbows allow one or two bends. This is not so much a long thin skylight as a short thick fiber optic cable. To learn more about this lighting see www.sunpipe.com.

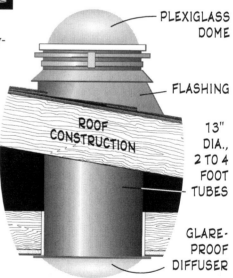

PLEXIGLASS DOME

FLASHING

ROOF CONSTRUCTION

13" DIA., 2 TO 4 FOOT TUBES

GLARE-PROOF DIFFUSER

6-9. The Sunpipe®

Lighting

Speaking of fiber optics, another clever daylighter is the Parans FO Suntracker. This contains 64 fiber optic cables whose upper ends connect to roof-mounted fresnel lenses that track the sun through the day and whose lower ends deliver light through a ceiling fixture below.[5] You might want to check this item's price before buying one, but seeing the company's video of its operation is better than paying twelve bucks to see a movie. Step under the marquee at www.huvco.com.

An exciting use of daylighting is to mount behind a window or skylight a motorized shade activated by a photocell which maintains a desired lighting level behind the glass no matter how sunny or cloudy the sky is outside. One company makes such a shade that can be up to 20 feet wide and 225 square feet in area. It can also be screened to limit the sun shining through it, can be installed inside or outside new or old windows, is easily programmable, and offers precise operation with electronic keypads. Known as the Sivoia QED (for quiet electronic drive), it is sold by Lutron Electronics (www.lutron.com/shadingsolutions). This company has been cleverly manipulating light like this for decades.

Speaking of decades, another fine example of programmed daylighting, dating back to 1962, is the 125-foot-tall aluminum louvers on the south facade of the Hall of Records in Los Angeles. As the hot southern California sun moves across the sky, computerized photocells (in 1962!) rotate these huge fins on their vertical axes to block the sun's glare and reduce heat transmission through the glass. By always remaining at least slightly open they allow a soft ambient light to enter interior spaces, which reduces eye fatigue caused by intense contrasts of light and dark. The louvers have a reflective silver coating and are hollow inside, so the heat they absorb convects upward, away from the glazing. The system's designer, the distinguished architect Richard Neutra, said, "All technical things are auxiliary to human well-being and an aid to vitality." Well said for any age.[6]

Artificial Lighting

An artificial light is a glass bulb that contains a filament or has a phosphor coating on the glass's inner surface. When electricity passes through the filament or excites the phosphor, the bulb glows brightly. Phosphor-activated bulbs require a ballast, a small transformer that creates the high voltage needed to excite the phosphor and maintains even voltage afterward. But some ballasts hum, some take a few seconds to excite the phosphor, they don't dim well, and they introduce harmonic distortion in the wiring.

A bulb's brightness is measured by its wattage. A Christmas tree light may be five watts while a large floodlight may be a thousand. But two kinds of bulbs of the same brightness can have different wattages. An 85-watt fluorescent bulb is as bright as a 300-watt incandescent bulb, and a 35-watt low-pressure sodium bulb is as bright as both. In any bulb much of the wattage that enters the bulb is emitted as heat and only a portion leaves as light, and even part of the light is absorbed by the fixture the bulb is mounted in. This energy distribution is sketched below. A bulb's heat and fixture losses often determine which illumination is best for a given task.

Two more lighting criteria are *rated life* (how long a bulb will burn) and *depreciation* (how well a bulb maintains its brightness

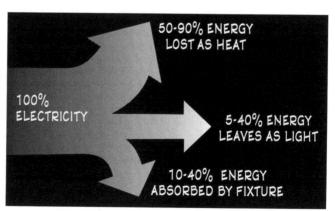

6-10. Energy distribution in a light bulb

100% ELECTRICITY

50-90% ENERGY LOST AS HEAT

5-40% ENERGY LEAVES AS LIGHT

10-40% ENERGY ABSORBED BY FIXTURE

during its life). Some bulbs lose nearly half their brightness as they age, and it often costs less to replace them when their light dims to a prescribed percentage of their initial output.

Another variable is *dimmability*. One bulb may be dimmable to zero percent of full brightness, another to only 20 percent, and another not at all. When a light is dimmed to 50 percent it still consumes about 70 percent of the energy at full brightness, so dimming doesn't save as much energy as you may think.

Also important is a bulb's *CRI* (color rendering index): its ability to render colors accurately. Incandescent and quartz bulbs render all colors quite well, metal halide bulbs render greens and blues well, and low-pressure sodium bulbs render only yellow. Color rendering hardly matters for highway lighting, but it means everything if you're displaying clothes in a storewindow or matching a picture's colors at a printing press.

What all this adds up to is that every bulb has a certain personality, one endowed with certain attributes yet afflicted with certain debilities; and a designer's task is to find the one right light from many choices that is best for the space it will brighten. Common choices, and a few uncommon ones, are detailed below.

Incandescent (*I*). Known to engineers as *I* lights, this is the bulb that began it all. It may be *clear* (the brightest), *frosted* (these emit slightly diffuse light), or *white* (these emit highly diffuse light). One line of "IQ" bulbs has energy-saving microchips in their bases that enable the lights to turn off after 30 minutes (good for closets, storerooms, and bathrooms), turn off after 6 hours (allows a home to look occupied during evenings), and dim from 60 to 5 watts over 10 minutes (good for hallway night lighting). A few characteristics of incandescent bulbs are:

Ballast .... no   *Wattage* ... 5 to 1,000
Rated life ...... 750 to 1,500 hours
Depreciation ... less than 5 percent before burn-out
Dimmability .... to 0 percent of full brightness
CRI .... renders all colors well

➕ Available in many types and sizes, easy to install, starts instantly, requires no ballasts, operates in any temperature and humidity. Lowest initial cost, which allows easy stockpiling and easy replacement of burnouts.

➖ High operating cost, high heat loss, short life.

Fluorescent (F). These long thin bulbs are made as tubes, circles, U-s, and corkscrew-shaped *CFLs*. All provide excellent short-distance illumination. Different coatings inside the bulbs enable them to render certain colors well, as follows:

Warm white	enhances reds and yellows
Cool white	enhances greens and blues
Daylight	simulates overcast sky
Triphosphor	renders all colors fairly well
Black	used in bug zappers
Blacklight-blue	violet decorative light
Grow lamp, tanning lamp	emits ultraviolet rays

In these bulbs each on-off cycle slightly erodes the electrodes in the ends of the tubes and consumes an amount of energy equal to about 15 minutes run time, so *F* bulbs are a poor choice for short lighting periods. They are usually installed in stores and offices where they burn all day. Never use these bulbs to illuminate rotating machinery, as they can create a strobe effect that can make rapidly rotating machinery look as if it isn't moving.

Ballast	yes
Wattage	4 to 120
Rated life	about 10,000 hours
Depreciation	20 to 35 percent during rated life
Dimmability	dimming requires ballasts, is poor below 20 percent, and shortens bulb life
CRI	renders most colors generally well

➕ A soft, low, shadowless light. Many bulb types can be fitted into a single fixture, allowing spaces with different lighting requirements to have one standard fixture for

different bulbs. The most economical short-distance illumination for long periods. Low heat allows bulbs to be
touched and located near flammable materials.

- Fluorescent bulbs contain mercury, which raises safety
  issues and creates disposal problems. Some may take a
  few seconds to start and/or reach full brightness, and
  all but *CFLs* require large obtrusive fixtures. Most burn
  less efficiently above 100° F and below 60° F, making them
  unsuitable in unheated garages in cold regions and for
  most outdoor lighting. In multi-bulb fixtures, if one light
  or ballast fails, all other components degenerate.

Light-Emitting Diode (*LED*).[7] No longer are these lights limited to off-on indicators on photocopiers and computers. They
have escaped the bounds of fringe technology and now appear in
buildings as security lights, emergency exit lights, and museum
exhibit lighting. A few thousand have been mounted in a 25-foot-
long nightclub marquee, and 18 million have been fashioned into
an eight-story billboard in Times Square. These lights cost a lot,
but their operation saves a lot of money. Consider this installation in a parking area for a shopping plaza in New Hampshire: 28
400-watt metal halide and high-pressure sodium lights were
replaced with 25 two-level (217 and 78 watt) LEDs equipped with
motion sensors that turn on the lower-wattage lights when the lot
is little-used such as late at night. This retrofit cost $45,000, but
electrical consumption was reduced 62 percent.[8] The projected
return on investment for the project was originally four years,
but rising energy costs and unexpected maintenance savings
reduced the projection to less than three years.

Ballast .... no   *Wattage* ... 1.2 to 224
Rated life ...... 40,000 to 50,000 hours
Depreciation ... loses 35 to 50 percent at 50,000 hours
Dimmability .... to 20 percent of full brightness
CRI .... renders all colors medium well

Architecture Laid Bare!

A controversy exists regarding the comparative economies of incandescent (*I*) lights, *CFL*s, and lately *LED*s. Let's first compare *I* lights versus *CFL*s. *I* lights emit only about 9 percent of their wattage as light and the rest as heat, while *CFL*s emit about 34 percent; so *CFL*s burn almost four times more efficiently than incandescents. A 60-watt *I* light also burns for about 1,000 hours while a 14-watt *CFL* (about as bright as a 60-watt *I* light) burns for about 10,000 hours; so a continuously burning *CFL* will last about as long as ten *I* lights burning one after the other. Thus if a 60-watt *I* light costs 80 cents each while a 14-watt *CFL* costs $4.99 each (local hardware store prices), and the utility charges 12 cents per kilowatt-hour, the life-cycle cost of each light is:

BULB	INITIAL COST	OPERATING COST		LIFE-CYCLE COST
I light	0.80 × 10 +	10,000 × 0.12 × 60/1000	=	$80.00
CFL	4.99 × 1 +	10,000 × 0.12 × 14/1000	=	$21.79

No contest, wouldn't you say?

But wait. That 91 percent of an *I* light's wattage that is emitted as heat ... where does it go? If it is cold outside, that heat will *not* be lost, because it will reduce by an equal amount the heat needed to warm the room the light is in. Therefore, if the temperature outdoors is less than 65 degrees —as it is in the evening during most of the year in most places in the United States when people at home turn on the lights— *the heat emitted by incandescent bulbs is useful heat*. But this varies greatly. In northern Montana, evening temperatures rarely remain above 65 degrees all year round, while in southern Florida they rarely fall below 65 degrees all year round. Considering this alone, one might say *I* lights are economical in Montana and uneconomical in Florida.

Also as mentioned earlier, when a fluorescent light is turned on its electrodes erode slightly and the bulb consumes an amount of energy equal to about 15 minutes' burn time. So if a *CFL* is turned on and off frequently it will last much less than 10,000 hours, and if it burns for only short periods (as when you go to the bathroom at night) it may use more energy than an *I* light. *I* lights

Lighting

don't have these problems. Furthermore,

1. When some *CFL*s are turned on, they emit an ashy glow for a few minutes that is unpleasant to read by.
2. *CFL*s aren't fully dimmable, and dimming shortens bulb life.
3. *CFL*s grow weaker as they age; after 10,000 hours they typically are only 60 percent as bright as when new. *I* lights remain nearly as bright as new until they burn out.
4. *CFL*s often break before they burn out; and what good is a bulb that could last ten years if some kid breaks it in two?
5. When a *CFL* breaks it creates a dangerous disposal problem. This doesn't occur with *I* lights.
6. *CFL*s don't work as well as *I* lights in cold weather.

These debits of *CFL*s were succinctly summarized by a local contractor who recently said to a friend of mine: "Everyone in America knows incandescents are better than *CFL*s except consumers." These shadowy details were also brought to light in a front-page article in the May 29, 2009, *New York Times* titled "The Bulb that Saved the Planet May Be Less than Billed". *CFL*s are usually a better choice when installed in hard-to-reach areas, in warm regions, where electrical rates are high, and where they remain on for long periods; but incandescents are usually better where it is cold much of the year, where they could be easily broken, and where lights are on briefly (another example being occupancy-sensor-activated floodlights overlooking a turnaround that turn on when a car enters the turnaround and turn off when the car leaves). These plusses are why many people legitimately prefer the old lumen lemon —and why it is a crime for governments to pass laws outlawing them. Beyond this, one cannot state one blanket conclusion for every use of these bulbs everywhere.

You may have noted that all the above examples are for residences. What about businesses? Here many of the criteria favorable to incandescents are reversed. Businesses usually operate during the day when temperatures are higher than the daily average, their lights are often turned on and off once a day and

Architecture Laid Bare!

remain on for hours, and they are typically installed in ceilings where they aren't easily broken. These pluses make fluorescent bulbs more cost-effective than *I* lights in most commercial occupancies, and is why they are common there.

To many, an obvious debit of *CFLs* is that they contain mercury. But even this may be the opposite of what most of the public may believe; because the EPA recently stated that where electricity is generated by coal-fired utilities, since coal contains mercury and *I* lights burn much less efficiently than *CFLs*, *I* lights actually cause more mercury to be released into the environment per kilowatt consumed than CFLs. Plus, the mercury released by *I* lights ends up in the atmosphere instead of landfills. This is the kind of dilemma that plagues serious environmentalists day and night. Just when you think you've got an issue figured out, you learn something new that puts you back at square one!

Now let's compare *CFLs* with *LEDs*. *LEDs* are smaller, light up instantly to full brightness, consume less power per watt, generate less heat, can turn on and off frequently without shortening their lives, are fully dimmable, and have no ballasts. But *LEDs* cost considerably more, their rated life is halved with every 10° Centigrade increase above room temperature (they usually work best in cool temperatures), and they may not fit into a fixture you buy them for. I learned this last fact the hard way: when I recently bought one for my drafting lamp, I couldn't screw the bulb in because its wide base wouldn't fit into the lamp's conical reflector. I tried screwing the bulb into my bedside lamp, but the bulb was so low that I couldn't refit the shade because its bottom hit the lamp's base. If you consider buying an *LED* light, first, if you can, test one in the fixture you plan to use it in.

So you can make the wisest decisions with these three bulbs, figure 6-11 compares their properties. Some of you will find one bulb to be best for a certain situation while others will find another —and everyone of you should be able to buy all three.

No matter which bulb you use, three ways to economize their use anytime anywhere are:

242

Lighting

	INCANDESCENT	CFL	LED
EQUIV. WATTS	60 watts	14 watts	10.5 watts
COST: SUPERMARKET HARDWARE STO. ELEC. SUPPLY	$1.50 0.80 0.50	$2.99 4.99 2.45	$30 (mail order)
BRIGHTNESS (LUMENS)	800 lm	625 lm after 3,000 hr	575 lm
RATED LIFE	≈ 1,000 hrs	≈ 10,000 hrs	≈ 45,000 hrs
DIMMING RANGE	full dimming	90-20%	full dimming
TIME TO REACH FULL BRIGHT- NESS	instant	30 seconds to 3 minutes	instant
BRIGHTNESS DIMS WITH AGE?	dims slightly with age	dims to 40% with age	dims to 70% with age
COLOR RENDERING	near 100	77-85	80-90
BULB TEMPERATURE	burns if touched	warm to the touch	cool to the touch
TEMPERATURE PERFORMANCE	unaffected by cold	reaches full bright slower & ages faster in cold	ages faster in warm temperatures
EST. ENERGY COST, $ PER 50,000 HRS OF OPERATION	$400	$109	$93

6-11. A comparison of incandescent, CFL, and *LED* bulbs

☞ Locate the bulb closer to the area it illuminates.

☞ Turn fewer of them on.

☞ Leave them on for a shorter time.

Architecture Laid Bare!

The next few lights to be discussed are more common in commercial buildings and outdoor installations.

Quartz (*Q*). Also *tungsten* or *halogen* bulbs, these have the highest *CRI* of any bulb which makes them the top choice for exhibiting objects in museums, displaying merchandise in storewindows, matching fabrics, comparing paint colors, and proofreading fine print. Since these bulbs burn hot, tend to explode when they break, and emit UV light (they can sunburn people with sensitive skin who remain near them), they are usually ceiling-mounted in cowled and ventilated reflectors with UV-inhibiting facings that project well below the ceiling yet above the reach of occupants. Some bulbs operate on 12 or 24 volts, which requires a small transformer but these wires won't shock someone even when wet, which makes them safe for landscape lighting. If you touch a quartz bulb when it is cold (as when you fit it into a socket), clean it with isopropyl alcohol afterward, or your skin's oils will damage the bulb when it is hot, and your fingerprints may be hugely magnified on a surface illuminated by the light.

> *Ballast* .... no   *Wattage* ... 20 to 2,000
> *Rated life* ...... 1,500 to 2,500 hours
> *Depreciation* ... less than 5 percent before burn-out
> *Dimmability* .... to 0 percent of full brightness
> *CRI* .... renders all colors very well

➕ Smaller, more efficient, and longer-lasting than *I* bulbs of equal wattage. Output depreciates little during rated life.

➖ UV radiation is undesirable for illuminating paintings and textiles. Voltage variations (i.e. brownouts) can degrade performance and shorten life.

High-density discharge (*HID*). These bulbs are efficient and long-lasting. However, most when turned on take 3 to 5 minutes to reach full output, and if power is interrupted the bulb must cool 5 to 10 minutes before it can restart; so they are generally used

244

where they will burn for several hours. They are installed in high ceilings in warehouses, superstores, and the like. Outdoors they are located above streets, parking, and recreation areas. Since they burn hot and their pressurized bulbs typically explode with hot glass particles if they break or contact any liquid, they are enclosed in metal fixtures with protruding mounts. All these bulbs contain mercury and other toxins. There are four kinds:

Mercury Vapor (MV): These emit a blue-green light, which makes them ideal for night-lighting foliage and weathered copper exteriors; but they'll make those porterhouse steaks at the supermarket look like spoiled meat. Since they emit ultraviolet light, they require UV-inhibiting lenses where people will be near them; and in gymnasiums they are shielded with metal cages.

Ballast . . . . yes	*Wattage* . . . 50 to 1,000
Rated life . . . . . . 14,000 to 24,000 hours	
Depreciation . . typically 50 percent at end of life	
Dimmability . . . to 50 percent of full brightness; dimming creates color shifts in the light	
CRI . . . . renders greens and blues well, reds poorly	

Metal Halide (MH): These are smaller and produce better-quality light than *MV* bulbs. They offer the best combined efficiency, color rendering ability, and long life of all lights and so are used for long-burning general commercial illumination. They should have UV-blocking lenses where people are nearby, and as they age their color shifts toward blue, which is a relamping indicator.

Ballast . . . . yes	*Wattage* . . . 175 to 1,500
Rated life . . . . . . 7,500 to 20,000 hours	
Depreciation . . . loses up to 40 percent at end of life	
Dimmability . . . . to 50 percent of full brightness	
CRI . . . . renders greens and violets well, reds and oranges poorly	

Architecture Laid Bare!

Low-pressure sodium (LPS or SOX): This is the most efficient
of all bulbs, but its drab yellow light makes all other colors look dull. However, the light is more of a soft glow
which produces less glare and creates sharp images on
surveillance TV monitors. It is used for roadways, tun-
nels, security areas, and other places where economy is
more important than color clarity. This light also penetrates fog well and promotes plant growth indoors, so it
is used in vehicular headlights and greenhouses. When
the lamp turns off it rapidly returns to full brightness.

Ballast .... yes   *Wattage* ... 10 to 180
Rated life ...... up to 18,000 hours
Depreciation ... brightness does not decline with age
Dimmability .... to 50 percent of full brightness
CRI .... renders only yellow, and all other
                    colors look like shades of yellow

High-pressure sodium (HPS): These bulbs are smaller than *LPS*
lights and most don't last as long, but they render colors
reasonably well and their light depreciates little with
age. They are installed in streetlights, parking garages,
security areas, and other places requiring steady high-
output lighting where color rendering is unimportant.

Ballast .... yes   *Wattage* ... 35 to 1,000
Rated life ...... 10,000 to 24,000 hours
Depreciation ... less than 20 percent at end of life
Dimmability .... poor precise dimming
CRI .... renders oranges, yellows, and greens
                    a little above average, violets poorly

➕ High outputs, high efficiencies, long lives. They are little
affected by large temperature changes, so they are a
good outdoor lighting.

➖ Some have lengthy warmup and restrike times. No good
near flammable materials.

246

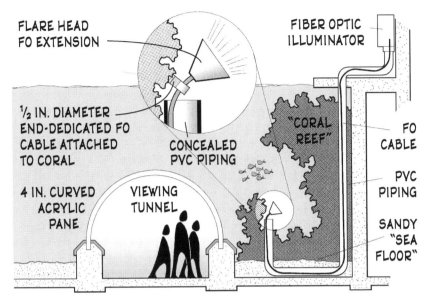

FLARE HEAD
FO EXTENSION

FIBER OPTIC
ILLUMINATOR

½ IN. DIAMETER
END-DEDICATED FO
CABLE ATTACHED
TO CORAL

CONCEALED
PVC PIPING

"CORAL
REEF"

FO
CABLE

4 IN. CURVED
ACRYLIC
PANE

VIEWING
TUNNEL

PVC
PIPING

SANDY
"SEA
FLOOR"

6-12. Clever use of fiber optic cable

Fiber optic (*FO*). Imagine a tube whose inside is so mirror-like that a light aimed into one end is barely diminished as it emerges from the other. This is the rudimentary "fiber optic". The tube is about as thick as fishing line, it can be up to 70 feet long, and many can be bundled to provide a fairly strong light if the bends are slight. Some *FO* cables are clad in reinforcing and insulation that make them more resistant to crushing and damage by heat. There are two kinds:

End-dedicated FO cable: This sends light into one end of the cable and out the other. It is installed where it is difficult or dangerous to install electrical wiring, in corrosive environments, where static is a problem, where light is desired but UV radiation is not (i.e. museum exhibit cases), and where danger of electric shock exists from water or moisture (as in fountains, aquariums, swimming pools, and medical applications). A clever use of this lighting appears in figure 6-12.

247

Architecture Laid Bare!

Side-dedicated FO cable: This sends light into a cable with translucent walls that transmit the light which makes the cable glow. It is used in chandeliers, signs, artwork, scientific applications, luminous railings and ceiling-mounted directional guides in theaters and nightclubs, and even in light-transmitting concrete.

You won't find fiber optic cable at the local hardware store. It requires specialists to design and install (you may find a few in the phone book or on the internet), and it is costly.

Neon. This is a gas-filled glass tube that emits a cool but dazzling light whose voltage is regulated by a small transformer. The tubes may be any shape, many colors are available, and reflectors can be mounted along the tubes to direct the light. The lights are designed as follows: an architect draws the desired layout and selects the colors; then a fabricator selects the components, bends the glass in a shop, and assembles the fixture on-site. These lights often appear in restaurants and retail stores, but are unsuited for general illumination due to their low intensities and dangerously high voltages. This illumination is often

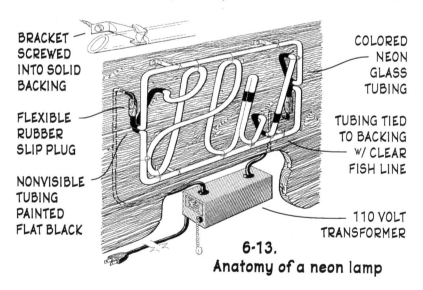

BRACKET SCREWED INTO SOLID BACKING

COLORED NEON GLASS TUBING

FLEXIBLE RUBBER SLIP PLUG

TUBING TIED TO BACKING W/ CLEAR FISH LINE

NONVISIBLE TUBING PAINTED FLAT BLACK

110 VOLT TRANSFORMER

6-13.
Anatomy of a neon lamp

Lighting

combined with flashers, fading, and animation devices to create exciting effects. Some building codes do not allow neon lighting in residential areas because it may distract passing drivers.

Light Ribbon. Imagine a light that is only one-fiftieth an inch thick and up to 22 inches wide that can be bent like cardboard and tucked into a corner. Such a light exists. It is bright enough to read by, is dimmable to 3 percent of full brightness, consumes little power, generates no heat, comes in seven colors, and can be 1,500 feet long. A strip of this too-good-to-be-true illumination appears below. It can cover whole ceilings and walls as long as they are flat or single-curved surfaces. Known as *El Lightstrip*, it is made by RSA Lighting of Chatsworth, CA.

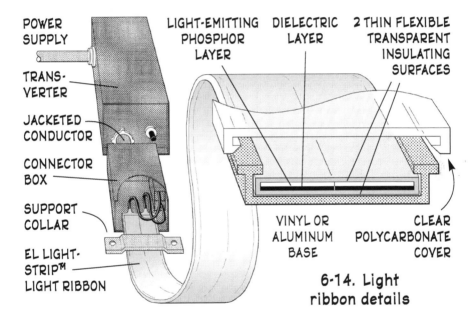

POWER SUPPLY

TRANS-VERTER

JACKETED CONDUCTOR

CONNECTOR BOX

SUPPORT COLLAR

EL LIGHT-STRIP™ LIGHT RIBBON

LIGHT-EMITTING PHOSPHOR LAYER

DIELECTRIC LAYER

2 THIN FLEXIBLE TRANSPARENT INSULATING SURFACES

VINYL OR ALUMINUM BASE

CLEAR POLYCARBONATE COVER

6-14. Light ribbon details

Sulphur Light. This is a hollow quartz sphere mounted on a long thin stem which together is about the size of a Tootsie-Pop. The light is extremely bright for its size: a 1,000-watt bulb generates 125,000 lumens, which is a little like storing a lightning bolt in a ping-pong ball. This light renders colors similarly as sunlight, it is efficient, it lasts up to 20,000 hours, its brightness doesn't diminish with age, and plants grow well under it. But before you run out and buy one of these beauties for your favorite reading lamp you might want to check the price. One vendor sells them for 2,300 bucks apiece. But he does offer "quality discounts for volume purchases". I bet. For a free look, try www.nlites.co.uk /sulphur-plasma.htm.

Modern technology has spawned several other unusual lights: the **Rope Light** (a flexible clear plastic tube containing tiny lights that blink and flash), **LiveWire Lighting** (a wirelike electroluminescent conductor that comes in ten colors), the **Honeycomb Light** (a hexagonally patterned "chickenwire light" whose weatherproof strands contain tiny linear lights), and the **Spark Light** (a string of pencil-tip-sized bulbs that produce shimmering and sparkling light). Even LEDs have gotten into this act with *LED* **strip lights**. All can create a carnival array of effects. Try googling these gems on the internet.

Luminaires

An essential part of any light bulb is the fixture or luminaire it is mounted in —what Mark Twain described as "plenty of daylight in a box."[9] Each has one or more sockets, a mount of some kind, and a cord to the power supply. Each may also have a protective enclosure, a reflector that directs the light,

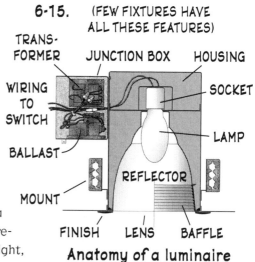

6-15. (FEW FIXTURES HAVE ALL THESE FEATURES)

TRANS-FORMER   JUNCTION BOX   HOUSING

WIRING TO SWITCH   SOCKET

BALLAST   LAMP

MOUNT   REFLECTOR

FINISH   LENS   BAFFLE

Anatomy of a luminaire

Lighting

and a protective lens. These components are assembled in a myriad ways to satisfy every lighting requirement or personal taste.

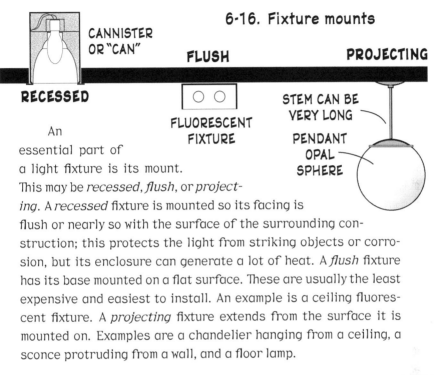

6-16. Fixture mounts

CANNISTER OR "CAN"

FLUSH

PROJECTING

RECESSED

FLUORESCENT FIXTURE

STEM CAN BE VERY LONG

PENDANT OPAL SPHERE

An essential part of a light fixture is its mount. This may be *recessed*, *flush*, or *projecting*. A *recessed* fixture is mounted so its facing is flush or nearly so with the surface of the surrounding construction; this protects the light from striking objects or corrosion, but its enclosure can generate a lot of heat. A *flush* fixture has its base mounted on a flat surface. These are usually the least expensive and easiest to install. An example is a ceiling fluorescent fixture. A *projecting* fixture extends from the surface it is mounted on. Examples are a chandelier hanging from a ceiling, a sconce protruding from a wall, and a floor lamp.

ELLIPSE	PARABOLA	HYPERBOLA	DIFFUSE
RAYS AIM INWARD	RAYS ARE PARALLEL	RAYS AIM OUTWARD	RAYS ARE RANDOM

6-17. Fixture reflectors

Another important part of a light fixture is the shape of its reflector. An *elliptical* reflector focuses the fixture's light inward. Surgeons use these because they aim lots of light onto the site of an operation. A *parabolic* reflector emits the light's rays in parallel or nearly so: useful for searchlights and spot-lights. A *hyperbolic* reflector spreads the rays outward: nice for lights that brighten large areas. A *diffuse* reflector sends the rays randomly over the illuminated scene. These usually work well for general illumination and tend to be inexpensive.

A luminaire may be a *point*, *line*, or *area* light source. A *point* source contains a single bulb that radiates light from one spot. Common is the incandescent bulb. A *line* light source contains a tube-like bulb that creates a long linear light. Familiar here is the fluorescent tube. An *area* light source has one or more bulbs mounted behind a prominent translucent facing that emits a diffuse light. Examples vary in size from EXIT signs to theater marquees.

Every light fixture has a *switch*. Behind this tiny lever may lurk an amazing array of controls. Chief of this tribe is the *dimmer*. Some are automated so when a cloud passes over the sun and reduces the light entering a window, the dimmer increases the artificial light by the same amount to maintain even illumination indoors. One dimmer can do this for dozens of luminaires. An automated dimmer should have a manual override, and its eye should have a clear view of the glazing through which the daylight enters. Such "illumistats" offer more efficient lighting, reduced energy use, less heat loss, lower cooling bills, longer bulb and ballast life, and lower maintenance costs —plus more desirable illumination and better working conditions.

Another useful "dimmer" is the occupancy sensor. Each of these little sentinels has an eye that notifies host controls down at computer headquarters to turn on the lights when someone enters an area and turn them off when the last person leaves, saving energy when the space is vacant. Each sensor is usually mounted near a room's entrance where it replaces the usual snap switch and has a manual override. They are also installed out-doors, where their usually adjustable coverage patterns may include service entrances, property fences, and driveways. They can activate interior and exterior lights, intrusion alarms, even a

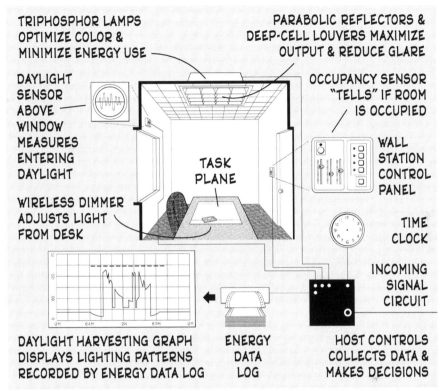

TRIPHOSPHOR LAMPS OPTIMIZE COLOR & MINIMIZE ENERGY USE

PARABOLIC REFLECTORS & DEEP-CELL LOUVERS MAXIMIZE OUTPUT & REDUCE GLARE

DAYLIGHT SENSOR ABOVE WINDOW MEASURES ENTERING DAYLIGHT

OCCUPANCY SENSOR "TELLS" IF ROOM IS OCCUPIED

TASK PLANE

WALL STATION CONTROL PANEL

WIRELESS DIMMER ADJUSTS LIGHT FROM DESK

TIME CLOCK

INCOMING SIGNAL CIRCUIT

DAYLIGHT HARVESTING GRAPH DISPLAYS LIGHTING PATTERNS RECORDED BY ENERGY DATA LOG

ENERGY DATA LOG

HOST CONTROLS COLLECTS DATA & MAKES DECISIONS

6-18. A dazzling array of automated lighting controls

bedside notifier beside a sleeping occupant; and they can be operated offsite by cellphones that allow an arriving homeowner to activate everything from opening the garage door to turning on the light inside the front door before leaving the car. In commercial spaces they may be programmed for almost any activity. Examples:

☞ An auditorium requires lighting controls for entry, slide projection, speaker, and intermissions with each scene activated by controls at entrances, in the projection booth, and via wireless transmission at the podium.

☞ A church requires lighting controls for regular daytime,

regular evening, solemn daytime holiday, solemn evening holiday, joyous daytime holiday, joyous evening holiday, wedding, and funeral services; with each scene having activators at the pulpit, organ, choir, vestibule, and usher's station.

☞ The landscape lighting for a corporate office needs to be turned on at sunset, dimmed at 11 P.M., and turned off at dawn, and should include scenarios for daylight savings time, leap years, and Christmas lighting.

One company that has done this work for decades is Lutron (www .lutron.com). They offer a dazzling array of switching, dimming, and shading controls that can combine with audiovisual aids, stage, security, and building management systems for offices, convention centers, hotels, campuses, stadiums, even yachts.

An occupancy sensor could also be connected to the illuminated area's heating and cooling systems, and turn these energy consumers off when the room is vacated.

Indoor Lighting

Each part of a room that contains a light (including windows and skylights) is a "larger light fixture" whose construction may be shaped and sur-faced to direct its light most advanta-geously to the area it illuminates. These con-structions are known as *lighting environ-ments*. Each can make a space look larger and be smaller at the same time, which reduces the cost to construct it

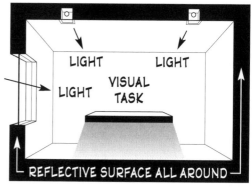

6-19. The "larger light fixture"

Lighting

and keep it comfortable, and each often conceals the light so it won't shine in your eyes. Common lighting environments appear below. They can be combined in an infinity of imaginative ways.

Canopies and Soffits. These are overhangs whose undersides contain bulbs that brighten the area below. They provide excellent downlighting for counters, desks, vanities, workplaces, walls, niches, and other small areas. Fluorescents and LEDs often work well here due to their small size and low heat output.

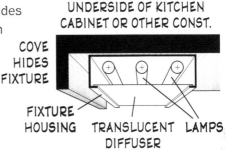

6-20. Soffit lighting

Ceiling Systems. In this lighting, areas of ceiling-mounted fixtures have just below them either sheets of milky plexiglass that widely diffuse the light or patterns of tiny eggcratelike openings (also known as *polycube louvers*) that throw the light straight down into the spaces below. The louvers can be white, clear, silver, even black. This lighting is common in commercial offices. The illuminated areas tend to look dimmer around their edges, which is countered by mounting the outer two rows of fixtures closer together. Enclosing walls should be lightly colored.

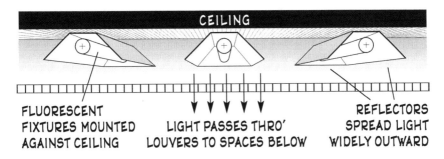

6-21. Uniform ceiling illumination

Coffers. These are usually ceiling recesses in which the lights are mounted on any inner surface. They are usually rectangular but can be any shape, their sides usually incline in toward the top, all inner surfaces are reflective, and shallow coves around their bases help hide the lights. This construction often mimics a skylight.

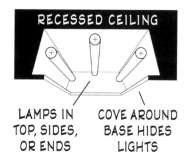

RECESSED CEILING

LAMPS IN TOP, SIDES, OR ENDS

COVE AROUND BASE HIDES LIGHTS

6-22. Coffer lighting

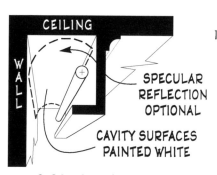

CEILING

WALL

SPECULAR REFLECTION OPTIONAL

CAVITY SURFACES PAINTED WHITE

6-23. Cornice lighting

Cornices. A cornice is a row of lights mounted behind a vertical projection near the seam of a wall and ceiling or roof eave where the lights unobtrusively brighten the wall and areas below. This recessed border lighting is usually horizontal, but can be vertical, inclined, and curved as well as straight.

Coves. A cove is much like a cornice except the projection near the meeting of wall and ceiling is horizontal and the concealed lights brighten the ceiling which makes it look larger. This recessed border lighting may be linear, circular, or elliptical. It works well with a slightly domed ceiling — perhaps one painted sky blue, with a few clouds painted on it and a chevron of geese flying south.

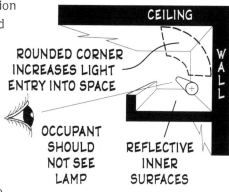

CEILING

ROUNDED CORNER INCREASES LIGHT ENTRY INTO SPACE

WALL

OCCUPANT SHOULD NOT SEE LAMP

REFLECTIVE INNER SURFACES

6-24. Cove lighting

Lighting

Fixed Luminaires. The generic "light fixture," these are usually mounted on a wall or ceiling. They can have almost any kind of mount and reflector, and are often operated by a wall switch or occupancy sensor. Examples are as varied as porcelain sockets, chandeliers, cannister lights, and exit lights.

Portable Luminaires. This easily moved fixture typically has a base that sets on a flat surface, a translucent shade that reduces side glare, and a cord plugged into a nearby outlet that may be operated by a switch on the fixture or on a nearby wall. The base may be tall, as in a floor lamp, and the shade is often a focal point in itself, an elegant example being the Tiffany lamp.

Floods and Spots. Also known as *PAR lamps*, these include incandescent, quartz, and metal halide bulbs whose reflectors concentrate their rays into conical beams of strong light that vary from about 3 to 130 degrees. Floods have the wider beams and spots the smaller. Each has a beam-spread designation such as PAR 55 ◄ 60°, which is a 55-watt flood whose beam is 60 degrees wide. These lights can have elliptical beamspreads, one being an MH 500 ◄ 10 × 26° lamp (a 500-watt metal halide lamp whose elliptical beam is 10 degrees wide in one axis and 26 degrees in the other). If you have been at a concert and seen a long thin shaft of light shining from the back of the audience onto the performer onstage, that light is a *collimated pencil beam spot*. These are also used as searchlights.

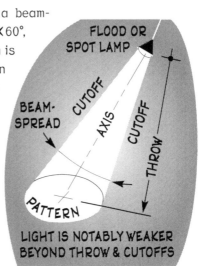

6-26. Floods & spots

Architecture Laid Bare!

Floodlights can be fitted with blinders that can make their beams fit almost any shape, such as the frame of a painting or edge of sculpture in a museum. Floods and spots are usually 100 percent dimmable and this is often an important part of one's design.

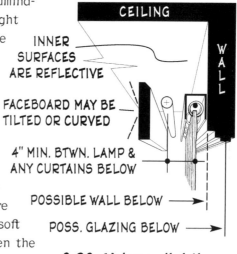

Sconces. A sconce is a wall-mounted light with a translucent or opaque shade that redirects the light against the surface behind the bulb to create a gentle light in the spaces nearby. The cleverest sconce I ever saw was in a 19th-century pony express depot renovated into a night club near Parker, Arizona. The broken handles of several old prospector's spades were embedded in the adobe wall below the fixtures. Aside from romanticizing the old west, this soft light cast a radiant glow on the nearby seating and aisles.

6-27

Valances. In this illumination a wall-mounted light source (usually one or more fluorescent tubes) is concealed by a faceboard that sends a soft light onto the ceiling above and the wall below. The faceboard may be tilted, curved, translucent, or opaque. Valences work well above large mirrors in bathrooms, where they bathe the ceiling with soft reflective light and brighten the mirror and vanity below.

CEILING

INNER SURFACES ARE REFLECTIVE

FACEBOARD MAY BE TILTED OR CURVED

W A L L

4" MIN. BTWN. LAMP & ANY CURTAINS BELOW

POSSIBLE WALL BELOW →

POSS. GLAZING BELOW →

6-28. Valence lighting

Lighting

Grazing and Washing. With this illumination one or more lights aim at a small angle across a flat rough surface such as stone, brick, tile, or drapery to reveal its texture. With *glazing* the lights' angle of incidence is so low (usually one to five degrees) that it turns a rough surface into an area of pebbly shadows or slightly recessed mortar joints into patterns of sharp lines. With *washing* the lights' angle of incidence is a little greater (usually 10 to 20 degrees) which smooths rough surfaces and produces a soft glow. Both illuminations add a sense of space to a surface's flatness and make it look larger. This lighting generally enhances the nature of walls, but it can be used to liven horizontal areas. As a sample, in a night club horizontal grazing can brighten a dance floor and highlight the dancers' feet. A related wall washing on long facades is *scalloping.* This is created by aiming several uniformly spaced uplights or downlights at low angles across the height of the wall.

You can see what grazing and washing look like by doing the following. At night go into your bathroom with

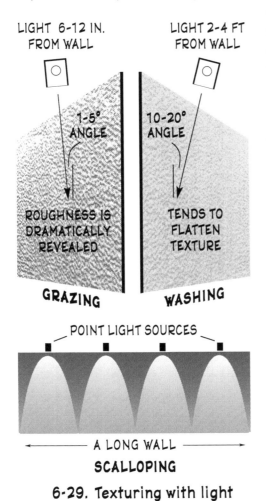

LIGHT 6-12 IN. FROM WALL

1-5° ANGLE

ROUGHNESS IS DRAMATICALLY REVEALED

GRAZING

LIGHT 2-4 FT FROM WALL

10-20° ANGLE

TENDS TO FLATTEN TEXTURE

WASHING

POINT LIGHT SOURCES

A LONG WALL

SCALLOPING

6-29. Texturing with light

a flashlight, step into the tub, hold the light close to the wall above the tub, and aim it across the tiles. If you hold the light close to the wall, this is glazing: the light shining across the tiles will reveal the slightest irregularity (it could make it look like a poor-quality job). If you hold the light a few inches farther from the wall, this is washing: it will make the wall look flat and neatly tiled. With this experiment you will also see that precise aim of the light is important.

Emergency Lighting. In commercial buildings this illumination is installed near exit doors, stairway entries, floor level changes, major corridor intersections, and abrupt changes in direction. Each fixture should be operable by a battery or generator that activates within 10 seconds after an electric power failure and maintains required brightness for at least 90 minutes. A common exit light today is the *LED* display EXIT sign. Less common is the *corner guard light*, a thin lamp mounted on the outer corner of a hallway just above the floor; when activated by a nearby smoke alarm this lamp emits a strong strobe light that penetrates smoke better than normal lighting. Exit lights can be connected to computer programs that periodically test them, log their operation, and record their maintenance.

One kind of emergency lighting consumes no energy, has no bulbs, is nontoxic, and requires no computerized controls. This is *luminous escape route trim*: a photoluminescent tape that glows in the dark. Sold as Luminous Tape WT-022 by Ningbo Teagol Packing Tools Co. (pay them a visit at www.packing-bag.com or www.teagol tools.com), the tape is sold as adhesive-backed sheets that can be cut into arrows, strips, signs, and other shapes then applied to floors, wall bases, tread nosings, stair rails, and door frames. If the lights are off, the tape glows enough to guide occupants through spaces that otherwise would be dark. But this appliqué can do much more. Imagine a sleepy resident going to the bathroom in the middle of the night in which the doorknob, doorframe, a row of floor tiles leading to the toilet, and the toilet

6-30. Luminous escape route trim

itself are decked out in a nocturnal bunting that could raise this normally anxious act to a festive occasion. Such guidance would be a delight to a child who needs to go to the potty at night, as well as a homeowner who wants to investigate a noise outside without turning on the lights. And it would be a boon to tenants and employees of nursing homes, hospitals, and retirement communities. Used these ways, luminous escape route trim is nothing less than a new interior landscape, one that could have as profound an effect on nocturnal living as did the candle ages ago.

Video Conferences. In this lighting environment a person appears before a camcorder mounted on a computer in which appears a small image of the subject so s/he can remain focused

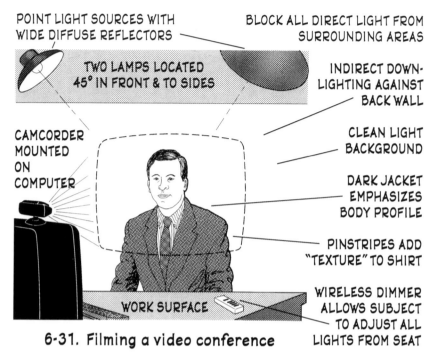

POINT LIGHT SOURCES WITH WIDE DIFFUSE REFLECTORS

BLOCK ALL DIRECT LIGHT FROM SURROUNDING AREAS

TWO LAMPS LOCATED 45° IN FRONT & TO SIDES

INDIRECT DOWN-LIGHTING AGAINST BACK WALL

CAMCORDER MOUNTED ON COMPUTER

CLEAN LIGHT BACKGROUND

DARK JACKET EMPHASIZES BODY PROFILE

PINSTRIPES ADD "TEXTURE" TO SHIRT

WORK SURFACE

WIRELESS DIMMER ALLOWS SUBJECT TO ADJUST ALL LIGHTS FROM SEAT

6-31. Filming a video conference

and framed during telecasting. This environment is best brightened by two ceiling-mounted downlights aimed about 45 degrees from the speaker's front and sides that highlight the face, sheen the hair, and profile the torso. The wall behind should be lightly colored and backlit enough to contrast the subject's profile. Any glare arriving from nearby windows should be blocked with a lightly colored fabric that diffuses the entering light. The subject should avoid wearing baggy clothes, glittery jewelry, tinted glasses, lots of white (this reflects too much light and makes the face look dark), and lots of black (this causes the face to be overexposed). If the subject is overweight, s/he should lean forward slightly to hide the gut and any rolls in the neck and make the body look smaller. Subjects should wear light makeup, even men, to soften glare and enhance skin tones.

Here are a few tips for illuminating indoor areas.

Lighting

Air, undesirable. Where air is humid, dusty, or polluted, fixtures should be enclosed and sealed.

Ceilings. Bulbs mounted in high ceilings must be brighter than lower bulbs to provide equal light in areas below. By mounting the fixtures on chains or pendants that lower the light closer to visual tasks, the bulbs' wattage can be lower, which saves energy. Attractive ceilings can be revealed by uplights with diffuse reflectors, while unattractive ceilings (such as open ceilings with exposed structure and ducting) can have every surface painted flat back and receive no uplighting.

Cleaning. Many spaces with low lighting such as restaurants, night clubs, and theaters should have 60 footcandles (fc) of floor-level illumination for articulate cleaning.

Control rooms. These should have ceiling lights with diffuse reflectors. The lights should be dimmable to 10 to 15 fc where dials are illuminated and 150 fc where they aren't.

Corridors. Illumination should be about 20 percent of that in the rooms the corridors serve. Spill light from transoms, French doors, and clerestories can reduce lighting loads in these narrow areas.

Elevators. Doors should receive 75 fc for safe entry, and interiors should receive 30 fc to reveal faces and signage.

Entrances. Lighting should be in front of the door at an angle that reveals faces and brightens the door.

Floor level changes. Each change in level should be illuminated both ways. Stairway lights should be in front of the lowest step but far enough back to reveal all treads and nosings, and landings should be clearly defined.

Lecturers and Speakers. Dominant lighting should arrive optimally about 45 degrees from the speaker's front and sides. Secondary lighting should not be overhead (this can give the speaker raccoon eyes) but should aim 35 to 45 degrees down from the front to highlight the face and hair and profile the upper torso. A narrow spot downlight should brighten the lectern top, and on the lectern should be controls for dimming audience lighting and activating projector lighting. Background surfaces should be light to contrast the speaker in front.

Maintenance. Bulbs should be easily changed, and fixtures should be easily cleaned. Avoid fixtures whose servicing requires catwalks or intrepid workers.

Paintings. Each typically requires one or two accurately aimed overhead spots of high intensity with adjustable shutters that enable the light's edges to align with the painting's frame. The light should be above the line of viewers' vision.

Public areas. In lobbies, halls, and foyers, lights should have wide beams that aim at signage. Highlight any parts of public areas seen through windows from outdoors.

Rest rooms. Mount long luminaires above mirrors to illuminate people's fronts. Above commercial toilets install line lights with their longest dimensions perpendicular to the partitions so they don't cast shadows on the seats.

Outdoor Lighting

When the sun sets, outdoor lighting rises to the fore. Here the radiating photons aren't enclosed by a big reflective container; hence the illuminated scene looks brighter while all around is black, which creates harsher contrasts. Since these can hurt one's eyes, outdoor light sources should be concealed behind shrubbery or low walls, tucked into cornices or under eaves, or mounted out of view on roofs. The best lights for such scenes are typically small floods with narrow well-aimed beams. All wiring should be sleeved in rustproof metal conduits and located underground or well away from vehicular and pedestrian routes. There are three general kinds of outdoor lighting:

Landmark lighting. This brightens facades, monuments, and other prominences, and is especially effective on light-colored surfaces with slight indents or projections that cast lines of shadow which model their forms. Precise angles between the viewed scene, observers, and lights are important, and they usually require onsite adjusting to maximize their effect. The lights should be concealed, to minimize glare and lend mystery to the effect. A few small lights are often better than one large.

6-32

A delightful variation of landmark lighting is *patch lighting*. This brightens a focal area while blackening its surround, an example being an entrance at night. Here two or more floods are mounted near the base of an entrance like footlights before a stage so their crisscrossing rays minimize shadows in the scene's center while maximizing them on the sides. The lights should be dimmable from indoors, so visitors won't be blinded by the lights as they leave.

6-33. Patch lighting

Landscape lighting. There are two basic landscape lighting strategies: *organic* and *rational.* Organic design utilizes natural shapes and free arrangements: its aim is to conform man to Nature's grandeur. Rational design uses geometric shapes and formal layouts: its aim is to fit Nature to man's ideals. The two do not mix well. Either way, it often takes four seasons of readjusting the luminaires to achieve the optimal effect. An excellent guide for landscape lighting is Frank Lloyd Wright's dictum: "Take care of the terminals and the rest will take care of itself." [10] By first determining how terrestrial terminals as steps, landings, overlooks, and pathway corners should be illuminated, brightening the areas between becomes much easier.

Figure 6-35 below shows several methods of brightening a tree at night. Considering that *daylighting* is what the tree looks like during a sunny day, *frontlighting* illuminates its foliage from

DAYLIGHTING   FRONTLIGHTING   SIDELIGHTING

BACKLIGHTING   UPLIGHTING   DOWNLIGHTING

6-34. Methods of lighting at night

Lighting

the front, usually with two spots located to each side that empha-size the tree's form and highlight its character. *Sidelighting* emphasizes the tree's texture and edges, creates shadows that accentuate depth, and enhances the tree's movement when ex-posed to breezes. *Backlighting* aims from behind the tree, which profiles its foliage, gives it a translucent glow, and adds depth to the scene. *Uplighting* highlights the heart of the foliage, partic-ularly the way the branches radiate from the trunk, and *down-lighting* emphasizes the foliage's crown.

A related night-lighting strategy is *moonlighting*: a soft downlighting that emulates the silvery glow of a full moon. A good light source for creating this effect is a low-wattage metal halide bulb mounted in a parabolic reflector faced with a blue filter.

A landscape that people will walk in at night should have *pathway lights* placed along pedestrian routes. The lights should be mounted low and aim downward, away from the eyes and toward the feet, with part of the emitted light diffusing upward to reveal adjacent foliage. Occupancy sensors are often important here. By turning lights on as you approach them and turning them off after you leave, these controls save energy and save you the anx-iety of finding a switch in the dark to turn them on. A clever path-way lighting is in Oglebay Park in Wheeling, West Virginia. There a row of knee-high concrete mushrooms have lights mounted under each cap. This and two other lovely pathway lights appear below.

MUSHROOM   DROOPING TULIP   LANTERN W/ SHIELD

6-35. Three lovely pathway lights

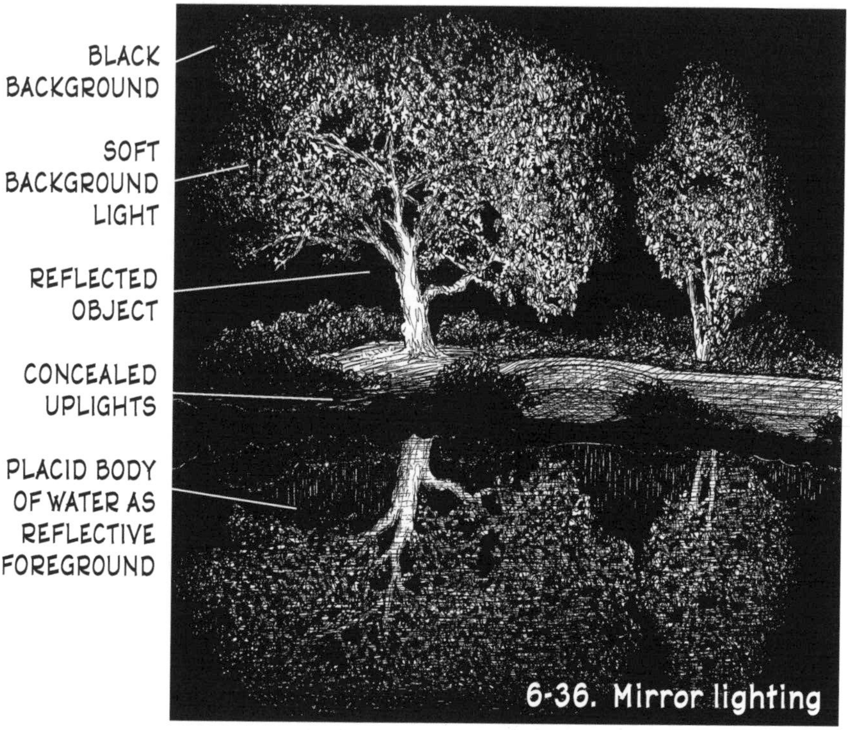

BLACK
BACKGROUND

SOFT
BACKGROUND
LIGHT

REFLECTED
OBJECT

CONCEALED
UPLIGHTS

PLACID BODY
OF WATER AS
REFLECTIVE
FOREGROUND

6-36. Mirror lighting

Another exciting nocturnal strategy is *mirror lighting*. This reflects an interesting scene in a pool or other placid body of water as appears above. This illumination is composed as follows:

1. Set the water's surface as a dark reflective foreground in which no light shines on, in, or from under the water.
2. Locate the reflected scene a little back of and directly behind the water.
3. Locate behind the water and in front of and a little to each side of the reflected scene recessed uplighting that highlights the object's texture.
4. Just behind the reflected scene add a small amount of soft background light.
6. Blacken the remaining background.

Lighting

Moving water offers an illuminating challenge at night. If the water is a fountain or falls over a rough surface, it is *aerated* and is best lit from behind to make it glow. If the water falls over a smooth edge, it is *solid* and looks best when lit from in front.

Security Lighting. This illumination is presently undergoing revolutionary changes due to computerization. Gone is the old yellow flood mounted high on a building's cornice, a garish star in the firmament, glaring down on a turnaround or service yard for up to 15 hours a day and annoying the neighbors more than protecting the premises. Now this lighting can be fitted with adjustable shutters and combined with motion sensors, intrusion alarms, battery packs, remote TV surveillance, "lived-in look" indoor lighting scenarios, and other features that can satisfy the security requirements for almost any scene whether the occupants are present or absent.

For example, imagine a husband and wife returning home late at night. By operating a handheld remote before leaving the car they can turn on the lights over the garage door, in the garage, by the front door, and in the foyer behind —as if the house is welcoming them home. Once inside the front door they can remotely turn off all unneeded lights before taking another step. One can even have a "digital barking dog" which, when activated by someone prowling outside, plays a high-fidelity recording of a loudly barking canine. Three companies that sell these woofers are www.guarddog.net, www.entrybell.com, and www.elights.com.

Or, imagine a sleeping person who is wakened by a strange noise outside at night. When s/he turns on a programmed surveillance console by the bed, the console activates floodlights mounted under the roof and video cameras under each light. By operating a few directional buttons below a video display on the console, the person can scan every area around the house and check digital readouts of every window and door. If necessary s/he can press a button that notifies the police. By pressing another button, s/he can tell the programmer to reset everything if the noise was only a raccoon knocking over a garbage can.

Or, imagine an off-hour security system installed at a tool-and-die shop in a high-crime urban area. Mounted high on each facade are wide-beam floods that cover the service yard, loading dock, truck parking area, and material storage area. Below each light is a motion detector whose coverage area matches that of the light, and each light is fitted with an adjustable glare shield that controls light trespass to neighboring buildings. The lights are connected to programmed circuitry that turns them off from dawn to dusk, dims them from dusk to dawn, and turns them on fully if motion is detected at night — then the system activates a siren mounted under the roof and notifies the police department. The system even notifies the facility manager when a light burns out or other component malfunctions. A few more security lighting guidelines are:

☞ Illuminate all parts of the area; don't leave dark spots where an intruder could hide. Illuminate each area from two directions to minimize shadows. Aim lamps at entries and other critical areas.

☞ Mount outdoor lights on poles 10 to 16 feet above walks and 14 to 25 feet above parking areas. The

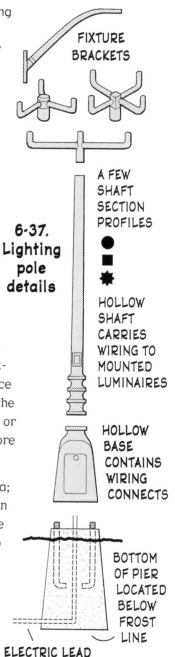

6-37. Lighting pole details

FIXTURE BRACKETS

A FEW SHAFT SECTION PROFILES

HOLLOW SHAFT CARRIES WIRING TO MOUNTED LUMINAIRES

HOLLOW BASE CONTAINS WIRING CONNECTS

BOTTOM OF PIER LOCATED BELOW FROST LINE

ELECTRIC LEAD

Lighting

lights on top should be several feet from any foliage and the poles' bases should be five feet from driveway edges and parking areas. The best fixtures have simple mounts, easily replaceable bulbs, and battery packs that maintain operation during power outages. Tall mounts require fewer lamps and they minimize shadows cast by obstructions; though they require bulbs of higher wattage to maintain the same brightness as lower-mounted bulbs. Several smaller lights usually create more uniform light than one large. The construction of a typical lighting pole appears in figure 6-37.

Every outdoor light fixture should be easily accessible for changing bulbs and cleaning, and they should have strong housings and special connections that resist damage by vandals and weather. The best housings are aluminum, brass, or copper (this weathers to a lovely verdigris patina), and the best lenses have heat-resistant glass and watertight rims. Facings can also have shields that create sharp cutoffs of almost any shape, and colored lenses or filters can liven the color of outdoor objects in the enveloping blackness. But like food seasonings, colored filters should be used sparingly. Other effective "light shields" are broad-leaved plants and highly textured foliage placed around the luminaire to soften its rays and reflect part of their light into adjacent areas.

Outdoor lighting often requires switches indoors. These are best located on the wall by the door leading to the illuminated scene, or by a nearby window through which one can view the scene before stepping outside. Switches and dimmers may also be installed outdoors near terraces and recreation areas. Such controls could be operable from both indoors and outdoors with two-way switches and/or hand-held remotes.

Although night lighting can make the darker half of one's day more enjoyable, there is one kind of night lighting that should stop. This is the habit of many commercial establishments to keep their lights burning at night —as exhibited by whole urban skylines lit up bright as a forest fire which at the same time blots one of the most wondrous illuminations of all: starlight from the galaxies embroidered across the firmament. All this nocturnal lighting pocks our planet with dots so bright that when seen from a satellite at night western Europe, the eastern United States, and Japan appear as vast nebulae of light. Indeed, all the energy this nation could save with compact fluorescent lights, waterless urinals, and lo-flo showerheads is hardly a watt compared to what it would save if its businesses turned off their lights at night. How can we claim to be serious about conserving energy when we give this wasteful habit a free pass?

All this excess lighting does more than waste energy. Skylines of windows lit brightly at night baffle migrating birds, which by disorienting and exhausting them after they've lost their way kills millions of avians in this nation alone every year. We even have an eyewitness account of this disorientation that is nearly 140 years old. See what Mark Twain said in 1883 during the infant days of electricity:

> We had a succession of black nights, going up the river, and it was observable that whenever we landed, and suddenly inundated the trees with the intense sunburst of the electric light, a certain curious effect was always produced: hundreds of birds flocked instantly out from the masses of shining green foliage, and went careering hither and thither through the white rays, and often a songbird tuned up and fell to singing. We judged that they mistook this superb artificial day for the genuine article.[11]

Nightlighting also makes migrating birds think the days are longer, which induces them to migrate earlier; then they arrive at their destinations too early to nest successfully. Nature's casualties caused by such blights of brightness are many. Sea turtles, having a natural disposition for dark beaches, find fewer places to nest. Nocturnal mammals become easier targets for predators. Frogs, fishes, and other marshy creatures have their circadian rhythms disrupted. The biggest cause of all these environmental disorders, says *National Geographic*, is "bad lighting design, which allows artificial light to shine outward and upward into the sky." [12]

Now that we have sensors that can extinguish a room's lights when occupants leave, every municipality in America should pass a law —one whose violation could be detected at a glance— decreeing that vacated office spaces, unused recreation areas, and empty parking lots must turn off their lights at night. No more "Bright lights, big cities!" Municipalities could further reduce this watt-wasting by passing ordinances mandating that public light fixtures shine less brightly and aim downward, that private porch lights be recessed in ceilings, entrance lights be shielded, and streets have lower lighting levels and energy-saving light curfews. If local governments and businesses are looking for ways to trim their budgets in these hard times, you would think they would be the first to adopt such directives.

Notes

Plumbing

A building is a container that holds a lot of water. And every drop that flows from every faucet must be pure. This requires an amazing variety of pipes and related components, all of which are far more complicated and delicate than the act they eventuate would suggest and which can be very dangerous when every part doesn't work perfectly well. To confirm this we need look no further than the weekend of July 21, 1976, where at an American Legion convention in a hotel in Philadelphia a germ crept into the water supply and killed 34 people —and gave birth to the term, *Legionnaire's Disease*.

Fixtures

The central character in this system's parade of purity is the *plumbing fixture*. Here is where all the purifying reaches a climax —and where it ends. Each such receptacle typically has:

☞ A hot and cold *faucet*, each with a valve below the handle.

☞ A smooth nonabsorbent *basin*.

☞ A *drain*, preferably with a strainer in it.

☞ A *trap*, a U-shaped pipe below the drain that keeps noxious gases from rising into the fixture through the drain.

☞ A *vent* extending up from just below the trap that conveys any accumulating waste gases through the building's roof.

☞ A *flood rim*, a small hole near the top of the basin that keeps it from overflowing and connects to a small pipe descending outside the basin to the drain.

☞ An *air gap*, at least one inch of vertical space between the flood rim and the faucets that keeps water rising in the basin from possibly contaminating the water supply.

274

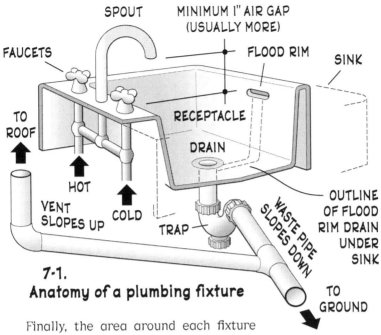

SPOUT MINIMUM 1" AIR GAP (USUALLY MORE)

FAUCETS FLOOD RIM SINK

TO ROOF RECEPTACLE

DRAIN

HOT OUTLINE OF FLOOD RIM DRAIN UNDER SINK

VENT SLOPES UP COLD TRAP WASTE PIPE SLOPES DOWN

TO GROUND

7-1.

Anatomy of a plumbing fixture

Finally, the area around each fixture must be spacious, well-illuminated, and well-ventilated. All these are not coveted luxuries, but code-mandated necessities that ensure the purity of every drop lurking behind every valve in every faucet in every building.

Water pouring from a faucet not only must be pure; it must have pressure. Too little, and it may take seemingly forever to fill a coffeepot with water. Too much, and a pipe or fitting may burst. In between, 20 to 50 pounds per square inch should exist at every spout. If the water arrives from a public street, its pressure is maintained by the municipality that delivers the water. If the water comes from a well drilled on the property, the pressure is maintained by a pump immersed in the well and a tank inside the building. Since water's pressure decreases by about four-tenths of a pound per square inch (psi) for every foot the water flows upward and by about one-tenth of a pound per square inch for every yard it flows outward, maintaining proper pressure at every faucet in tall and long buildings may require booster pumps at vertical or horizontal intervals along the water supply.

A hot topic in plumbing these days is *no-touch controls*. These automatically turn on a fixture's water as you approach and turn it off as you leave. Theoretically they are easier to use, are sanitary, and conserve water. But here I would like to ask someone I can trust —You: how often does a no-touch faucet fail to turn on when you waggle your fingers before it, or stop running while your hands hover under the spout, or keep running after you step away? Why not simply install a foot pump with a hot and cold pedal at the sink's base? Many sinks in rural parks have these "toe-touch controls", and The Chicago Faucet Shoppe (www.chicagofaucetshoppe.com) sells them. These devices contain no costly electronics, consume no electricity, require only a few footpresses to wash your hands, and pressing both pedals gives you warm water.

FAUCET

12 VAC WIRING

MICROCONTROLS

DUAL BEAM

LONG-RANGE SINGLE BEAM

SHORT-RANGE SINGLE BEAM

7-2. No-touch controls for lavatories

And toilets ... last winter I entered a toilet stall in a public rest room in Albany, New York, and when I found no hook on the door to hang my overcoat I stepped back to open the door to find another stall. The toilet flushed. When I stepped into the next stall and found a hook on its door, I removed my overcoat before sitting down. The toilet flushed. After using the fixture, I stood up to leave. The toilet flushed. After removing my overcoat from the hook and putting it on, I opened the door to leave. The toilet flushed. Four flushes in one trip to the john? Foot-operated toilets in airplanes —another *toe-touch control*— conserve water much better than this. Why doesn't LEED award points on their checklist for these inexpensive and easily operable devices —instead of costly clumsy controls that waste water, waste electricity to deliver it, and waste money to maintain?

Another misguided effort at water conservation occurs in showers. Some environmentalists say: "Install lo-flo showerheads." But what happens when you take a shower? First you wet yourself down, then you wash your body, then you rinse yourself off. If conserving water is the object, then while washing your body —soaping your skin and shampooing your hair— why not *turn off the water*, so you don't wash the soap *off* while trying to put it *on*? This simple act (known in the army as a military shower) could save much of the gallonage you guzzle when showering —and much of your patience in putting up with long drizzly showers. My health club has a solution here: a lever on the showerhead that lets you cut the water off without changing the hot and cold settings. When you start to soap yourself down, you flip the lever up; when you're through soaping, you flip the lever down. This is the kind of simple common sense that is missing in many green products today.

But the worst no-touch culprit is waterless urinals. When urine enters one of these receptacles, it sinks beneath a layer of lighter-than-water liquid and drains through a siphonic trap in back to eliminate the need for flushing. But only half the public uses this fixture, the other half uses it only half the time, and even then a quart of water is all it takes to flush the fluid away. A waterless urinal has other debits: (1) the covering liquid must be periodically replenished; (2) the siphonic trap contains a cartridge which must be periodically replaced; (3) the urinal's walls aren't washed after each use which makes them smell so they must be periodically cleaned with an antiseptic spray; (4) undiluted urine tends to crystallize in the fixtures' drains which can clog or corrode them so they must be periodically flushed with Drain-O or similar chemical; and (5) cigaret butts, chewing gum, and other debris tend to get thrown into these trash cans which must be removed. All these added liquids, cartridges, cleaners, and flushers plus the people paid to maintain them could be replaced with a simple "lo-flo" urinal that uses a quart per flush and no chemicals.[1] This conservation of water and other resources also conserves one's patience, and cultivates the kind of respect that would lead a skeptical citizen to embrace environmental concepts instead of scorn them.

Delivering pure water at every fixture in a building has other considerations that affect a plumbing system's design:

Water quality. Does the water contain any microbes, minerals, or particulates? Prior to designing a building's plumbing system, the designer should have a sample of the water supply tested by a laboratory. This may indicate that the water requires softeners, filters, and other conditioners to ensure that the water not only is pure but tastes good, won't corrode or leave residues in the piping, and won't damage machinery or anything in them (like clothes in a washing machine).

Public versus private occupancies. Public fixtures generally experience more touching and banging than private ones. They should have sturdier and stubbier handles and spouts, rounder corners, concealed piping, and shutoff valves accessible only to service personnel.

Transient versus static occupancies. Transient occupants (visitors to restaurants, stores, lecture halls, etc.) normally use a fixture once while static occupants (residents in homes, students in schools, workers in businesses, etc.) use the same fixture often. In transient occupancies fixtures should be simple and comply with ADA (handicapped) guidelines, while ones in static occupancies may have decorative features that satisfy users' tastes.

Occupancy use patterns. Different occupancies often require different fixtures. A kindergarten needs an 11-inch-high kiddie toilet in a lavatory next to each classroom, while an elementary school requires low and high toilets and sinks in separate-sex rest rooms next to a public hallway. Also women, due to anatomical differences and more restrictive clothing, usually spend twice as much time in public rest rooms per visit as men, and 90 percent of women wash their hands afterward while only 30 percent of men do. This indicates (if you do the math) that for every two toilets, two urinals, and three sinks in a public men's room there should be eight toilets and nine sinks in a womens' room nearby. This *potty parity module* should be a code mandate for public rest rooms everywhere —and another item LEED should include on its checklist.

Wipedown versus washdown cleaning. Wipedown cleaning involves wiping fixtures with a rag or other handheld item, while washdown cleaning uses hoses to clean fixtures and the floors below. A washdown area requires a floor that descends gently to a central drain and is rimmed by an integral (no crack between floor and base) baseboard at least four inches high. Although such floors appear in health clubs and large public rest rooms, they are a good idea for homes too, where they can be easily cleaned during those "once-a-century supermesses."

As for fixtures, here's a few ways to make them more useful:

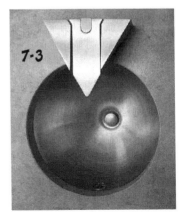

7-3

Sinks ... each should have a drain with a basket strainer and paddle handles (not knobs) that are easy to use when your hands are messy or arthritic, as is the gorgeous "ADA-compliant" model on the right designed by Frank Lloyd Wright.[2] At least one sink on every floor should also have

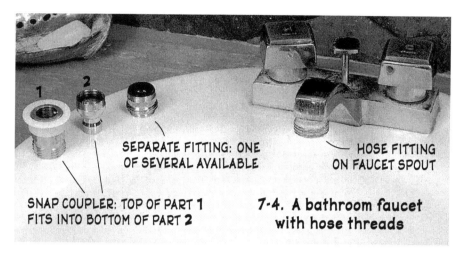

SEPARATE FITTING: ONE
OF SEVERAL AVAILABLE

HOSE FITTING
ON FAUCET SPOUT

SNAP COUPLER: TOP OF PART **1**
FITS INTO BOTTOM OF PART **2**

**7-4. A bathroom faucet
with hose threads**

spigot threads on its spout so a hose can be screwed onto
it. These are available in almost any hardware store. Two
appear in the photo above. They enable you to do everything from washing the family dog in a bathtub to fighting
fires in nearby rooms.

Bathtubs ... give each tub two sturdy handlebars to enable anyone with old or slippery feet to safely enter and leave. In
the wall above the tub replace the puny soap dish with an
expansive three-shelf recess 3 inches deep, 12 inches
wide, and 24 inches high that can hold all kinds of soaps
and shampoos. The shelves can be pieces of stainless
steel a tilesetter slips between the tiles' mortar joints.

Showers ... Make this bathing booth a roomy 38 × 54 inches, set
a triangular seat in a corner opposite the controls, make
at least one wall translucent so light can enter while preserving privacy, and install a floor sill low enough to allow
someone to enter in a wheelchair.

Toilets ... know the difference between *flush tank* toilets (ones
with a boxy tank behind the seat) and *flush valve* toilets
(ones with only a lever behind the seat which when
pressed creates a roar of cascading water in the bowl).

Plumbing

Flush tank toilets consume much less water per flush but require a 2 to 3 minute wait between flushes. Flush valve toilets are typically installed near public assembly areas where several people can use them quickly.

One toilet needs no water at all to flush: the *compostable privy*. This descendant of the ancestral outhouse can now be located indoors and is odor-free. These "in-houses" are described below in a nonpromotional manner whose primary intent is to satisfy those who may be curious about their nature and use.[3]

A compostable toilet combines two age-old activities: going to the bathroom and decomposing organic waste. Regarding the kind of unit that fits into a normal bathroom (larger models exist for multiple bathrooms) each is about the size of a barrel laid on its side and has a standard cover and seat on top in whose center is a waste inlet port about 4 inches wide and 9 inches front-to-back. This hole is kept in alignment with the center of the seat by a click lock on a rotatable drum below. If a man wants to urinate, he doesn't have to sit down, but he might want to since this toilet's inlet port is notably smaller than a normal toilet bowl with its seat raised. Beneath the seat are three chambers:

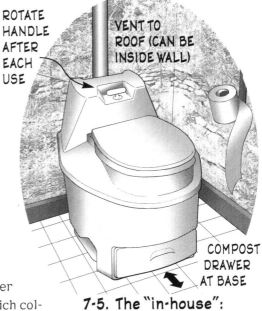

ROTATE HANDLE AFTER EACH USE

VENT TO ROOF (CAN BE INSIDE WALL)

COMPOST DRAWER AT BASE

7-5. The "in-house": a modern privy

1. A cylindrical digester where the toilet waste decomposes.
2. An evaporating chamber under the digester which collects excess moisture leaking

from the decomposing waste. This liquid either drains though a small pipe descending from the chamber's back or evaporates and rises up a vent through the building's roof. Some models have small fans and heaters to speed up the composting and evaporation (these accessories diminish this product's energy advantages unless they are powered by natural energy). If the region experiences freezing weather the vent should be insulated to keep ice from forming inside. You also can't turn the drum if the compost inside is frozen. In fact, every part of these toilets —their shape, look, and any pretensions toward decor— are made to accommodate those who seek normally comfortable lives.

3. A finishing drawer where the decomposed waste in the digester is periodically emptied.

Each unit comes with a pint-size jar of micro-mix (this inoculates the compost with aerobic bacteria) and a large bag of bulking agent (this mixes with the waste and releases carbon to sustain the reaction). The toilet operates like this:

1. Before using it, add a few tablespoons of micro-mix and a cup of bulking agent to prime the composting process.

2. After each bowel movement, toss the toilet paper into the inlet port and add half a cup of bulking agent (or a total of one cup per person each day of use). Never toss in any kleenex, paper towels, tampons, and other refuse because they won't decompose.

3. Every two or three days, rotate the drum four to six revolutions (it's best to mark these dates on a calendar mounted on a wall by the toilet). This mixes the waste with the bulking agent and aerates it.

4. Every month or so (when the drum is about half full), empty the compost into the finishing drawer by rotating the drum backwards until at least most of the compost has emptied into the drawer below. Again, circle the dates

on a calendar. Don't worry if the compost's recent deposits haven't decomposed, because they continue to do so in the drawer. Each time you empty the drum into the drawer, open the drawer a little to see how full it is. If the drawer is too full, scoop out some of the contents and dump them back into the inlet port on top.

5.   Once a month, add a few more tablespoons of micro-mix; because the microbes in the digester may die off if the compost dries out, the toilet isn't used for several days, or someone taking antibiotics uses it. When you run out of micro-mix or bulking agent, you usually buy more from the company that sold you the toilet.

6.   Every few months or so, pull out the finishing drawer and empty it (usually about as often as you buy a new bag of bulking agent). The compost can be used as a fertilizer for trees, shrubs, and flowers, but you shouldn't grow vegetables in it as it may contain pathogens.

Compostable toilets are a viable alternative to standard water closets in cabins, hunting lodges, and other small buildings located where water is scarce, surface bedrock or a high water table exists in the vicinity of the building, bodies of water are close by, or electricity and septic systems aren't available. Two sellers of these units are sun-mar.com and enviro-let.com.

Supply Plumbing

This is the pipes and related components that deliver water to the fixtures. Common pipe materials are detailed below:

Copper. This reddish-brown metal is strong and light, is easily cut, and its connections can be soldered which is quicker than threading but not as strong. Copper pipe is made in four wall thicknesses: K (the thickest and strongest, it can be used underground), L (thinner than K, it can't be used underground), M (thinner than *L*, it is commonly used in small buildings), and *DWV* (the thinnest and weakest: it is used only for nonpressurized drain, waste, and vent piping). For any size pipe each wall thickness has the same diameter, which allows tees, sleeves, and other fittings to connect pipes of the same diameter that have different wall thicknesses. Thus for a given diameter the thicker-walled pipes weigh more, cost more, are stronger, and hold less water than thinner-walled pipes: all important design criteria for engineers. The above pipes cannot be bent, but a fifth type, *flexible copper tubing*, is a soft copper with small diameters that can be bent by strong hands. It is used to connect *K*, *L*, or *M* type copper piping to fixtures in confined areas.

- ⊕ Lightweight, easy to install, versatile, resists rust, is highly resistant to air and salt water.
- ⊖ Cannot convey liquids or gases at high pressures or velocities, cannot carry steam or highly acidic or alkaline wastes, cannot be exposed to corrosive soils.

Steel. This is the strongest pipe, but it is harder to cut than copper and its connections must be threaded, both of which increase labor costs. As with copper, each diameter has several wall thicknesses and the outer diameter is always the same for each thickness so fittings of the same diameter can connect pipes with different wall thicknesses. Steel piping may be *galvanized, black pipe*, or *stainless steel*. Galvanized pipe has a protective zinc coating that minimizes rust and corrosion, but any minerals in the water may react with the galvanizing and form scale which can clog the pipe. Galvanized pipe also cannot be used in gas lines because the gas causes the zinc to flake off and again clog the pipe. This pipe is commonly used as handrails. Black pipe has a black oxide surface which can rust and corrode so it is usually covered with a protective oil which makes it messy to handle. It is used for circulating hot water in boiler systems and conveying gases in commercial facilities, but it cannot be used for drinkable water or waste drainage. Some of these pipes have very thick walls and can resist very high pressures. Stainless steel pipe is used for noncorrosive piping in food, pharmaceutical, petrochemical, and other industries. Due to its silvery streamlined appearance it is also used as railings, posts, and other aesthetic applications.

➕ Best for high temperatures, pressures, and velocities; requires the least support; lowest coefficient of expansion.

➖ Expensive, heavy, brittle in very cold temperatures.

When copper and steel pipes are fitted together (as when new copper pipe extends from galvanized pipe in an old building), the copper will dissolve the steel until the two metals no longer touch due to galvanic corrosion (which means the connection will soon leak badly) unless the metals are joined with a *dielectric union*, as appears in figure 7-6.

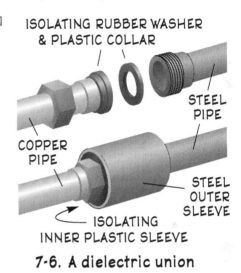

7-6. A dielectric union

Plastic. This piping costs less than copper and steel, it is easily cut with a hacksaw and easily connected with quick-drying solvent, but it is much weaker. There are several kinds:

PVC (polyvinyl chloride, the pipe's material), a rigid white pipe used for cold water supply, drains, and vents.

ABS (acrylonitrile-butadiene-styrene), a rigid black pipe used for drains and vents.

CPVC (chlorinated polyvinyl chloride), a strong cream-colored pipe used for hot and cold water supply.

PE (polyethylene), a black flexible tubing that can be snaked around corners and resists corrosive soils.

⊕ Lighter and less costly than steel or copper; resists most groundwater acids and alkalis. Best for irrigation and other unsleeved low-pressure underground installations where the piping won't freeze.

⊖ Easily cracked or crushed; expands or shrinks greatly with changes in temperature; is brittle at low temperatures, loses strength above 180° F; cannot withstand high pressures. Plastic pipe flexes when water is turned off which makes it prone to fatigue-cracking over time, so it requires frequent supports. Not allowed for commercial plumbing or natural gas piping.

A new kind of plastic piping that is gaining popularity these days is **PEX** *(crosslinked polyethylene) tubing,* a flexible corrosion-resistant piping that is useful for small plumbing systems (i.e. in cottages and campground bath houses), radiant floor heating, snow melting, and irrigation.[4] It comes in red, blue, and white and is made in $^3/_8$, $^1/_2$, $^5/_8$, $^3/_4$, and 1 inch diameters, all of which can connect to the same diameters in copper pipes.

⊕ Costs less than copper and is easier to install, not brittle at low temperatures, not prone to fatigue cracking, can be fairly easily connected to copper and other plastic pipes, can be fitted into tight corners.

⊖ Requires special handtools, should not be buried underground, is susceptible to damage by greases and oils, deteriorates when exposed to UV rays, is NG for high pressures, can be used only for small-diameter piping.

Cast iron. This heavy corrosion-resistant pipe is used only for waste, drain, and other non-pressurized piping. Common diameters are 2 to 6 inches and unit lengths are 3 to 4 feet.

⊕ Low material cost; easy to assemble; unaffected by fire; resistant to subsurface corrosion.

⊖ Heavy; high labor installation costs; cannot convey liquids under pressure.

Plumbing

A crucial act of plumbing is laying the supply main in a trench leading into the building. Many things can go wrong here, all to be concealed when the trench is backfilled. If you ever need this work done, visit the site with a camera and a tape measure while the trench is still open. During your burial watch, look for the following:

☞ If the supply main and sewer main connect to municipal conduits out front, is the water main located above the sewer main as in figure 7-7? The supply main should be at least 6 inches above and 12 inches to the side of the sewer main. Fail to do this, and years later you may need to re-lay the pipes because a cracked sewer main is leaking into a cracked water main.

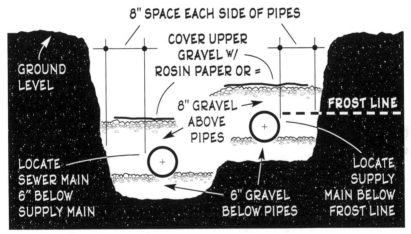

7-7. Location of water and sewer mains in a trench

☞ Is the supply main located below the local frost line? Know this depth for your area (your building department can tell you). Measure the trench's depth, which should equal the depth of the frost line plus the diameter of the largest pipe.

☞ Is six inches of gravel laid below the pipes? This mini-

287

mizes rupturing some future day due to expansion and contraction due to earth temperature changes, settling subsoils caused by water saturation, and/or vibrations from heavy vehicular traffic.

☞ After the pipes are laid, is eight inches of gravel added on top? The reasons are the same as for the gravel below.

☞ Is the gravel on top covered with resin paper (a pinkish-brown water-repellent paper) or 90-pound roofing felt before the trench is backfilled? This keeps the airspaces between the gravel from filling with silt over the years.

☞ Where driveways or other roads will cross the piping, is the pipe sleeved with heavy conduit whose diameter is at least 4 inches larger? This is cheap insurance against the pipes crushing someday.

☞ As the supply main enters the building, does it sleeve through the foundation wall just above the footing? It should not enter the building below the footing. This may require the bottom of the footing to be as much as a foot below the frost line, as sketched below.

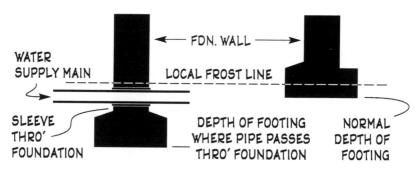

7-8. Location of supply main at foundation wall

You may need to be a scientist to understand all this, but you don't need to be one to tell a contractor to do what this page says.

Once the supply main enters the building, here are a few more things to look for just inside, fortunately more at your leisure. Not every building needs each item listed below.

Plumbing

☞ A *shutoff valve* for emptying the whole system if necessary, with a floor drain below the valve.

☞ An easily readable *water meter*.

☞ An easily readable *water pressure gauge*.

☞ A *backflow valve* that keeps water from flowing back into and possibly contaminating the water supply.

☞ A *strainer* with shutoff valves fore and aft that traps particulate matter which may be suspended in the waterflow.

☞ If the area gets really cold in winter, a *heater* governed by a thermostat set at forty-five degrees.

From the service entrance to each fixture, every linear foot of piping, hot and cold and young and old, should:

☞ Have at least six inches between hot and cold pipes and both should be insulated: hot pipes to minimize heat loss, and cold pipes to prevent surface condensation. The insulation should have vapor barriers on its outer surfaces and all seams should be sealed with duct-tape or equal.

☞ Allow space for pipe movement due to thermal expansion. Any temperature changes inside or outside can shorten or lengthen the pipe up to two inches per hundred feet.

☞ Slope up or down at $1/4$ inch per linear foot ($3/8$ inch is better). Every low point should have a *blowout valve* and a floor drain below, as in figure 7-9, and plenty of space around it for opening and closing.

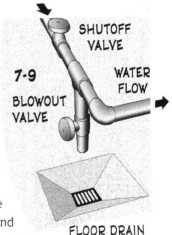

SHUTOFF VALVE

7-9

WATER FLOW

BLOWOUT VALVE

FLOOR DRAIN

☞ Be accessible for maintenance and any future upgrading. If you can't walk along the pipe with a tool box in hand, the pipe needs more access area around it.

☞ Provide adequate support along the pipe depending on its diameter and contained weight. The supports should

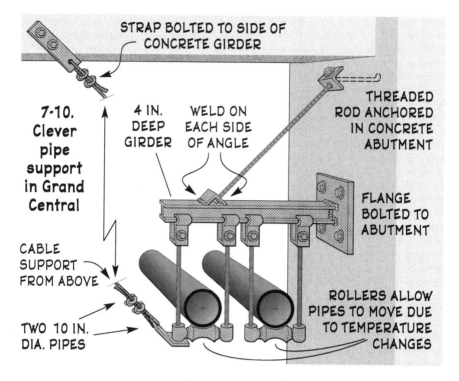

STRAP BOLTED TO SIDE OF
CONCRETE GIRDER

7-10.
Clever
pipe
support
in Grand
Central

4 IN.   WELD ON
DEEP   EACH SIDE
GIRDER OF ANGLE

THREADED
ROD ANCHORED
IN CONCRETE
ABUTMENT

FLANGE
BOLTED TO
ABUTMENT

CABLE
SUPPORT
FROM ABOVE

TWO 10 IN.
DIA. PIPES

ROLLERS ALLOW
PIPES TO MOVE DUE
TO TEMPERATURE
CHANGES

hold the pipe snugly while allowing it to slide laterally, be close enough to prevent pipe sags between them, and be at least a few inches from tees, elbows, and other fittings. In large buildings pipe supports can be elaborate. Above the tracks in Grand Central Station is the pipe support you see in figure 7-10. It holds two large pipes where they cannot be supported with standard hangers.

☞ Have a *tattletale gauge* that tells if any part of the supply piping has a leak (especially handy if the dripping is under a floor or behind a wall where it can't be seen or heard; finding such a detected leak is another matter). This gauge contains a red triangle that spins when all the faucets are turned off and a pipe leaks somewhere; it is usually mounted on the supply main just inside the building.

Plumbing

Hot and cold water supply plumbing requires a number of components to ensure that the water arriving at the fixtures has adequate pressure and is free of impurities, as follows:

Pumps. A pump is a motor-driven impeller fitted with an inlet pipe and a backflow valve on one side and a discharge pipe on the other. It usually pumps a liquid or gas at a specified pressure. A plumbing system usually needs one of these machines to deliver water at an adequate pressure to every fixture in the building. In urban areas, this machine is usually located outside the building and is operated by the municipality that supplies the water. In suburban and rural areas, the pump is typically a long cylinder about 4 inches in diameter that is lowered into a drilled well where it resides a few dozen feet above the well's bottom so silt and sand possibly stirred up by its sucking won't abrade the pump's working parts. This machine pushes water sometimes hundreds of feet upward into the building and often works for decades without servicing.

Drilling a well for a submersible pump is a mysterious exercise, because the well must strike enough

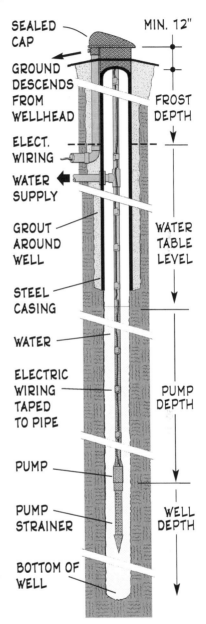

7-11. A drilled well with submersible pump

291

water to satisfy the served building's water demands in gallons per minute (gpm), and you never know what you'll find until you get there. If the amount is too low, a faucet may sputter if someone takes a shower while the dishwasher is running. If the amount is too high you will spend more money than you should. A simple rule of thumb for determining a small building's water demands is to add up its plumbing fixtures (sinks, tubs, toilets, washers, outdoor hose bibbs, and the like) and multiply the sum by two-thirds. If the building will have 12 fixtures, the well should deliver about 8 gpm. If the occupancy includes a hot tub, swimming pool, irrigation, or industrial operations, you better get a professional to do this divining for you. Later when the well driller sets up his rig and begins to drill, you cross your fingers and pray. I tried this on my property; but it didn't work. When the driller struck 3 gpm at 240 feet, I, thinking of the 18 fixtures in my planned domicile, said keep drilling. He didn't find another drop until 592 feet, where he struck 13 gpm. On my property that's 60 feet below sea level. I almost expected the water to be salty. My excavator, a drinking man, said that for what I paid for my well they should have put scotch in it.

In a drilled well the electrically operated pump draws water from deep in the ground like a big soda straw. In my well the water rises to about 50 feet from the top (it's a little higher in winter and lower in summer) and the pump is 450 feet down, so the water rises about 400 feet above the pump. If this pillar of liquid is 8 inches in diameter, a little number-crunching says it holds 1,020 gallons of water, plus a few thousand gallons more reside in the ground around the pipe. This is a big tank of water for a little house.

One kind of pump requires no electricity whatever to move water upward: the *ram pump*. This machine is located near a fairly large creek, and it uses the momentum of a large amount of water flowing downstream to push a small amount of water upstream. Who says water can't flow uphill? Here's how it works:

1. The upper end of a large inlet pipe, typically 100 feet long

Plumbing

and 2 to 4 inches in diameter, is submerged in the creek upstream (see drawing below); then the water in the pipe rushes downhill into a cylindrical chamber where the water's momentum opens flapper valve **A** and closes float valve **B**, then the water rising through the flapper valve "rams" against the air in a dome which compresses the air: this is the *ram* cycle.

2. An instant later the compressed air rams back against the water which closes flapper valve **A** and opens backflow valve **C** through which flows some of the rammed water uphill to a reservoir: this is the *pump* cycle. When flapper valve **A** closes, this also creates a slight vacuum in the chamber below which opens float valve **B**, then the excess water in the chamber flows into the outlet pipe. Then the cycle begins anew.

RAM CYCLE

1. WATER'S MOMENTUM IN DRIVE PIPE OPENS VALVE **A** & CLOSES VALVE **B**, THEN RISING WATER RAMS AGAINST AIR IN DOME.

PUMP CYCLE

2. WHEN AIR IN DOME RAMS BACK IT CLOSES VALVE **A** & OPENS VALVE **C** & WATER ENTERS DELIVERY PIPE. THIS LOWERS THE PRESSURE BELOW VALVE **A** WHICH OPENS VALVE **B** THRO' WHICH EXCESS WATER ESCAPES TO OUTLET PIPE.

7-12. How a ram pump works [5]

Architecture Laid Bare!

If you want to build a house above a large creek and supply it with water without using electricity, this is one way to do it. The pump is often housed in a shed which muffles its constant clanking. The drive pipe must be strong (galvanized steel is a good choice), and the delivery pipe cannot be exposed plastic (critters from rats to bears will nibble holes in it). For more information see:

www.rampumps.com (they sell a book)
www.i4at.org/lib2/hydropump.htm
www.clemson.edu/irrig/equip/ram
www.animatedsoftware.com/ram_pump
www.ncollier.com/rams
YouTube has several videos of ram pumps in action

Pressure Tanks. When a pump delivers water to a building, it usually fills a sealed tank about three-quarters full which compresses the air above to a specified maximum pressure (perhaps 55 psi), then the pump turns off. As the water below is used, the tank's pressure lowers until it falls below a specified minimum pressure (perhaps 45 psi), then the pump turns back on to refill the tank. This operation ensures that water is available when it is used faster than the pump can deliver it and it keeps the pump from running constantly to satisfy the building's water demands. The tank may be small as a thermos-size hydrocell unit fitted under a hot tub, or as large as a bedroom-size reservoir mounted on the roof of a hotel. A popular size for small buildings is a rust-resistant metal cylinder about two feet thick and five feet tall. On its top is a pressure relief valve which relieves the air pressure if it becomes dangerously high, and an air valve for recharging the air when necessary.

Valves. These are the traffic lights of plumbing: they tell the fluids when they can stop and go. They are chiefly used to isolate part of a system when it needs servicing or repair. One is installed on the supply main just inside the building, at the base of risers (vertical pipes serving a number of fixtures on upper floors), and

Plumbing

before and after each plumbing component. Each should have adequate service area around it, and the floor below should be waterproof and drainable. There are five kinds of valves:

Globe valves. The common hose bibb or spigot valve, like the one on the side of your house. Its round handle offers precise regulation of flow. Useful in cold regions is a *frostproof sill cock,* an 8 to 12 inch pipe with the handle on one end and the valve on the other that is mounted in an exterior wall with the handle outdoors and the valve inside behind the insulation where it won't freeze.

Gate valves. These have handwheel handles and perpendicular-to-flow closures. They usually operate fully open or closed, and are used for isolating plumbing zones or components that need infrequent servicing or repair.

Pressure relief or PRV valves. Each typically has a nut handle that is turned with a wrench which allows precise pressure control by authorized personnel. They are mounted on water heaters and pressure tanks to keep them from exploding if the pressure exceeds a prescribed level.

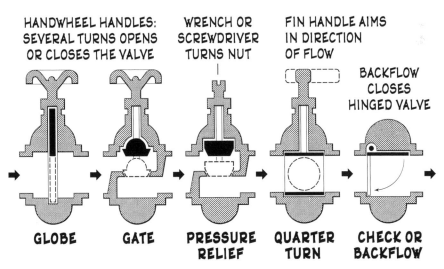

HANDWHEEL HANDLES: SEVERAL TURNS OPENS OR CLOSES THE VALVE

WRENCH OR SCREWDRIVER TURNS NUT

FIN HANDLE AIMS IN DIRECTION OF FLOW

BACKFLOW CLOSES HINGED VALVE

GLOBE   GATE   PRESSURE RELIEF   QUARTER TURN   CHECK OR BACKFLOW

7-13. The five basic valves

Quarter-turn valves. Also known as *ball, plug,* or *butterfly* valves, each has a blade handle that opens with a quarter turn in the direction of flow. They are used for maintaining full-open or full-close flows.

Check valves. Also known as *swing, lift,* or *backflow* valves, these have hinged discs that lay against the incoming opening where they allow full flow when the water is running and close if the flow stops or reverses. They eliminate possible contamination of the water supply upstream that could result from backflow in the pipe.

Water hammer arresters. A serious piping plague in some buildings is water hammer. It occurs in long straight runs when a faucet is closed, which can cause the long cylinder of water in the pipe to suddenly slam into the faucet's valve like a battering ram —then a pressure wave rebounds back through the piping, straining every fitting along the way and sounding like someone is hitting the pipe with a hammer. If a pipe suddenly starts leaking or a pump rattles on its mount after years of perfect service, it may be caused by a straw-that-broke-the-camel's-back failure due to water hammer. This problem makes plastic piping a poor choice for all but small low-pressure plumbing, it makes steel the first choice for large-diameter piping, and it emphasizes why all pipes should be snugly supported at short intervals. To eliminate water hammer on long straight runs, water hammer arresters as sketched in figure 7-14 may be mounted before bends and diameter reductions. Each typically has a standard tire valve which allows the air inside to be recharged; so each should be accessible for periodic testing and servicing.

Water hammer arrester 7-14

Plumbing

Water Purifiers. Most buildings in this country have pure water, but some do not. Then a chemist prescribes a method of removing them. If the impurities are pathogens, they are usually killed with chemicals. If they are particles that damage piping, leave rings in toilet bowls, stain washed clothes, and the like, they are usually removed with a filter installed on the supply main before the water flows to any fixture. The best systems have two filters installed either parallel or in series so one still operates while the other is serviced, as sketched in figure 7-15. On the internet is a chart that lists ten brands of water filters and their prices, capacities, and eleven impurities that each filter does or does not remove (see www.waterfiltercomparisons.com). Common filters are:

Cellulose cartridges. This is typically a thermos-size fuzzy white cylinder fitted into a transparent container through which the cylinder is inspected. When it darkens to a certain shade it is considered to be saturated with impurities and is replaced. The cartridge removes particles as small as 5 microns including iron, chlorine, giardia (a diarrhea-causing protozoa), and some bacteria.

Activated charcoal. Here the water passes through a filter or charcoal bed that removes noxious tastes, odors, and colors plus some toxins and bacteria. Sizes range from cellulose cartridges to tanks larger than hot water heaters.

Gravity beds. Here beds of sand or diatomaceous earth strain particles, large bacteria, scale, grit, and similar impuri-

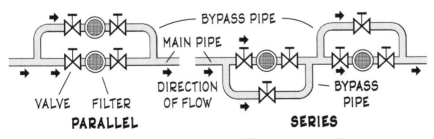

7-15. Parallel and series filter installations

ties out of large volumes of water. The beds may be $2\frac{1}{2}$ to 3 feet deep and 3 to 10 feet in diameter while the water rises another 3 to 5 feet above. The strained water may be used for bathing but not drinking. When the bed becomes saturated it is cleansed by backwashing, which today can be activated by computerized controls.

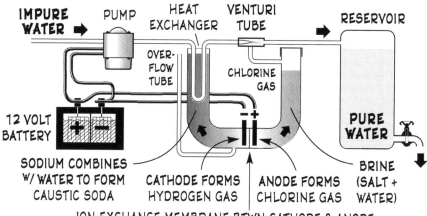

IMPURE WATER ➡ PUMP HEAT EXCHANGER VENTURI TUBE RESERVOIR

OVER-FLOW TUBE CHLORINE GAS

12 VOLT BATTERY PURE WATER

SODIUM COMBINES W/ WATER TO FORM CAUSTIC SODA   CATHODE FORMS HYDROGEN GAS   ANODE FORMS CHLORINE GAS   BRINE (SALT + WATER)

ION-EXCHANGE MEMBRANE BTWN CATHODE & ANODE KEEPS HYDROGEN & CHLORINE FROM COMBINING

7-16. Making pure water with salt and a car battery [6]

In remote areas one can purify water with a suitcase of chemistry lab equipment, a handful of table salt, and a 12-volt car battery as diagrammed above. After the water is strained (a tee-shirt folded twice over is usually adequate) (1) the salt is mixed with water, (2) electricity from the battery electrolyzes the salt into chlorine and hydrogen, (3) the chlorine is atomized in a Venturi tube (a short tube with a narrow neck), and (4) the atomized chlorine purifies the water flowing through the tube. The system is easy to set up and operate, and it is claimed to purify up to 50 gallons of water per minute. It is used in rural environments worldwide and you can buy it on the internet.

According to *National Geographic*, purifying water is even simpler than this. It suggests: Retrieve a discarded water bottle.

Plumbing

Remove the label and fill with water that "is not too murky" from a creek or puddle. Place the bottle on a piece of metal in full sunlight. In six hours the sun's UV rays will kill viruses, bacteria, and parasites in the water, making it safe to drink. This article even had a photo of 59 filled bottles arranged on a sheet of corrugated roofing. [7]

Water softeners. The groundwater in more than half the United States contains dissolved calcium, magnesium, and a few lesser compounds. In buildings this *hard water* can clog supply pipes and components and fixtures, leave unsightly rings in toilets and pots and pans, keep soap from lathering, and leave deposits inside boilers and heat exchangers where they inhibit heat transfer. All this is eliminated by *water softening*, a process that passes the hard water through a tank filled with sodium-saturated beads known as *zeolite* that replace the calcium and magnesium ions in the water. When the beads become saturated with calcium and magnesium, the tank is backwashed with brine that recharges the beads with sodium and flushes the calcium and magnesium ions away. The removed ions rarely clog drains because they can no longer adhere to surfaces, the ions don't harm septic tanks because they actually stimulate anaerobic activity, and they apparently improve soil percolation in leaching fields. This chemical process does not remove iron from the water, which is commonly done with filters.

Water softeners in small buildings are usually a pair of cylindrical tanks about four feet tall that are installed by professionals who test the water, size the softener, adjust its settings so neither too little nor too much backwashing occurs (too little and the water is still hard, too much and the water tastes salty), and sell you more zeolite when you need it. Larger systems are available. For more info take a look at www.culligan.com, easywater.com, www.lenntech.com, and watersoftenerscompared.com.

However, water softeners do not have a clean bill of health. Since they dose the treated water with sodium they are not recommended for infants, people on salt-restricted diets, and the eld-erly; and the chloride-tainted wastewater is difficult to purify at water treatment facilities. These deficiencies have led to the de-velopment of the *physical water conditioner*,[8] a small electronic device that is clamped onto the water supply main and passes a low-energy electromagnetic field through the flowing water that keeps the suspend-ed calcium and magnesium ions from crust-ing in the pipes. Where the water later evaporates on a surface such as a glass shower screen, the suspended particles may spot the glass but usually are easily wiped off. These devices cost a fraction of a water softener; they require no bags of salt and no filters and need little mainte-nance; they use only a tiny amount of ener-gy; they extend the life of pipes and the appliances they serve; they remove hard

COURTESY OF **SoPhTec**

7-17. A physical water conditioner

water deposits from inside boilers, heat exchangers, cooling tow-ers, food service equipment, car wash plumbing systems, irriga-tion emitter heads, and dehumidifiers; and they can even remove existing scale from inside pipes, fittings, and componentry. On the minus side, they work unpredictably, their performance parame-ters presently are poorly defined, they don't enable soap to lath-er better, and added units usually must be installed on the outlets of water reservoirs because the counter-ion charges tend to wear off while the water resides in the tank. In summary, this product presently exists in that netherworld of having not yet proven that it works fully as claimed, yet seems too important not to mention.

Water heaters. In small buildings this is commonly a cylin-drical tank whose water is heated by electricity or natural gas. For domestic water the optimal temperature is 120° F, but for com-mercial water the temperature is often 170° which is needed to kill *Legionella* bacilli. Each tank has a *draw capacity* (maximum gal-

Plumbing

lons per hour of water the unit can heat), a *recovery rate* (maximum gallons per hour the unit can replenish used hot water), and an *input rating* (maximum energy the unit's heater uses, measured in kilowatt-hours for electricity and Btus per hour for natural gas). When the tank is "full", it really is only about 85 percent full; because water expands as it heats up (when 53 gallons of water heats from 40 to 140 degrees it becomes 54 gallons) and the tank must have a cushion of compressible air on top or it could explode. A water heater's capacity is typically in gallons of cold water it will hold plus the volume of the air above.

As you can see in figure 7-18 on page 303, a gas water heater has an incoming gas line and pilot dial at its base, while an electric water heater has one or two plate-like anode shields mounted on its side. A gas unit requires outdoor ventilation, has a continuously burning pilot light which consumes energy, has a slightly larger diameter than an electric unit of the same capacity because of the flue rising through its center, it requires a flue above the unit that usually rises through the building, and it loses some heat up the flue (more energy lost). However, an electric unit requires a 240-volt electrical service (if the occupancy already has a clothes dryer this drawback is negated), heats water only about half as fast, and costs more to run.

A recently developed gas water heater that is more efficient than the above models is the *condensing water heater*.[9] This has a helical tube immersed in the cylindrical tank through which rise the hot gases from the burner at the tank's base, then the water around the tube absorbs much of the gas's heat that would normally go up the flue. The increased efficiency allows a smaller tank to supply the same amount of hot water. But these units cost a lot, and they require a small pipe to remove the water condensate that forms inside the helical tube, which means they also require a system of drainage that is more sophisticated than a garden hose trailing out a garage door.

Another efficient unit is the *heat pump water heater*.[10] This warms water by compressing and expanding a refrigerant in a closed loop (this operation is described on page 388). When the unit is surrounded by 60-degree air it can heat water to 140 degrees. An electric resistance element serves as a backup if the surrounding air is too cold or when the occupants use a lot of water. This operation does have its share of minuses. Each unit needs at least 1,000 cubic feet of airspace (about the size of a bedroom) to run efficiently, it should not be installed near a boiler or furnace, it produces up to five gallons of water condensate per day which must be drained, and the compression cycle creates cool dry air which tends to limit these units' cost-effectiveness to warm humid climates. These units also cost at least $1,500 plus installation costs (about half as much as for standard units); but their increased efficiency often returns the extra outlay in a few years, plus $1,500 in tax credits are usually available for one's installation.[10] By the way, a $1,500 tax credit doesn't mean you get $1,500 back; it means you pay taxes on $1,500 less income; so if you're in a 20 percent tax bracket you get only $300 back.

A water heater's capacity depends on the number of plumbing fixtures it serves and the temperature of the heated water. The higher the temperature, the smaller the heater and the less it will weigh and cost; but the more it will cost to operate because more heat will migrate from the residing water through the tank's surface. To retard this flow, today's water heaters have two or three inches of insulation wrapped between the tank and the casing. But this is nowhere near enough in this age of escalating energy costs. These days it would pay to fit another ten inches around the tank. But this is easier said than done, because most water heaters are crammed into a corner among other mechanical equipment where someone can hardly slip a finger around it. Here is where a little planning can lead to big savings, as follows:

☞ Make sure the door to the heater (and all doors lead-

Plumbing

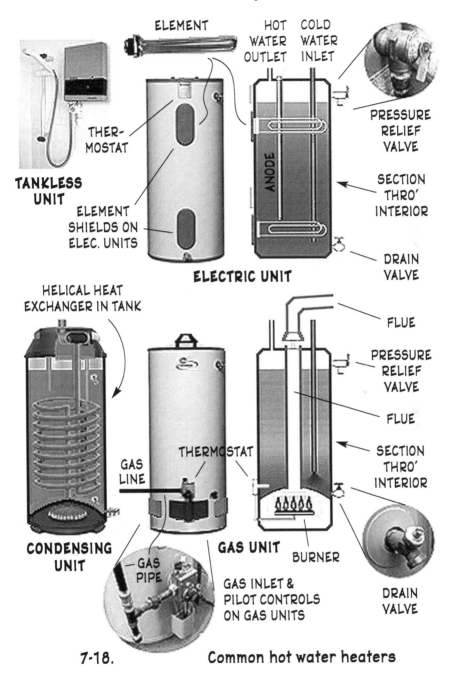

ELEMENT

HOT COLD
WATER WATER
OUTLET INLET

THER-MOSTAT

TANKLESS UNIT

ELEMENT SHIELDS ON ELEC. UNITS

ANODE

PRESSURE RELIEF VALVE

SECTION THRO' INTERIOR

DRAIN VALVE

ELECTRIC UNIT

HELICAL HEAT EXCHANGER IN TANK

FLUE

PRESSURE RELIEF VALVE

FLUE

SECTION THRO' INTERIOR

GAS LINE

THERMOSTAT

CONDENSING UNIT

GAS PIPE

GAS UNIT

BURNER

GAS INLET & PILOT CONTROLS ON GAS UNITS

DRAIN VALVE

7-18.   Common hot water heaters

303

ing to this door) are wide enough for the heater to fit through. Make the door's clear width the heater's diameter plus 4 inches (larger if future upgrading is a possibility). Then when a flue corrodes or an anode burns out every decade or so the unit can be easily replaced.

☞ Mark a dot on the floor, scribe a thirty-inch radius around it, add a two-foot aisle on two adjacent sides, center the water heater on the center of the area (not the dot), and don't put anything else in this area.

☞ Install in this area a waterproof floor that slopes gently to a central drain.

When a small number of infrequently used plumbing fixtures are located a few dozen feet from a water heater, the hot water residing in the long pipes while the fixtures are off cools; then when a faucet is turned on, it may take seemingly forever for the cold water to flow out of the pipe before hot water arrives at the spout, which also means the first few gallons of delivered water are heated twice. Enter the *tankless water heater*, alias the *point-of-use* or *on-demand water heater*.[11] These small units (some can be mounted under a sink) can save considerable energy and patience in the above scenario by delivering hot water in ten or twenty seconds after a faucet is turned on. They also take up virtually no floorspace and have computerized controls that monitor performance. However, these units require two vents to the outdoors (one to draw in fresh air for combustion and one at least two horizontal feet away to exhaust the combusted gases). Also if someone turns on the water again just after it has been turned off (as when a showertaker turns the water off while soaping one's skin and shampooing one's hair) the unit might not restart until the control sequence has completed its purge cycle which may take a few minutes. The units also cost a lot: around a thousand dollars plus perhaps another thousand for installation which usually includes new electrical outlets, larger gas pipes, and added ventilation. These installations also mean the

Plumbing

installer must be an expert in water, gas, and electrical installations —not your neighborhood handyman. It may take several years for one of these burners to recoup its initial investment. Here a dime of design might be worth a dollar of construction; or the installation may be more thankless than tankless.

7-19. Hot showers in the wilderness

FLUE CAP   COPPER COIL IN DUCT   PIPING FROM CREEK

ADJUSTABLE SPIGOT VALVE   PIPE FROM COIL   BURNER UNDER COIL   FIREBRICK BASE   5 GALLON PROPANE JUG

There is one more on-demand water heater which surely you have never seen in a catalog but which is too enchanting not to mention here. Back in 1969 when I was a carpenter on the house in Big Sur that I described in the chapter on electricity, Reeford Shea, the contractor, built an ingenious wilderness shower as sketched above. The shower was located beside the trunk of a huge oak tree with a thick branch extending overhead under whose spreading foliage one could view the fabled Big Sur coast. First Reeford bent a length of flexible copper tubing into a coil

305

about 6 inches thick and 15 inches high, mounted the coil inside a length of furnace duct, and set a used stove burner under the coil. Second, he ran a 200-foot length of pipe uphill to a creek to create adequate water pressure at the showerhead, and connected the pipe's lower end to the bottom of the copper coil. Third, he ran a length of copper pipe from the top of the coil to the tree, up its trunk through a spigot valve mounted at chest height, and out under the overhanging branch to the showerhead. Fourth, he connected to the burner a five-gallon propane jug which was periodically refilled from a large propane tank on the premises. To take a shower one would do the following. (1) Open the spigot valve on the treetrunk to start the water running. (2) Open the gas valve on the propane jug and light the burner. (3) After waiting half a minute for the water to warm up, adjust the valve on the treetrunk to obtain the right temperature: if the water is too cold, close the valve slightly which slows the waterflow through the heating coil which raises the water's temperature; if the water is too hot, open the valve slightly to increase the waterflow which lowers its temperature. Before showering you had to open the valve before lighting the burner, and after showering you had to turn the burner off before closing the water valve; but this was a small price to pay for such boundless luxury.

Another way to heat water for a building's plumbing fixtures is with the sun. This involves mounting a network of small pipes on a flat surface about the size of a sheet of plywood, covering the pipes with glazing, backing them with insulation and a structural substrate, and aiming the panel south. Cold water enters the bottom of the sun-exposed pipes, flows upward via convection as it is warmed, and exits from the top. For speedier results you could drive the water with a small pump, which could be run by a few photoelectric cells. It is best to empty the solar-heated water into a standard hot water heater whose burner keeps the liquid hot during cloudy weather and at night. If this reservoir is above the collectors, the heated water will flow naturally into it via *thermosiphoning* (natural upward movement of a heated fluid when it

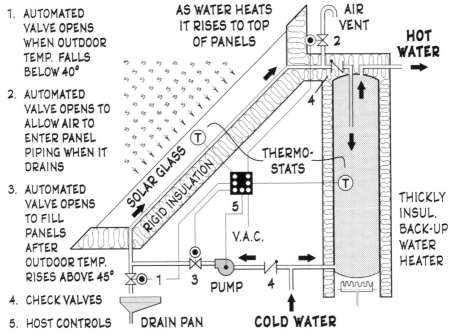

1. AUTOMATED VALVE OPENS WHEN OUTDOOR TEMP. FALLS BELOW 40°

2. AUTOMATED VALVE OPENS TO ALLOW AIR TO ENTER PANEL PIPING WHEN IT DRAINS

3. AUTOMATED VALVE OPENS TO FILL PANELS AFTER OUTDOOR TEMP. RISES ABOVE 45°

4. CHECK VALVES

5. HOST CONTROLS

AS WATER HEATS IT RISES TO TOP OF PANELS

AIR VENT

HOT WATER

SOLAR GLASS

RIGID INSULATION

THERMO-STATS

V.A.C.

PUMP

DRAIN PAN

COLD WATER

THICKLY INSUL. BACK-UP WATER HEATER

7-20. Making hot water from sunshine

expands and becomes lighter) into the tank. This technology is decades old; in 1940 half the houses in Florida had solar water heaters built much as described above. [12]

In these panels the best piping is usually flexible copper tubing because it conducts heat well, won't rust, and can be bent by hand. Inside the panels the tubing should be slightly flattened to widen its area of exposure while still allowing water to flow through it, and the tubes and exposed surfaces between them should be painted or electroplated with a blackish *selective surface* or *low-E coating* that absorbs incident shortwave energy while radiating little of the converted longwave energy. If you are technically adept or know someone who is, another way to create a highly absorptive surface is to immerse the copper tubing in nitric acid then a solution of copper sulphate dissolved in hydrochloric acid: the resulting deep black surface will absorb nearly 100 percent of incident sunlight. In these panels the best glazing is tempered glass (it resists breakage from falling branches), the best insulation around the panels is usually styrofoam or other rigid insulation (they are physically strong and water-repellent), and the pipes outside the panels and the holding tank should be thickly insulated. In this age of computerization the panels can also be equipped with programmed thermisters that activate shutoff valves which drain the panels when the outdoor temperature falls below about 35 degrees and refill the pipes when the temperature rises.[13] But these computerized controls apparently have a few wrinkles which still need to be ironed out: recent users have reported they often fail due to clogging, deposits, corrosion, computer breakdowns, and power outages. One improvement these systems could have is a "dead man" control that automatically drains the pipes via gravity when anything goes wrong, then the valves can be manually reset later. Better no free hot water for a day than a broken system.

If the ground near the south side of a building to be served by solar water heaters receives plenty of sunshine, instead of locating the collectors on the roof consider mounting them on the ground or even as a long awning over the first-floor windows. The advantages of these locations are described beginning on page 211 in the section on photovoltaic cells.

To size a solar water heating system, one can engage in all manner of meticulous analysis to determine the optimal area of panels for a given occupancy. A quicker way that is just as approximate at least for residences is to use the map graph in figure 7-21. This says a conservation-minded family of four living in central Missouri would need about 20 square feet of panel area per person, or 4 × 20 = 80 square feet for the family. Since a conservation-minded person would use about 15 gallons of hot water per day, panels this size in this locality would supply this foursome with 4 × 15 = 60 gallons of hot water per day, which becomes the capacity of the system's holding tank/backup water heater. The panels' optimal tilt for year-round sungathering (as indicat-

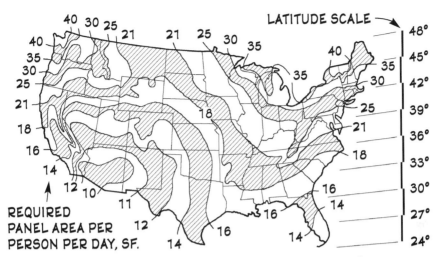

7-21. Solar water heating area map graph

ed by figure 5-17 on page 211) is the local latitude plus 5 degrees; so in central Missouri, at about 38 degrees north latitude, the back of the panels should tilt up about 43 degrees above horizontal. If you want more hot water in winter (when you would likely need it most) at the expense of making less the whole year, tilt the panels to the local latitude plus 20 degrees, which in central Missouri would be around 58 degrees. The panels could have adjustable tilts (these could be reset monthly if desired), which would be more expensive but more efficient.

These systems work best if occupants space their use of hot water throughout the day, bathe at the end of the day rather than early in the morning, and wait for sunny days to launder clothes.

An organization called the Solar Rating and Certification Corp. (SRCC) publishes a catalog that provides design guidelines and lists the specifications for some 500 certified solar water heating systems. Take a look at www.solar-rating.org.

Today's engineers have developed another solar water heater: the *evacuated tube collector*.[14] This system's elemental unit is a finned copper pipe mounted in a long thin glass tube usually about 3 inches round and 60 inches long from which the air is removed to create a thermos-like vacuum inside the tube. Compared to a flat plate collector, a rack of these suncatchers is easier to install, operates more efficiently at higher water temperatures, performs more constantly year-round, and is less likely to freeze. Another subtle advantage is that while thermosiphoning can increase the efficiency of solar water heating panels, these physics play no role in the operation of evacuated tubes. On the minus side, a rack of evacuated tubes may cost more, is more likely to be damaged by wind and hail, snow can't slide off or be raked off easily, and the tubes tend to work for about 15 years while flat plates commonly last for 30. Generally plates perform better at lower temperatures and tubes do better in high. Commercial buildings with large flat roofs in warm climates may be the place for this technology. As a sample, the flat roof of a large jail in Texas has 12,000 evacuated tubes mounted on it. [15]

7-22. Evacuated tube collectors

Irrigation. Some people like lush green lawns so much they will water them with networks of buried pipes mounted with patterns of sprinkler heads amid the blades of grass. LEED even awards credits for irrigation systems that emphasize water-efficient landscaping (2 points), innovative wastewater technologies (1 point), and water use reduction (2 points). In other words, all a LEED point-seeker needs to do with this environmentally destructive construction is use a few high-efficiency nozzles, a couple moisture sensors, and a little recycled water to earn *five full points* toward earning certification.[16] But building irrigation systems does more than (1) dig up the environment onsite to bury the pipes and (2) dig up more environment elsewhere to make them. (3) They deplete local water tables (some of the water may replenish groundwater levels immediately below, but grass is a greedy drinker); (4) they consume more water than would natural flora of equal area; (5) they consume energy to supply the water; (6) they are often accompanied with fertilizers and (7) pesticides that both consume energy to make and often drain into nearby waterways and kill fish and aquatic plants; and (8) they are often manicured by noisy gas-powered mowers, weed wackers, and leaf blowers that consume lots of embodied energy to make and lots of fossil fuel to run and which also pollute the air above the plants.

The optimal solution? Let lawns grow! Lawn foliage is only a few inches deep and typically has only one or two species of plants, while shrubs are a few feet deep and may have dozens of species, and forests are sixty to eighty feet deep and typically have a hundred different plants —and the thicker and more varied an area's foliage the more diverse is its wildlife, which is the most singular indication of a healthy environment because it enriches that natural foundation on which all life depends. High piles of foliage also absorb more airborne impurities, more carbon dioxide, more water, and more heat than any lawn ever could. And when have you ever seen a forest being irrigated? Letting lawns grow also takes less time, takes less money, consumes less water, and due to the biomass it creates the net embodied energy consumed is minus! A homeowner may like a plot of lawn close to the house for kids and pets to romp on, or want a thirty-foot band of grass patched with terraces and turnarounds around the house to protect it from possible wildfires —but let every area beyond be a *no-mow zone*. Better yet, talk your neighbors into doing the same; because the real value of the taller foliage is not just converting one grassy property but whole neighborhoods of properties; because when the taller foliage of adjacent properties conjoin, islands of wilderness in a sea of grass suddenly become islands of grass in a sea of wilderness; then the animals and plants residing in these habitats can move around more and form the kind of communities they need to thrive, which increases the biodiversity that leads to healthy environments.[17]

Architecture Laid Bare!

Here LEED would better serve the public by *subtracting* points for irrigation systems, and awarding points for growing original flora watered by the sky (2 points), covering an area with native and not alien plants (2 points), and employing innovative *non*-water technologies (2 points); and each of these features would not be a token representation but would exist throughout the system. Surely an organization that promotes lo-flo shower-heads could promote lo-flo landscapes!

Cisterns. In the late 1800s, many a rural home had a *cistern* that collected rainfall from the roof to use for irrigating, bathing, washing clothes, flushing toilets, even cooking. The roof runoff drained into one or more downspouts with a strainer at the base of each and filled a reservoir often bigger than a bedroom that typically had thick masonry walls built deep in the ground, a hatch in the roof through which one could enter and clean the inside, and a concrete floor sloping to a drain that passed through a shutoff valve outside and emptied some distance beyond. This construction appears below.

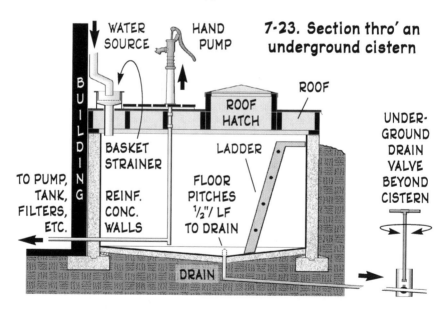

7-23. Section thro' an underground cistern

WATER SOURCE

HAND PUMP

ROOF

BUILDING

ROOF HATCH

UNDER-GROUND DRAIN VALVE BEYOND CISTERN

BASKET STRAINER

LADDER

TO PUMP, TANK, FILTERS, ETC.

REINF. CONC. WALLS

FLOOR PITCHES ½"/ LF TO DRAIN

DRAIN

Plumbing

Even today, virtually every building in America has a cistern in it. When you are sitting on a toilet you are leaning your back against it. During plumbing breakdowns or when the electric power fails, this reservoir of drinkable water is available merely by lifting its top. Another simple cistern many a house could have is a barrel placed under a gutter downspout. A single mother in Oregon built a reservoir like this. She mounted nine 60-gallon barrels on one side of her house and six 30-gallon barrels on another side.[18] When the first barrel fills, the overflow fills the next barrel until up to 740 gallons are stored. She uses these sizable casks primarily to water her garden during Oregon's dry summers. Opportunities like this exist almost everywhere in America today, and often you can obtain the containers for free. The benefits of these systems can only increase in the future, as burgeoning populations impose ever-increasing demands on water and the energy often consumed to deliver it.

Cisterns are typically built as follows: [19]

1. Know where the water will come from. If from a roof, the best is usually unpainted metal. Not so good are oil-coated metals (these leach oil), metals with soldered seams (these leach lead), asphalt shingles (these leach toxins), or wood shakes (these leach tannin). If the water will come from a creek, get a sample assayed by a professional laboratory.
2. Determine the water source's patterns of availability. Droughts in summer? Ice in winter? If the source is a creek, does it run dry part of the year? What are the local maximum, minimum, and average monthly rainfalls? Best for cisterning is rain that varies from occasional cloudbursts to nothing for weeks, and worst is light infrequent rains. If the source is a creek, it would be kind to the frogs and fish to leave two-thirds of the waterflow in its bed.
3. Know how the water will be used.
4. Decide whether the cistern will be above or below grade. Above-grade models require no excavating and cost less,

but their bulky shapes often blemish the landscape. Above-grade fiberglass tanks should be roofed to protect them from UV decomposition. Below-grade models won't freeze and are out of view.

5. Size the cistern. Figure about 750 gallons or 100 cubic feet per person per month (7.48 gal = 1 cf). If you have the space, multiply this by the year's average longest dry spell plus one month. If the construction will require a foundation, it should be designed by an engineer.

6. If the cistern will be fed by downspouts, use large half-round gutters (6 inches is nice) and round downspouts (5 inches at least) that can carry large volumes of water and are less likely to clog. If the spouts will empty into one or more barrels, each spout should fit snugly into a lid that keeps out rodents and breeding mosquitoes. If the lid is wood and unlatched, any overflow will raise this buoyant cover until water runs over the barrel's rim.

7. Install a filter between the water source and the cistern. The best filters have a holding tank that collects the first 30 to 40 gallons of water (the dirtiest), then cleaner water flows through the filter into the cistern. For more information on this component check the *filtering roofwasher* at www.waterfiltrationcompany.com.

8. Think of how you will draw water from the cistern. The old ones had a cast iron hand pump mounted on top. Today's models are more apt to have a pump and pressure tank, but a nice-looking old-timey hand pump can be bought on the internet. To look at a few, google pitcher pumps.

9. To make drinkable water, pass the cisterned water through three sediment filters rated at perhaps 25, 5, and 0.5 microns plus a bacteria-killing UV filter.[20]

Good sources for cistern fittings are suppliers of fittings for swimming pools, which of course are a type of cistern. Pay attention to minor components such as float switches, check valves, and computerized controls, and try to get a few experienced professionals on your team before taking the plunge.

My favorite cistern is a large above-ground model in California to which the owner added a faux front door and windows, clapboard siding, and a shingle roof to make the big ugly tank look like a pretty cottage in his back yard.

Nonwater Plumbing

Plumbing also conveys fluids other than water, as follows. All these systems are designed by professional engineers.

Pure Water. It may surprise you to know there are different kinds of pure water. One may be 100 percent free of minerals, while another may be completely free of organic matter. These systems usually have stainless steel piping, include a distiller, and serve medical or industrial facilities.

Nonwater liquids. This plumbing carries such liquids as milk in dairies and chemicals in industrial facilities. In each system, meticulous specifications and a detailed list of required componentry are essential for successful design.

Fuel Oils and Gases. In these systems a flammable liquid or gas is stored in a pressurized tank which may be small as a bucket or large as a railroad tanker car. From the tank the fuel flows through one or more copper or brass pipes (never iron or steel because they can create sparks when struck) to machines in homes, commercial buildings, and industrial facilities. If your house has a gas stove or gas water heater, you have one of these systems. In the tank is onsite, it is capped with a gauge, regulator, and shutoff valve and it should be located outdoors in a sheltered well-ventilated area, accessible by a truck but not where vehicles can bump into it, and placed away from windows or other openings where leaking gas could enter. Since fuel gases often contain moisture, if any fuel gas pipe exists outdoors or passes through unheated indoor areas where temperatures could fall below freezing, beware of any sags in the line. The moisture will collect there and freeze, which could crack the pipe, which would allow the gas to leak, which could cause an explosion. This piping should always slope slightly up or down through such areas.

When a network of piping carries petroleums, chemicals, toxins, and other environmentally damaging fluids it requires a dizzying array of subcomponents as follows:

☞ Sensor cables under each fuel tank and every linear foot of piping that notify host controls of any leakage.

☞ A reclamation tank for any collected leakage.

☞ A catch basin under each access port.

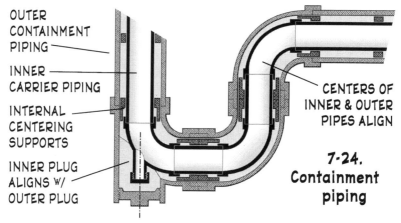

OUTER CONTAINMENT PIPING

INNER CARRIER PIPING

INTERNAL CENTERING SUPPORTS

INNER PLUG ALIGNS W/ OUTER PLUG

CENTERS OF INNER & OUTER PIPES ALIGN

7-24. Containment piping

☞ A concentric enclosure of larger pipes known as *containment piping* that protects the carrier piping from damage and keeps any leaks from escaping into surrounding areas, as appears below. The outer piping is sometimes made of clear plastic which is unsurpassed for visual display.

☞ Filters and oil/water separators that remove any impurities and moisture from the line.

☞ Circulators that keep the fuel flowing slowly through the filters and separators so it will be fresh at all times.

☞ Automated monitors and alarms.

Plumbing

☞ Computerized visual readouts of the whole system.
☞ All the above is duplicated in case one system fails.

When a fuel tank or pipe leaks, it must be dug out and every teaspoon of tainted soil removed and hauled away in special trucks by licensed operators (not dump trucks by the neighborhood excavator) to a dedicated burn plant (not the local landfill). Failure to do this in the past has led to the ground in some places to becoming so saturated with toxins that water drawn from any drilled well in the area is unsafe to drink. Whole regions of eastern Europe are like this today. We must not let this happen here.

Medical Gases. These systems convey gases as oxygen, compressed air, vacuum air, helium, nitrous oxide, ethylene, and cyclopropane (the last three are anæsthesias) in hospitals, dental offices, medical clinics, and many industrial and scientific facilities. The gases are stored in steel cylinders similar to oxyacetylene welding tanks or large pressurized reservoirs located at least 50 feet outdoors from which extend one or more brass or thick copper pipes. Each outlet requires a shutoff valve and a quick-coupler mounted 4 to 5 feet above the floor.

Compressed Air. In these systems a pump compresses ambient air and stores it in a pressurized tank, then steel pipes (not copper or plastic) extend to outlets with quick-couplers to which connect hoses that operate power tools, inflate tires, and/or clean small areas. Compressed air tools carry no shock risk, run cooler, are less of a fire hazard, and are more dependable in dirty environments than electrical tools. Since air heats when compressed, in large systems the compressor may require jacketing with circulating water or refrigeration. Though compressed air is noncombustible it vigorously supports combustion, so each system must incorporate fire safety measures.

Vacuum Air. Here a pump removes air from a sealed tank from which one or more pipes extend to valved stubs to which are connected hoses that suck loose matter from in front of the nozzles. This system is used to clean large homes, apartments, hotels, and laboratories. In hospitals it cleans instruments, removes fluids from surgical incisions, and sucks spent heavier-than-air anesthesia gases from operating room floors. Since the detritus is often messy, each system typically has a separator (a second tank with a filter that keeps collected particulates from entering the pump), an exhaust that vents any noxious odors into unoccupied areas outdoors, and dismantleable componentry so each piece can be cleaned or unclogged if necessary. Since air cools when its pressure lowers, in large systems the pump may cake with ice which may require heat to remove.

Fire Suppression

Nearly every method of extinguishing a fire in and around buildings uses plumbing. These networks of pipes can do more than put out fires. They can contain sensors that alarm occupants, notify local fire departments, activate HVAC dampers and other fire controls, and reveal escape routes. Common systems are:

Water. Every small building should have mounted on opposite facades a pair of *frostproof sill cocks* whose spigots won't freeze in cold weather, and near each should be a hose rack. The hose should be rubber (not vinyl, which tends to kink) with nickel-plated couplings (not plastic, which tends to break if a car rolls over them). If vandalism is a concern, install the spigot and rack just inside a garage door or service entrance (below each should be a concrete or tile floor that slopes to a drain); then the water can be applied anywhere the hose can extend indoors. Every floor should also have a bathroom faucet with hose threads on it.

⊕ Good for most general fires; common in almost every occupancy; most occupants are familiar with its use. Fixtures are unobtrusive and commonplace. Inexpensive to use; doesn't require replacing or refilling afterwards.

- Will not quench burning electrical equipment, flammable liquids, fats, oils, and some chemicals and metals. Can water-damage unburned materials and construction.

Handheld Extinguishers. These chemical-filled cylinders are mounted in accessible locations near fire hazards. When a fire erupts, an occupant dismounts the extinguisher and discharges its contents at the base of the fire. Each unit typically operates for 12 to 30 seconds and covers distances from 10 to 30 feet. Larger cart-mounted units are used by trained personnel in airports, docks, and marinas. There are eight classes of handheld extinguishers:

Class *A* ... these extinguish burning clothes, woods, rubbers, foliage, and many plastics. Each has a number before its "*A*" designation which when multiplied by 1.25 indicates the unit's quenching power compared to gallons of water: e.g. a 20*A* extinguisher will quench the same fire as 20 × 1.25 = 25 gallons of water. Why somebody added the 1.25 to the designation number I do not know.

Class B ... these suppress burning oils, tars, paints, fuels, some plastics, and other flammable liquids and gases. Pouring water on these fires will only make them spread. The number preceding the "*B*" designation indicates the extinguisher's power in square feet of area: e.g. a 40*B* unit will suppress about 40 square feet of deep-liquid fire.

Class C ... these put out electrical fires erupting in computers, telecom equipment, motors, lighting, and appliances. Pouring water on an electrical fire is potentially lethal, because the current can climb the stream of water and electrocute the person holding the hose.

Class BC ... these contain dry chemicals that put out oil and electrical fires. They cover the flames with a nonflammable blanket that reduces reignition, but on electrical fires they leave a harmful residue on equipment.

Class ABC ... these work on woods, papers, oils, and electrical wiring. On electrical fires they leave a harmful residue.

CO_2 *(carbon dioxide)* ... these extinguishers emit a cloudlike gas that puts out oil, gas, and electrical fires. It leaves no harmful residue on electrical equipment.

Class *D* ... these suppress burning chemicals from acetylene to xylene as well as flammable metals as sodium, potassium, magnesium, and powdered aluminum.

Class *F* ... these extinguish kitchen fires caused by cooking oils, greasy skillets, and dirty hoods. When these fires are small they can be suppressed with baking soda.

When using a fire extinguisher aim at the fire's base, squeeze the lever slowly, and sweep from side to side. If the fire looks like it is out, wait to make sure; because a doused fire may reignite.

⊕   A versatile method of suppressing small incipient fires by untrained personnel. Units are lightweight and are easily mounted, relocated, and refilled. Installation requires little building expense.

⊖   Good for only small fires. Each extinguisher must be used only for the type of fire it will suppress.

Standpipe systems. Here a large vertical pipe known as a *standpipe* rises through the building, then on each floor extends one or more pipes to *firehose racks*: wall-mounted cabinets with glass doors that contain a 50 to 100 foot canvas firehose and often a fire extinguisher and a fire axe. This system is like putting a fire hydrant on every floor, one operable by occupants as well as firefighters. Firehose racks are required in every building more than 90 feet tall, but are worth the

COURTESY OF POTTER ROEMER

7-25. Fire hose rack

reduced insurance premiums in many commercial occupancies.

➕ Good for suppressing fires quenchable by water and where fires may occur during periods of occupancy. Required in buildings whose upper floors can't be reached by ground-level firefighting equipment.

➖ **NG** for oil or electrical fires. High-velocity streams of water can damage furnishings. Required water reservoir is heavy which poses structural problems if on the roof.

Fire sprinklers. When a fire breaks out indoors, hot gases rise to the ceiling then billow outward, superheating the ceiling structure and causing it to lose strength until it may fall under its own weight. Ceiling-mounted water sprinklers suppress more than 90 percent of such fires. In these systems rows of small nozzles extend just under the ceiling or next to walls and each nozzle is plugged with a chunk of wax. When the wax melts at a specified temperature, the spraying water suppresses the flames below. The water flowing through the pipes may also activate audible and visual alarms, which in some systems will close supply air ducts, open exhaust air ducts near the flames, and notify local fire and police departments. When a fire erupts usually only a few heads open. Afterwards their thermal fuses are replaced.

There are three types of sprinkler heads: *upright* (aims the spray upward), *pendant* (aims the spray downward), and *sidewall* (aims the spray horizontally), as sketched in figure 7-26 on the next page. The heads can be combined. Each must be located away from lights and other heat sources and cannot be painted. Sprinklers may be fed by the main water supply, or during a loss of electric power the water may arrive from a *siamese connection*, a Y-shaped hydrant mounted outside the building where a parked fire truck pumps in the water. Floors covered by sprinklers should be waterproof and slope to drains. Standpipes and fire sprinklers are often combined.

➕ Good in large open areas (usually required in commercial

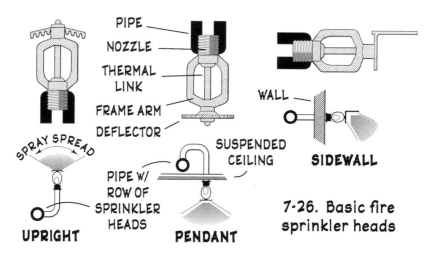

7-26. Basic fire sprinkler heads

areas of 1,500 square feet or more) and where fires are likely to occur during off-hours.

● **NG** for electrical or oil fires or where valuable contents could be damaged by water. Systems require adequate water supply and floor drainage.

Presently a movement is afoot to require fire sprinklers in residences. Is this a good idea? Let's examine the facts.

Statistics indicate that occupants are less likely to die in fires and less damage will occur in homes equipped with fire sprinklers. When large old residences are converted into institutional occupancies, local codes mandate that sprinkler systems be installed throughout indoor areas. In new homes, advocates of these systems claim they will replace expensive fire hydrants and their required water mains along public roads.

However, these sprinklers (1) often require separate plumbing, or else every pipe and fitting leading to the sprinkler plumbing may need to be enlarged; (2) the pipes must be steel with threaded connections (not copper with soldered connections or plastic): (3) the systems must be inspected annually and maintained by code-approved specialists; (4) on rare occasions they don't work when they should and work when they shouldn't; and (5) they will *not* eliminate street hydrants and their required water mains because hydrants are needed to put out brushfires and clean debris off roads after accidents. Also, occupants can more easily flee from a two-story house with openable windows than from a tall building with fixed panes. And hear the opinion of a thoughtful reader with ten years' construction experience with Habitat for Humanity who responded to a magazine article that advocated home sprinkler systems:

> It seems to me that other issues would be better addressed, such as old faulty wiring, outdated and unsafe heating systems, and poorly maintained structures. Even the numbers of fatalities from residential fires, while tragic, does not necessarily support mandatory sprinklers. Most often, the first line of lifesaving defense is a functioning smoke detector. It would be interesting to correlate the number of deaths quoted in the story with the percentage that occurred in homes protected by proper smoke detectors; my assumption would be not many. [21]

The final verdict? You should be able to examine the facts and decide for yourself. Some residences (perhaps multistory wood dwellings with multiple tenants) might be made safer with this plumbing, while in others it would be a waste of money. Another clue: Might those who urge these systems be likely to profit handsomely from their making or installing?

Carbon Dioxide. This system has a pressurized tank filled with CO_2 from which extends pipes fitted with nozzles. Each system may be a short pipe aimed at an important piece of equipment, or several pipes branching to a number of spray heads. These systems are installed where possibly large electrical fires can't be suppressed by handheld extinguishers or where flammable liquids and valuable contents prohibit the use of water. The areas served should keep the heavier-than-air suffocating gas from flowing into nearby lower floor areas.

➕ Can be used on Class *B* (flammable liquid) and *C* (electrical) fires. Good for chases, display cases, voids above suspended ceilings, and other confined and unoccupied areas. Has no residual effects on food or equipment, does not conduct electricity, leaves no residue.

➖ Ineffective on organic materials; **NG** for reactive metals, metal hydrides, and certain flammable chemicals. Good for small surface fires only. **NG** outdoors and in highly ventilated indoor areas. High concentrations of CO_2 can cause loss of consciousness, making this gas potentially lethal to occupants, animals, and firefighters.

Halon Alternatives. On Jan. 1, 1996, domestic production and importing of Halon 1301 was banned. Since then several environmentally acceptable replacements have been developed. Some have brand names while others are identified by chemical names or numeric notations, a few being Inergen (IG-541), Argonite (IG-55), FM200, FE25, and FE13. There are two general kinds: (1) gases stored under pressure which when activated discharge through one or more nozzles as a heavier-than-air mist that smothers and cools the fire; and (2) streaming agents that produce sprays, mists, fogs, or high-velocity jets that cover the fire. All have lower fire-quenching capabilities than Halon 1301; hence their use requires enlargening former reservoirs, piping, and nozzles. These agents do not conduct electricity, can extinguish hard-to-reach fires, are nontoxic so they can be used in occupied areas, can be used to protect sensitive electronic equipment, and require little cleaning afterward.

➕ Lightweight, fairly nontoxic. Good for putting out electrical fires in small spaces containing valuable contents.

➖ **NG** for large fires. Most will not extinguish burning metals or self-oxidizing materials. High concentrations can be a health hazard. Some agents that are stored in cylinders must be removed and refilled offsite after each use.

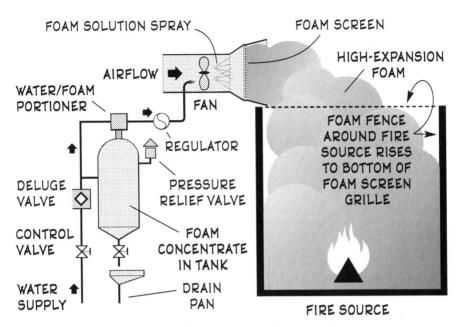

7-27. Foam fire suppression system

Foams. Here a detergent concentrate is stored under pressure, then when activated the concentrate mixes with water and the sudsy solution is driven by a large blower through a nylon net which creates an avalanche of foam that advances across burning areas to prevent oxygen from feeding the flames. These systems are installed in assembly lines, aircraft hangars, and other open industrial occupancies where fires may involve flammable liquids. Since the foam is 99 percent air, occupants and firefighters may advance through it safely. Later the foam is easily rinsed away.

➕ Lightweight, fast-operating, and usually won't damage delicate machinery. The foam will not harm anyone trapped in the building or putting out the fire.

➖ **NG** outdoors, in areas with windy or turbulent air, and highly ventilated areas. Foam must be rinsed away afterward or it can cause maintenance and moisture damage.

Waste Plumbing

Most plumbing fixtures require a drain to carry the effluent down and a vent to carry any noxious gases up. The drains combine downstream like tributaries of a river into one main that leaves the building at its base, and the vents combine similarly upward until one or more stacks rise above the roof. In both systems, pipe diameters cannot decrease in the direction of flow. Figure 7-28 (essentially a miniature of figure 7-1) shows how these pipes extend from a fixture. A waste plumbing system's parts are further detailed below:

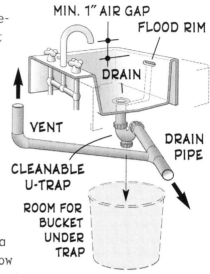

7-28. Waste plumbing components

Drain. This is a hole in the lowest part of the basin that receives the swirling effluent. It should have a plug, cap, or a small basket strainer that catches large particles and is easily removed for cleaning.

Trap. This is a tube with a U-shaped bend at its bottom that is located below the drain where the most recent effluent settles to form a liquid seal that keeps any noxious gases downstream from rising through the drain and indoors. This little snare can also capture small heavy objects, such as diamond rings and other baubles; so every trap should have a threaded plug at its base and room for a bucket directly below. Traps under showers and bathtubs can be reached from the floor below. If a shower or tub rests on a ground-level concrete slab, you better not drop any valuables down their drains.

Drain pipe. This conveys the effluent downstream from the fix-

326

ture. Each requires cleanouts that enable every linear foot to be cleared in case it becomes clogged. Any drain pipe running uphill requires mechanical pumping.

Vent. This pipe stems from below each trap where it collects any noxious waste gases rising in the drain pipe and conveys them upward through the roof. Where each penetrates the roof it must be open at the top, but needn't be capped because rain falling into it descends to the drain pipe at its base; but it should be covered with $\frac{1}{4}$ inch wire mesh to keep tree debris, birds, rodents, and snakes from entering. A vent may also extend through a facade just below the roof, then it must be recessed within the plane of the facade and the recess's base must slope steeply enough to keep birds, snow, and ice off it. A vent should never open into an attic or other unfinished indoor space even if ventilated, because the vented gases are noxious.

In Arctic regions a vent's top may require frost closure protection. This is done by (1) extending the vent only 1 or 2 inches above the roof, (2) enlargening its diameter just below the roof, (3) installing flashing with an airspace between the vent and the building, and/or (4) encircling the vent at roof level with hot-water tubing or electrical heat tracing cable. In Arctic regions vents are often installed in a building's sides where someone can knock off any icicles and frost boles that form.

In Arctic and high montane regions where temperatures go below minus 40 degrees, weird things can happen where air moisture exits a building. Icicles can form at tiny holes in a facade, and moisture leaking through an exterior doorknob can cause it to freeze solid. Then one's "house key" may be an electric blow dryer hanging outside the door, with a second dryer hanging inside for getting out. If you plan to build "north of 66", consult a few local authorities before breaking ground —which itself is not easy because it's permafrost. [22] For more information check the

Architecture Laid Bare!

Department of Energy at www.eere.energy.gov.

There are five kinds of plumbing waste. Each requires different treatment after draining from the fixtures, as follows:

1. *Clearwater.* Essentially clear but undrinkable water. This includes rainfall from roofs, HVAC condensates, water residues from industrial operations, cold water draining from a fixture while someone waits for hot water to arrive, and the like. When this waste doesn't mix with other wastes downstream it can flow in channels, troughs, trenches and other open watercourses, and it can empty into cisterns, ponds, streams, and marshes. When filtered this fluid can be reused in fire sprinklers, toilets, and urinals, and for washing cars and clothes.

2. *Graywater.* Water draining from sinks, showers, tubs, clothes washers, cooling towers, and the like. It is undrinkable and may have a slight odor and pose a health hazard, hence it must empty into closed drains and requires venting. But it can bypass septic tanks and sewers, be filtered, and be reused in industrial operations and to flush toilets. If this fluid contains hot water, it offers possibilities for heat reclamation in holding tanks. One such tank already exists in most houses: the bathtub. If you take a bath when it's cold outside and let the water remain in the tub overnight, the water's escaping heat can keep the bathroom and a nearby bedroom at near-room temperature during twelve hours of 20-degree outdoor weather.

3. *Brownwater.* Effluent draining from toilets and urinals, food scraps from restaurants, mulch from hospital sinks and grinders, and the like. This unsightly and smelly waste must empty into closed drains that flow into septic tanks or public sewer systems.

4. *Blackwater.* Chemicals and toxic liquids draining from usually commercial or industrial operations. Even in resi-

dences this waste should drain into dedicated containers and be taken to recycling facilities. Blackwater should never empty into public watercourses, and residents should never pour it down household plumbing drains.

5. *Grease.* Oils from machines, fats from restaurants, and the like. This matter adheres to surfaces, is largely water-insoluble, and is often flammable. In restaurants and food processing plants, waste greases and oils typically drain into tanks that contain meshed panels to which the grease adheres as it cools, then the remaining liquid (considered as brownwater) flows downstream and the panels laden with fats and solids are periodically removed and replaced. The tank is often a cubic yard in size and may be concrete, stainless steel, or fiberglass. It usually has an acid-resistant finish on the inside, a coat of bitumen (a tar-like waterproofing) on the outside, and a manhole on top with plenty of floorspace around it. The tank's volume should allow the entering effluent to sub-side without agitating the effluent already there, and the tank's depth should allow suspended particles to rise or sink before being disturbed by the next-arriving effluent.

    In residences, try to keep bacon fats and kitchen oils out of sewers and septic systems.

Wastes 1 through 4 above may combine with any higher number but not a lower number: i.e. waste 2 may combine and be treated with wastes 3 or 4, but not waste 1. Otherwise it becomes much more expensive to separate them.

When clearwater or graywater is used to irrigate crops, flush toilets, and the like, the enabling apparatus is a *graywater recycling system*. The approximate daily volume draining into the system is its *potential supply*, and the approximate daily volume of treated water desired is the system's *potential demand*. The two should approximately equal each other. The system's collection tank should be sized to hold twice the daily potential supply, and its contents should be retained no more than 72 hours.

Figure 7-29 shows a large graywater recycling system that operates by gravity. On top is a roof that sheds rainwater, and just below are a bathtub, two sinks, and a clothes washer. These fixtures drain into an optional heat exchanger which captures heat from the wastewater, then the wastewater and roof runoff drain into a collection tank that has (1) an accessible and replaceable fine-mesh filter (an old nylon stocking works well here) that removes visible particles from the water, (2) a roof vent, and (3) an overflow pipe that empties into the building's waste plumbing. From here the graywater drains into a filter bed which removes microparticles, then the filtered water descends through a main water supply pipe which increases the filtered water's volume if it is insufficient to serve the intended fixtures downstream (the supply pipe is fitted with a backflow valve to keep the slightly impure filtered water from possibly contaminating the supply water). Then the filtered water may either empty into irrigation systems

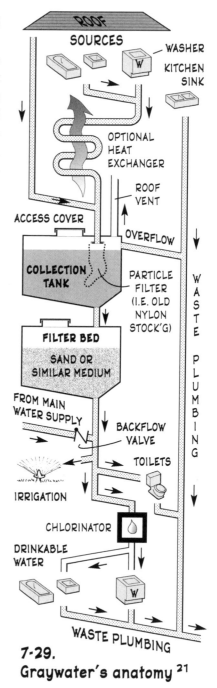

7-29.
Graywater's anatomy [21]

and toilets or enter a chlorinator that kills any microbes in the water which makes it drinkable. The only energy this system uses is a few watts of electricity to run the chlorinator. [23]

If a graywater recycler does not work by gravity, it will likely *increase* energy costs rather than decrease them. Such a counterproductive converter appeared in a recent magazine, as follows: It was installed under a bathroom sink and used a small pump to lift the used water from under the sink to the top of a toilet nearby. This monument to Pollyana will consume more energy to pump the water than it will save by reusing the water, plus a patch of environment somewhere was despoiled in making the pump. To make this gadget work by gravity one must (1) raise the sink from vanity height (usually 30 inches) to kitchen counter height (usually 36 inches); (2) install a toilet with a lower tank; (3) install a kiddie toilet (the kind used in nursery schools) which is only 11 inches high instead of 18 and is surprisingly comfortable for a grownup to sit on; and/or (4) mount the toilet a step or two below the floor under the sink.

One more aspect of the above magazine article merits a dishonorable mention. The article was supposedly written by a journalist who practices the principles of truth and integrity that are the acme of objective reportage. Yet the journalist colluded with the magazine's editor to claim that a certain device would solve a problem when it definitely would not. The magazine even included an impressive technicolor photograph that was so realistically alluring that it would be hard for an unknowing layman to see the truth behind the ruse. How can the public get honest facts about a serious issue when journalists and magazine editors act as irresponsibly as this?

A few plumbing waste components are required in many occupancies as described below.

Floor Drains. These remove water collecting on flat roofs or floors before they can damage nearby construction or furnishings. Where wasteflow may contain oils and sediments, a floor

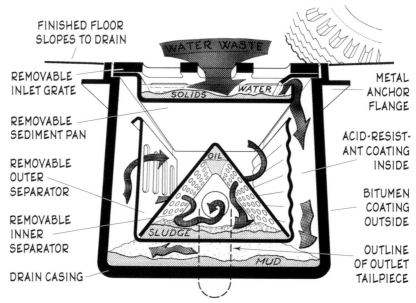

FINISHED FLOOR
SLOPES TO DRAIN

REMOVABLE
INLET GRATE

REMOVABLE
SEDIMENT PAN

REMOVABLE
OUTER
SEPARATOR

REMOVABLE
INNER
SEPARATOR

DRAIN CASING

METAL
ANCHOR
FLANGE

ACID-RESIST-
ANT COATING
INSIDE

BITUMEN
COATING
OUTSIDE

OUTLINE
OF OUTLET
TAILPIECE

WATER WASTE

SOLIDS   WATER

OIL

SLUDGE

MUD

7-30. Commercial floor drain details and operation

drain may be a cubic-foot-size metal casing with an acid-resistant finish inside and a coat of bitumen outside. One of these
beauties appears above. On its top at floor level sits a removable
cast iron inlet grate, just below lies a removable sediment pan
that collects solids without impeding wasteflow, and a few inches
further down rest two removable separators that collect sludge
and oil.

Every commercial kitchen should have a floor drain in front
of the sinks (not a bad idea for residential kitchens and areas in
front of washing machines either). Each such drain requires a
trap, vent, and drain; and the drained floor area should be rimmed
by an integral baseboard at least 4 inches high and descend ¼
inch per foot in all directions toward the drain.

Ejectors.[24] In buildings where a few plumbing fixtures exist
below the sewer main, ejectors pump the effluent up to the sewer.
This reservoir is generally sized to hold a day's supply of efflu-

ent, built of a nondegradable material, installed with an alarm
that warns of any malfunc-
tion, and is usually in-
stalled in pairs lest one
fails. If the tank isn't
concrete or other heavy
material it must be
anchored to a concrete
base to keep the tank
from buoying up when it
contains mostly air. The
tank's top must have a
removable manhole with
plenty of floorspace around
it plus a hose bibb and hose rack
nearby. Three companies that sell

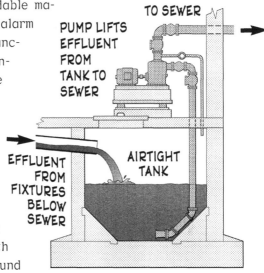

7-31. Ejector details

ejectors are Liberty Pumps, Gorman-Rupp, and Goulds Pumps.

When clear water waste (usually from groundwater seepage, stormwater, or minor flooding) collects in the lower part of a base-ment or crawl space of a small building and needs to be pumped outdoors to a higher elevation, this is typically done with a *sump pump*. This is an electric motor attached to a small pump that sucks water collecting in an often bucket-sized sump pit and delivers it to the higher elevation. This drainage can be open and doesn't require vent-ing. Most units will pump up to 15 feet vertically before they lose power. The pit and pipes may

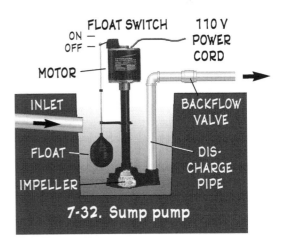

7-32. Sump pump

need to be periodically cleaned of dirt, gravel, sand, and other debris (which means the unit should have adequate service area around it), and one's operation should be periodically tested.

Cleanouts.[25] These are Y or T fittings with a threaded plug in one stem that can be removed to allow the waste pipe downstream to be inspected or cleaned. These openings must be located at every change of direction of 45 degrees or more, no more than 75 feet apart, and within 5 feet of where the waste main exits the building. Today a plumber can insert a video camera into a cleanout to locate any buildup before it becomes a stoppage. For such colonoscopies deep in a building's bowels the practitioner needs plenty of elbow room: at least 6 × 6 feet of waterproof floor area with a central drain, a nearby door to facilitate entry of personnel and equipment, plus a hose bibb and a hose rack on a wall nearby for cleaning.

PLUG / WASTE / AT EACH CHANGE IN DIRECTION, HORIZONTAL OR VERTICAL / AT THE BASE OF WASTE STACKS / PLUG / MAX. 75 FT. BTWN PLUGS

7-33. Cleanout locations

Septic Systems. A septic tank is a reservoir shaped like a large concrete box that is located below grade where it collects effluent from a usually small building. As the effluent empties into the tank, any heavier-than-water solids settle on the bottom and lighter-than-water solids form a sludge on top, then the clarified effluent discharges through an overflow pipe into a *leaching field*: a network of underground 4-inch diameter footing drains with penny-size holes along their sides known as *perforated drain tiles* through which the effluent seeps into the surrounding soil. The drains are laid below frost level in trenches filled with at least six inches of gravel, and the solids and sludge are pumped out of the tank every few years. These systems are designed by a chain of events which typically unfold as follows:

1. The septic tank and leaching field are located at least 100 feet from any wells, streams, and lakes. Both should be in grassy open terrain, not under parking areas or where heavy loads could compact the soil above the drains. If trees exist in the area they and especially the major part of their roots are usually removed.

2. The septic tank is sized based on the number of occupants served. In residences this is usually done by counting up the bedrooms and in commercial buildings by counting the plumbing fixtures.

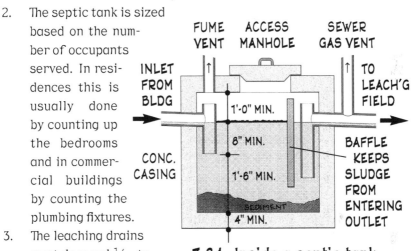

7-34. Inside a septic tank

3. The leaching drains must descend $1/16$ to $3/8$ inch per foot from the septic tank. Their length is determined by the tank's size and how porous the soil is in the vicinity of the drains. To determine the latter, a plumbing inspector digs a bucket-size hole in the soil, an act of discovery known as a percolation test or *perc test*, then fills the hole with water and with a stopwatch times how fast the water sinks into the soil. The longer this takes, the longer the drains must be according to code-mandated formulae. In hard clay a perc test result may be so poor that truckloads of gravel and porous soil must be dumped onto the leaching area to create adequately permeable soil.

335

4. To make sure the earth where the leaching drains will be laid is deep enough to bury the drains below frost level plus six inches of gravel under them, an excavator digs several 5-to-6 foot deep holes where the drains are to be laid, an act of discovery known as a *deep-hole test*. If solid rock or ledge is found too near the ground's surface, truckloads of gravel and dirt may have to be dumped over the leaching field's area to create a legal depth.

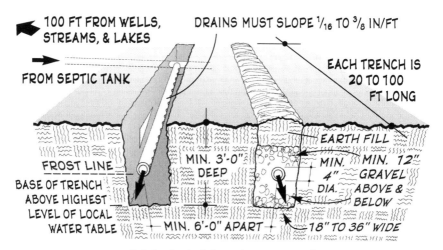

7-35. Outside a leaching field

Septic systems usually receive effluent from buildings whose water supply is a drilled well. Hence the system and well create an ecological "Round River" that returns the used water nearly to where it was drawn, transforming the intervening earth into a huge three-dimensional filter often a cubic acre in size that keeps the well water perpetually pure. So a well/septic system doesn't really consume water (it consumes a small amount of electricity): it merely borrows water from one place and returns it to another. Any foliage above the leaching drains —a garden maybe?— is also made more luxuriant by the fertilizing effluent: a completion of another of Nature's cycles. Here is Green Architecture at its best.

Plumbing

Regarding plumbing waste that empties into a public sewer, research conducted by the Institute of Land and Water Research at Penn State University in the 1960s found that if the effluent of a typical city of 100,000 is treated in a manmade lake, it would require 1,290 acres of area to purify the water. But if the same effluent empties into a forest where it would filter down through the foliage, strain through the topsoil, and flow out its streams, it would require only 129 acres to purify it.

As usual Nature trumps industry, if you give It a chance.

Notes

Climate

A building's indoor spaces are warmed in winter, cooled in summer, freshened when stale, and otherwise made comfortable by devices that create the opposite effect of the weather outdoors no matter how it rages every hour of the year. However, making these devices serve their masters comfortably well begins by analyzing what happens ninety-three million miles away.

The Site

As the earth tilts on its axis during its annual rotations around the sun, at any latitude this bright orb crosses the sky at a significantly higher altitude in summer than in winter. In summer it also rises earlier well north of east and sets later well north of west, and in winter it rises later well south of east and sets earlier well south of west. There are clever ways to manipulate these solar trajectories to your advantage.

8-1. Using sun angles to design an overhang

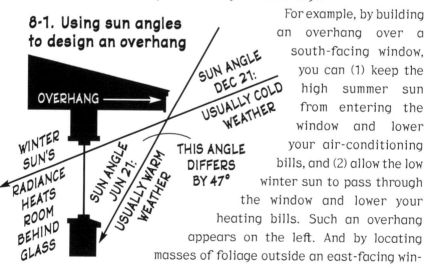

OVERHANG

SUN ANGLE DEC 21: USUALLY COLD WEATHER

WINTER SUN'S RADIANCE HEATS ROOM BEHIND GLASS

SUN ANGLE JUN 21: USUALLY WARM WEATHER

THIS ANGLE DIFFERS BY 47°

For example, by building an overhang over a south-facing window, you can (1) keep the high summer sun from entering the window and lower your air-conditioning bills, and (2) allow the low winter sun to pass through the window and lower your heating bills. Such an overhang appears on the left. And by locating masses of foliage outside an east-facing window, you can block the summer sun rising north of east that would pass before this opening during the morning from throwing a lot of heat and glare into the room behind. But in winter, the sun rising south of east would shine only obliquely on the glass during the morning and you wouldn't want to block what little light it could add to the room behind. Such a window appears below. A mirror image of these conditions exists in windows facing west.

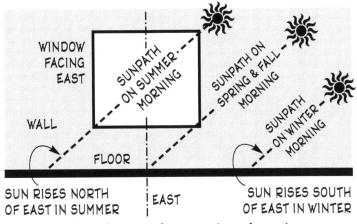

8-2. Sun angles, east and west

    This is how architects design a building's openings to save you money. By knowing how high above the horizon and what direction the sun will be every hour of the day during the year around a planned building, they can design overhangs over south-facing windows and locate barriers in front of east- and west-facing windows in ways that will appreciably reduce the building's cooling bills in summer and heating bills in winter.

    However, the sky doesn't always cooperate in these matters. Summer days can be cool, winter days can be warm, and clouds can hide the sun any time all year round. And the sun's highest trajectories across the sky don't occur on the average hottest days of the year, nor do its lowest trajectories occur on the coldest days. As a sample, on August 20 and April 20 the sun's trajectories across the sky are the same; but where I live, the average noonday temperature on August 20 is 78° while on April 20 it is only 56°. In early September I normally wouldn't want the sun shining on my windows, but in early April I would want all the free heat I could get. This shows that however well a fixed overhang may work, a movable overhang will work considerably better. But movable overhangs cost more. This is the kind of balancing act one must perform when designing a building to take advantage of the weather: either spend some money for a solution that will work some of the time, or spend more money for a solution that will work more of the time. Hence when you design for climate, you are gambling. But unlike the wagering that occurs in Las Vegas, where the "house" odds are always against you, when wagering against the weather, if you know the prevailing probabilities and bet on them, the "house" odds will be in your favor.

One kind of movable "overhang" over southerly windows that automatically allows the sun to shine on them in April and shades them in September is deciduous foliage. Such trees rising on the south side of a house or low commercial building will shade its windows in summer and let the sun shine through them in winter. This device also is pleasant to look at, and does anything but despoil the environment in its making.

Nearer than the sun but still some distance from a planned building is another climatic factor: wind. These air currents flow over land much the way water flows over the bed of a stream. Where the terrain is smooth, the air flows evenly; where the terrain is rough, the air flows fast over the high spots and slow over the low. Over low depressions these drafts often form stagnant "air ponds" that are clammy as a cave compared to the air fifty feet away: you wouldn't want to locate a building here, in warm weather or cold. Breezes also speed up when they slide down hills, fall over bluffs, or sluice though city streets and other narrow openings; and they slow down when they flow up hills, run into cliffs, and spread into parks and other open areas. Breezes are also slowed by masses of foliage, which cool the air below during the day and warm it slightly at night. How forest foliage affects

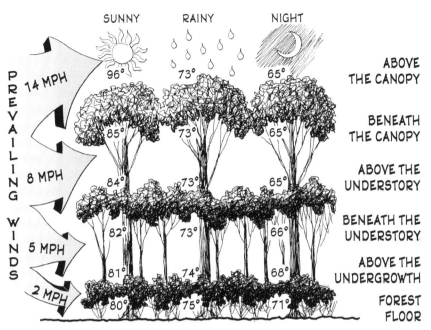

8-3. How forest foliage affects microclimate

air speeds and temperatures appears in the above drawing.

Prevailing winds also tend to bring cooler air from the north-west and warmer air from the southwest. In northerly latitudes during most of the year these breezes are unwelcome when cold and welcome when warm, and in southerly latitudes the reverse is true. The smart thing to do here is open a building to local pre-vailing breezes where they are desired, and shield them when they are not. Desirable openings are flat terrain, low ground covers, tall shade trees around a building, large casement windows locat-ed in facades where their opened sashes can scoop passing air indoors, and roof-mounted belvederes that can draw stuffy indoor air up from below. A lot of houses in warm climates are built this way. Desirable shields are rises in terrain, tall solid fences and other windbreaks, clusters of evergreen trees around a building, small high-silled windows, and recessed entrance doors. A lot of houses in cold climates are constructed this way. A few such open-

341

DISCOURAGING BREEZES WITH SHIELDS

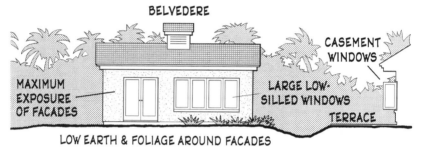

ENCOURAGING BREEZES WITH OPENINGS

8-4. Wind shields and openings around a building

ings and shields appear in figure 8-4. In temperate climates where temperatures are usually hot in summer and cold in winter, one can locate high-branched deciduous trees and other openings around a two- or three-story building's southern half, and place low-branched evergreens and other shields around the northern half. These natural strategies can lower a building's heating and cooling bills as much as adding one or two inches of insulation in its roof and outer walls. In fact, our old friend Frank Lloyd Wright said: "I think it far better to go *with* the natural climate than try to fix a special artificial climate of your own."[1]

Nearer than prevailing winds from a planned building is another natural element that affects life indoors: the ground. A marvelous tool exists for analyzing this: United States Geodetic

342

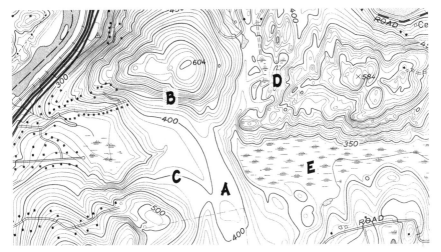

8-5. Part of a U.S. Geodetic survey map

Survey maps, also known as *topographic* or *topo maps*. The government publishes these for nearly everywhere in the country. They are drawn to a scale of 1 inch equals 2,000 feet, and they show forests in green, water in blue, elevation contours in brown, and roads, railroads, buildings, and other landmarks in black. Part of a USGS map appears above. Where topographic contours are far apart, as at **A**, the land is flat or nearly so, and where contours are close together, as at **B**, the land is steep. Flat land may seem like a good place to build, but water sometimes doesn't drain well in these places. The steeper the slope, usually the nicer the view downhill, but the more you will likely pay for a foundation and a driveway. Gentle slopes, like the one at **C**, usually offer the best of both worlds. Rugged terrain, as around **D**, can cause all kinds of trouble unless they are carefully analyzed. And see the grassy symbols in the flat area around **E**? That's a marsh. You probably couldn't build there if you wanted because most building codes won't let you. In this map are several streets, an interstate highway, a railroad, a river, and the corner of a lake. See if you can find them. When designing a building, an architect usually obtains the USGS map where the building will be located, enlarges

343

the area around the planned building, and draws the enlarged contours on the site plan.

Also affecting the climate around a building is the temperature of the ground's surface. As appears in figure 8-6, on a sunny day when the ambient air is 80 degrees, since light surfaces are more reflective and cooler than dark, the air over a meadow may be 75°, above bare earth 88°, over a pond 73°, above a lawn 78°, over rocks or concrete 98°, above asphalt 120°, and over a wood deck 85°.

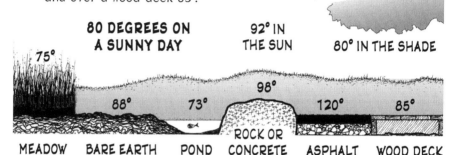

80 DEGREES ON A SUNNY DAY   **92° IN THE SUN**   **80° IN THE SHADE**

75°   88°   73°   98°   120°   85°

MEADOW   BARE EARTH   POND   ROCK OR CONCRETE   ASPHALT   WOOD DECK

8-6. How ground surfaces affect the temperature above

Knowing these things can indicate the best location for turn-arounds, terraces, decks, yards, and gardens around a building. As a sample, in warm regions you wouldn't want to locate hot surfaces around the south side of a building. Also the difference in temperature between a shady area and a sunny area only a few feet away is about 12 degrees. If it is 80 degrees Fahrenheit on a sunny day, a thermometer will read 80 in the shade and 92 in the sun. Hence a sunlit side of a building will be 12 degrees warmer than if shaded. This consideration is how well-placed foliage, especially deciduous foliage, can reduce a building's cooling bills in summer and its heating bills in winter.

Another important ground temperature is the one twenty feet below. All year round at this depth the temperature is approximately that of the local annual temperature and the local groundwater. Hear what a noted engineer says about this:

Climate

> In wells 30 to 60 feet deep, the water temperature is 2° F to
> 3° F above the annual mean temperature of the area. Well
> water decreases in temperature about 1° F for every 64 feet
> in depth. [2]

If you come across a text that says the temperature of the ground several feet below its surface is "always about 50 degrees" or "55 degrees" (as have three texts I've recently read) —give it a cold shoulder and seek your information elsewhere; because if it doesn't have this fact right it probably has others wrong too. Groundwater in Miami is obviously warmer (about 74°) than in Minneapolis (about 43°), which means a house in Miami requires only about 60 percent of the energy to heat to 120 degrees water drawn from a drilled well as does the same house in Minneapolis. An engineer needs to know these things before sizing a hot water heater, a furnace boiler, or any number of industrial operations. If you know these things, you can make sure an architect or engineer knows them too, and even inform your friends.

Speaking of water, one landscape feature that buildings should stay away from is streams. A whispery brook may seem the epitome of tranquility —but it can rise up and steal a house during a rare superstorm. If you consider building along a stream, see if the ground extending back from each bank is fairly level a few dozen feet or so to a second bank that slopes steeply uphill. That second bank was created by a few thousand years of once-a-century superstorms. Always remember that the stream owns the first mortgage on the level land between the outer banks. And here's a well-kept secret about America's most famous creekside residence: Frank Lloyd Wright's Fallingwater. Its foundation rising out of the creek absorbs water via capillary action, the way a towel draped over the side of a bathtub sucks water from inside the tub, and in the rooms upstairs the moisture in the air condenses on the cold stone walls the way it condenses on the side of a cocktail glass. At least one of my architecture school professors said this around 1960 (this defect may have been remedied by now). This historic house also experiences floods. Once during a violent storm the creek rose so high that it submerged the cantilevers on the second floor. The architecture above looked like a houseboat on a lake. It's a testimony to Wright's structural genius that the building didn't wash away. But the owners lost a lot of furnishings and had to scoop tons of mud from the flooded floors. So the moral here is: Keep your house away from creeks and streams, and they will keep trouble away from you.

With this insight it would be pertinent to say a word about the familiar expression, "once-a-century superstorm". A nebulous concept if there ever was one. In 1986 I built a pond below my house. Meticulous analysis on my part indicated I should install a big 36-inch-diameter culvert below the pond's outflow basin to carry the drainage of a once-a-century superstorm. Then in 1989 —only three years later— came Flood Floyd. At the height of this hurricane's rainfall the culvert was filled with thundering outflow and spilling over one side of the pond was a 7 inch deep sheet of water 70 feet wide! Fortunately I had "disobeyed" the building department's order to build a three-foot wide spillway beside the pond and instead made a 75 × 30 foot area of ground alongside the pond 12 inches lower, covered it with layer of softball-size rocks, covered the rocks with 4 inches of topsoil, and seeded the soil with hardy meadow grass. Here the designer, instead of whining to the authorities about a seemingly excessive order, allowed it to give power to his imagination to create a "soft path" solution that carried six times more water than the culvert.

A building's designer should also consider the nature of the ground up to several hundred feet away. Large areas of pavement around shopping centers and factories (roofs too if they are flat and dark) increase temperatures in the wake of prevailing winds. And the air on the lee side of expressways and airports is slightly more toxic. Here you wouldn't want to locate an elementary school playground, or maybe even one in your back yard. Also regarding any property you may buy, before writing a check pay it a lengthy visit and see if any noises bother you. Thirty years ago

Climate

I inspected a house for a couple who wanted to buy it. The place was a gem. But during the three hours we were there, we continually heard the drone of vehicles on an expressway hidden behind a grove of trees beyond the back yard. When the wife said, "I can't stand that traffic," I knew the noise had killed the sale.

The Shell Game

Once you've analyzed the weather and the landscape around a building, your next line of defense toward making its indoor spaces economically comfortable every hour of the year is insulating its lowest floor, outer walls, and roof: what is known as the *building envelope*. This cutaneous construction may contain three kinds of insulation:

Batts ... fluffy masses of spun glass that are fitted into voids in the construction.

Sheets ... lightweight rigid sheets such as styrofoam and urethane that are fastened to walls and roofs and laid under concrete slabs.

Fills ... lightweight granules or foams that are usually poured or sprayed into construction voids.

A big question with insulation is how thick should it be? Before speculating on the answer, let's state some facts:

☞ Insulation is a one-time cost that reduces a lifetime cost.

☞ A prevailing myth in building construction is that every added inch of insulation is slightly less effective and after perhaps 6 or 8 inches or so you reach a point of no return where any further thickness won't pay for itself. Not true. First, the point of no return is more like 20 inches. Second, the tipping point will *not* occur at a conceptual "added inch of insulation" but where the accumulating insulation suddenly requires a different and costlier construction to hold it. Due to continuing rises in energy prices, we will soon need to put *many* more inches of insulation in today's building envelopes, and this will require new methods of construction. (More about this two pages from now).

☞ The greater the temperature difference between the inside and outside of a building, the faster the heat flows through the building envelope (inward in hot weather, outward in cold); while the thicker the insulation in the envelope, the slower the heat flows.

But all the above facts are befuddled by five little letters:
water

Here's the problem. Air contains a certain amount of water, usually as a vapor suspended in the air, measured as *humidity*. If the temperature of air goes down, its humidity goes up, until it reaches 100 percent. If the temperature keeps going down, the water begins to drop out of the air because it can't hold any more, and this moisture deposits on nearby surfaces.

Now when heat flows through an exterior wall wherever there are any seams, cracks, and pores in the construction, part of the migrating heat is carried through these openings by the air which, remember, also contains water. As the air flows through the wall and its temperature lowers, the air cools and its humidity rises until it reaches 100 percent; then the water begins to drop out of the air and deposit on the wall's construction. In the old days when energy was cheap and nobody thought much about insulation, all the air flowing through the envelope not only deposited moisture in the construction as the air cooled, the flowing air also carried away the deposited moisture.

But during the energy crisis of the late Seventies, somebody got the bright idea that the way to stop a lot of heat escaping from a building in winter was to wrap it in an airtight membrane known as a *vapor barrier*. This stopped the heat flowing with the air —but it also stopped any flowing air from carrying away the deposited moisture. If this water cannot escape, it will rot the

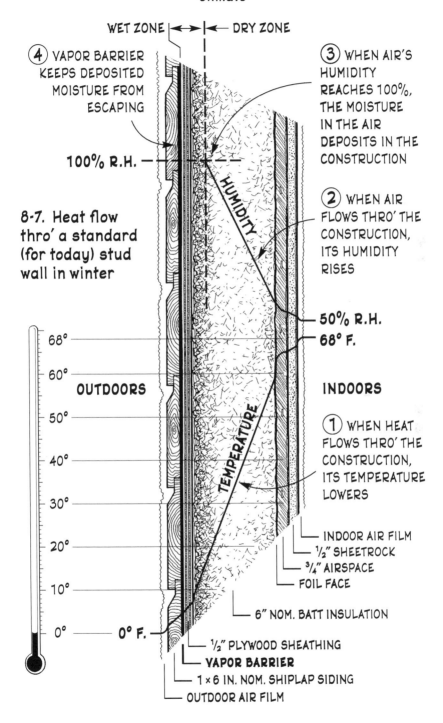

Climate

WET ZONE |←→|←— DRY ZONE

④ VAPOR BARRIER KEEPS DEPOSITED MOISTURE FROM ESCAPING

③ WHEN AIR'S HUMIDITY REACHES 100%, THE MOISTURE IN THE AIR DEPOSITS IN THE CONSTRUCTION

100% R.H. —

HUMIDITY

8-7. Heat flow thro' a standard (for today) stud wall in winter

② WHEN AIR FLOWS THRO' THE CONSTRUCTION, ITS HUMIDITY RISES

50% R.H.
68° F.

68°

60°

OUTDOORS

INDOORS

50°

① WHEN HEAT FLOWS THRO' THE CONSTRUCTION, ITS TEMPERATURE LOWERS

40°

TEMPERATURE

30°

20°

INDOOR AIR FILM
½" SHEETROCK
¾" AIRSPACE
FOIL FACE

10°

6" NOM. BATT INSULATION

0°   0° F.

½" PLYWOOD SHEATHING
VAPOR BARRIER
1 × 6 IN. NOM. SHIPLAP SIDING
OUTDOOR AIR FILM

wood, rust the nails, dampen the batt insulation which ruins its ability to insulate, and act as cajun seasoning to a host of molds, mildews, carpenter ants, and termites that love the nourishment of lignin —until after a few years a building's outer construction will begin to stink, look awful, and fall apart all at the same time. In this respect we're like B'rer Rabbit and the tar baby: de more we try to get unstuck-up, de more stucker-up we get!

If the shell of a building you live or work in is clad in Tyvek or one of its filmy kin, it is likely rotting around you *right now* and you don't even know it yet. As the price of fossil fuels continues to rise and buildings continue to be clad in moisture-trapping vapor barriers, this situation has become perhaps the most insidious economic issue confronting American buildings today. Hear what Joseph Lstiburek, Ph.D., says of these thermodynamics:

> Less energy flow [i.e. heat] from the inside to the outside means the materials on the outside of the building are colder in the winter. The colder the materials on the outside of the building become, the wetter they become and the wetter they stay. This is not good. ... Think of it this way. For every 100 units of energy you save on the efficiency and on the cooling side, you will need to give back about 20 units of energy to be dry. You are still 80 units ahead. The problem is that if you are greedy and want the entire 100 units, your building fails and your occupants become uncomfortable. [3]

Is there *any* way to notably reduce the heat flowing through a building envelope *without* trapping moisture in it?

There is!

It is the *Insulation Cage*, a wall construction that contains thick insulation, allows enough air to flow through the construction and carry away any deposited moisture, and is relatively easy and economical to build. [4] Its construction appears in figure 8-8. This 12-inch thick thermal armor has two 2×4-inch stud walls, each $3\frac{1}{2}$ inches thick, with a 5-inch airspace between —and no water-trapping vapor barrier around it. The outer and inner stud

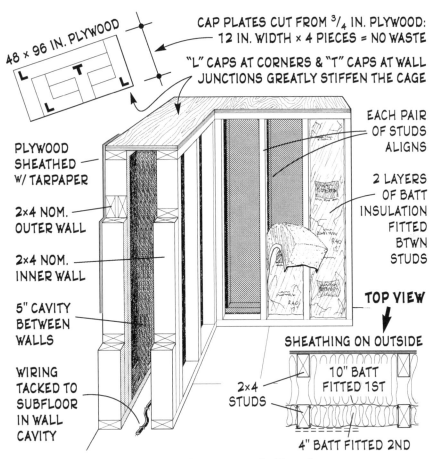

48 × 96 IN. PLYWOOD

CAP PLATES CUT FROM ³/₄ IN. PLYWOOD:
12 IN. WIDTH × 4 PIECES = NO WASTE

"L" CAPS AT CORNERS & "T" CAPS AT WALL
JUNCTIONS GREATLY STIFFEN THE CAGE

PLYWOOD
SHEATHED
W/ TARPAPER

2×4 NOM.
OUTER WALL

2×4 NOM.
INNER WALL

5" CAVITY
BETWEEN
WALLS

WIRING
TACKED TO
SUBFLOOR
IN WALL
CAVITY

EACH PAIR
OF STUDS
ALIGNS

2 LAYERS
OF BATT
INSULATION
FITTED
BTWN
STUDS

TOP VIEW

SHEATHING ON OUTSIDE

2×4
STUDS

10" BATT
FITTED 1ST

4" BATT FITTED 2ND

8-8. The wondrous Insulation Cage

walls are built separately (the studs of each should align); and since each wall is light they can be built quickly. This was a major problem with the 12-inch superinsulated walls developed in the late 1970s: each took a huge amount of labor to build. I know, because I built one once —and Lord, I never spent so much time doing so little good. I found that while three men could easily raise a sixteen foot length of 2×4 stud framing with a window in it, the same three men could barely raise a *six* foot length of 2×12 nominal stud framing with a window in it because it was so much heavier. The logistics of this are as follows: If you can lift 100 pounds and you need to lift 90 pounds (i.e. raise a 4-inch wall) you can do it; but if you need to lift 270 pounds (i.e. raise a 12-inch wall) you can't do it and you must find another way to get the job done; but if you need to lift 90 pounds twice (i.e. raise two 4-inch walls), you can do it. This is why the Insulation Cage is easy to build, because it is not one heavy 12-inch wall so much as it is two light 4-inch walls.

The Insulation Cage has another big thermal advantage: the 5 inches between the two stud walls eliminates another heat loss known as *perimeter heat flow*. In standard stud framing, heat conducts through the studs between the insulation and the plates along the wall's tops and bottoms; and since heat conducts through wood about four times faster than through fiberglass batts, nearly 40 percent of all the heat flowing through standard stud framing flows through the pieces of wood between, above, and below the insulation. This doesn't happen in the Insulation Cage. As a result, only *three-tenths* as much heat flows through this construction as through a normal 6-inch stud wall. This means every thousand dollars of heating bills out of your pocket becomes three hundred dollars!

The Insulation Cage has other advantages that every carpenter will appreciate. The 2-inch-nominal cap plate normally nailed on top of the two stud walls to hold them together is replaced by a 12-inch-wide strip of ¾-inch plywood which alone has five advantages: (1) the plywood is lighter and easier to cut than a 2×12; (2) the plywood's laminated ¾ inch thickness is stronger laterally than a 2×12 is across the grain; (3) a ¾-inch plywood cap won't shrink vertically over time as will most 2-inch nominal lumber, (4) four 12-inch wide pieces of plywood can be cut from one 48-inch wide sheet with no waste; and (5) where walls meet at 90-degree corners and tee intersections, the plywood can be cut into L and T shapes that will make these junctions so rigid they won't budge if you bump a truck into them. As for the five-inch airspace between the two walls, it alone has four construction advantages: (1) the space dampens noise transmission through the walls; (2) it makes the walls more impervious to fire because half the wood is 5 inches from the other half and the batts between them won't burn; (3) the space allows electricians to lay the wall's wiring on the floor between the two walls without wasting time drilling holes in every stud which also weakens them and without wasting more time pulling the wires through the studs which also can damage the wire's cladding; and (4) electric outlets mounted in the inner stud walls will no longer be notorious infiltrators of air because the boxes' backs are shrouded with several inches of insulation.

The Insulation Cage is built as described below. If you ever need this work done and don't want to do it yourself, hand these pages to a contractor or carpenter and s/he will know what to do.

1. Build the outer 2×4 stud wall including its sheathing as it has always been done, but leave off the cap plate.

2. Build the inner stud wall as you built the outer one. The studs in the two walls should align. With this framing nobody needs to learn any new construction techniques or how to use any new tools.

3. Nail the $\frac{3}{4}$-inch plywood cap plates onto the two walls.

4. Fit two layers of batt insulation between the studs as follows. (1) fit 10-inch nominal batts (actual thickness = $9\frac{1}{2}$ inches) all the way in between each pair of double studs and staple the batts' paper flanges along the back edges of the inner studs. (2) fit 4-inch nominal batts (actual thickness = $3\frac{1}{2}$ inches) in front of each 10-inch batt —to create a snug 13-in-12 inches of superinsulation. The slightly compressed batts will slow heat flow better because they eliminate airspaces that often remain around their corners in standard installations.

5. Apply all interior and exterior finishes as with normal framing —except for those awful vapor barriers. Instead, cover the plywood sheathing with easy-to-apply tarpaper,

which protects the framing from rain and allows it to
breathe through its seams. Tarpaper also costs about 4¢
per square foot compared to 11¢ for Tyvek.[4]

Not only is the Insulation Cage economical to build, thermally
superior, and impervious to rot, it is stronger than any 2×6 framing. I wouldn't wish this on anyone, but if a tornado swept through
a neighborhood of houses framed with Insulation Cages, more
homes would be standing afterwards.

Another advantage of the Insulation Cage is that instead of
mounting baseboard heating units against a floor's exterior walls
where some of the heat will escape through the unit's backs
directly outdoors, the units can be mounted against interior walls
where the heat escaping out the units' backs will remain indoors.
Then your energy bills will be another ten percent or so less.
Today's baseboard heaters are located around a floor's perimeter
because then the heat spreads evenly from one side of the building to the other; but if the Cage holds in the heat three times better, the heat between the walls will spread more evenly and it will
make much less difference if the heaters are centrally located.

Finally the Cage not only eliminates moisture damage and
lowers heating bills when heat flows outward through the building
envelope in cold weather, it also eliminates moisture damage and
lowers cooling bills when heat flows inward in warm weather —
because the thermodynamics of one is the reverse of the other.

In wood framing, some say the studs should be 24 inches
apart instead of 16. Unlike what the 16/24 ratio implies, you will
not reduce the number of studs in the walls by one-third because
the reduction occurs only between the wall's openings and its
corners. In a typical 12-foot-long stud wall with a door or window,
you will rarely save more than two studs. At the same time the
wider spacing makes exterior and interior finishes flimsier and it
offers less support for cabinets, shelves, and large pictures
installed inside. Altogether the wider spacing is a fine example of
being penny-wise and pound-foolish.

Another popular idea is to clad a building with several inch-es of rigid insulation. Though this insulation is thermally strong, it has a few weaknesses:

☞ It is difficult to fasten exterior finishes to the insulation's and the insulation to the wall inside. This is typically done by attaching a metal clip to the side of a furring strip to which the exte-rior finish is nailed, then inserting a long steel screw (up to 14 inches if needed)

METAL CLIP **LONG STEEL SCREW** **EXTER. SHEATH'G**

EXTER. FINISH

2×4 STUD

2×2 FURRING STRIP **LAYERS OF RIGID INSULATION** **INTER. FINISH**

8-9. Framing for rigid insulation

through the clip and the layers of foam into a stud behind, as sketched at right. To secure this connection you must drive the screw blindly through all those layers of insula-tion into the stud's *center* —not to either side where it would often split the stud's edge and form a weak connec-tion. This is a mighty narrow target for a woodbutcher to hit 49 out of 50 times —unless the targets are timbers.

☞ Since steel is a poor insulator, each long screw acts like a thermal soda straw that sucks heat through it several hundred times faster than through the surrounding foam insulation. In this construction this conductance can amount to a significant perimeter heat loss.

☞ Some rigid foams burn, then they emit large volumes of a deadly gas. Before using this insulation, take a tiny chunk outside, light it and take a whiff of the fumes. *Then* decide if you would like to enclose you and your loved ones and/or business colleagues in this material.

Rigid insulation does have a place in building construction. It is between an outer and inner masonry wall and under concrete floors. There the thermal barrier won't burn, no perimeter heat will flow through it, and nothing can rot.

The Insulation Cage also indicates the limitations of another insulation that has received a lot of promoting these days: spray-in foam.[5] This product's installers —the gun guys— have to wear oxygen respirators and head-to-toe protective suits because as they apply the foam, expanding droplets fly into the air and stick to light fixtures, electrical outlets, floor registers, doors, windows, tools laying around —you name it. In one installation the owner decided to photograph the work for his records; the goo flying from the guns got in his hair and ruined his camera. Yet a knowledgeable person must monitor this work because: (1) the gun guys must mix the foam's ingredients precisely because off-ratio mixes have considerably lower R-values (R-value is a measure of heat flow through a material: the higher the R-value the better the material0 insulates) (2) installations of more than two inches require several passes because thicker applications will release too much heat in the foam and can char it; (3) if too much foam is applied between the studs, the excess must be laboriously trimmed from the studs' inner faces or the walls' interior finishes will look lumpy; and (4) if too little foam is applied you won't get what you paid for. If you decide to use this material, insist that the gun guys bring along an extra uniform for you or another knowledgeable person to put on before the motes begin to fly. This work also requires far more electricity to operate the drum warmers, proportioning machines, and foam pumps than it takes a few laborers to install batt insulation with power staplers; and if the installation is off-grid, it requires renting a trailer-mounted generator for the day. Old buildings have another problem. If the foam is sprayed through holes drilled in the interior finish (the usual method, rather than removing the finishes to expose the framing), it is virtually impossible to fill every void between the studs below the wires running between the electrical outlets —and every little hole in the insulation drains heat the way the little hole in the bottom of a sink drains all the water.

Climate

Using spray-in foams can also create bureaucratic hassles. Some manufacturers prohibit applying foams at more than certain thicknesses, which makes some code authorities prohibit the same; then there go the advantages of superinsulation. Some building inspectors also demand a letter from an engineer stating that the framing is strong enough to support the foam (never heard this done with cottony batts); some officials have voiced fire and health safety concerns because most foams support combustion and emit toxic gases; and some foams void shingle and roof venting warranties. To top it off, for all these headaches you often pay two or three times what you'd pay for semi-skilled laborers to install fiberglass batts.

Insulation Cages are great for new buildings. What about old ones? This is a serious consideration, because there is no way all the king's contractors and all the king's crews can tear down all the millions of existing energy-wasteful buildings in this nation and replace them with new ones that consume a third as much energy. So if we are to solve this nation's energy crisis, *we must find ways to make existing buildings energy-efficient.* But how?

What other solution is there than to thicken the existing exterior walls? With not just six inches of insulation, but *twelve* inches. This can be done in three ways. (1) Tear down the existing walls and replace them with thicker ones. (2) Thicken the existing walls from the outside. (3) Thicken the existing walls from the inside. Choice 1 requires more work and more disruption of the building's use during the work. Choice 2, being outdoors, would be affected by bad weather. So let's hone in on choice 3.

If a building has lots of wasted space inside which is made more efficient as described in chapter 3, you would probably have plenty of room around the inside of the exterior walls to build a second wall up to a foot thick and fill it with as much insulation. This work could be done indoors one room at a time, so occupants could still use most of the building. One kind of building today would be perfect for this. McMansions! The bloated spaces in these wigwams of modern wasteful society could easily endure a little liposuction inside their skins, especially if the remaining interior becomes more sveltely comfortable. This construction could be performed as sketched in figure 8-10, as follows:

1. Remove the interior finish from the exterior walls and the floors and ceilings $9\frac{1}{2}$ inches back in from the walls.
2. Fit pieces of batt insulation into the voids between the ceiling framing above the wall and the floor framing below for 16 inches in from the wall.
3. Erect a second 2×4 stud wall $9\frac{1}{2}$ inches in from the existing wall.
4. Insert 10-inch thick batt insulation into the new wall.
5. Refinish the new wall same as the old, according to taste.

As usual, all this isn't as simple as this glib description suggests. For one thing, you'll have to remove the electrical outlets and wiring in the old walls and reinstall them in the new ones (but any electrician can do this). A more serious matter is if any closets are in the exterior walls. You'll probably have to tear them out and reframe them $9\frac{1}{2}$ inches further indoors, or relocate them somewhere else. Also, framing the second wall around existing windows and exterior doors would require a skilled carpenter.

As for thickening a building's exterior walls from the outside, this may be a better choice if the spaces inside are already compactly designed. One way to do this is to

1. Strip the exterior finish from the outer wall but leave the sheathing since it helps support the building.
2. Remove any Tyvek or similar vapor barrier if any.
3. Drill $\frac{3}{4}$-inch holes 16 inches apart vertically in the sheathing between each pair of studs. These "nostrils" will help the wall breathe.
4. Build a $9\frac{1}{2}$ inch ledge at the wall's base just below the first floor. This can be done several ways depending on the existing construction.
5. Along the ledge's outer edge, frame a 2 × 4 stud wall for

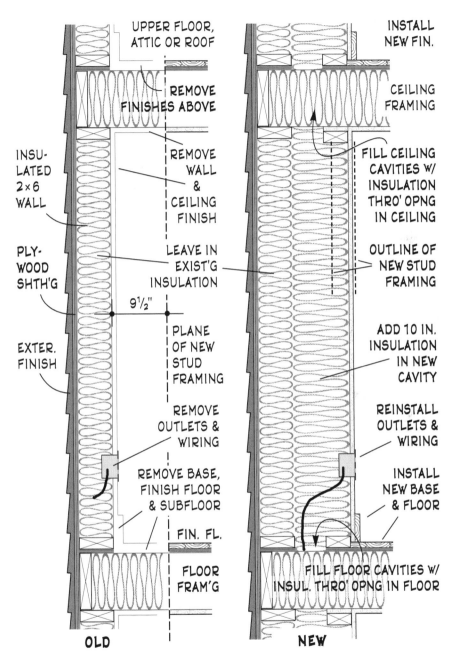

8-10. Thickening existing exterior walls from indoors

each floor up to its ceiling or the roof's eave.

6. Insert 10-inch batts from the outside between the studs.
7. Sheath the studs, add the exterior finish, clean up, and you're done.

What about roofs? If a building has a wood truss roof, you can lay thick batts on the existing insulation in the attic to create sixteen full inches of insulation. But if the roof has short eaves, a problem may occur where the trusses' ends meet the top of the exterior wall and the eave of the roof. At this triple intersection a constriction would prevent installing the full depth of insulation. One solution appears in figure 8-11, whose construction would proceed as follows.

1. Remove the lowest 2 or 3 feet of roofing and its sheathing up from the roof's eave.
2. Mount on each exposed rafter or truss strut a triangular cleat whose outer edge is high enough to allow a roof vent to fit above the new insulation to be laid in the attic. Each cleat should be the same thickness as the strut or rafter it rides on and is held in place by small $3/8$-inch plywood gussets nailed to its sides.
3. Resheath and reshingle the roof the same as before.

Now all this work may look too difficult to think of doing it yourself. It may even look too difficult to think of *anyone* doing it. But any carpenter worth his framing square can do it. Besides, think of all the money you'll save someday when energy prices are five times what they are now. Then, remembering that ancient day when you haltingly took these pages to a local builder, you'll look back at what you did and smile.

A note on asphalt shingles. These are usually replaced every ten to fifteen years and they create 10 million tons of waste per year. Enter Enviroshakes and Panelshakes. Made from waste wood fibers, old tires, used milk jugs and other recycled products, these shingles have a brownish-gray hue that weathers to a sil-

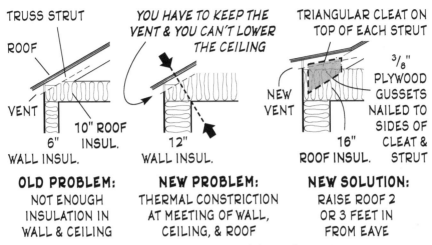

OLD PROBLEM:
NOT ENOUGH
INSULATION IN
WALL & CEILING

NEW PROBLEM:
THERMAL CONSTRICTION
AT MEETING OF WALL,
CEILING, & ROOF

NEW SOLUTION:
RAISE ROOF 2
OR 3 FEET IN
FROM EAVE

8-11. Superinsulating old roof eaves

ver-gray similar to cedar shakes. They are easy to install, are maintenance-free, require no added treatment or preservatives, and are fire-, mold-, and insect-resistant. They claim to be competitively priced and last more than 50 years. To learn more about this product, visit www.enviroshake.com.

As the decades go by and energy prices keep escalating, these constructions will become increasingly practical and grow ever more popular. In fact, if I wanted to stack my chips on the one "dark horse" idea in this book that presently seems the most far-fetched but fifty years from now will prove to be the most practical, thickening existing building envelopes would be it. Here is where magazines like *Fine Homebuilding*, *Home Power*, and *Consulting-Specifying Engineer* can perform a noble service for our nation's tired, our poor, our huddled masses yearning to be free of wretched energy woes, by encouraging the public and professionals to do the kind of work as described above.

As if the past can show a quicker path to the future: out in south central Colorado, at 8,000 feet above sea level where temperatures soar above a hundred degrees in summer and plunge below minus thirty degrees in winter, is a small town with a frontier command post of the same name: Fort Garland. Built in 1858 to garrison 100 soldiers commanded by Kit Carson, this fort (which today is a historical landmark that is open to visitors) has several long buildings whose thick adobe outer walls retard heat flow in this area of climatic extremes. How thick are these walls?

Twenty-four inches. In the corner of each room is a little fireplace to keep the occupants toasty warm. Each windowsill is so wide that one can sit on it and enjoy a view of several fourteen-thousand-foot peaks that stab the azure a few miles away.

Those oldtimers sure knew what they were doing 150 years ago. Certainly we can do as well in the near future.

Those five earlier-mentioned letters —w a t e r— that can wreck havoc in small buildings can do the same in large ones. Witness this scenario gone awry at the Imperial Polk County Courthouse in Bartow, Florida, completed in 1987 for $37 million.

This "Showcase Courthouse," a ten-story edifice with two three-story wings, possessed all the architectural elegance associated with halls of justice. The building's roof, rising above its prominent cornice at a graceful 3-in-12 pitch, was attractive clay tile laid on a rolled roofing cap sheet over a composite decking of rigid insulation and cement fiberboard. The building's facades were stylish brick backed by concrete block walls, whose outer faces were covered with asphalt waterproofing and whose inner faces were covered with rigid insulation mounted on strips of metal furring finished with gypsum board; and every window mounted in the facades was rimmed with PVC flashing. Inside, all lobby and corridor walls were clad in the finest marble veneer, all the courtrooms and judges' chambers were paneled with custom millwork, all other interiors were finished with attractive vinyl wallcovering, and most of the floors were covered with broadloom carpet. The state-of-the-art HVAC system included 67 chilled-water air-handling units that were oversized to accommodate any cooling demand in central Florida's hot humid climate and were governed by digital controls that provided optimal interior environments for every interior space. One would think nothing could possibly go wrong with such advanced technology and familiar construction whose durability had been proven over time ....

Soon after the building opened, it was found that rainwater didn't drain properly from the roof —because a 3-in-12 pitch is too shallow for clay tile. This water leaked through numerous cracks in the improperly installed cap sheets under the clay tile, and the accumulating moisture delaminated the decking below. From there the water drained into exterior walls, where it became trapped between the walls of brick veneer (which were poorly built with clogged or missing weepholes) and concrete block (which were developing cracks due to a lack of control joints and whose waterproofing was the thin brushed-on kind instead of the thick troweled-on kind); so the accumulating water couldn't escape outdoors through the bricks' weep holes and instead entered indoors through the porous concrete blocks. More water entered around the windows where the PVC flashing didn't extend to the brick facing and lacked turned edges at the windowsills' ends. Soon the migrating moisture had saturated ceiling tiles, gypsum wallboard, and broadloom carpeting; and this flow was increased by the oversized HVAC system that removed more air out of indoor spaces than it drew in through its outside air intakes. The intakes were also protected by insect screens rather than bird screens with larger mesh openings, so the smaller openings became clogged with dust and debris which decreased the supply air even more. Humidity levels constantly rose above 80 percent. Occupants complained.

The HVAC system was retrofitted with thermostatic controls that automatically adjusted chilled water temperatures. Still, the system failed to dehumidify interior spaces adequately, which prevented thorough redrying of interior finishes and their underlying construction. Mold bloomed in the sheets of gypsum behind the marble facing in the lobbies and corridors. Since the seams in the marble facing hadn't been adequately sealed, the humid indoor air entered the cavities behind the facing which caused the mold blooming behind the gypsum to flourish. Similar colonies of mold flourished behind the vinyl wall covering and millwork paneling throughout the building. Occupants experienced stinging eyes, runny noses, wheezing, coughing, shortness of breath, chest tightness, headaches, drowsiness, asthma, allergies, and other symptoms of "Sick Building Syndrome".

Investigations followed. The vinyl wall covering —which was found to have acted as a vapor barrier between the facade construction and interior spaces— was removed from every exterior wall and the damaged gypboard behind was repaired.

Still, complaints increased. Consultants were called in. They found massive blooms of *Aspergillus versicolor* and *Stachybotrys atra* throughout the building. In July, 1992, only five years after the building opened, the local health department condemned the edifice as a threat to human health and ordered it closed.

Massive reconstruction began. All contaminated materials were removed by methods similar to asbestos remediation. Every piece of construction removed was HEPA-vacuumed, double-sealed, and placed in secured dumpsters by workers wearing full-face respirators and Tyvek suits. Much of the marble and millwork finish was removed to reach the contaminated materials behind. 500,000 square feet of ceiling tile were removed and shredded onsite. Six miles of flexible ductwork were removed and carted away. Every article of furniture was HEPA-vacuumed prior to temporary storage offsite. Every file and document in the whole building was cleaned —one page at a time— on specially constructed vacuum tables. All interior surfaces, light fixtures, piping, and remaining ducting were thoroughly recleaned by hand. All the clay tile roofing and underlying cap sheets were removed and each piece of delaminated decking was repaired or replaced, then a batten-seam copper roof was laid over a rubberized asphalt membrane. Every square foot of the building's ten-story brick facades was scaffolded and 800,000 bricks were removed and new brick facades built with proper control joints, anchors, and ties; all improperly built concrete block walls were removed and replaced, all cracks in the remaining walls were filled with mortar, and thick asphalt waterproofing was troweled onto every wall; and every window was removed, cleaned, remounted on new subframing, and rimmed with copper flashing with turned edges at the sills' ends. Inside, all 67 of the HVAC system's chilled-water air handlers were removed and replaced with new units that forced longer cooling cycles and increased dehumidification.

Early in 1996 —eight years after initially opening— the building was reoccupied. What was the remedial expense of this travesty of faulty design, incompetent construction, and inadequate supervision that occurred in this 37 million dollar edifice? Another 37 million dollars! The citizens of Polk County collected $13 million from the architect, engineers, contractor, and subcontractors, plus $25.8 million from the builder's insurance carrier. [6]

A pyrrhic victory, if ever there was one.

The moral here? If a building's climate control system *and* the parent construction aren't meticulously designed and constructed —not according to certain notions of "standard practice" but to *the dictates of the laws of physics*— problems may occur that not only can damage the climate control system but also can damage the building at great cost to the owner and great suffering of the occupants —whether courthouse, condominium, or cottage.

In this age of energy-efficiency another method of building the top of a building is taking root: green roofs. On such "upland" terrain one can grow foods from strawberries to cornstalks, enjoy the view, even have fountains and topiary —whatever one's fancy and budget will allow. LEED awards points for this construction, on the grounds that it "can reduce roof temperatures from summertime highs of 150 degrees to less than 80 degrees ... can reduce energy demand by more than 50 percent annually ... can minimize impact on microclimate and natural surroundings ... can increase oxygen through photosynthesis."

"Can"? That little three-letter word as recruited above could also mean "might not", probably won't", "wouldn't in a million years", and a host of other adverse implications. In fact, each of the four conditions listed above "can" under a minority of circumstances prevail. However, while LEED awards points for green roofs, it does not make the following points about certain majority aspects of this construction:

1. Green roofs cost a lot: typically 15 to 25 dollars per square foot on top of one's initial cost. This could tilt the scales of this shelter's potential cost-effectiveness from positive to negative.

2. These roofs weigh a lot: usually 40 to 80 pounds per square foot, some as much as 200 psf; and all supporting structure below down to the ground must be made larger. To indicate how deceptive some promotions of green roofs have been regarding this, consider the recently built green roof on the Chicago City Hall, an impressive project that received rave reviews in numerous architectural magazines. However, only one of these periodicals mentioned (in a short sentence sequestered deep in its text) that what made all this heavy construction possible was that the building was originally designed to support the construction of an added floor; and the weight of the green roof replaced what would have otherwise been the weight of the future floor without requir-

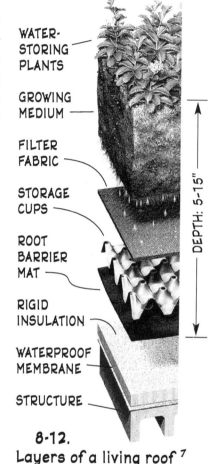

WATER-
STORING
PLANTS

GROWING
MEDIUM

FILTER
FABRIC

STORAGE
CUPS

ROOT
BARRIER
MAT

RIGID
INSULATION

WATERPROOF
MEMBRANE

STRUCTURE

DEPTH: 5-15"

8-12.
Layers of a living roof [7]

ing any revisions in all the structure below. Every article about this roof should have made this vital point clear. Or else —again— when someone who constructs this idea learns that it or some other ecologically promoted concept isn't what s/he was led to believe, the tide of one's opinion will likely turn from delight to dissent, and in the company of one's colleagues s/he will colloquially cast a vote *against* rather than *for* the reality —often with a fervor that far outweighs any feeling s/he might have otherwise expressed; for in such scenarios, censure generally outpaces praise.

3. The topsoil can erode and the subsoil can slip during heavy rains. Though LEED's guidebook says, "All garden roofs decrease stormwater runoff volumes substantially," this is false: garden roofs may decrease stormwater runoff during short light rains; but during severe storms when the roof's soil has become saturated, stormwater runoff will *not* be less than on standard roofs and this is when topsoils and subsoils will likely erode and slip. [8]

4. After construction most green roofs need almost daily horticultural attention: mowing, weeding, erosion control, and precise watering (enough to encourage growing but not enough to initiate erosion and slippage).

5. Green roofs attract bugs, rodents, and other members of a thriving ecosystem, even on tall buildings.

6. Green roofs require access —not by a ladder over a gutter but by a railed central staircase. A good central entry is a stairwell that rises into a small greenhouse with a door from which you step onto the roof. Also, occupiable areas should be enclosed by chest-high parapets; and any walkways or terraces should be masonry and not wood which requires waterproofing above, airspaces below, and toxic rot-proofing all around.

7. These roofs often require electric outlets, landscape lights, hose outlets, and related mechanical equipment.

8. The roof substrate can leak, and when it does it is difficult and expensive to repair.
9. It may surprise you to know that a green roof can be a fire hazard. If the roof's vegetation turns brown due to lack of water, a brush fire could start there and spread indoors or to other buildings. Section 317 of the 2012 International Fire Code now addresses this possibility.

LEED's guidebook also says (A) "Some green roofs have grasses and plants that require no watering," (False: all plants, even cactus, require some watering, which means monitoring, which means access); (B) "All types of green roofs have longer lifetimes than conventional roofs," (False: if they do last longer it is because they must be constantly maintained in ways that are not required with standard roofs); (C) "Green roofs provide lower maintenance than standard roofs." Hah! See (4) above.

If you want a green roof to increase a building's insulating ability and decrease its water runoff, there are better and cheaper ways to do these things. Hear this reproof of this architecture by the esteemed building scientist, Joseph Lstiburek, Ph.D.:

> Vegetative roofs? Grass and dirt are not energy efficient. Work with me here. Which saves more energy: two inches of dirt or two inches of insulation? Which saves more energy: grass or a white-colored membrane? Which is more expensive and does not save energy: grass and dirt, or insulation and a white-colored membrane? Which needs to be watered to keep the grass from dying and blowing away? [9]

On the other hand, if you love gardens and want to transform a barren tract wracked with violent temperature extremes into a meadowy landscape that blooms with wildflowers, bustles with butterflies and birds, is threaded with pleasant walks and patched with relaxing terraces, and offers fine views above the bugs and closer to the stars, then you deserve all the joys that gardens can give you, all the praise that periodicals may rain on you, and all the points that LEED may award you.

Climate

One bona fide technique that will improve the thermal performance of many a roof is to do what Joseph Lstiburek mentioned above: paint it white. The July 30, 2009, *New York Times* had a front-page article on this. It said such roofs not only are "An energy saver but also a way to help cool the planet ... These materials reflect as much as 90 percent of the sun's heat energy ... Studies show that white roofs reduce air-conditioning costs by 20 percent or more." Even Frank Lloyd Wright got into this act — years before anyone else did— by saying: "A white-topped roof is economical partly because white, of course, reflects heat rather than absorbs it."[10] As for the possibility that white roofs could lead to higher heating bills in winter, *Home Power* magazine says: "Summertime air-conditioning savings from choosing a light-colored roof will most likely outweigh the heat gained in winter by using a dark-colored roof [because] the winter sun is available for a shorter part of the day, is lower in the sky, and its light passes through more atmosphere than that of the summer sun."[11]

Three months before the *New York Times* article appeared, I painted 2,400 square feet of my house's roof with SolarFlex 287 SF, a thick white elastomeric roof coating made by the Henry Company of El Segundo, California. During the past two summers the rooms below have been notably cooler than in previous years, and they weren't any cooler during winter.

Making Indoor Spaces Comfortable

After analyzing the sun, wind, ground, and a building's insulated shell, you are ready to select the machines that will create the opposite effect of the weather outdoors and keep every indoor space comfortable every hour of the year. The best systems not only consume a minimum of fossil fuels, they consume less embodied energy in their making, packaging, and transporting to the site; they require minimum servicing; they are long-lived; and when they die many of their parts and materials can be recycled. Since climate control systems essentially do only what they are told, first we need to know what to tell them. Here are the parameters of indoor human comfort that define their operation:

Temperature: 65 to 77 degrees year-round, as measured by a thermostat.

Humidity: 45 to 55 percent year-round, as measured by a humidistat, which is often part of a thermostat.

Ventilation: At least 10 feet per minute (fast enough to keep air from feeling stuffy) but no more than 50 fpm (which will blow papers off a desk). Indoor air should also flow from "sweet" areas (spaces that rarely produce noxious gases or odors) to "sour" areas (spaces that commonly produce noxious gases or odors). When a sweet and sour zone are located near each other, as a dining room next to a kitchen or a bedroom beside a bath, the air should flow from the sweet zone to the sour zone. In buildings with HVAC systems this can be done by mounting an air supply register in the sweet zone low on the wall farthest from the door-in-common and mounting a return register in the sour zone in the ceiling farthest from the door, then locating just inside the supply and return air ducts *static air pressure (s.a.p.) sensors* calibrated to be positive in sweet zones and negative in sour zones. Then these detectors "tell" host controls down at computer headquarters to send sweet air out of the supply register and pull sour air into the return register.

Carbon dioxide: 300 to 600 parts per million (ppm). A human exhale contains about 38,000 ppm (3.8 percent) CO_2, while outdoor rural air has around 400 ppm and urban air about 550 ppm. Though people in an unventilated room will deplete its oxygen and increase its carbon dioxide at equal rates, they will feel uncomfortable if the oxygen level lowers from a normal 21 percent to 16 percent but will feel equally uncomfortable if the CO_2 level rises from a normal 0.04 percent to 0.15 percent —one-fiftieth the depletion of oxygen. Hence CO_2 is a better indicator of indoor fresh air. In large buildings with no openable windows, CO_2 sensors may be installed inside return air ducts in each zone. When the sensor detects excess CO_2, it informs host controls to deliver more outdoor air to the zone until its CO_2 level is lowered to acceptable levels.

Pollution: This includes dusts, odors, molds, microbes, noxious gases, chemicals, aerosols, hydrocarbons, and products of combustion. Today, computerized sensors mounted in a building's interior spaces can be programmed to detect almost any pollutant, then the sensors inform host controls to activate the HVAC system's motors, dampers, and other controls when necessary.

However, these sensors only detect. They do nothing about the problems that put the pollutants indoors in the first place. This has become a serious situation, because in recent years building interiors have become flooded with a cocktail of toxins that are known to cause allergic reactions, asthma, behavioral breakdowns, birth defects, endocrine disruptions, infertility, even cancer. These substances include *volatile organic compounds* (VOCs) in interior paints, adhesives, and finishes; *formaldehydes* in particleboard subfloors, plywood panelings, fiberboard drawer fronts, masonite drawer bottoms, composition countertops, oriented strand board (OSB) sheathings, and other pressed waste-wood products; *phthalate plasticizers* in vinyl wallpapers, plastic glazing, and curtain liners; *halogenated flame retardants* in foam insulations, drapes, furniture fabrics and foams, carpets and their underlayments; plus the usual potpurri of dusts and excess moisture. Also significant is the amount of a toxin in a material. This is why OSB is much worse than plywood, because OSB contains high concentrations of formaldehyde while plywood's layers of formaldehyde-laden glue are thin as paper. The problem described above is worsened by (1) new untested products and materials arriving from Asia and (2) domestic laws that allow manufacturers to list toxic chemicals as "trade secrets" on their products' safety data sheets —some of which the makers have the gall to call "green" alternatives!

Moreover, in today's interiors the effects of many toxins are worsened by airtight envelopes —which in more porous days would allow the menacing molecules to seep through the shells' seams and cracks to the outdoors. But in today's Tyvek-clad confines, if you try to remove these toxins by, say, turning on a stove hood fan, you're apt to pull a cloud of ashes out of your fireplace as the makeup air flows down the flue and stirs the ashes. Another such effort, reported by the author of the article I obtained much of this information from,[12] caused the air conditioner of an Energy Star-rated residence to pull lawn-mower clippings through the air conditioner's supply duct and deposited the clippings on the indoor furniture. This is why an all-too-common "solution" for removing toxins from interiors —hiring an engineer to specify oversize ventilation blowers— often only makes the problem worse.

This dilemma of incarcerating occupants in cells contaminated with toxins underlines three major themes that appear throughout this book. (1) Whatever building materials you use, use *less* of them, (2) use natural materials as often as possible, and (3) don't wrap your interiors in Tyvek or other suffocating vapor barriers. If you are about to construct a new building or improve an old one, pay a visit to www.epa.gov, make a list of toxic "chemicals of concern" and the products that contain them, and insist that whoever constructs your new confines to avoid using these materials. Also try the Kitchen Cabinet Manufacturers Association at www.kcma.org, which lists some products that contain low amounts of toxins. Whatever you do, Good Luck, and may the "Force" be with you.

Climate

Three common components of climate control systems are thermostats, ducts, and registers, as detailed below.

Thermostats. A thermostat is a dial switch that an occupant adjusts to obtain a desired air temperature, humidity, or other indoor comfort condition; then the switch turns on the machinery that satisfies the desired condition and turns the machinery off when the condition is satisfied. With the advent of computerized controls, this little sentinel has seemingly acquired a mind of its own. Today it can have touchpad keys and an attractive display like the one in figure 8-13 on page 385 that includes:

☞ Settings that govern heating and cooling for morning, daytime, evening, and sleep scenarios as well as daylight savings time. In figure 8-13 scenario settings for SLEEP, WAKE, EVENING, and MODE (weekday, weekend, or vacation) are arranged around a 24-hour clock dial and each scenario has a LO and HI temperature setting with tiny *up* (▲) and *down* (▼) pads for setting the desired temperature.

☞ Programs for 7-day, 5-2 day (i.e. five week days and two weekend days), 5-1-1 day, and vacation modes.

☞ Indicators that tell when to install or replace air filters.

☞ A programmer that includes instructions, a multiple-language selector, and memory storage.

Some of these prizes can even be operated via voice control offsite. As a sample, if you're driving to a winter hideaway, a half hour before arriving you can pull off the highway, pull out your cellphone, and order the thermostat's digital controls to turn on the entry and landscape lights as you pull into the driveway, raise the indoor temperature from a freeze-protective 42 degrees to 70 degrees so the building is warm when you enter, and activate the coffeemate so fresh-brewed coffee is waiting when you step into the kitchen. A few companies who make these devices are Honeywell (yourhome.honeywell.com), Robertshaw (robertshaw.com),

Trane (trane.com), and Carrier (residential.carrier.com).

A thermostat should be located on an inside wall, be exposed to the area it governs, be positioned away from lights and other heat sources, and be placed where its coverage won't be blocked by an opened door or other movable object.

In large commercial buildings, computerized thermostats can control temperature, humidity, ventilation, carbon dioxide, pollution, and air pressure for each room or zone; they can operate smoke controls and other life safety systems; and they can even trend facility operations for maintenance personnel. One innovation they have spawned is a more efficient design of HVAC systems known as *multiple module redundant design*. This involves replacing a large whole-building HVAC unit with several smaller units of the same capacity plus one more small unit. Example: if a building's design heating load is 1,000,000 Btus per hour, instead of one large 1,000,000 Btu/hr unit the building would have five + one = six 200,000 Btu/hr units. Then during most of the time when heating and cooling loads are notably less than maximum, instead of one big unit running which consumes a lot of energy, one or more smaller units operate by a process known as *step-firing*. This consumes less energy overall, each unit runs less which means it lasts longer and requires less maintenance, any one unit can be serviced on the fly without disabling the whole system, the smaller units require less headroom which means the whole building can be lower, and the units can be arranged more flexibly instead of in "one-clunker" locations.

Ducts. A duct is a usually long round, square, or rectangular tube that may be small as your arm or larger than a residential hallway laid on its side. Each may be made of hot-dipped galvanized sheet steel (the surface with a spangle finish), aluminum (used for indoor swimming pool exhausts and in numerous industrial applications), copper (installed as decorative ducting in restaurant stove hoods and the like), or stainless steel (used for kitchen and laboratory fume hoods). Ducts conveying certain

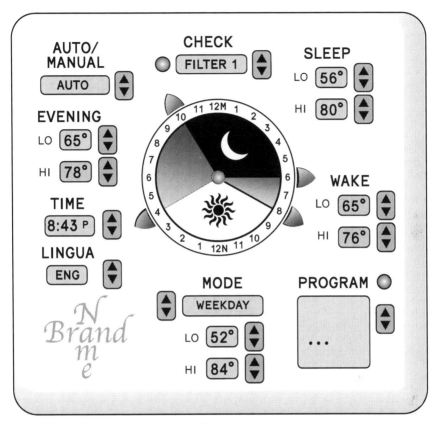

8-13. Tomorrow's thermostat today

chemical exhausts may be lined with polyvinyl chloride or other nonreactive inner surface. Ducts are also made of fabrics, where the air flows through the weave along its length which allows the air to disperse evenly through the spaces served, and screened registers can be sewn into the fabric where large amounts of air are required.[13] Fabric ducts are quiet, flexible, and lightweight. Many colors and textures are available.

Metal ducts have a number of fittings as sketched in figure 8-14. Of special note are *splitter dampers* and *mixing boxes*. A splitter damper is a thermostat-controlled vane that varies the airflow where a duct divides into two smaller ducts with varying heating or cooling requirements; this can happen in two adjacent rooms on each side of a corner when the sun shines into one room while the other is cast in shade. A mixing box blends proper proportions of hot and cold air where heating and cooling ducts meet to supply one room or zone with air. Also note the pieces of *Spiropipe*: this is a strong spirally braced tubing that can convey high volumes of air faster than 6,000 feet per minute (that's a hurricane-like 70 miles an hour). Every length of duct must be structurally support-ed (large ones can weigh hundreds of pounds per linear foot), each duct should have access portals along its length that allow in-spection and cleaning of every linear foot inside, and each should be wrapped with 1 or 2 inches of insulation clad with a vapor bar-rier on the inside. The insulation reduces heat loss in heating ducts, eliminates condensation and corrosion in cooling ducts, and absorbs such annoying duct noises as rumbles and whistles.

Another "duct" in some commercial buildings is the *under-floor supply plenum*. This is a crawlspace-like area under a raised finished floor through which run pipes to plumbing fixtures and wires to plug outlets in the floors, then air flows through the remaining void to the rooms above. These subspaces allow quick adding and removing of mechanical conveyances simply by remov-ing one or more floor panels above. LEED even awards points for their construction on the grounds that they eliminate ducting and reduce the costs of renovation caused by frequent changes in occupancy. But hear what our esteemed building scientist, Joseph Lstiburek, Ph.D, says of this counterfeit energy conserver:

> What's "green" about underfloor supply plenums? How do they save any energy? They sure as heck don't contribute to indoor air quality. Do you want to breathe air delivered in a ductless void under a floor that cannot be cleaned? Even if you can clean them, they are filled with services, so they are filthy. And, they are expensive. The building must be taller, which burns up resources and money. But, it's green. Says who? [14]

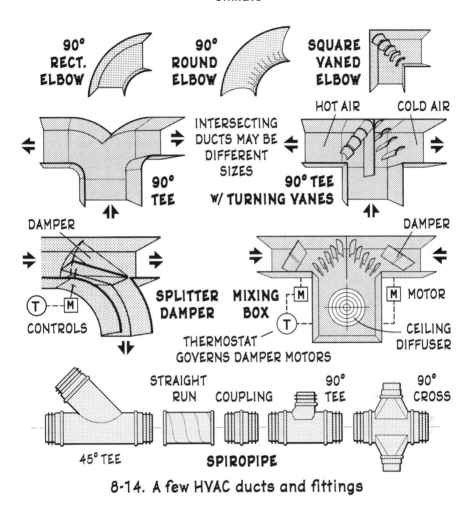

8-14. A few HVAC ducts and fittings

Underfloor supply plenums also leak air around their perimeters and through the seams between the finished floor panels. This assembly could be called poundwise and ton foolish (as in tons of wasted air conditioning load).

Registers. A register is a vaned grille that fits over the end of a duct where it enters a room or zone. They are often installed in pairs: a supply and a return for each area served. The two should be the same size and ideally located in opposite walls, one

377

near the ceiling and one near the floor, and where opened doors and furniture will not obstruct them. A few registers appear below. The arrows on the vanes show the directions they send the air. Supply grilles should direct air across walls and floors without creating drafts and their vanes should spread the air evenly into the space. A supply duct register is often designated by its *throw*: the distance it can propel air into a space, which generally should be about three-quarters across the room. Register throw ranges are listed in product catalogs.

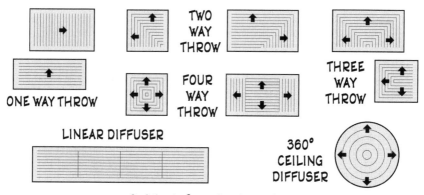

8-15. A few duct registers

Choosing a climate control system depends largely on the owner's goals, which may be (1) low initial cost, (2) low operating cost, (3) adequate level of performance that matches the competition, or (4) the ultimate in performance no matter what the cost. A simple way (simple? None of this is simple) to compare the total life cycle costs of two or more systems is with the formula:

Total cost = initial cost + (useful life × operating cost)

Initial cost = price of product + cost to install it

Useful life = number of years an installation will operate before replacing (generally 20 years)

Oper. cost = annual fuel expenses (unit cost × amount used) + annual maintenance expenses (cost of cleaning, replaced parts, etc.)

Climate

The following is a catalog of common (and a few to-be common) climate control systems. Though some have worked well for
decades, a new logistic may soon render a few of them obsolete.
This is the changing ratio of material costs to fuel costs. Consider water baseboard heaters. In the old days when fuel was
cheap, the water was heated in a boiler with thin walls and no
insulation, because then the materials cost more than the fuel.
But now it costs less to make the boiler than to heat the water it
holds, and the materials are a fixed one-time cost while the heat
is an escalating lifetime cost. So today's boiler has thick walls
and is clad in insulation, both of which also allow it to be smaller,
and its operation has efficient controls. This is a different
machine than the one that warmed your grandparents, and it may
demote the elder model to installation in a landfill.

Electric Heating. This system involves mounting against
the base of a wall a long heating element as pictured below, which
converts electricity into heat that radiates into adjacent spaces.
When these units are located against an exterior wall, part of the
heat conducts through the unit's back directly outdoors. In
superinsulated buildings the units can be installed against interior walls as earlier described.

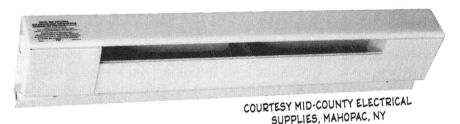

COURTESY MID-COUNTY ELECTRICAL
SUPPLIES, MAHOPAC, NY

8-16. An electric baseboard heating unit

In buildings with baseboard heaters mounted against exterior walls, consider locating each a few inches out from the wall
and above the floor, as appears in figure 8-16 on the next page. As
the air behind the heater is warmed it rises, which draws cooler

air on the floor via a *convective air loop* that carries the heat accumulating behind the heater into the spaces above before it escapes through the wall behind. This is one reason why the old cast iron steam radiators worked fairly well: they stood on short legs that held these heaters a few inches above the floor and out from the wall behind, which allowed convected air to flow under and behind the units which lessened the heat lost through the wall.

OUTER WALL

NEW CAP PLATE

2x4 SPACERS PLACED 32" APART

BASE-BOARD HEATER

CONVECTIVE LOOP

OLD BASE PLATE

FLOOR

CONVECTIVE

3½"

3½"

8-17. A little way to save a lot of heat

Three other electric heaters are *floor inserts* (units fitted into floors with the grilles level with the floors), *spots* (these usually small units are installed almost anywhere to heat the areas they face), and *heat tracing cables* (electric wires installed along water pipes and roof eaves to keep them from freezing; they are also embedded in entrance aprons to melt snow and ice).

- ⊕ Units are compact, noiseless, odorless, and easily installed. They occupy little space, require no central units that occupy a roomful of space that costs money to build, have no moving elements, require no ducts or flues, and need little servicing or maintenance.
- ⊖ Units do not humidify, filter, or ventilate air. Operating costs are high in areas with high electric rates. Areas around the units must be clear of furniture, drapes, etc. Fin covers are easily bent and often do not fit well.

Hot water heating. In this system a boiler heats water that is pumped through pipes to rooms or zones with baseboard heating units. This is your typical household furnace-fed water baseboard heating system. The baseboard units look much like the electric unit in figure 8-16, except that behind the unit's front panel is a pipe instead of a wire. The system's boiler can also heat domestic hot water, swimming pools, hot tubs, and radiant floors; and the fuel may be gas, oil, even waste wood such as scrap lumber, sawdust, recycled paper, and crop residues. The piping loops are usually configured as baseboard units, but they can be shaped to satisfy almost any spot heating demand. As a sample, I once saw a hot water heating loop configured as a row of towel racks in a bathroom; as it heated the room it dried the towels.

⊕ Works well in small buildings with high heating and low cooling loads. Each zone can have different temperature settings and water circulating rates. Plumbing runs require less space than ducting. The thermal plume in the boiler flue offers opportunities for heat reclamation.

⊖ Requires a flue. Does not humidify, filter, or ventilate air. The central heating system takes up a roomful of space which costs money to build. Plumbing must be protected from freezing in winter and condensation in summer.

Electric heating and cooling. This is typically a compact unit having registers with adjustable vanes that is mounted under a window or in a wall where it heats, cools, filters, and ventilates the air in its zone. You've probably seen these units under windows in motels. When producing cooling air it usually creates a condensate which drips onto the ground outside.

⊕ Small through-the-wall units are easy to install and require only an electrical outlet to run. Useful in buildings with many small rooms that require individual climate controls; economical in areas with low electric rates.

⊖ NG in large spaces; operating costs are high in areas with high electric rates. Any condensate pans require periodic cleaning which requires service access. Many units do not control ambient humidity levels.

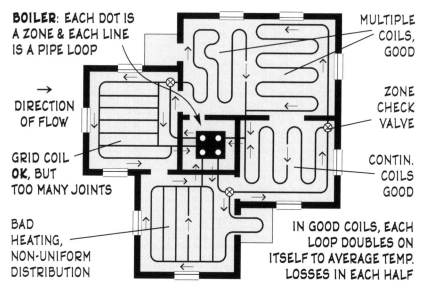

BOILER: EACH DOT IS A ZONE & EACH LINE IS A PIPE LOOP

→
DIRECTION
OF FLOW

GRID COIL
OK, BUT
TOO MANY JOINTS

BAD
HEATING,
NON-UNIFORM
DISTRIBUTION

MULTIPLE
COILS,
GOOD

ZONE
CHECK
VALVE

CONTIN.
COILS
GOOD

IN GOOD COILS, EACH
LOOP DOUBLES ON
ITSELF TO AVERAGE TEMP.
LOSSES IN EACH HALF

8-18. Four radiant floor heating layouts

Radiant Floor Heating. In these systems a central boiler heats water that flows through piping loops embedded in concrete floors from where the heat radiates into the spaces above, as pictured above. For the heating loops flexible plastic tubing is gaining popularity because it is light, costs less, is flexible and easily bent, and won't corrode.

➊ Feasible in one-floor buildings with large rooms and slab-on-grade construction; eliminates drafts; doesn't circulate dust and other airborne contaminants.

➋ High initial cost; requires precise construction; settling problems can crack concrete and break pipes which are expensive to repair. **NG** if the water contains chemicals that deposit in the pipes.

Radiant Ceiling Heating. In this system a gas such as propane or butane is ignited in a ceiling-mounted firebox through which flows fan-driven air into a large-diameter metal tube that has a U-bend at its end so the tube doubles on itself to average

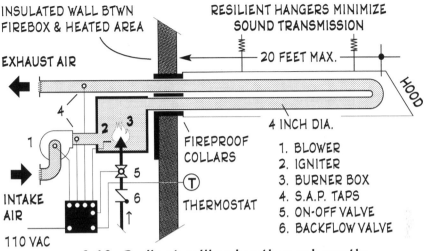

INSULATED WALL BTWN
FIREBOX & HEATED AREA

RESILIENT HANGERS MINIMIZE
SOUND TRANSMISSION

EXHAUST AIR

20 FEET MAX.

HOOD

4 INCH DIA.

4

2   3

1

FIREPROOF
COLLARS

1. BLOWER
2. IGNITER
3. BURNER BOX
4. S.A.P. TAPS
5. ON-OFF VALVE
6. BACKFLOW VALVE

5

6

(T)

THERMOSTAT

INTAKE
AIR

110 VAC

8-19. Radiant ceiling heating schematic

heat losses along its length. The double pipe may be up to 20 feet long and has a reflective hood above which directs the radiance downward. The units are mounted 4 to 6 feet above the area to be served, and chain hangers allow easy raising, lowering, and relo- cating to satisfy changing occupancies. This heating works best where ceilings are high, floors are concrete, large exterior doors are often opened, occupants engage in mild physical activity, and the presence of airborne dust makes air systems undesirable. This system appears above.

Two smaller ceiling units are *infrared heaters* and *quartz lamp heaters*. An infrared heater resembles a fluorescent light fixture and has a heating element up to six feet long. To see 58 companies who make these popular units visit www.thomasnet.com and type infrared heaters in the Product/Service pane at the top of the page. A q*uartz lamp heater* has one or two tubular quartz lamps up to about 40 inches long mounted in a narrow reflector. Two companies that sell them are Thermaline (thermaline.com) and Fostoria (fostoria-industries.com). All these units run on electricity from 110 to 480 volts. When operating they also pro- vide low-level lighting.

- ⊕ Units run quietly and cleanly; they have no ducts, vents, blowers, or moving parts; and they produce no airborne pollutants. Smaller units are suitable for small spaces that require low-level lighting at night.
- ⊖ NG above areas containing flammable materials, volatile gases, or cooling operations such as ice skating rinks, supermarkets with open freezers, etc. Correct location is critical. Units must be well away from lights, utility conveyances, and structural members.

Air heating. This is generally a furnace which heats air that flows through ducts to occupied spaces, and some systems have return air ducts. This is your standard residential duct heating system. Supply ducts should be insulated and supply registers be near floors. In cold regions a two or three inch-diameter fresh air pipe should run from outdoors to within 24 inches of the furnace's air intake. The pipe's outer opening should be screened with $\frac{1}{4}$-inch mesh, it should face down so it won't collect water, and the area below should be clear of foliage and any accumulating snow. The furnace area should be partitioned from adjacent spaces and its door(s) weatherstripped.

- ⊕ Can ventilate, humidify, and filter incoming air. Practical in homes and small buildings in cold regions. The flue's thermal plume offers opportunities for heat reclamation.
- ⊖ Bulky furnace, thick ducting, and required flue are costly and take up space which costs money to build. Registers must be well located. The airflow stirs stir up dust, which can be undesirable for occupants with allergies and where airborne dust may interfere with industrial operations.

Air Cooling. This is usually a large air conditioner mounted on a flat commercial roof from which extend one or more ducts that serve the floorspaces below, and some units have return air ducts. Another common installation is a ground-level concrete pad located in a usually foliage-enclosed area behind a commercial building. Trailer-size units can also be rented for large summertime temporary events. All these units work like big refrigerators, and their mechanics have changed little since the 1950s. The water removed from the cooled air generally empties into drain pans that must be accessible for periodic cleaning. Three makers of these systems are NuTemp (nutemp.com), Carrier (commercial.carrier.com), and Lennox (lennoxcommercial.com).

⊕ Compact; easily installed; good for one-story buildings with large floor areas. Units operate quietly, have computerized controls, and are easily maintained. Can humidify, filter, and freshen air. Some units have a small capacity for heating. Runs efficiently in warm climates.

⊖ Impractical in regions with mild summers and cold winters and for buildings more than three stories tall.

Air Heating/Cooling. This is your big-building HVAC system. One appears on the next page. It operates as follows. (1) Fresh outdoor air and stale return air enter one end of an *air handling unit* (or *AH unit*), a long box that may be as big as a mobile home; (2) the air is preheated in cold weather, precooled in warm weather, humidified if too dry, dehumidified if too moist, and filtered to remove impurities; (3) at the AH unit's other end a large motor-driven fan drives the air into the primary duct; and (4) the air flows through a network of increasingly smaller branch ducts at each floor and outlet ducts in each room or zone. The AH unit is usually located on the building's roof a short distance from a *cooling tower*, a tall vented enclosure that cools the water heated in the AH unit's precooling section. The fresh air intake vents of both components usually face prevailing winds. These systems can satisfy a variety of heating and cooling loads, especially where both heating and cooling are needed in adjacent rooms or zones. They maintain desirable temperatures and humidities and fresh air, remove odors and particulates from interior air, and have computerized fire controls.

An air heating/cooling system can also be small. One model is

Architecture Laid Bare!

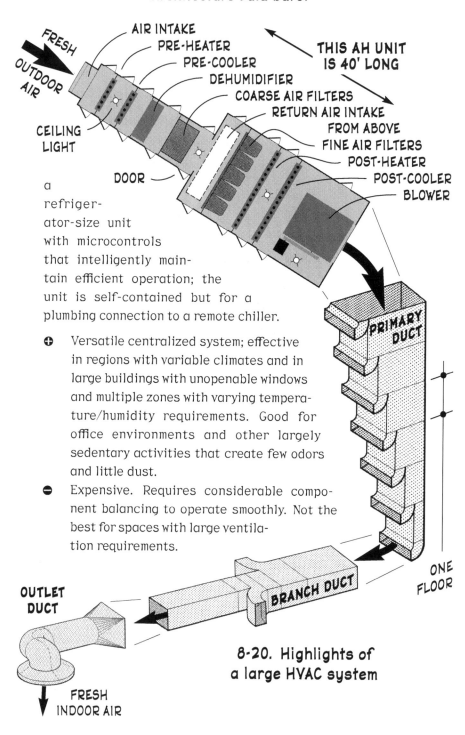

FRESH OUTDOOR AIR

AIR INTAKE
PRE-HEATER
PRE-COOLER
DEHUMIDIFIER
COARSE AIR FILTERS
RETURN AIR INTAKE FROM ABOVE
FINE AIR FILTERS
POST-HEATER
POST-COOLER
BLOWER

THIS AH UNIT IS 40' LONG

CEILING LIGHT

DOOR

a refrigerator-size unit with microcontrols that intelligently maintain efficient operation; the unit is self-contained but for a plumbing connection to a remote chiller.

➕ Versatile centralized system; effective in regions with variable climates and in large buildings with unopenable windows and multiple zones with varying temperature/humidity requirements. Good for office environments and other largely sedentary activities that create few odors and little dust.

➖ Expensive. Requires considerable component balancing to operate smoothly. Not the best for spaces with large ventilation requirements.

PRIMARY DUCT

ONE FLOOR

OUTLET DUCT

BRANCH DUCT

FRESH INDOOR AIR

8-20. Highlights of a large HVAC system

Climate

Air-Water Heating/Cooling. These systems are much like air heating/cooling systems except the ducted air flows at high velocities through pipelike tubes called Spiropipes that are notably smaller than sheet-metal ducts. The smaller tubes allow a building's floor-to-floor dimensions to be lower, which in tall buildings can significantly reduce construction costs. The system's air handling units are much like those in air HVAC systems, although they require more powerful fans and motors to drive the air through the smaller ducts. They can also satisfy a greater variety of heating and cooling loads.

⊕ Versatile, centralized system. Small ducting requires less space for installation, making it desirable in tall buildings and other structures with minimum spatial requirements for mechanical equipment.

⊖ Complicated, costly. Feasible only in large buildings.

Steam heating. This is much like hot water baseboard heating except the water is heated to above its boiling point and delivers more energy in a smaller volume to each room or zone. To handle the high heat and pressure involved, the boiler is usually cast iron and the pipe loops are heavy steel with threaded and sealed connections. All pipes are thickly insulated to minimize heat loss, to keep condensation from forming on them, and to keep anyone touching the pipes from being burned. A century ago these systems appeared in many buildings. Today's systems can be large enough to heat whole groups of buildings, college campuses being a favored item. The biggest in this country has five generating plants and 105 miles of steam mains that serve 1,800 buildings including the Empire State Building and the United Nations. At the other extreme, in the Susan Dana house in Illinois that Frank Lloyd Wright designed in 1904, he laid a steam radiator on its side under a kitchen counter to serve as a warming oven.

⊕ More compact than other systems of comparable capacity.

Leftover steam from industrial or other large operations can be used for cooking, sterilizing, running small industrial processes, and driving generators.

● Complicated; high steam pressures can cause explosions; safety devices and controls are required. Supply water impurities can cause boilers to corrode. Pipes can freeze, and can be noisy if not accurately sized. These systems require precise design and installation by engineering specialists. Today's systems are usually practical only for large buildings or groups of buildings.

Heat Pump. Imagine a machine that makes cold air out of hot and hot air out of cold. That's what a heat pump does. The way it performs this thermal sleight-of-hand is like this. (1) It takes a container of Btus —heat— and *compresses* them, which moves the Btus closer together which makes them hot; (2) the hot Btus enter a second container called a *radiator* that is colder outside, then, since heat travels from hot to cold, a lot of the Btus in the radiator pass through its thin walls and warm the Btus outside; (3) the warmed Btus outside the radiator are driven by a fan into a room which makes it warmer; (4) the Btus in the radiator enter a third container where they are *expanded*, which moves them apart which makes them cold; (5) the cold Btus enter a fourth container called an *absorber* where the Btus outside are warmer, then some of the Btus outside pass through the container's thin walls and warm the Btus inside. Then the cycle begins anew. So instead of creating heat by burning fossil fuel, a heat pump *moves* heat from one place to another in a way that consumes much less energy.

But this is only half the story. This cycling can be *reversed* to make the heater work as a cooler. All it takes is a reversing valve, which appears as a black circle with a white **X** in it in the upper center of figure 8-21. When the circle turns one way the Btus flow clockwise and the pump pulls heat from outdoors and sends it indoors; when the circle turns the other way the Btus flow counterclockwise and the pump pulls heat from indoors and

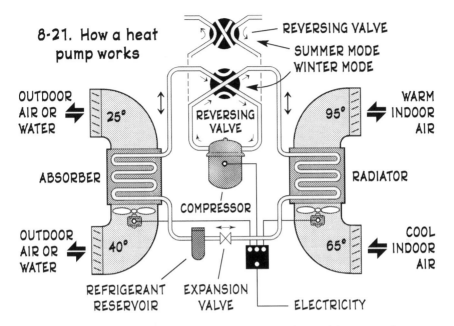

8-21. How a heat pump works

REVERSING VALVE
SUMMER MODE
WINTER MODE

OUTDOOR AIR OR WATER   25°

WARM INDOOR AIR   95°

REVERSING VALVE

ABSORBER   RADIATOR

COMPRESSOR

OUTDOOR AIR OR WATER   40°

COOL INDOOR AIR   65°

REFRIGERANT RESERVOIR   EXPANSION VALVE   ELECTRICITY

sends it outdoors. That's all it takes for this machine to make a room warm in winter and cool in summer. You probably have one of these machines in your house right now: your refrigerator. If you installed a reversing valve in it, you could use your ice cube tray as a warming oven.

But all this cleverness has a catch. Below about 35 degrees, all this heat-moving becomes so sluggish that it consumes as much fossil fuel as a furnace to create useful heat. So heat pumps don't work well in areas where temperatures go below freezing. But this catch has an "uncatch": If the absorber is buried several feet in earth or water that remains above 35 degrees in winter, the cycle will work efficiently. This fact of physics has spawned three kinds of heat pumps: *air-to-air* (the radiator and absorber are exposed to the air above ground, your standard system), *water-source heat pumps* (the absorber is immersed in water), and *ground-source* (the absorber is buried in the ground).[15] In water-source systems, the absorber is often long pipes immersed vertically a few hundred feet into one or more wells drilled on the property or the pipes are laid horizontally in a several-foot-deep body of water. In ground-source systems, the absorber is often many loops of horizontal pipe buried under several feet of earth. If you live in cold country and have a sizable pond or large swimming pool at least 10 feet deep, a water-source heat pump may be a viable option. But a ground-source system can be a chancy venture because (1) burying the pipes usually requires an environmentally destructive excavation 30 by 40 feet in area and several feet deep (you'll regret doing this even more if you run into ledges or bedrock); (2) every linear foot of pipe has to be carefully covered with earth for the first foot or so (puncture one pipe and you might not know about it until you're done then you have to start over), and (3) the excavated earth must be returned above the loops and replanted. All this can add up to big bucks and big headaches. Other than this, heat pump technology is as old as a second-hand refrigerator.

Heat pumps are also used in a variety of industrial operations. If you would like to read what a thousand users of 35 different brands of heat pumps have said about their operation, take a long look at www.furnacecompare.com/heatpumps/reviews.

When a walk-in freezer (a type of heat pump) is located on the ground, the floor must be thickly insulated and have a ventilated crawlspace under it, or equal. Otherwise the earth below may freeze and expand which can raise the floor several inches.

- ✚ Units operate quietly and occupy less space than most other systems. Air-source heat pumps are economical where winter temps remain above 35° F for prolonged periods. Water-source units work in colder climates where a body of water at least several feet deep is nearby.
- ✚ Systems must be carefully planned and built before their operating economies can be realized. Immersing the absorber pipes in a drilled well or burying them in the ground is expensive. If the absorber pipes are metal they may corrode when exposed to chemically impure water,

Climate

salty air in coastal installations, or corrosive gases in industrial environments. Impractical in large multi-zoned buildings.

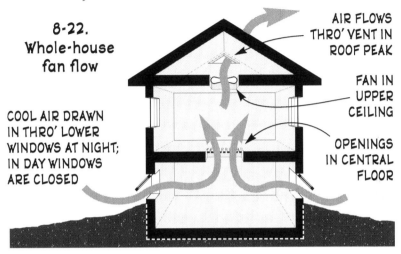

8-22.
Whole-house
fan flow

AIR FLOWS
THRO' VENT IN
ROOF PEAK

FAN IN
UPPER
CEILING

COOL AIR DRAWN
IN THRO' LOWER
WINDOWS AT NIGHT;
IN DAY WINDOWS
ARE CLOSED

OPENINGS
IN CENTRAL
FLOOR

Fans.[16] Like heat pumps, a fan also moves heat instead of produces it, often nearly as cheaply as the cost of a match. In a small building up to three floors tall, one of these bladed whirlers mounted near the center of the ceiling in the top floor can pull stuffy stale air up from the spaces below. If the air around the lower floor is cool and a few windows exist here, the windows can be opened to let cool fresh air indoors. This works well where outdoor temperatures fall into the sixties or low seventies at night, then in the morning when the house is filled with cool air the fan is turned off and the lower windows closed. The more thickly insulated the building's outer walls and roof, the longer the air indoors stays cool. The best fans are activated by a thermostat and faced with louvers that close by gravity and open when fan-driven air pushes against them, which also keeps dust, debris, and rodents from entering indoors. A ceiling fan can be quite large. The one over the swimming pool in the Holiday Inn Express in Middleton, Wisconsin, has twelve blades and is 24 feet in diameter.

Architecture Laid Bare!

Humidification. Most likely the first humidifier used in American buildings was a pan of water on a Franklin stove. This technology is little changed today, though now it can be governed with digital controls. Some of today's models are nearly as small as a pan of water: one under-the-counter model measures only 9.5 × 8.7 × 7.7 inches yet has four flexible hoses that can deliver humidified air to computer cabinets, museum exhibit cases, and other small enclosures. In large units, outlets should be at least 18 inches below ceilings and 8 feet from any seated occupants, and the humidistat should be well away from the outlets. Humidifiers are often installed in low-velocity HVAC systems to maintain hygroscopic environments in textile mills, printing plants, and the like. In every system pure water is essential because it minimizes nozzle-head buildup and suspension of impurities in the humidified air.

A common humidifier is the *evaporative cooler*. This sends a mist of cool water into hot dry air that lowers its temperature. If you have ever draped a wet towel over your head while under a hot sun you have manufactured a portable evaporative cooler. You do the same, minus the towel, when your body sweats in hot weather. In desert regions evaporative coolers are often accompanied by louvered doors, concrete block screens, and other perforated constructions that foster natural air circulation while preserving privacy. An innovative evaporative cooling system is installed on the 250,000 square foot flat roof of a factory in Greenville, South Carolina. A network of pipes with dozens of sprayheads creates a mist that lowers the ambient temperature above the roof which reduces the air-conditioning costs in the spaces below by a cool $13,000 a year. [17]

A method of humidifying air in high deserts where nightly temperatures may be 40 degrees cooler than midday is *night roof spray cooling*. As sketched in figure 8-23, a network of small sprinklers trickles water onto a smooth slightly sloping roof at night, the chilled water is reservoired, and the next day it circulates through cooling coils indoors. The system is simple and eas-

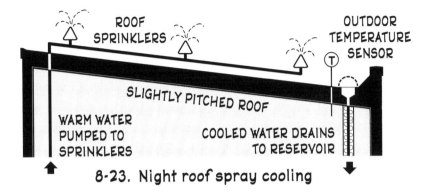

8-23. Night roof spray cooling

ily built, is operable with computerized controls, and protects the building from fire. An experienced manufacturer of these systems is Integrated Comfort, Inc. of Davis, CA (www.ics1hvac.com).

- ➕ Good for cooling interiors with gentle airflow in hot dry weather. Can add moisture to spaces in cold dry weather or where industrial operations require excess moisture to be removed from interior air.
- ➖ NG where interior air is humid or flows fast. Overdesign can create condensation problems.

Dehumidification. This involves removing water from warm humid air which makes it feel cooler, and can also inhibit rusting of metals, minimize rotting in wood, and eliminate slippery floors in moist interiors. These systems are common in food prep areas, supermarkets, indoor swimming pools, household basements, and other occupancies that accumulate unwanted moisture. The humidifier should be located on the floor because the air below the level of its intake vent generally remains moist.

There are two kinds of dehumidifiers: *chillers* and *absorbers*. Chillers refrigerate air to below a prescribed dew point which causes moisture to fall out of the air. They are used in small buildings in southerly and lowland regions where air is often warm and humid. They also remove excess moisture in basements and other rooms filled with cold clammy air which keeps mildew and other fungi from rotting wood, ruining clothes, and making every-thing smell bad. Absorbers, also known as *desiccant dehumidi-fiers*, remove water from the air with moisture-absorbing desic-cants that later have the moisture removed from them. In one model the desiccant is spread on a porous wheel that cycles slow-ly through two half-circular ducts, one flowing with humid air whose moisture is removed by the desiccant, the other flowing with hot dry air that absorbs the collected moisture. An innova-tive desiccant dehumidifier is in the Borden facility in North-brook, Illinois, which produces 1,000,000 boxes of Cracker Jacks each day. As the corn pops it liberates moisture which if not quickly removed would be absorbed by the hygroscopic caramel and form a gooey brick inside the package —not the "surprise in every box" one would want. By passing desiccant-dried cold air over the popping corn until it is sealed in its cartons the system removes up to 2,200 pounds of water per hour from the facility's assembly lines.[18]

⊕   Cools interiors in warm humid weather. Efficiently main-tains comfortable temperature and humidity where cook-ing, swimming, industrial operations, and other activities produce moisture that can't easily be vented outdoors.

⊖   NG in dry climates and where interiors create dust or air-borne particles that are removed by large volumes of cir-culating air. Since adding or subtracting moisture from air expands or contracts its volume, this system is not very good in buildings with unopenable windows.

Heat Exchanger. In almost every building some of the ener-gy consumed to keep occupants comfortable escapes up a flue as hot gases, through a vent as warm air, or down a drain as warm waste water. Reclaiming this lost heat and reusing it offers tan-talizing opportunities for reducing energy bills in such buildings. The heat is typically recovered by a *heat exchanger*, a radiator-like device containing a network of small pipes through which passes a fluid that absorbs the heat flowing around them, as appears in figure 8-24. These installations are often practical in industrial operations where much otherwise wasted heat can be reused to create hot water, heat interiors, and speed up chemical reactions.

➕ Economical where mechanical operations emit large amounts of wasted heat. Usually easily and economically built to known specifications. Many different models and types.

➖ They require space to install and maintain where space is often unavailable; are usually only 50 to 85 percent efficient.

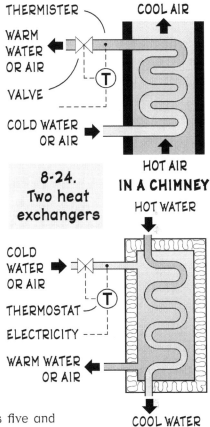

8-24.
Two heat
exchangers

THERMISTER
COOL AIR
WARM WATER OR AIR
VALVE
COLD WATER OR AIR

HOT AIR
IN A CHIMNEY
HOT WATER

COLD WATER OR AIR
THERMOSTAT
ELECTRICITY
WARM WATER OR AIR

COOL WATER
BELOW A BATHTUB

Solar Energy. In chapters five and seven we discussed how to use the sun to make electricity and hot water. Here we will discuss how to use the sun to heat indoor spaces.

When sun shines on a pane of glass, no matter how cold the air is outside, the sun's electromagnetic rays will pass through the glass and heat the air indoors. Using this energy to heat interiors can be more than 80 percent efficient. But this force is fickle. (1) A passing cloud can reduce it to nearly nothing. (2) If the sun is near the horizon or well east or west of the glazing, its power is greatly reduced. (3) The sun doesn't shine at night when its heat is usually needed most. In many regions in winter, all this adds up to an average of only three or four hours of useful sungathering per day. During all the other winter hours any collected radiance will flow right back outdoors —and take a lot of your fossil fuel dollars with it.

But there is a way to lure those free Btus from the sky and trap them indoors. Though the ideal system doesn't exist yet, its parts do, sometimes nearly under your nose, and they can be assembled by anyone who is handy with tools. So, with a little sleuthing here and a little imagination there, on the next few pages we are going to engage in a pioneering effort —and create this ideal system. Let's begin with a large area of south-facing glass and locate panels of movable insulation behind the glass. What else should this ideal system have?

☞ The panels should cover all the glass when closed and obstruct none of the glass when open.

☞ The panels should open quickly and automatically when the sun is shining, and close similarly when the sun becomes too weak to heat or doesn't shine.

☞ Assuming the building's other outer surfaces are Insulation Cages or equally thick thermal barriers, the panels should contain 10 inches of insulation —for to be maximally effective, this movable insulation's R-value must approach that of the building's other outer surfaces.

☞ The insulation should be translucent, so that when closed during the day it won't darken the rooms behind.

What a tall order we've made for ourselves! But let's get to work before discouraging ourselves with negative thoughts.

Regarding making the panels of movable insulation cover all the solar glass, one way to do this has been hanging around in your house for years. It's that homely furnishing residing in a few cobwebby corners of your garage's ceiling: the overhead sliding door. This portal's hinged horizontal panels form a solid wall when closed and they lay flat against the ceiling when open. The one in your garage might not be big enough to mount behind a large area of solar glass when closed, but the one in your local

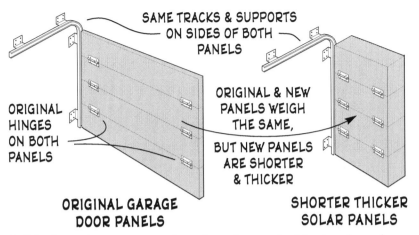

SAME TRACKS & SUPPORTS
ON SIDES OF BOTH
PANELS

ORIGINAL & NEW
PANELS WEIGH
THE SAME,

ORIGINAL
HINGES
ON BOTH
PANELS

BUT NEW PANELS
ARE SHORTER
& THICKER

ORIGINAL GARAGE
DOOR PANELS

SHORTER THICKER
SOLAR PANELS

8-25. Reusing garage door hardware behind solar glass

fire station would. Some of these doors are thirty feet wide and eighteen feet high. But what we want most from these doors is not their size but their hardware: the hinges that hold the panels together, and the wheels and tracks along the sides that guide them up and down. So here's how to use this hardware:

1. Disassemble a wide overhead garage door and weigh its panels, which are typically 20 inches high.
2. Build boxlike panels 10 inches deep that when filled with insulation will be the same height and weight as the original panels but will be notably shorter in length.
3. Fill the panels' cavities with 10 inches of insulation.
4. Reassemble the panels with the original hardware. They should weigh the same and operate the same as the original panels but may be only six to eight feet wide. This assembly is sketched above. If the area of solar glass is wider, make more than one system.

The above idea is not new. I should know, because in 1979 I received a government grant to build one. Though I was granted the funds to construct one of these systems, I couldn't build it because I couldn't find a homeowner who wanted an "ugly garage door" in the living room. But this is a different day. One open-minded company (www.raynor.com) now makes overhead doors that are up to 3 inches thick, 32 feet long, and 24 feet high that have "an extruded polyethylene insulation thermally bonded between two steel skins that has an R-value of 17.05." Though this is getting up there, it is not as much as the R-values of 35 or so that are possible with the construction outlined above.

Now let's discuss how to make the insulation open and close quickly and automatically. The motivater of this movement is the *thermal sensor* or *thermistor*, a dime-size metal bulb that records the temperature around it and wires the thermal data to a computer processor. If three thermistors are mounted around the panels of movable insulation as shown in figure 8-26, they can make the panels automatically open when the sun shines and automatically close when it doesn't as follows:

1. Locate a *solar* thermistor T_s in the space between the solar glass and the panels so the thermistor is exposed to the sun's trajectories across the southern sky.
2. Locate an *indoor* thermistor T_I near the center of the indoor space that will be heated by the solar glass.
3. Locate an *outdoor* thermistor T_o under the north eave where it will be shaded from the sun all year round.
4. Wire the thermistors to a programmed controller that connects to electric motors that operate the panels.

The controller can be programmed by a computer programmer (of which there are many these days) to open and close automatically as follows. When the thermistor between the panels and the solar glass is warmer than the indoor thermistor when the outdoor thermistor under the north eave is above 65 degrees, the panels close to keep the unwanted heat outdoors; and when the solar thermistor is cooler than the indoor thermistor when the outdoor thermistor is above 65 degrees, the panels open to let any excess heat indoors escape. This is the system's **summer mode**. When the thermistor between the panels and the solar glass is warmer than the indoor thermistor when the outdoor thermistor under the north eave is below 65 degrees, the panels open and let the sun's radiance enter indoors; and when the solar thermistor is cooler than the indoor thermistor when the outdoor thermistor is below 65 degrees, the panels close to keep the heat indoors. This is the system's **winter mode**. These electronics will work automatically all year round. This idea also is not new, because in 1986 I was granted a patent for it (USP 4443978). It has expired, so help yourself.

SUMMER MODE: T_o IS ABOVE 65°:
WHEN T_s IS ABOVE T_i, PANELS CLOSE.
WHEN T_s IS BELOW T_i, PANELS OPEN.

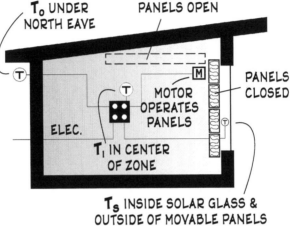

T_s INSIDE SOLAR GLASS &
OUTSIDE OF MOVABLE PANELS

WINTER MODE: T_o IS BELOW 65°:
WHEN T_s IS ABOVE T_i, PANELS OPEN.
WHEN T_s IS BELOW T_i, PANELS CLOSE.

8-26. Electronic operation of movable solar panels

As for making the solar panels translucent, a simple material has probably laying around your house or place of work for years: bubblepak. A sheet of these tiny enclosed airspaces is a good insulator. If you stack many sheets of this material until they are ten inches thick and sandwich between them cellophane-like sheets of electrostatic inhibitor such as Heat Mirror®, (see www.southwall.com), you will have a translucent insulation with a hefty R-value. I once conducted a comparative "hot-box" test

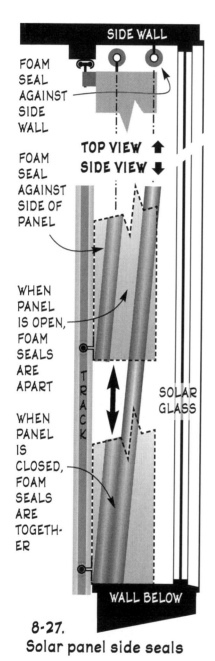

8-27.
Solar panel side seals

between six-inch-thick packets of this insulation and styrofoam, and my invention was superior. This idea also is not new. I received a patent for it (USP 4796404), also expired, in 1989.

When the panels close, they should form a seal with the adjacent walls so heat won't leak around the sides. One way to do this is to mount matching pairs of foam pipe insulation at a slight tilt along the panels' sides with one foam attached to the panels and the other to the wall, as sketched in figure 8-27. When the panels close, the two foams come together to form a snug seal along the panels' edges.

Another movable translucent insulation already on the market is the *cellshade*, as sketched in figure 8-28A. This contains a number of slatlike cells that compress when the shade is raised and open when the shade is lowered to form a barrier of translucent insulation. However, this thermal barrier's R-value is only about 3 or 4, which may be okay for buildings with old-timey R-11 insulation in their walls but not for superinsulated ones. But if the shade's cells are thick, as in the "photoshopped" version in fig-

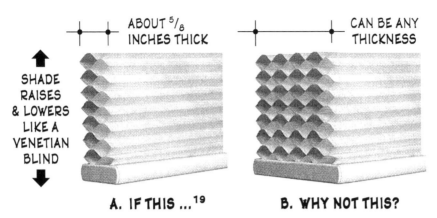

ABOUT ⁵/₈ INCHES THICK

CAN BE ANY THICKNESS

SHADE RAISES & LOWERS LIKE A VENETIAN BLIND

A. IF THIS ...[19]

B. WHY NOT THIS?

8-28. Tomorrow's movable translucent insulation

ure 8-28B, it could have almost any R-value. Maybe if enough customers tell the folks over at www.baliblinds.com about this idea, they'll start making them this way.

And here's a final solar gem: a fiberglass greenhouse whose roof is capped with a vent that opens automatically when the sun shines on an attached tube of beeswax. The sun heats the wax, which makes it expand, which opens the vent. When the weather cools, the wax contracts and the vent handlessly closes. Hot and cool at the same time! In imaginative hands this idea could have all kinds of applications. Take a look at www.solargem greenhouses.com.[20]

CHECK THE TUBE THAT OPENS THE VENT

8-29. Look, no hands or wires!

Architecture Laid Bare!

Thermal Massing. Every material —solid, liquid, or gas— has an ability to hold heat. Indeed, when you are in a room everything around you —the air, every object from a pencil to a sofa, and every enclosing wall and ceiling and floor— holds a certain quantity of heat. The higher the temperature, the more heat each material holds. When you raise the setting on the room's thermostat, more heat enters the room and warms the air, then the Btus in the air migrate into every solid in the room, raising the temperature of each until every molecule in the room is the same temperature. When you lower the thermostat, the heat first flows out of the air through the enclosing building envelope, then heat flows out of every solid in the room back into the air, until again every molecule in the room is the same temperature. Since wood absorbs about 1,000 times more heat than an equal volume of air, masonry about 1,750 times more, steel nearly 3,200 times more, and water 3,400 times more, when you turn up the room's thermostat, only a small amount of the heat entering the room remains in the air while most of it flows into the thermally denser solids.

On a recent winter day I came across a wonderful example of these thermodynamics. At a local auto body shop, the proprietor put every piece of scrap metal from his work on top of a large woodstove in his shop. He also said that at home he keeps an anvil on his woodstove, where "it soaks up a lot of heat at night, and gives it back in the day."

Now let's take two rooms, each the same size with lots of glass in the south wall and panels of thick movable insulation behind, and fill one room with a few barrels of thermally dense water and let the other room remain empty. When the sun shines through both areas of solar glass, the panels open and the sun's radiance fills both rooms with heat. In the empty room all the heat remains in the air, so its temperature will be notably higher; but in the other room the water will absorb much of the heat which will keep the air's temperature from rising as much. Now, since the greater the temperature difference between indoors and outdoors the faster the heat flows through the enclosing construc-

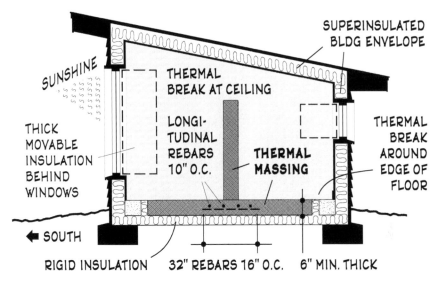

8-30. Effective thermal massing

tion, the empty room with the higher air temperature will lose considerably more heat through its enclosing construction. In fact, from late afternoon through a cold night until early the next morning, the temperature in the empty room may lower thirty degrees while the temperature in the room containing the water may lower only five degrees. Obviously it would take correspondingly less fossil fuel keep the room containing the water warm overnight. In summer when it is hot outside, all the above thermodynamics occur in reverse; then it would take less energy to keep the room containing the water cool.

In the room containing the water, the water should be located near the room's center where it can heat the most air. If the water is located near an exterior wall, the water's heat will flow more quickly outdoors. Also, since the water absorbs the air's heat through its surface, this mass will reservoir heat better if it has a high surface-to-volume ratio; so a barrel of water won't absorb and release as much heat as an equal volume of tall thin columns of water. But containers of water can leak. For this reason long thin walls of masonry, which store heat only half as well as water but won't leak, often work better as thermal massing.

Now let's put these physics to work with some well-designed architecture. Let's begin with a one-story house whose long south facade contains lots of solar glass with large panels of thick movable insulation mounted behind and whose roof and other exterior walls contain lots of insulation. Next let's build down the middle of the house a central wall of masonry that can store lots of heat, as appears in figure 8-30 on the previous page. This wall should be 6 to 8 inches thick, its ends should be several feet from the east and west walls, and its top should end a couple feet below the roof. The wall should be built on a 6-inch reinforced concrete floor (which also thermomasses well), the concrete under the wall should contain half-inch rebars spaced laterally and longitudinally as shown in figure 8-30, and beneath the concrete should be 4 inches of styrofoam insulation, which surprisingly can support 3,000 pounds per square foot. Styrofoam is also water-repellent, so it will keep ground moisture from wicking through the concrete (often a problem with this construction), and beneath the concrete the styrofoam won't burn.

As effective as this thermal construction is, it can be significantly improved by replacing the masonry with a superior thermomassing material known as *phase-change salts* or *eutectic salts*. One, named PCM 20T (see www.pcmenergy.com), is said to thermomass 50 to 80 times more heat than masonry if the temperature ranges above and below 68 degrees Fahrenheit. A few tall thin tubes of this powerful thermal sponge would absorb lots of heat during a sunny day and release it at night and in so doing maintain fairly even indoor temperatures all day long. PCM Energy makes three other phase-change salts that act similarly at around 64, 77, and 84 degrees. They are not the only makers of these materials.

The above thermodynamics can be improved even more by locating any baseboard heaters against the central wall. This was the way indoor heaters were installed a couple centuries ago —

when the heat source was a fireplace. In those days the hearth was near the center of the house where it could do the most good all the way around. That's the way it should be in any building, in any age. If you ever see a so-called "energy-efficient" house with a fireplace in an exterior wall, steer clear of the place because if it doesn't have this right it probably has other things wrong too.

Another fine method of thermomassing heat is with *electric thermal storage (ETS) units*. These are heating cabinets (one is $24\frac{1}{2}$ inches high, $10\frac{1}{2}$ inches deep, and 58 inches long) that contain an electric heating element mounted in a mass of high-density ceramic bricks. These prisms can sponge up a lot of Btus at night when electric utility rates may be lower, then the next day they radiate the stored Btus back into nearby spaces when electric rates are higher. An ETS unit can heat about 400 square feet of floor area and requires a 240-volt outlet. One manufacturer, the Steffes Corp. of Dickinson, ND (see www.steffes.com) also uses its bricks in a heat pump booster and a furnace.

Woodburners.[21] Heating with a woodstove that has a low emission rating (an EPA certification that lists how much smoke a wood-burner emits per unit of wood burned) is more efficient than even the fireplace detailed in Chapter 4, though not as romantic. The best woodstoves have a flat cooktop, an insulated metal flue, and an emission rating of about 4.0 grams of smoke per kilogram of wood burned. A conventional fireplace emits 50 to 80 gm/kg. Whatever unit you install, do not mount it on a raised hearth, as the air below won't flow into the fire and your feet will remain cold.

If your house has a standard fireplace in it, especially if in an exterior wall, think of unbuilding it. That's right; start at the chimney cap with a rented jackhammer and work your way down. In this age of spending money to save money this "unstallation" is a sure winner. You could save another bundle of bucks by recycling the bricks as a terrace and barbecue pit in the back yard.

Two other woodburners merit an honorable mention here. One is the *masonry heater* (some are known as Finnish stoves or

Russian stoves). This is a massive brick or rock construction that contains an enclosed firebox (the front may be pyrex glass so you can see the flames dancing inside) from where the produced heat twines through a maze of channels whose enclosing masonry absorbs the heat and radiates it into surrounding spaces. These units typically emit only 1 to 2 grams of particulate per hour, but they are expensive to build and weigh tons. For more information about them visit wikipedia, masonry heater; www.woodmasonry .com; and www.tempcast.com. The other honoree is the *woodburning furnace*. This has a thermostat that regulates the heat produced by controlling the air that enters the firebox. This heater is feasible where fuel oil is expensive and wood is plentiful. To learn more about them take a look at www.biomasscombustion.com and www.charmaster.com.

Ventilation

The best ventilator is an open window. Its cost is low, its "hands-on" technology is simple, it comes in many sizes, it is widely available —and you can't look out a furnace or an air conditioner. Especially adept is the

8-31. Casement ventilator

casement window. When half open it can scoop breezes flowing along a facade and send them indoors. Hear what Frank Lloyd Wright said of these little doors with big panes: "I fought for outswinging windows because they associated the house with the out of doors, gave free openings, outward. In other words the so-called 'casement' was simple, more human in use and effect, so more natural. If it had not existed I should have invented it." [22]

Another clever natural air freshener is the *turbine ventilator*. This little whirler works best when mounted on the peak of a roof. Prevailing breezes can turn its vanes as fast as 2,400 rpm, which can suck lots of stuffy warm air from below. A unit's size is based on the diameter of its neck, which may be 4 to 24 inches (the 4-inch model works well as a vent for a compostable toilet). The best models are aluminum (which won't rust) and have permanently lubricated and sealed steel ball bearings. They are nearly as easy to install as a stovepipe, and work best if the roofs aren't closed in by hills or foliage.

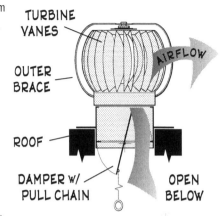

8-32. Turbine ventilator

Another clever rooftop ventilator is the *belvedere*. When this is perched on a roof's peak, prevailing breezes blowing through its vented sides create a slight vacuum in the flue-like void below that sucks stale hot air up from the spaces below like soda sucked up a straw. A belvedere needn't be as small as the one on the right. It can be as large as an observatory on a building's peak where occupants can enjoy views of the surrounding country-side. Then this perch's low walls may contain vents that let the air below rise around the edge of the floor.

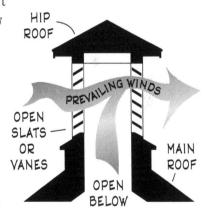

8-33. Belvedere

Another nifty natural ventilator is the *solar chimney*, a flue-like shaft with a tall pane of glass on the south side and an opening high on the north. When the sun shines on the glass it heats the air in the shaft which rises and draws stale stuffy air up from below. The taller the shaft, the taller the glass, the wider the shaft

407

from east to west, and the larger the opening, the faster the air rises inside and the cooler the air below. Imagine that: *cooling* with solar energy! Painting the north wall black also speeds up the airflow. If a house has a staircase with open risers and its ceiling is the roof, the tall narrow space enclosing the stairs would work magnificently as a solar chimney; as plenty of air would flow through the risers for the height of the stairs. Another possibility here is to build a real chimney like a solar chimney. Make the top of the flue rise four or five feet

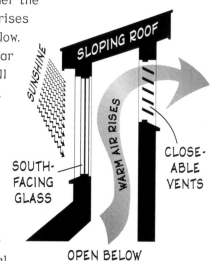

8-34. Solar chimney

above the roof, mount a tall narrow pane of Pyrex glass on the south side, open the top of the north side, and mount the cap at a steep tilt toward the north. I've never seen one of these babies built, but the physics behind its operation seem infallible. Besides, such visions never stopped Thomas Edison and Henry Ford from building what they thought would work. To say this cooler would function admirably as a flue above a fireplace in winter would be to vastly understate the facts.

With the roof ventilators described above, the warm air removed from the spaces below can be replaced by air drawn from the building's basement where it has been cooled by the surrounding ground. When these ventilators are installed in regions with cold winters, the openings on their undersides should be plugged with snug panels of thick insulation.

There are a number of ways to ventilate buildings with machines that run on fossil fuels. You can read all about them in other books.

Air Filtration

We breathe about 1,000 times an hour, and every breath should be a labor of love. Hence every lungful of indoor air should be filtered of *particulates* (dust, dander, pollen, lint, smoke, soot, and other minute solids), *microbes* (bacteria, viruses, spores, allergens, molds, fungi), *odors* (fumes, food aromas, vehicle exhausts, volatile gases from furniture and finishes), and *toxins*. Many of this nebula of impurities arrive from outdoors. If you live in a suburban or rural area, your domicile may already have the finest filter money can buy: foliage around the facades. Grasses, meadows, shrubs, and trees not only absorb carbon dioxide, they soak up sulphur dioxide, nitric oxide, and other airborne toxins and they generate oxygen which freshens the air even more. Nearly two hundred years ago, Washington Irving described the airy advantages of foliage exceedingly well when he said:

> As the leaves of trees are said to absorb all noxious qualities of the air, and breathe forth a purer atmosphere, so it seems as if they draw from us all sordid and angry passions, and breathe forth peace and philanthropy. There is a serene and settled majesty in woodland scenery that enters into the soul, and dilates and elevates it, and fills it with noble inclinations. [23]

Another fine filter a home may have —if it isn't wrapped in one of those awful vapor barriers— is its building envelope. This slightly porous construction will strain impurities from the small amounts of air infiltrating through it.

As for more mechanical filters, most are mat-like devices mounted in an HVAC duct where they strain impurities from the airflow. When one becomes clogged and can hold no more particles, it is cleaned in place, removed and cleaned, or discarded and replaced. There are a dozen or so different kinds, but not one removes every kind of impurity; so they are often combined to remove an acceptable percentage of whatever impurities are present. Filters are especially important in commercial buildings with nonopenable windows, as in them pollutants generated by the occupants and mechanical equipment inside cannot be removed via natural ventilation. A computerized method of filtering air involves mounting air pressure sensors before and after a filter mounted in a duct. As the filter cleans the airflow, the increasing number of trapped particles continually slows the airflow and the downstream sensor registers a continually lower air pressure; then when the filter becomes clogged, the downstream air pressure drops dramatically to a preset level which notifies service personnel that the filter should be changed. [24]

A filter is rated in terms of *arrestance* (ability to strain lint, dandruff, and dust), *efficiency* (ability to remove subvisible particles as carbon black, fly ash, and pollutants), *airstream velocity* (typically 125 to 150 feet per minute for high-efficiency filters, up to 500 fpm for medium-efficiency ones, and to 625 fpm for low-efficiency ones), *resistance* (how much the filter slows the airflow, requiring the HVAC system to have a correspondingly stronger blower fan and motor), and *lifespan*. All filters require access portals and adequate floor area outside so they can be easily inspected and maintained. Common filters today are:

Dry Media. These are typically 2 to 6 inch-deep frames filled with dry mats of cellulose, glass fibers, or other porous materials that fit across a duct's area where they strain particles out of the airflow. When a filter becomes clogged it is discarded. They are 5 to 30 percent efficient.

- ⊕ Good for low dust loads, prefiltering, and removing small amounts of microparticles; easily replaceable; low cost.
- ⊖ Inefficient; small holding capacity; high service cost; pores become increasingly clogged over time; short life. They do not filter microbes, gases, or odors.

Cleanable Media. These are similar to dry media filters except when they become clogged they are removed, cleaned or re-oiled, and reused. They are 65 to 80 percent efficient.

Climate

⊕ Simple, ecologically viable; requires no replacing.

⊖ Requires maintenance staff and cleaning space.

Aluminum Mesh. These are panels that contain layers of aluminum screens or meshes of different densities. The panels are strong enough to be mounted horizontally in ducts with large areas, they filter hot and greasy airflows, and can be removed and washed with detergents and chemicals. The metal screens also prevent electromagnetic interference from entering the ducting, which can be a problem in electronic environments. These are the best filters for restaurant stove hoods. Though they do not directly collect particles, microbes, and odors, these contaminants often adhere to the collected greases. They are 30 to 70 percent efficient.

⊕ Strong, nonflammable, reusable, durable, low resistance to airflows, good for high-velocity airflows. Ability to absorb hot particulates enables them to be installed in stove hoods, lab fume hoods, and some chimney flues. Also collects greases and gooey industrial impurities.

⊖ High initial cost, heavy.

Viscous Impingement. These filters contain a coarse medium such as spun glass fibers, metal screens, or expanded laths that force the airflow to change directions frequently as it passes through the medium, which is periodically covered with a tacky oil or grease that collects the impurities. Efficiencies vary widely.

⊕ Removes pollens, dusts, ashes, mists, oil smokes, and visible particles of high concentration. Large capacity; long life; needs little service; good pre-filter for other types.

⊖ Won't filter lints, viruses, bacteria, smoke, or toxins.

High-efficiency Particulate (HEPA). These filters have pleated blankets or mats with tiny pores that remove very small particles. Some are 99 percent efficient.

⊕ Removes fine particles and some bacterias and odors.

- Filter membranes can be a breeding ground for microbes; they are poor removers of most odors, gases, and microbes; they greatly reduce airflows of high velocities and require powerful blowers to be effective. They do not last long and require frequent changing.

Activated Charcoal. Also known as *carbon media*, these are replaceable panels or cartridges that have a foam or fabric medium filled with granulated carbon or activated charcoal. The carbon filters tiny particles and absorbs odors and heavy gases.

- Removes odors and toxins efficiently. Removes particles of all sizes, especially microparticles as smokes, certain microbes, most odors, and chemical toxins. Units can be installed in central systems as well as individual rooms.
- Greatly reduces airflow; requires frequent changing; breeds microbes. When carbon reaches its capacity for absorption it ceases to function as a filter.

Roll-type Disposable. These have a sheetlike filter mounted on a roll that is turned by a pressure-actuated motor. The filter rolls slowly through the airstream and as it becomes clogged it rewinds on a takeup spool. They are 20 to 50 percent efficient.

- Long-lasting; constantly cleans with constant airflow resistance; is an economical prefilter.
- Low efficiency; requires electricity to operate; must be promptly replaced when the feed roll is exhausted.

Ionic or Ionizing. These filters are usually set on tables or desks where they generate ions that induce airborne particles to adhere to each other until they are so heavy that they fall out of the air. They are often used in rooms filled with cigaret smoke and industrial inhalants. They are highly efficient but require lengthy exposure to large volumes of slowly circulating air.

- Removes low concentrations of smoke and particles from

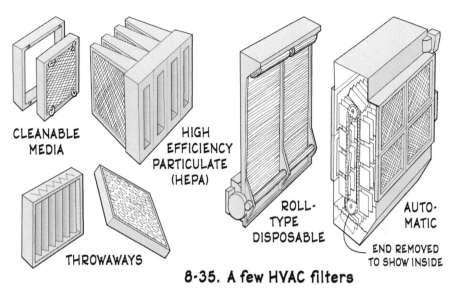

CLEANABLE MEDIA

HIGH EFFICIENCY PARTICULATE (HEPA)

ROLL-TYPE DISPOSABLE

AUTO-MATIC

END REMOVED TO SHOW INSIDE

THROWAWAYS

8-35. A few HVAC filters

large volumes of air. The ions travel freely through the air, and can improve air far from the filter.

- Undesirable when installed inside ducting or HVAC componentry; requires energy to operate. Since the particles fall out of the air, the treated area's floors, tables, and other flat surfaces require periodic cleaning.

Electrostatic. In these devices the airflow passes between two metal plates charged with up to 12,000 volts. The high voltage causes the charged particles to adhere to the plates which then rotate on a moving chain through an oil bath that removes the particles. They are used in smokestacks to remove particulate emissions, and are 75 to 90 percent efficient.

- Good for low-velocity and high-volume airflows. Removes microscopic particles; creates low resistance to airflow; induces low pressure drops within the airstream. Suitable where the filter is hard to reach or service is difficult.
- High initial and operating costs; requires extra space for transformer and rectifier; air exceeding 70 percent

413

humidity may adversely affect operation. **NG** in linty atmospheres and white rooms unless after-filters are used, which may be required to trap large particles that flake off the plates.

Automatic. These contain overlapping filter panels whose sides are attached to chains that move the panels across the airstream then through an oil bath. They remove medium and large particles well and are 80 to 90 percent efficient.

- ➕ Airflow resistance is fairly constant; filter is always clean.
- ➖ Costly; bulky; requires electricity to operate.

Ultraviolet. Here a beam of UV light passing through the duct destroys bacteria, molds, or fungi passing through the rays. Efficiency depends on intensity of light, volume of airflow, and length of exposure.

- ➕ Does not slow duct flow; requires no periodic cleaning; often used as a sanitizing agent in medical facilities.
- ➖ Removes no particulates; requires extra equipment and energy to operate; humans and animals must be shielded from exposure to the UV light.

Ozone. These devices introduce ozone (O_3) into a duct's airflow where the ozone's extra atom of oxygen attaches to microbes and organic gases, rendering them harmless and producing free oxygen. This action continues after the airflow has entered occupied spaces. Efficacy depends on air grille designs and room circulation patterns that mix the ozone with the arriving airflow.

A recently developed filter is the UV ozone filter, which combines the advantages of ultraviolet and ozone filters. For more information see www.o3ozone.com.

- ➕ Does not reduce duct flow; can be installed in central ducting or single rooms; requires no intermittent cleaning. Good when unwanted microbes or organic gases can be quantified and where considerable but not complete removal of the specified pollutant is satisfactory. Works best where pollutants are known and can be quantified, and where occupants will not be exposed to the ozone.

- ⊖ Has no effect on particulates; requires extra equipment and energy to operate; reacts slowly. Since inhaled ozone can damage one's lungs, this method requires precise quantifying of the pollutant and its remover. Has little or no effect on some chemicals and can produce irritating or harmful by-products when reacting with some chemicals.

←———— PARTICLE SIZE OR TYPE ————→

TYPE OF FILTER	Small	Medium	Large	Bacteria	Viruses	Fungi	Molds	Gases	Odors
Dry media	•	●	●						
Cleanable media	•	●	●						
Aluminum mesh	•	●	⬤		•	•		•	•
Viscous impingement		●	●		•	•		•	•
HEPA	⬤	●	●	•	•	•	•	•	•
Activated charcoal	⬤	●	●					⬤	⬤
Roll-type disposable	•	●	●						
Automatic	•	●	⬤						
Ionic or ionizing	⬤	●	●	●					
Electrostatic	⬤	●	•						
Ultraviolet				●	●	⬤	⬤	•	
Ozone				⬤	●	●	●	⬤	•

8-36. Ability of filters to remove air impurities

The chart above indicates the ability of different filters to remove certain impurities from interior air. The larger the dot beside a filter, the greater its ability to remove the impurity listed above the dot. This chart also reveals the compatibility of certain filters with others, so it facilitates combining certain filters to remove a variety of pollutants from indoor environments.

Acoustics

Otherwise comfortable and beautiful architecture can be made unbearable by unwanted sound. If you don't like what you see, you can close your eyes —but with sound you're trapped, prisoned by an invisible invader. If you have ever heard an annoying noise come through a wall from the room next door, you know what I mean. At other times you may not be able to hear a sound you want to hear. A lecturer's voice is feeble ... a minister's words sound fuzzy ... a cello's bass tones are harsh while its tenor tones are tinny. Another problem with sounds is subjectivity. There is no doubt when an overstressed beam fails or an overloaded circuit trips its breaker —but who's to say the sound that bothers you bothers me?

To better understand these elusive physics, let's first consider an aural event we all are familiar with: a hammer striking a nail. When the hammer's base strikes the nail's top, the colliding metals are slightly compressed —then they return to their original shapes so fast that they push out the air molecules around them, which pushes the molecules immediately beyond them, which pushes the next molecules outward and so on until the ever-widening spherical wavefront collides with a surface whose area may be a twentieth of a square inch that is buried deep in your ear. A pressure of $^1/_{500}$ of a pound will hurt these delicate membranes. Think about this the next time you clean your ear with a Q-tip. You also have not one but two of these receivers. If a sound comes toward the right side of your head, it enters your right ear first then travels around your head and enters your left ear about $^1/_{2000}$ of a second later. This tiny difference is enough for your eardrums to send separate signals to your brain which helps you locate the sound's source when you can't see it.

Still more happens here. When the wavefront radiating from

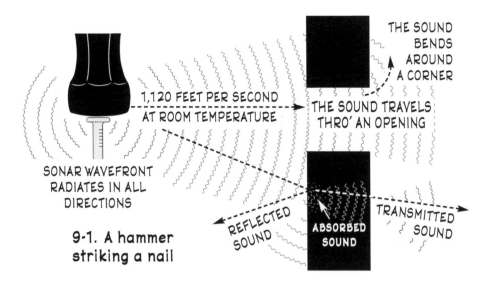

9-1. A hammer striking a nail

the hammerblow hits an enclosing surface of the room it is in, some of the sound reflects off the surface, some enters the construction behind and is absorbed, and some keeps traveling through the construction and emerges on the other side. The solid-borne sound even picks up speed; for while sound at room temperature travels through air at about 1,120 feet per second, it travels through wood at about 5,000 fps, concrete at 12,000 fps, and steel at 16,000 fps. Since such a wavefront is moving faster the instant it bursts from the wall's far side, for that instant it may sound even louder than when it entered the wall.

Still more sonar events occur here. The spherical wavefront radiating from the hammerblow keeps moving outward until, fatigued at having to plow through so many millions of molecules, it diminishes to less than your ability to hear it: a level known as the *threshold of hearing*. If an initially loud sound of 90 decibels is reduced to 3 decibels by sound-absorbing materials and you can't hear sounds below 6 decibels, you will no longer hear the sound even though it is still resonating somewhere; until finally the sound dies amid billions of moribund molecules to become nothing, damped by reality.

Airborne Sound

Airborne sound passes through the air. Figure 9-2 charts the intensity levels of a number of familiar sounds. Each is generally measured 3 feet from its source. In this chart the symbol ₫ stands for *decibel*. This is the "inch" by which sound is measured. Every sound, whether loud or soft, has a *source* (where it originates), a *path* (where it travels), and a *receiver* (where it ends), as described below.

Sound source. This is the aural event that originates the sound. An initial sound has an *intensity, frequency, diversity*, and *duration*, as further detailed below:

Intensity. This is a sound's loudness at its source, from the ticking of a watch to the roar of a jet engine, as measured in decibels (₫) by a sound meter located three feet from the source. A whisper is about 20 ₫, human conversation around 50 to 65 ₫, and a shout about 80 ₫. Hearing loud sounds for lengthy periods can permanently damage one's ears. OSHA (the Occupational Safety Hazard Association) has mandated that in industrial activities sound levels cannot exceed 115 ₫ (equal to a jackhammer three feet away) for 7 minutes, 105 ₫ (a chainsaw) for 20 minutes, 95 ₫ (a power mower) for one hour, and 85 ₫ (a truck engine) for eight hours.

Frequency. Also known as *pitch*, this is a sound's vibrations per second, measured in *Hertz* (Hz). This ranges from the beat of a bass drum at about 40 Hz to the shrill of a whistle at about 4,000 Hz. The human voice ranges from about 60 to 3,000 Hz, its dominant frequencies being around 500 Hz for men and 900 Hz for women. A musical note is a *pure* sound: one with a single frequency. A chord is an *integral* sound: several pure sounds that harmonize to create a uniform sound. Noise is *diverse* sound: a mix of nonharmonious sound frequencies.

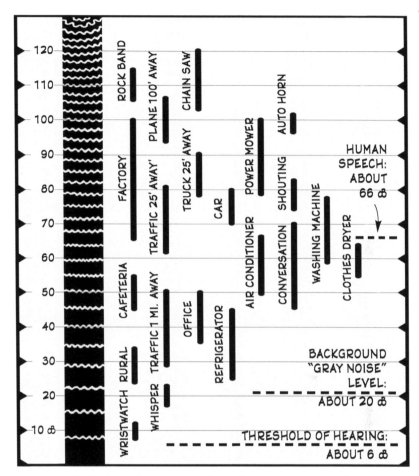

9-2. Loudness levels of common sounds

The lower a sound's frequency, the longer its wave. At room temperature, a low bass tone at 40 Hz is 28 feet long while a high tenor tone at 2,000 Hz is only about 6 inches long. The longer a low soundwave is, the harder it is to bend. You could say that uttering a low bass sound is like throwing a spear through the air while uttering a high tenor sound is like throwing a toothpick. This is why low-pitched sounds pass more readily through air, fabrics,

419

and other soft media while high-pitched sounds tend to be absorbed, and why from the ground an airplane engine is an ear-piercing whine when you board the plane and a low drone when you hear it high in the sky. Another example is rock music transmitting through a wall. On the wall's near side you may hear fingerpicking on the highest frets of the guitar, but on the far side you may hear only the drums. Since masonry absorbs long low soundwaves well and thick fabrics absorb short high soundwaves well, one way to absorb both sounds is to build an intervening wall of masonry and cover the side facing the sound with thick drapes.

Diversity. This is the tendency of a sound to be *singular* (the sound comes from one place, like a knock on a door) or *diffuse* (the sound comes from many places at once, like vehicular traffic on a city street or cheering spectators in a football stadium).

Duration. The sound's timespan, from a ping to a drone. It may be an *impulse sound* (an isolated event such as a door slam) or a *steady-state sound* (a continuous event such as a whirring fan). Some steady-state sounds are aggregates of impulse sounds, one being the closely spaced phonemes of speech that comprise human conversation.

Sound path. This is the direction an acoustic wavefront takes as it travels from its source. If the wave migrates through air or gas it is *airborne*, if it travels through a solid it is *solid-borne*. A soundwave may pass though water or other liquid, but this rarely happens in architecture. A migrating sound may change from airborne to solid-borne and back several times —as when an off-balance HVAC blower fan revolving at high speed creates an ear-piercing vibration (airborne) that passes through the blower's frame (solid-borne), resonates through the air beneath the frame (airborne), penetrates the concrete floor below (solid-borne), travels through the airspace between the underside of the floor and the top of the suspended ceiling below (airborne), passes through the suspended ceiling (solid-borne), and enters the office below (airborne) to annoy a person working at a desk. A sound like this, which may originally be 95 dB, is commonly reduced to tolerable levels as follows. First you can forget about the last 6 dB because it is below your threshold of hearing. Then all the tiny sounds coming from everywhere around you typically dissipate to a background "gray noise" level of about 20 dB; so the annoying sound needs to be lowered only about 70 dB to be unhearable. Next you can introduce a second sound that is more enjoyable to listen to, a method known as *masking*. Two examples are a fan and soft music, each of which occurs at about 35 dB. Now only about 35 dB remain to be lowered by the intervening construction. If you add 5 dB to be safe, a 40 dB acoustic barrier construction is fairly economical to build. If you don't turn on a fan or music, 75 dB is expensive to build. Of course, another solution here is to go upstairs and repair the off-balance blower fan.

Sounds in theaters, auditoriums, lecture halls, and other assembly areas require special attention. If any seats in the audience are more than about 60 feet from the sound source, the sound usually needs to be electronically amplified. This is generally done by locating a microphone near the sound source, mounting a cluster of megaphone-shaped loudspeakers 15 to 20 feet overhead, and aiming the speakers over the listening area. If any seats are more than 110 feet away, speakers are usually mounted above the seats at thirty feet intervals so listeners can hear the speaker almost instantly. In assembly areas soundwaves generally radiate from a performer onstage over the audience, reflect from enclosing surfaces, and return over the audience. Architects analyze these sonar patterns when designing theaters, lecture halls, and sometimes even classrooms, by taking a plan of the area, drawing radial lines out from the sound source over the audience to the area's enclosing surfaces, then drawing reflective lines from the enclosing surfaces back over the audience to see the patterns they make. This plotting is known as *ray tracing*, and the patterns are *ray diagrams*. Architects use this graphic data to determine optimal speaking positions, stage heights, loudspeaker locations, angles of sound reflectors mounted above the stage, and the shape of an assembly area's enclosing walls and ceiling.

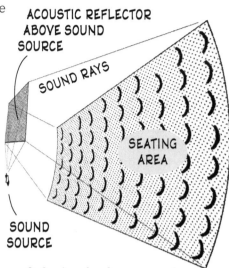

Another amplifier of sound is the human mouth. Shaped somewhat like a megaphone from larynx to lips, it could be called a mul-

9-3. Analyzing sound reception with ray tracing

tifrequency speaker horn mounted on a swivel base.

Sounds can take annoying routes, as the following anecdote will attest. Once when seated in my accountant's office, I heard voices coming seemingly out of nowhere that were nearly as loud as the accountant's voice as he sat behind his desk. In the ceiling near the wall behind him I noticed an HVAC supply air register. I stepped outside to investigate. In the office on the other side of the wall another accountant was conversing with a client, and in the ceiling above his head was another supply air register. The second conversation was entering the register above, migrating through a duct extending above the ceiling over the wall, and emerging from the register in my accountant's office: an example of *speaking tube noise*. Eliminating this violation of confidentiality involves reconfiguring the ducting and/or lining its inner surfaces with sound-deadening materials.

Another annoying acoustic event is *flanking sound*. An example is a noise that slips through a louver or loose trim in a door, moves down a hall to the next door with louvers or loose trim, and

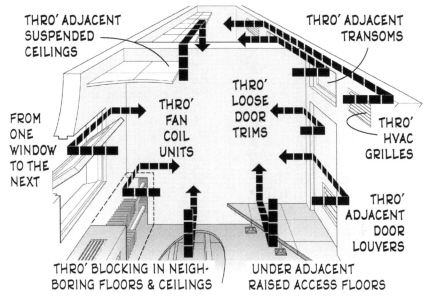

THRO' ADJACENT SUSPENDED CEILINGS

THRO' ADJACENT TRANSOMS

THRO' LOOSE DOOR TRIMS

THRO' FAN COIL UNITS

FROM ONE WINDOW TO THE NEXT

THRO' HVAC GRILLES

THRO' ADJACENT DOOR LOUVERS

THRO' BLOCKING IN NEIGH-BORING FLOORS & CEILINGS

UNDER ADJACENT RAISED ACCESS FLOORS

9-4. Flanking sound paths between adjacent spaces

slips through these openings to annoy occupants in the next room. Flanking sound can creep around walls between open windows, hop over walls between suspended ceilings, duck under walls between raised floors, and sneak through other openings in seemingly solid construction. It is prevented by filling, sealing, or eliminating any openings between adjacent spaces.

Receiver. This is where a sound ends. This includes your ears, surfaces a sound reflects from, and solids where a sound is absorbed. A sound arriving at an enclosing or *boundary surface* is *incident sound*, and the portion that returns from the surface is *reflected sound*. If a surface is smooth and flat, the reflected sound is a mirror image of the incident sound and is *articulate*. If the surface is rough or curved, the reflected sound is *dispersed*. Sometimes articulate sound is desirable, other times it is not. Consider a conference room. If it has a ceiling and plaster walls, several large windows on one side, a ceramic tile floor, and a dozen wooden chairs around a large table, the room may look attractive but its many hard surfaces will create a cacophony of sounds that will make a meeting here unpleasant. If the room's ceiling is covered with acoustic tile, the walls are hung with tapestries, the windows are fitted with drapes, the floor is laid with carpet, the wooden chairs are replaced with upholstered ones, and a long fabric runner is centered on the table, a meeting here will be much more pleasant and productive.

Another kind of reflected sound often occurs in assembly areas. If the room's walls and ceiling and walls are smooth, they may harshly echo the speaker's words: a phenomenon known as *reverberation*. A little reverberation is often desirable: in a concert hall it can make the music sound richer and more natural, and in a church it can make a minister's sermon seem more solemn. Sometimes an assembly area may need its enclosing surfaces to be highly reflective on one occasion and highly absorptive on another, as in an auditorium when a concert is scheduled one night and a lecture the next. Here the surfaces should be more absorbent the first night and more reflective the next. One way to do this is to cover the walls and ceilings with such flexibly reflective surfaces as retractable sound-absorbing fabrics (often known as *sails*) in the auditorium's ceiling and revolving sound-absorbent panels in the walls, as appear above. With these surfaces a room's acoustic properties can be quickly changed, even during a performance if necessary.

9-5. Sound behavior at different surfaces

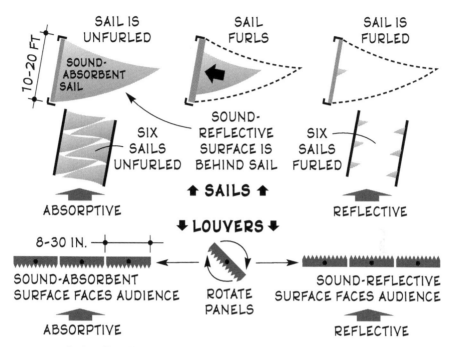

SAIL IS UNFURLED

10-20 FT

SOUND-ABSORBENT SAIL

SAIL FURLS

SAIL IS FURLED

SIX SAILS UNFURLED

SOUND-REFLECTIVE SURFACE IS BEHIND SAIL

SIX SAILS FURLED

↑ SAILS ↑

ABSORPTIVE

REFLECTIVE

↓ LOUVERS ↓

8-30 IN.

SOUND-ABSORBENT SURFACE FACES AUDIENCE

ROTATE PANELS

SOUND-REFLECTIVE SURFACE FACES AUDIENCE

ABSORPTIVE

REFLECTIVE

9-6. Flexible acoustics with louvers and sails

An extreme reverberation is *resonance*. This is a harmonic buildup of reflected sound whose wavelength is an exact multiple of the dimension of a space through which the wave travels. If a cellist performing in a chamber whose temperature is 69 degrees Fahrenheit plays a middle C (wavelength = 262 Hz which is 4.304 feet long) and the note's soundwave strikes a surface 21'-6¼" away (exactly five times the length of the soundwave), the reflected sound will add repeatedly to the original sound and make it much louder. This rarely occurs in such a space —but when it does it can be agonizing. You may have heard this when a person is speaking before a microphone and at a certain pitch (i.e. wavelength) the person's voice screeches awfully. To deal with this possibility the architect may have the space tested after its finishes are applied. Any offending surfaces are usually covered with absorptive and/or diffusing materials or rebuilt.

Architecture Laid Bare!

Another annoying reverberation is *oscillation*. This occurs when a soundwave strikes a thin or membranous material and makes it vibrate which can magnify the sound on the other side. These adverse acoustics can occur in back-to-back medicine cabinets in adjacent apartment bathrooms, back-to-back bookcases in adjacent offices, and in ducts where swiftly flowing air makes the sheet metal walls rumble. Oscillation is often the result of stingy budgets. Design remedies are:

☞ Build suspected membranes of thicker, heavier, and less elastic materials. Fabric-covered lead lining (also known as sheet lead) is best for critical situations.

☞ Make suspected areas smaller. One way is to glue a rib through the center of the offending membrane which divides it into two smaller areas that are less elastic.

☞ Frame the suspected membrane with resilient borders.

☞ Cushion one side with fiberglass insulation or other soft material.

☞ In large windows, install thermopane units whose panes have different thicknesses.

An important aspect of sound reception is a room's shape. Consider an empty living room shaped like a big box. A sound originating here may reverberate between its parallel surfaces and become a pitter-patter of echoes. You may have heard this the first time you stepped into your living room before the moving van arrived. This rebounding sound is usually eliminated by covering at least one of each opposing surface with unsmooth objects such as carpets and upholstered furniture on floors, drapes and shelves of differently sized books on the walls, acoustic tiles on the ceiling, and the like. A few solutions more commonly found in commercial interiors are curved surfaces, "lightning bolt" wall profiles, sloping floors or ceilings that keep opposing surfaces from being parallel, and walls covered with soft materials. Several such absorptive methods are employed in movie theaters. Their floors slope slightly and are carpeted, the side walls angle in toward the screen and are covered with drapes, the seats are upholstered with fabrics that resemble clothing so they will absorb sound fairly equally whether occupied or vacant, and the screen is perforated (if you stand close to it you can see the holes). All this leaves only a dominant sound arriving straight at you from the speakers at the screen. Home entertainment centers are often shaped and surfaced this way. In such a "performance environment" the "complex electro-acoustic interactions" should possess the "psychoacoustic sensations that critical listeners expect." The above-quoted expressions were coined by RPG Diffuser Systems (rpginc.com), a prominent designer of acoustic environments for commercial, entertainment, and research occupancies. Another company that does a fine job of making entertainment centers psychoacoustically sensational is Crutchfield Electronics, at crutchfield.com.

When an architect designs a theater, lecture hall, or other acoustically important space, s/he carefully selects its boundary surfaces from an acoustic palette of reflective materials (a few are concrete block, glass, and plaster) and absorptive materials (a few are carpets, drapes, and acoustic tile) and configures the room's shape to regulate the sounds occurring within.

Solid-borne Sound

Solid-borne sound migrates through a floor, wall, ceiling, or other solid construction and emerges in adjacent spaces. During a building's design these potentially annoying sounds may be reduced by isolating noisy areas from quiet ones as follows:

☞ Group noisy areas as entertainment and mechanical rooms in one part of a floorplan, group quiet areas as bedrooms and studies in another, and place neutral areas as stairs, corridors, and closets in between.

☞ In multifloor buildings stack noisy areas and quiet areas: in apartments place kitchens over kitchens and bedrooms over bedrooms. In hotels and motels don't locate sleeping areas next to elevator shafts.

Solid-borne sound is minimized by building interior floors, walls, and ceilings as described below and in figure 9-7:

☞ Select floor, wall, and ceiling finishes that reflect or absorb sounds rather than transmit them. Good sound reflectors are plaster, painted concrete block, and ceramic tile; slightly less so are exposed brick and masonry. Good sound absorbers are thick drapes, deep pile carpets with foam underlayments, and sheet lead (the best but expensive). Metals, glass, and plaster typically reflect much incident sound but the sound they absorb tends to be transmitted. Metal and plaster can be covered with drapes and/or backed with batt insulation. Wood is intermediate: it reflects, absorbs, and transmits fairly equal amounts of incident sound and is economical. Hardwoods reflect sound slightly more than softwoods and softwoods absorb slightly more.

☞ Interlayer soft materials with hard.

☞ Use textured interior finishes.

☞ Don't mount two electrical outlet boxes, medicine cabinets, or other thin-backed objects back-to-back.

☞ In acoustically critical spaces, staple half-inch strips of weatherstripping to the inner surfaces of joists, studs, and rafters before applying interior finishes.

☞ Between acoustically critical areas, build double-stud walls and fill with batt insulation. Stagger the studs rather than align them.

☞ In acoustically important construction the architect should specify fine workmanship and visit the site often with the client to make sure the work is done as specified.

Unfortunately, all the labor spent in designing sound-absorbent construction can be negated by loose trim around

LINE ALL DUCTS

SEAL ALL DUCT & PIPE ENTRY SEAMS IN WALLS & FLOORS

SEAL UNDER BASE PLATES

W/W CARPET ON UNDERLAY- MENT ON 3/4" PLYWOOD ON SLEEPERS ON RESILIENT MAT

BATTS OVER WALL ABOVE SUSP. CLG.

DOUBLE WALL OF STAGGERED STUDS W/ BATTS IN VOIDS

RESILIENT CLIPS BTWN. SHEETROCK & STUDS

BATTS IN ALL FRAMING CAVITIES

DOUBLE GLAZING

HARDWOOD FLOOR ON SLEEPERS W/ BATTS BTWN SLEEPERS

RAISED ACCESS FLOOR ON RESILIENT MAT

BATT BAFFLES IN ALL VOIDS AROUND CEILINGS

INSULATED CURTAIN WALL

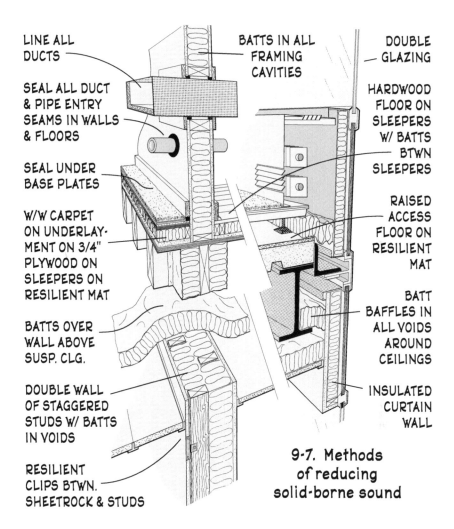

9-7. Methods of reducing solid-borne sound

doors and windows, open edges around suspended ceilings, seams around electrical outlets, and the like. You could say acoustic construction is only as strong as its weakest *leak*. An easy way to ferret out such "mouse sounds" (because they can wriggle through tiny spaces) is to wait until it's dark and shine a flash-light on one side of the suspected construction and see if any light appears on the other side. Sound leakage is usually most annoying with high-pitched sounds because, as alluded to earlier, their shorter wavefronts sneak through contorted soundpaths more easily.

An effective method of controlling sound in large open interiors is with shoulder-high walls covered with sound-absorbent fabrics, like the ones arranged around office cubicles in commercial environments. In these confines, sounds originating from people talking while seated tend to travel over the walls and aren't heard by seated persons beyond. This works better for low sounds than high because, again, lower sounds have longer wavefronts that don't bend as easily.

The American Society for Testing Materials (ASTM) has given a number of construction assemblies *Sound Transmission Class* (STC) ratings, wherein the higher the STC rating the more the construction reduces sound transmission through it. Constructions with STC ratings of around 45 are average, ones above STC 60 are highly absorbent but usually expensive, while ones below STC 35 tend to be cheap constructions that transmit sound.

Two solid-borne sounds, *impact noise* and *machine-borne sound*, require special attention as detailed below.

Impact noise. This occurs when an object sharply strikes a surface and creates a quick loud sound that passes through the construction behind. Examples are a door slamming against its frame, a woman's spike heels striking a hard floor, and a heavy object falling on a floor. The chief remedy for eliminating these annoyances is to cushion the impact at its source, as follows:

☞ Float wood floors on fiberglass batts, and cover wood and concrete floors with deep-pile carpets on foam pads.

☞ Leave a half-inch gap between a finished floor and its surrounding walls, fill the gap with seal sealer (thin fiberglass strips about 6 inches wide that every lumber company sells) and conceal the sealer with base molding.

☞ Staple lengths of weatherstripping to the tops of joists,

faces of studs and plates, and undersides of rafters before installing finishes in noise-producing areas.

☞ Suspend ceilings from resilient hangers and install drop-in or lay-in sound-absorbent panels.

As with STC ratings, ASTM has given a number of floor constructions *Impact Insulation Class* (IIC) ratings, in which the higher the IIC rating the more the construction absorbs impact sound. Constructions with IICs of at least 55 are installed between units in most hotels and apartments, and luxury units generally have values of 60 to 75. Two websites that list comparative ratings for construction assemblies are www.toolbase.org/PDF/CaseStudies/stc_icc_ratings.pdf (they give STC and IIC ratings for floor, wall, and ceiling constructions) and www.quietsolution.com/html/noise-samples (here you can listen to audio comparisons of twenty acoustic constructions).

Machine-borne sound. This sound originates in HVAC units, elevators, loosely mounted pipes, and other mechanical equipment. Sloppy installation of such mechanisms can turn an otherwise well-designed occupancy into a chaos of vibrations, rattles, rumblings, hammerings, buzzes, and whistles. A few remedies are described in the text below and figure 9-8 on the next page.[1]

☞ Install quietly operating machinery and locate it on vibration isolators or resilient mounts.

☞ Specify oil- or silicone-filled transformers for indoor installations (these don't hum as loudly) and quieter electronic ballasts for fluorescent and HID light fixtures.

☞ Reduce turbulent velocities in pipes and ducts by increasing their diameters.

☞ Fit ducts with fiberglass liners.

☞ Fit rubber grommets onto bolted connections.

☞ Fasten piping to solid construction with insulated mounts.

☞ Install flexible boots at the base of plenums.

☞ Install flexible couplings in pipes.

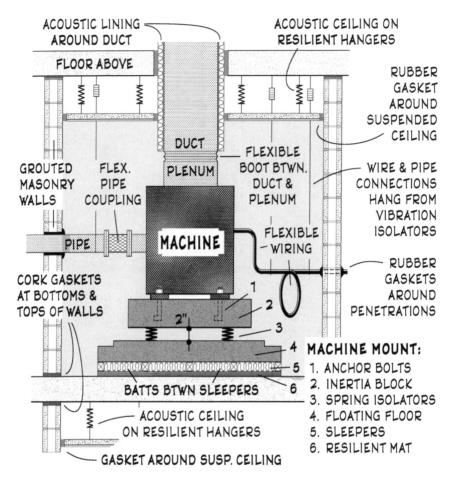

ACOUSTIC LINING AROUND DUCT

ACOUSTIC CEILING ON RESILIENT HANGERS

FLOOR ABOVE

RUBBER GASKET AROUND SUSPENDED CEILING

DUCT

PLENUM

FLEXIBLE BOOT BTWN. DUCT & PLENUM

WIRE & PIPE CONNECTIONS HANG FROM VIBRATION ISOLATORS

GROUTED MASONRY WALLS

FLEX. PIPE COUPLING

MACHINE

FLEXIBLE WIRING

PIPE

RUBBER GASKETS AROUND PENETRATIONS

CORK GASKETS AT BOTTOMS & TOPS OF WALLS

2"

1
2
3
4
5
6

BATTS BTWN SLEEPERS

ACOUSTIC CEILING ON RESILIENT HANGERS

GASKET AROUND SUSP. CEILING

MACHINE MOUNT:
1. ANCHOR BOLTS
2. INERTIA BLOCK
3. SPRING ISOLATORS
4. FLOATING FLOOR
5. SLEEPERS
6. RESILIENT MAT

9-8. Methods of isolating machine-borne sound

☞ Locate loops in wires extending from machinery.

☞ Install solid-core doors to mechanical areas and fit them with gasketed edges.

☞ Seal all penetrations through nearby walls or floors with gaskets, fillers, or caulking.

A clever eliminator of duct noise is the *active noise canceller*, as sketched in figure 9-9. In the duct near the noise's

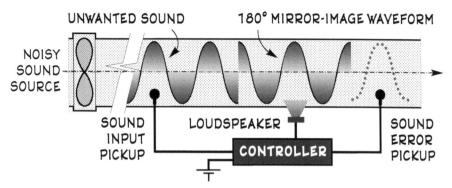

Fig. 9-9. Active noise controls in HVAC ducting[†]

source is mounted a sound pickup which records the offending sound and sends the data to a programmed controller, which creates a 180° mirror-image waveform that exits a loudspeaker mounted further down the duct which cancels the offending sound. These silencers can eliminate diverse sounds of several frequencies. They work best at low frequencies, usually the most annoying sounds in ducts. Two companies that make these devices are Digisonix/ Nelson Industries in Middleton, WI, and Noise Cancellation Technologies in Stamford, CT.

Outdoor Sound

As with lighting, the biggest difference between indoor and outdoor sound is that in the latter no reflective shape encloses the source and receiver. In such spaces the sound is usually weaker at near distances; so if the sound is a lecturer or musicians performing before an audience, the sound may need to be amplified more. Lack of enclosing surfaces also enables outdoor sound to travel farther, then the air absorbs the short high-pitched waves more readily than long low-pitched waves. This is why distant airplanes and foghorns sound so low.

Irregular topography and outdoor foliage tend to reflect and absorb sounds, but they can also concentrate sounds in ways that will amplify them. For example, three-eighths of a mile from where I live is a house which when the owners have a party I can hear it almost as if I'm in their front yard. This is because (1) the road between us is straight and curves just before each house so both are aligned with the axis of the road; (2) the terrain west of the road rises sharply and uniformly uphill; and (3) the terrain east of the road is covered with large trees whose foliage ends at the road. The result: a tunnel of open space between the two houses that funnels the sound from one to the other.

Outdoor sound is categorized as *outdoor-indoor sound* or *outdoor-outdoor sound*, as explained below.

Outdoor-indoor sound. This arrives from outside a building into interior spaces, chiefly through windows. If the sound is too harsh, the window may require special design. Consider the Seaport Hotel in Boston, where guests enjoy views of (but not sounds from) nearby Logan airport and Boston Harbor through large 5 × 7 foot windows, each a sandwich construction of $\frac{1}{4}$-inch glass, $\frac{3}{8}$-inch airspace, $\frac{9}{16}$-inch laminated glass, $4\frac{9}{32}$-inch airspace, and $\frac{3}{8}$-inch laminated glass fitted into an insulated aluminum frame. Each window weighs 800 pounds and can be opened for cleaning. Outdoor sound also enters interiors through exterior doors, wall vents, and utility connections. These sounds are minimized by sealing all seams, eliminating flanking paths, and mounting the openings in masonry or other solid construction.

Outdoor-outdoor sound. These sounds originate and remain outdoors. If a backyard or park should offer peace and quiet, it may be shielded from nearby annoying sounds by barriers that absorb much of the sound and deflect the rest upward. This is done by making the barrier construction thick, making its outer surface soft and rough (usually with masses of foliage), having the barrier rise well above the sight line between sound source and receiver, and placing the barrier near either the sound source or receiver. If possible make the barrier's side-to-

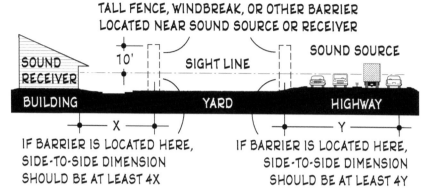

TALL FENCE, WINDBREAK, OR OTHER BARRIER
LOCATED NEAR SOUND SOURCE OR RECEIVER

9-10. An outdoor sound barrier

side dimension at least four times the length between the sound source or receiver, whichever is nearest. Practical solutions are rows of dense foliage, windbreaks, tall fences, thick ground covers, and varied terrain.

Altogether Now...

When it comes to consuming energy, America is ailing. The problem is so serious that if we all immediately started using efficient lightbulbs and the low-flo showerheads, this would be nowhere near enough to create a sustainable architecture because we are hemorrhaging energy in too many other ways.

But if you arrange efficient furniture in compactly designed spaces enclosed with thick insulation and whose south walls have large areas of glass backed with thick movable panels of translucent insulation, while you're helping the nation "go green" you'll save some of that "green" you put in your pocket, and you'll make yourself, your loved ones, and your business colleagues more comfortable at the same time.

Our nation has long had a word for such enterprising people. Pioneers.

So let's get digging.

Epilogue

Footnotes

Shades of Green

1. All citings of LEED directives are from the *LEED Certification Guidebook, Process management Guidebook for Projects in the District of Columbia* (Oct 2008); this publication is available on the internet.
2. *Plumbing Systems & Design* magazine, Jul/Aug 2010, p. 29: "To LEED or not to LEED: Cost Becomes the Question".
3. Frank Lloyd Wright, *On Architecture* (1941, Duell, Sloan, & Pierce, New York), p. 245.
4. *ASHRAE Journal*, Nov 2008, p. 28: quote by Joseph Lstiburek, Ph.D.
5. Frank Lloyd Wright, *A Testament* (1957, Horizon Press, New York); this quote is a combination of two short expressions on p. 203.
6. Frank Lloyd Wright, *The Natural House* (1954, Horizon Press), p. 141.
7. *The New York Times*, Aug 26, 2010, p. D6, column one.
8. Kevin Ireton, *Fine Homebuilding* magazine, Fall/Winter 2010, p. 10.
9. This quip appeared in the *ASHRAE Journal*, Nov 2008, p. 36, by Joseph Lstiburek, Ph.D.; it was credited to Henry Gifford of New York City.
10. The cited quotes are from Michelle Nijhuis' review of Maggie Koerth's book, *Before the Lights go out: Conquering the Energy Crisis before It Conquers Us*, *Audubon* magazine, May-June 2012, p. 94.
11. Martin Luther King, Jr., "Negroes Are Not Moving Too Fast", *The Saturday Evening Post*, Nov 7, 1964, p. 8.
12. *The Essential Frank Lloyd Wright: Critical Writings on Architecture*, Edited by Bruce Brooks Pfeiffer (2008, Princeton University Press, Princeton, NJ), "The Art and Craft of the Machine", p. 23.

Tools

1. Eugène-Emmanuel Viollet-le-Duc, *Lectures on Architecture* (1987, Dover Publications, New York); the first half of this quote is from Volume I, p. 268, the second half is from Volume II, p. 448.
2. *The Essential Frank Lloyd Wright: Critical Writings on Architecture*, Bruce Brooks Pfeiffer, ed. (2008, Princeton University Press), "Ausgeführte Bauten und Entwürfe von Frank Lloyd Wright", p. 65.
3. Some of the text on contract bidding was taken from *Fine Homebuilding* magazine, Summer 2010, p. 16: "A Slow Economy Doesn't

Footnotes

Change the Rules of Bidding".

4. *Plumbing Systems & Design* magazine, Sep 2008, p. 34: "Risky Business —PE Supervision by a Contractor's Engineer". The quoted passage was written by Donald Wise, President of Buildings and Construction Advisory, Inc., New York City.

Design

1. This and much similar data appearing throughout this book was taken from *Architectural Graphic Standards*, 10th Edition (John Wiley & Sons, New York).
2. *Home Power* magazine, Jun/Jul 2008, p. 22: "Hybrid Footprint".
3. Ulf Bossel, *Home Power* magazine, Aug/Sep 2006, p. 83.
4. *National Geographic* magazine, Oct 2007, p. 41.
5. *Scientific American* magazine, Jul 2009, p. 52: "Grassoline at the Pump".
6. Rudolf Arnheim, *The Dynamics of Architectural Form* (University of California Press, Berkeley, CA, 1977), p. 152.
7. *Fine Homebuilding* magazine, Feb/Mar 2005, p. 84: "Home Elevators".
8. *Fine Homebuilding* magazine, date unknown (approx. 2010), p. 18: "Great Ideas: The Food File".
9. *The New York Times*, Jan 15, 2009, p. D1, "24 Rooms Tucked into One".
10. This conversation occurred Oct. 15, 2002, with Larry Savino of Putnam Valley, NY.
11. Most of these suggestions were taken from the following sources: (1) a pamphlet, *It Can't Happen in My Home! Are You Sure?* (prepared by the Forest Service for the United States Department of Agriculture, 2002); and (2) *Fine Homebuilding* magazine, Apr/May 2004, p. 78: "Fire-Wise Construction".
12. Frank Lloyd Wright, source unknown.
13. Frank Lloyd Wright, source unknown. I believe I found this information in a museum display on the site of the Darwin Martin House in Buffalo, NY, in Oct 2009.
14. Frank Lloyd Wright, *The Future of Architecture* (1953, Horizon Press, NY), p. 70.
15. Frank Lloyd Wright, *The Natural House* (1954, Horizon Press, NY), p. 20. Wright said approximately the same thing in several of his writings.
16. *The Essential Frank Lloyd Wright: Critical Writings on Architecture*, Edited by Bruce Brooks Pfeiffer (2008, Princeton University Press, Princeton, NJ), "In The Cause of Architecture", p. 49.
17. Donald Hoffman, Frank Lloyd Wright's Hollyhock House (1992, Dover Publications, New York), p. 40.

18.   William Shakespeare, *Hamlet* (1973, Washington Square Press Edition, Pocket Books, New York), Act 3, Scene 1, line 59.
19.   Eugène-Emmanuel Viollet-le-Duc, *Lectures on Architecture* (1987, Dover Publications, New York), Volume I, p. 470.

Structure

1.   Frank Lloyd Wright, *The Natural House* (1954, Horizon Press), p. 147.
2.   This information was taken from the internet soon after the event occurred sometime in 2009. It is no longer posted there.
3.   An article on boxed wood trusses appeared in *Fine Homebuilding* magazine, Feb/Mar 2010, p. 36: "Exploring the Benefits of Engineered Floor Joists".
4.   The text that describes the design and construction of the Unitarian Church in Madison, WI, is based on my several visits to this building (on one occasion I entered above the first-floor ceiling and inspected the trusses above the nave with a flashlight) and the following texts: (1) *The Meeting House, First Unitarian Society, Madison, WI*, Mary Jane Hamilton (1991, Friends of the Meeting House, Madison, WI); and (2) *Architectural Forum* magazine, Dec 1952, p. 28.
5.   Frank Lloyd Wright, *The Natural House* (1954, Horizon Press, NY), p. 19.
6.   Eero Saarinen, *Shaping the Future* (2006, Yale University Press, New Haven, CT), p. 349.
7.   *The New York Times*, Jun 26, 2002, p. A1: "The Poison is Arsenic, and the Suspect Wood".
8.   Joseph Lstiburek, Ph.D., wrote a pithy article on the mold-engendering nature of OSB and other inferior constructions involving processed was-woods in the *ASHRAE Journal*, Aug 2007, p. 54: "The Material View of Mold". This article also sheds light on the moisture problems occurring in vapor-barrier-clad building envelopes that I describe in this book's p. 364, particularly where Dr. Lstiburek says, "The problem is that the same amount of water we've always had to deal with is hanging around longer in building materials that can't take it."
9.   The buckled steel column occurred in the Bullock & Jones Building in San Francisco during the 1906 earthquake and subsequent fire. The photo was by Richard Humphrey and appeared in the *USGS Report*, 1907. I found the photo on the internet.
10.   Taken from the internet at http://inhabitat.com/2010/06/sticky-rice.
11.   Photo taken by the author, April 1962.
12.   David Wright House, Phoenix, AZ; photo taken by the author, 1966.
13.   Frank Lloyd Wright, source unknown.

Footnotes

14. Frank Lloyd Wright, *The Natural House* (1954, Horizon Press, NY), p. 37.
15. *The New York Times*, Jan 20, 2011, p. D1: "A Love Affair Cools" by Christina Lewis.
16. *Fabric Architecture* magazine, Jul/Aug 2009, p. 11: "New Mesh-up".
17. Photo from *Fabric Architecture* magazine, Jul/Aug 2009, p. 30.
18. Photo of Kennedy Residence, Cave Creek, AZ, from *Fabric Architecture* magazine, issue date unknown (probably 2009), p. 30.
19. Photo from *Fabric Architecture* magazine, May/Jun 2009, p. 30.

Electrical

1. *Home Power* magazine, Feb/Mar 2011, p. 58: "High Efficiency Appliances: The Best of the Best".
2. *Ibid*, Dec 2010/Jan 2011, p. 66 has an article on grid-tied systems.
3. Much of the information on solar electric panels was taken from (1) *Fine Homebuilding* magazine, Dec 2007/Jan 2008, p. 55: "The New Age of Photovoltaics"; (2) *Home Power* magazine, Oct/Nov 2008, p. 72: "Pump Up the Power"; and (3) *Home Power* magazine, Apr/May 2005, p. 92: "Checklist for Designing & Installing a PV System".
4. *Home Power*, Aug/Sep 2010, p. 70: "PV Systems Simplified".
5. *Ibid*, Apr/May 2010, p. 114: "PV Ground-Mounting Strategies & Installation Tips".
6. *Home Power*, Aug/Sep 2010, p. 36.
7. *Home Power*, Apr/May 2009, Jun/Jul 2010, and Aug/Sep 2011 has articles on mounting PV modules on a roof or the ground.
8. Much of the information in this section was taken from (1) *What Can the Wind Do for Me?*, (2) *How does the Wind Make Electricity?*, and (3) *Wind Power and the Environment*, three pamphlets published by the Energy Center of Wisconsin, 2000.
9. *The Essential Frank Lloyd Wright: Critical Writings on Architecture*, Edited by Bruce Brooks Pfeiffer (2008, Princeton University Press, Princeton, NJ); the photo of Wright's Romeo and Juliet Windmill Tower was taken from p. 371 (FLLW Fdn# 9607.0012).
10. *Home Power*, Feb/Mar 2005, p. 64: "Wind Generator Tower Basics".
11. My source for Maurice Datchet's wind-powered heated clothing is lost. I believe it appeared in *Home Power* magazine. However, accounts of Mr. Seddon's heated clothing also appear on the internet.
12. Much of this section was taken from *Home Power*, (1) Oct/Nov 2004, Dec 2004/Jan 2005, Feb/Mar 2005, a three-part series titled "Intro to Hydropower"; (2) Feb/Mar 2007, p. 40: "Microhydro-Electric Systems Simplified"; (3) Apr/May 2008, p. 68: "Microhydro Intake Design"; (4)

Jun/Jul 2008, p. 56: "Pipeline Hydro-Electric Penstock Design"; (5) Aug/Sep 2009, p. 78: "Hydro Design Considerations".

13. *Home Power*, Dec 2010/Jan 2011, p. 82: "Off-Grid Batteries".

14. *Ibid*, p. 80: "Choosing the Best Batteries". Also useful is *Home Power* magazine, Aug/Sep 2006, p. 54: "Top Ten Battery Blunders."

15. *Home Power*, (1) Jun/Jul 2007, p. 50: "Battery Box Basics"; (2) Feb/Mar 2011, p. 96: "Battery Box Design".

Lighting

1. *LD + A Journal* (published by the Illumination Society of America), Jul 1996, p. 5: "Views on the Visual Environment".

2. *Fabric Architecture* magazine, Mar/Apr 2008, p. 48: "Time to Shine".

3. *The Essential Frank Lloyd Wright: Critical Writings on Architecture*, Edited by Bruce Brooks Pfeiffer (2008, Princeton University Press, Princeton, NJ), "In The Cause of Architecture VI: The Meaning of Materials—Glass", p. 138.

4. *Home Power* magazine, Oct/Nov 2005, p. 40: "Designing with Daylight".

5. *Building Design + Construction* magazine, Apr 2008, p. 46: "Fiber Optic Skylight".

6. http://en.wikipedia.org/wiki/Los_Angeles_County_Hall_of_Records. Mr. Neutra's quote was from another website which I failed to note at the time, and which now I believe is no longer posted on the internet.

7. Much of the data for LED bulbs was taken from (1) *TechZone* magazine, issues TZL101.us and TZL111.us, 2009 (Digikey Corporation); and (2) *Consulting-Specifying Engineer* magazine, Jan/Feb 2011, p. 27, "Specifying LEDs in Lighting Design".

8. *Home Power*, Oct/Nov 2010, p. 32: "Saving Energy with LED Lighting".

9. Mark Twain, *Life on the Mississippi* (1987, The World's Best Reading Series, Reader's Digest Association, Inc., Pleasantville, NY), p. 178.

10. *Frank Lloyd Wright, Writings and Buildings*, selected by Edgar Kaufmann and Ben Raeburn (1960, Meridian Books, New York), p. 229.

11. Mark Twain, *Life on the Mississippi* (1987, The World's Best Reading Series, Reader's Digest Association, Inc., Pleasantville, NY), p. 296.

12. *National Geographic* magazine, Nov 2008, p. 102: "Our Vanishing Night". The quoted passage is from p. 106.

Plumbing

1. *Plumbing Systems & Design* magazine, (1) Jul/Aug 2008, p. 42: "Water-Free Urinals? I'm Having Second Thoughts", and (2) Oct 2008, p. 42:

Footnotes

"Water-Free Urinals —A Brand-new Gap!"

2. This sink and faucet is in a Wright-designed residence in the Midwest.

3. The information on composting toilets was obtained from *Composting Toilets*, a 2009-2010 catalog published by Sun-Mar Corp. and several telephone interviews with Chris Muir of this company.

4. *Fine Homebuilding* mag., Jun/Jul 2006, p. 71: "Is Copper on the Way Out?"

5. *Home Power* magazine, Apr/May 2005, p. 52: "Ram Pump Reprise".

6. *Plumbing Systems & Design* magazine, Sep 2008, p. 20: "Preventing Illness and Saving Lives in Developing Countries".

7. *National Geographic* magazine, date (approx. 2010) and page unknown: "High Marks for Clean Water".

8. *Plumbing Systems & Design*, Nov 2010, p. 26: "Taking the Salt out of Softening".

9. *Plumbing Systems & Design*, Nov 2010, p. 12: "Water Heaters, Part I: Storage, Tankless, and Condensing Types".

10. *Fine Homebuilding*, Jun/Jul 2010, page 44: "Heat Pump Water Heaters".

11. Most of the information on tankless water heaters was taken from (1) *Fine Homebuilding*, Feb/mar 2010, p. 53: "Upgrade to a Tankless Water Heater"; (2) *Plumbing Systems & Design* magazine, Mar 2008, p. 40: "Tankless Water Heaters"; (3) *Fine Homebuilding* magazine, Dec 2007/Jan 2008, p. 83: "Why Add a Tank to a Tankless Water Heater?"; and (4) *Home Power* magazine, Apr/May 2007, p. 74: "Choosing a Tankless Water Heater".

12. Much of the data on solar water heating is from (1) *Home Power*, Jun/Jul 2005, p. 18: "Solar Hot Water Simplified"; (2) *Home Power*, Apr/May 2008, p. 42: "Single-Tank Solar Water Systems"; (3) *Home Power*, Jun/Jul 2008, p. 92: "Solar Hot Water Heating Systems Buyer's Guide"; and (4) *Fine Homebuilding*, Apr/May 2008, p. 76: "Solar Hot Water".

13. *Plumbing Systems & Design*, Mar 2011, p. 15: "How to Overcome Freezing & Stagnation" [in solar water heating systems].

14. *Plumbing Systems & Design*, Jan/Feb 2011, p. 13: "Solar Thermal System Design, Part 1: Solar Thermal Applications and Modern Solar Collectors." Evacuated tube collectors are described on p. 15.

15. Three sources of information on solar water heating systems are (1) wikipedia: solar water heating; (2) three articles in *Plumbing System Design*, issues February, March, and April 2011; and (3) an article in *Home Power* issue 140 (Dec. 2010/Jan. 2011) on closed loop systems (these contain a heat exchanger containing antifreeze which transfers much of the heat collected in the panels to the water) which has several color photos that would be useful for any flat plate system. A number of internet websites describe the above systems.

16. *Fine Homebuilding*, Fall/Winter 2010, p. 10: "How About a Low-Flow Landscape?"

17. An important book, *Bringing Nature Home*, by Douglas W. Tallamy (2007, Timber Press, Portland, OR) details how to develop lawned properties into diverse wildernesses.

18. *Home Power*, Feb/Mar 2009, p. 52.

19. *Fine Homebuilding*, Oct/Nov 2001, p. 84: "Rainwater-Collection Systems".

20. *Ibid*, Spring/Summer 2010, p. 42: "Harvesting Raindrops".

21. Robert Meyer, *Fine Homebuilding*, Feb/Mar 2010, p. 10.

22. *ASHRAE Journal*, (1) Apr 2009, p. 362: "High-Rise Igloos"; and (2) Feb 2009, p. 56: "Building in Extreme Cold".

23. *Plumbing Systems & Design* magazine, Oct 2008, p. 38: "Graywater Systems".

24. *Ibid*, Jan/Feb 2011, p. 10: "What Plumbing Designers Need to Know About Sump & Ejector Basins".

25. *Ibid*, Jan/Feb 2009, p. 28: "Cleanouts".

Climate

1. Frank Lloyd Wright, *The Natural House* (1954, Horizon Press, NY), p. 178.

2. Joseph Messina, CPD, *Plumbing Systems & Design* magazine, Mar 2010, p. 12: "A Deep Issue: Well Water Temperature".

3. *ASHRAE Journal*, Aug 2008, p. 60–64: "Energy Flows Across Enclosures".

4. Although I described the Insulation Cage in detail thirty years ago in my 1981 publication, *The Ecological House*, pp. 81–85, similar information on this construction appeared in *Fine Homebuilding* magazine, Dec 2009/Jan 2010, p. 69: "Double Stud Walls are Tried and True".

5. *Fine Homebuilding* magazine, Feb/Mar 2009 (1) p. 32: "Spray Foam: What Do You Really Know?", and (2) p. 60: "Prepping for Spray Foam".

6. The story of the Imperial County Courthouse in Bartow, FL, is from *Engineering Systems* magazine, Jan 1996, p. 25: "The High Cost of IAQ".

7. Some of the information for this section was taken from *National Geographic* magazine, May 2009, p. 84: "Up on the Roof". The drawing I adapted from a color illustration on p. 91.

8. *Building Design + Construction* magazine, Feb 2007, p. 48: "Five Tips on Building a Sloped Green Roof".

9. *ASHRAE Journal*, Nov 2008, p. 34: quote by Joseph Lstiburek, Ph.D.

10. Frank Lloyd Wright, *The Natural House* (1954, Horizon Press, NY), p. 159.

11. *Home Power*, Aug/Sep 2009, p. 35: "Cool Roofs for Your Climate?"

Footnotes

12. *Fine Homebuilding*, fall/winter 2011, p. 12: "Healthful homes need more than a huge hood fan".
13. *Fabric Architecture*, Mar/Apr 2002, p. 48: "Going With The Flow".
14. *ASHRAE Journal*, Nov 2008, p. 30, quote by Joseph Lstiburek, Ph.D.
15. *Home Power*, Dec 2010/Jan 2011, p. 74: "Using the Earth's Heat" [to operate heat pumps].
16. *Ibid*, p. 98: "Cheaper, Effective Cooling with Whole-House Fans".
17. *Engineering Systems* magazine, Jun 1995, p. 20: "Case in Proof".
` 18. Ibid, Sep 1994, –Issues & Events".
19. *Home Power*, Aug/Sep 2010, p. 107, photo of solar shade.
20. Idid, Aug/Sep 2008, p. 118-20.
21. Several kinds of woodburners are described in *Fine Homebuilding* magazine, Oct/Nov 2008, p. 40: "Is Wood Heat the Answer?"
22. Frank Lloyd Wright, *The Natural House* (1954, Horizon Press, NY), p. 40.
23. Washington Irving, *Bracebridge Hall*, p. 73, (1991, The Library of America Series, Volume 52).
24. Much of the information on air filters was taken from the *Handbook of Air Conditioning System Design*, prepared by the Carrier Air Conditioning Company (1965, McGraw-Hill, New York), p. 6-51 to 59.

Acoustics

1. Much of the information in this section and figure 9-9 was taken from the *ASHRAE Journal*, Aug 2007, p. 30: "Vibration from HVAC & R Equipment".

Some of the information appearing in *Architecture Laid Bare!* was taken from my previous publications, *The Ecological House* (1981) Morgan & Morgan, Ardsley, New York), *Architectural Engineering Design: Structural Systems* (2002, McGraw-Hill, New York) and *Architectural Engineering Design: Mechanical Systems* (2002, McGraw-Hill, New York).

To keep this reference about the myriad subtleties and nuances of an everyday subject from being thousands of pages long, it must necessarily be a summary of many of the topics it covers, which often distills its mission to one of direction more than execution. Fortunately a more extensive reference exists today for delving more depthfully into almost any architectural subject listed in the following index: the internet.

Index

90-pound roofing felt, 145–46

Index

panel of electrical circuit breakers, 188–89

Brownfield development, method of building on inferior sites advocated by LEED, 21–22, 130–31

Brownwater, type of water waste, 328

Bubble fabric structures, 182–83

Bubblepak, use as translucent insulation, 399–400

Building envelope, insulated construction in outer surfaces of a building, 19, 29, 206, 347–61, 402, 409

Bureaubed, efficient furniture, 95–96

Busbar, electrical conductor, 191

BX cable, electrical conductor, 191

C

Cable, also *conductor*, conductor of electricity, 190–91, 196–97, 199, 202;
ethernet cable, 200;
in fabric structures, 179–81;
fiber optic cable, see *fiber optics*;
heat tracing cable, 327, 380;
sensor cables in containment piping, plumbing, 316;
wind tower cables, 214–15

Caisson, deep columnar structure in soft soil under a building, 130

Canopy, also *soffit*, lighting environment, 255

Cantilever, as beam structure, 133, 163, 346

Carbon dioxide, 78, 205, 311, 374, 409;
amount in air, 370;
combustion product, 174;
type of fire suppression, 320, 323–24

Caryatids, columns shaped as female figures, Athens, Greece, 136

Casement window, as ventilator, 341, 406

CCA, toxic wood preservative, 146

Ceiling system, lighting environment, 255

Cellshade, movable translucent insulation, 400–01

Cement, ingredient of concrete, 158

CFL, type of fluorescent light, 97, 238–43

Change Order, legal document for enacting changes in construction, 56

Chiller, type of dehumidifier, 393–94;
part of HVAC system, 386

Chimney flue, used as chimney cap, 166–67;
used as solar chimney, 408

Chinese sheetrock, toxic use in USA, 27–28

CINVA RAM, portable mold for making adobe bricks, 177–78

Circuit box, see *breaker box*

Circuit breaker, electrical, 188–89

Circuits, electrical, 188, 193–98

Circulation, of air in climate control systems, 374–77, 384–87;
of people in or near buildings, 79–86

Cistern, onsite reservoir of water, 312–315

Cleanouts, waste plumbing, 334

Clearwater, type of water waste, 328

Clustering, of homes, 24–25

Coffer, lighting environment, 256

Color rendering index (*CRI*), ability of a light to portray colors accurately, 237–39, 243, 244–46

Column, type of structure, 136–138

Composite decking, see *metal decking*

Compostable privy, 281–83

Compressed air, nonwater plumbing, 317

Computers, use in architecture, 47, 103, 116, 235, 260, 298, 314, 316, 371, 385, 393;
re regulating fresh airflow in ducts, 370;
re eliminating annoying sounds in ducts, 433;
re electrical systems, 195–198, 200;
re operating filters in ducts, 409;
re operating lighting systems, 252–54, 269–70;
re operating no-touch controls in plumbing fixtures, 276–78;

Index

Architecture Laid Bare!

Index

451

Index

Architecture Laid Bare!

Physical water conditioner, remover of
unwanted minerals in water, 300

Pier, small footing in buildings, 137

Pilaster, type of column structure, 137

Piles, deep columnar supports in soft soil
under a building, 130, 137

Pipes, common ~ used in plumbing systems,
283–88

Pisa, leaning Tower of, Italy, 127

Plans, see *architectural plans*

Plastic pipes, in plumbing systems, 285–86

Plumbing fixtures, 274–83

Plywood, as structure, 137, 150, 306;
use in concrete formwork, 159–61;
use in Insulation Cage, 351–54, 360;
toxins in ~, 150, 371

Point light source, type of lighting, 252

Poles, type of wood structure, 152–53

Ponding, structural load created by water
collecting on flat roofs, 141–42

Portland cement, in concrete, 158

Portman, John, designer of pod elevators
in tall buildings, 83

Post, type of column structure, 137

Post-and-beam construction, see *timber
frame construction*

Power density (PD) ratio, quantifier of
biomass in environment, 25–26

Preservatives, wood, 146–47

Pressure tanks, in plumbing systems, 294

Primary cable, also *primary*, electrical
conductor, 188–89

Pumps, in plumbing systems, 291–294

Pure water, type of nonwater plumbing, 315

PV arrays, see *photovoltaic cells*

Q

Quartz (Q) light bulbs, type of lighting, 244

R

Radiant ceiling heating, 382–83

Radiant floor heating, 381–82

Rafter, roof beam, 133, 138, 360–61

Raised access floor, see *underfloor supply
plenum*

Ram pump, type of water pump, 292–94

Ramp, type of inclined circulation, 81

Ray tracing, method of analyzing sound
paths in assembly areas, 421–22

Reactive power, see *electromagnetic interference*

Rebar, also *reinforcing rod* or *reinforcement*, use in concrete, 158–59

Recycling, reusing discarded building
materials, 117–125, 184–87

Reflectors, surfaces in a light fixture that
send a bulb's light in desirable
directions, 250–52

Registers, vaned grilles at ends of ducts
in climate control systems, 377–78

Renewable energies (sun, wind, water) that
generate electricity, 205–25

Resonance, type of sound, 425–26

Reverberation, type of sound, 424–26

Ribbon windows, long narrow windows that
distribute light evenly indoors,
98, 121, 124, 212, 233

Rigid frame, type of structural bracing, 140

Rigid insulation, also *rigid foam insulation*,
347, 354–55, 403–04

Roadsigns, for driveways, 70–71

Romex cable, also *NM (nonmetallic) cable*,
electrical conductor, 190–91

Ronchamp Chapel, designed by Le
Corbusier, France, 116, 230

Rope Light, novelty lighting, 250

"Round river", recycling concept, 336

R-value, a building material's insulating
ability, 19, 356, 396, 398, 400, 401

S

Saarinen, Eero, architect, 82–83, 116, 136

Sag curve, type of vertical curve in
driveways, 67–69

Sail fabrics, see *fabrics, type of structure*

Index

Architecture Laid Bare!